Ellen Terry

Roger Manvell

Ellen Terry

HEINEMANN : LONDON

William Heinemann Ltd
LONDON MELBOURNE TORONTO
CAPE TOWN AUCKLAND

First published 1968
Reprinted 1968
Copyright © Roger Manvell 1968
434 45000 6

Printed in Great Britain by
Cox & Wyman Ltd.,
London, Fakenham and Reading

Acknowledgements

I want to thank especially Edward Craig, the grandson of Ellen Terry, and Laurence Irving, grandson of Henry Irving, for their generosity, both in time and help. In the preparation of this book, I have turned to them constantly for guidance, and although the conclusions I have reached about Ellen Terry in her various relationships are wholly my own, I believe that the evidence I have received from them has enabled me to arrive at a much fairer judgment than might otherwise have been possible. Edward Craig as a child lived with his grandmother for some years and shared a great bond of sympathy with her. Although so young, he came to know her intimately.

I am also most grateful to Mrs Molly Thomas, curator of the Ellen Terry Museum at Smallhythe in Kent, and to the National Trust, to which the property now belongs, for giving me every help during the period my wife and I were working there; to Miss Jean Scott Rogers and Miss Jennifer Aylmer, respectively Administrator and acting-curator of the British Theatre Museum Archives and Library in London who have helped me continuously; to Miss Mary Garnham, Mrs Enid M. Forster and Miss Dorothy Livermore of the British Drama League Library; to Wilfrid Blunt, curator of the Watts Gallery at Compton near Guildford in Surrey; and to the staff of the Enthoven Collection at the Victoria and Albert Museum. I am grateful, too, to Ernest Lindgren and Colin Ford of the National Film Archive for their assistance in connexion with the films in which Ellen Terry appeared and which are preserved in the Archive.

I have received help from many other people, and I hope that I have not forgotten to acknowledge this individually in the Notes to the chapters. But I would like to conclude by thanking my wife for her great help during the period of research at Smallhythe, and Miss Annette Wiggins for undertaking the typing of a difficult manuscript.

ROGER MANVELL

The author and publishers are grateful to the following for permission to quote from copyright material: to Mr W. D'Arcy Hart of Gilbert Samuel & Co., literary executors for Ellen Terry, for the quotations from *Memoirs* by Edith Craig and Christopher St John and for the extracts from unpublished letters and notes by Ellen Terry; to The Society of Authors for the quotations from *A Correspondence* by Ellen Terry and Bernard Shaw; and from *Pen Portraits and Reviews* by Bernard Shaw; to Hulton Publications Limited for the quotations from *Index* by Edward Gordon Craig; to Hutchinson and Co. for the quotations from *Autobiography* by John Martin-Harvey and *Ellen Terry and Her Secret Self* by Edward Gordon Craig.

NOTE ON THE DATE OF ELLEN TERRY'S BIRTH

Throughout her life, Ellen Terry regarded the date of her birth as 27 February 1848. This date appears in her Memoirs, and was the date she always used for legal and other formal purposes. She never took the trouble to check this in the Register of births in the district of St Johns and St Michaels, Coventry, where on page 9 for the year 1847, entry number 44 records that she was born there on 27 February of that year. Her name is given as Alice Ellen Terry; her father is named as Ben Terry, profession, Comedian; her mother appears as Sarah Terry, formerly Ballard. Their address is entered simply as Smithford St, Coventry, and the date of registration was 29 March 1847. A photostat copy of this entry can be seen at Smallhythe.

Ellen Terry was therefore exactly one year older than she believed herself to be.

R.M.

Contents

Contents

vii

Illustrations

ix

I

BEGINNINGS

It was early in 1874, during the winter, that Charles Reade, the famous Victorian novelist, playwright and man of the theatre found himself face to face with Ellen Terry in a country lane. The meeting happened entirely by chance when Reade was out hunting in the countryside near Harpenden, north of London, where Ellen was then living. He had not seen her for six years. He had loved and admired her as a young actress, and had been almost like a foster-father to her during her adolescence on the stage. Yet in her early twenties she had suddenly deserted the theatre, and all her friends and relatives, and run away to live alone with her lover, Edward Godwin.

She had borne two children to the man she could not marry. She was still at this time the wife of the celebrated artist, George Frederic Watts, whom she married when she was only sixteen. The marriage had lasted a bare ten months and had ended in legal separation. Her life with Godwin, the sheer exuberant fun of living in the country with her babies and her animals, was all that she believed she wanted. If Godwin had not been deeply in debt she would certainly have resisted Reade's insistence that she return to London at once and star in a play he was about to direct. He saw immediately the publicity value of restoring her to the theatre where she was still remembered with such affection. With an instinctive desire to ease her domestic problems, she demanded forty pounds a week, and got it.

This was how Ellen Terry returned to the stage and resumed the career to which she had been dedicated from childhood in the hard school of the mid-Victorian theatre. She had to face London society at the age of twenty-seven with two illegitimate children. But if she had left the theatre as a young and untried girl obsessed by a love affair, she returned an experienced woman who was to become not merely a famous actress but one of the great liberating personalities of her time.

Yet she had begun life in the humblest circumstances, the daughter of strolling players working in a period when the theatre still retained characteristics which dated back to the eighteenth century. She had been brought up from her earliest years to live entirely in and for the theatre, the stage her only school. It was to provide a uniquely suitable education for a woman whose name was to stand for everything that a girl might dream of becoming during the Victorian era.

Every night before they left their lodgings for the theatre, Ben and Sarah Terry would pull a mattress from their bed and lay it on the floor for the children to sleep on. There Nellie, Ben's favourite daughter, would lie down beside the empty bed waiting for her father to come back after the long hours of work in the theatre. Then she would sleep peacefully, holding his hand through the night.[1]

Ellen was the fourth child of Ben and Sarah Terry, who were to be the founders of the most distinguished family in the history of the British theatre. Their four daughters, Kate, Ellen, Marion and Florence, were all to appear upon the stage, and Fred, the youngest of their sons, was also to become a famous actor. Yet neither Ben nor Sarah, though highly professional, if impoverished, provincial players, had the theatre in their blood. Both came from Portsmouth. Sarah, born in 1817, was the daughter of Peter Ballard, a builder and a lay preacher for the Wesleyan congregation; her mother belonged to a reasonably well-connected Scottish family, who had from the first opposed their daughter's love for Ben, the son of a local Irish publican. Ben was a year younger than Sarah. The Terry family was respectable enough, and they were indeed good Wesleyans, but the Ballards considered young Ben too unstable to marry their beautiful daughter. Besides, Ben's Uncle James had been sentenced for smuggling and had died far away at sea, while his elder brother, Thomas, was often seen drunk at the Fortune of War. This was the tavern managed by Ben's mother, Catherine, after her husband's death. George, another of Ben's brothers, played a violin at the local theatre, which in 1836 had been closed because 'unseemly and improper conduct' had occurred in its precincts. It had reopened in 1837 under the professional management of William Shalders, to whom Ben became indebted for his introduction to the backstage working of a theatre. He hung about until, among other jobs, he became a drummer in the theatre orchestra. There was every reason, perhaps, during 1837 for the Scottish parents of Ellen Terry's future mother to oppose their daughter's growing infatuation for young Ben Terry, with his Irish exuberance and his quite undesirable occupation.

Nevertheless, on 1 September 1838 Ben and Sarah asserted their legal independence and got married in a church. Both of them claimed to be twenty-one, and felt free now to do as they pleased, though Ben, in point of fact, was still two weeks under age; which demonstrates their eagerness to be wed. Their parents were not present at the ceremony and, certainly in the case of the Ballards, had not been told it was to happen. Ben described himself in the marriage register as a 'Gentleman', though actors were scarcely so regarded in the year Victoria became Queen. He had nothing to offer his bride but the rigours of life as a travelling player, and the burden of a quarter-century's recurrent childbearing. Starting in 1839 with the arrival of Benjamin and ending only in 1864 with the birth of Fred, Sarah endured eleven confinements, not counting her miscarriages.

At the age of twenty-one, Ben and Sarah made a handsome pair of strolling players, and Ben at least was to become an established supporting actor in the Victorian theatre. That he had great feeling for his profession can never be in doubt. He was an ebullient, stylish man, gay in manner and not easily defeated. Though he had a ready eye for any pretty woman, he was devoted to his wife and cared for his many children with an indefatigable pride. His earnings as an actor could rarely have exceeded one pound a week in the initial years, and from being an enthusiastic amateur he resolutely made himself into a competent professional, fostering his wife and growing family in the process. Though never a brilliant performer, he had a fine voice and he knew how to place his children to advantage in the theatre. Above all, he gave them a thorough elementary grounding in stage technique and practice. There was not that much difference between the lively ale-house in which he had been brought up and the small and dirty provincial playhouses, only too often frequented by shouting hooligans and their girls. Ben was well used to playing the fiddle while perched upon a table in the bar of his mother's tavern, the Fortune of War, back home in Portsmouth. 'Ben, play us a tune,' the drinkers would shout, crying out the song they wanted, and Ben, at home alike with the fiddle or drums, learned the art of entertainment in the heart of a family audience without airs or pretences.

Descriptions of Ben and Sarah in their youth are difficult to come by, but John Coleman, the biographer of the dramatist Charles Reade, met them on 'the Worcester Circuit' and remembered Ben as 'a handsome, fine-looking, brown-haired man, and the wife as a tall, graceful creature, with an abundance of fair hair, and with big blue eyes set in a charming face'. Which is how you might expect the mother of Ellen Terry to look.

Though Sarah between her recurrent pregnancies performed regularly on the stage to earn an extra few shillings to help keep a roof above her children's heads and food inside their bellies, she had more looks than talent as far as the theatre was concerned. For her, it always mattered more to be acknowledged a gentlewoman, and her great qualities were soon evident as those of an itinerant housewife and a firm if patient mother rather than those of an actress. She worshipped her wilful Irish husband. She had faith in his talent as an actor and recognized his value as a proud and loving father whose fire and wayward enthusiasms contrasted with her quietude and gentility, and who, however difficult life became, never lost heart. Together Ben and Sarah created an environment for their children which turned the poorest attic into the happy turmoil of a well-conducted home. They struggled to rear their intelligent, excitable children with all the strict discipline of the normal middle-class Victorian household.

In nineteenth-century England there was no recognized training for the theatre except that of working in it. For this reason, such limited theatrical enterprises as existed in the 1830s tended to be dominated by a handful of theatrical managers who had achieved either fame or a measure of distinction in London and the provinces. They usually married actresses and sometimes, as in the case of Roger Kemble and Edmund Kean, founded families of players, though none to match the theatrical dynasty of the Terrys. In addition, they gathered round them companies of supporting actors less talented or fortunate than themselves, and recruited younger players who appeared likely to shape well and were prepared to work day and night for meagre payment. In return for this willing servitude, the more conscientious actor-managers and their actress wives taught the younger generation, and it was common for children literally to be brought up on the stage, with the theatre as their sole disciplined education. Neither Kate nor Ellen Terry ever went to school, but when the family's income increased in later years it became possible to give the younger children a formal education.[2]

By the time Ellen was born Ben was a fully established supporting actor, well used to travelling with his wife from town to town to secure what minor work he could. He appeared in stock seasons with Macready, who admired his elocution, and during these earlier years he performed in both Edinburgh and Glasgow and became known and liked by audiences in Scotland. Sarah, particularly at first, appeared on the stage with her husband. She used the stage name of Miss Yerret[3] – Terry spelt backwards. In 1844 (the year Kate, her first daughter, was born on 21 April) she played Charity to Ben's Mark Tapley at the Liverpool Theatre Royal in a dramatization of *Martin Chuzzlewit*. In 1847, the year of Ellen's birth in Coventry, she appeared as '4th Singing Witch' in a production of *Macbeth* at the Glasgow Theatre Royal. Ben was in Coventry with Sarah when, on 27 February 1847, the midwife was summoned to their lodgings near the theatre to deliver Mrs Terry of her fifth child, whom she called Ellen – the name she had already given to an earlier daughter who had died in infancy. When the family moved to Glasgow, the new baby at its mother's breast, Benjamin, the first-born, was eight years old and Kate, Ellen's elder sister, was three. Two other daughters had died soon after birth.

Everyone who knew her agreed that Sarah was a magnificent mother. Ellen describes how Sarah Terry would bundle her babies up in a shawl when they were still too small to be left in the care of the landlady, and take them with her to the theatre, to sleep in the dressing-room or in the actors' green room while the play was in progress. So Benjamin, Kate and Ellen spent their childhood on the road, living in hired lodgings when not actually in the theatre itself. They became used to the constant movement of their parents and the absence of any roof they could call their permanent home.

While Ellen was still a baby Kate was beginning her theatrical training under her father's careful and exacting tutelage; according to her sister she appeared on the stage before she was four, dancing a hornpipe in a diminutive sailor-suit.

Kate's great talent as a child actress led to the temporary splitting-up of the family in 1852 and eventually to the easing of their financial difficulties. When Ellen and her father stayed together in Liverpool, where Ben was under a long-term contract with a stock company, Sarah went to live in London to look after the rest of the children. At first they lived in lodgings in Camden Town. Kate was engaged to play in Charles Kean's company, her first role that of Prince Arthur in *King John,* a part she had already played in Edinburgh. She was to stay with Kean until 1859. This left Ellen, aged only five, in the hands of her father for a considerable period. She cooked his breakfasts and did what domestic work she could. 'He never ceased teaching me to be useful, alert, and quiet,' she wrote later. 'Sometimes he hastened my perceptive powers with a slipper, and always corrected me if I pronounced any word in a slipshod fashion. He himself was a beautiful elocutionist, and if I now speak any language well it is in no small degree due to my early training.' They did not join the rest of the family in London until the close of 1853, when Ben was invited to join Kean's company at the Princess's Theatre in Oxford Street.

It is significant that the family was divided up in this particular way during these important, formative years in their daughter's life. Ellen was Ben's favourite daughter, and in many ways she took after him and shared his vigorous, erratic Irish temperament. Kate had more of Sarah's nature; although she was to become a celebrated actress, she was quite ready at the height of her fame to leave the stage and become a genteel and comfortable housewife with social pretensions of a kind that could never have appealed to Ellen's undisciplined temperament. These long months away from her mother's restraining influence must to some extent have saved Ellen from acquiring the Victorian inhibitions normally imposed upon a child. She learnt the value of independence at an early age. She claims in her Memoirs that she lived alone with her father for as long as two years, but it would seem that the period must have been much shorter, or at any rate interrupted, since the records show that Ben appeared at the Princess's Theatre in September 1852 (before joining Kean's company on a more permanent basis in 1853).[4]

Kate in the meantime was doing well in London. To be working as a member of Charles Kean's company was in itself a distinction. She repeated in London the success she had had in Edinburgh as Prince Arthur, and even played the part at a Command performance at Windsor Castle. Whatever may be said about Queen Victoria's shortcomings as a supporter of the arts, she helped in her own way to raise the social status of the theatre. Once the obsolete privilege of exclusive patronage by royal licence had been withdrawn from the Covent Garden and Drury Lane theatres, she extended her patronage to successful companies by establishing Command performances.

Ellen was born in 1847. The royal restrictions on the freedom of the theatre imposed during the seventeenth century had been abolished only four years earlier, in 1843. All that now survived of these restrictions was the prerogative of the Lord

Chamberlain of the Queen's Household to censor plays performed in the theatres of the British Isles. Until 1843 the two London theatres enjoying official royal patronage – Covent Garden and Drury Lane – were the only houses where so-called 'legitimate' drama could be performed under Royal Patent, or licence. All other theatres in London were limited to staging opera, burlettas, spectacles, and other 'illegitimate' shows. The legitimate drama, however, flourished in the provinces where, during the eighteenth century, royal patents were granted to theatres in such places as Bath, York, Liverpool, Manchester and Bristol, the Lord Chamberlain licensing further theatres in places of royal residence such as Brighton and Windsor. But in London the development of the theatre had been held back by the royal patents; by 1850 the capital had barely twenty theatres to cater for the growing needs of its rapidly increasing population, which had grown from less than a million in 1800 to well over two million by 1850. By this time, too, public transport was developing in the cities and in the country as a whole, and accustoming larger numbers of people to make the effort to leave their homes and patronize entertainments which might formerly have seemed out of reach.

The existence of the royal controls had been in most respects a grave disadvantage to the development of the theatre as a whole, however much they may have heightened the prestige of the two Theatres Royal at Covent Garden and Drury Lane. The writers of new theatrical scripts were largely hacks paid a small sum to produce an actable scenario with dialogue and if necessary, songs. Audiences were mostly a rough and ready lot, with the respectable middle classes conspicuously absent. The second half of the nineteenth century was to see the British theatre and its increasingly middle-class audiences gradually respond to their new freedom until almost at the turn of the nineteenth century the British theatre could begin to take its place, rather late in the day, alongside the new drama already well established during the 1880s and 1890s in other European countries, the drama of Ibsen, Tolstoy, Turgenev, Chekhov and Strindberg.

Meanwhile, new theatres had to be built, new methods of

atmospheric lighting and staging exploited,[5] so that new audiences from the middle and upper classes could be attracted to patronize the theatre instead of being fearful of moral contamination from its stages. The whole conception of acting was to change during these fifty years, passing from the old-fashioned 'heroics' of the eighteenth and early nineteenth-century melodrama to the naturalism of performance needed for the 'modern' plays designed for 'modern' audiences, the plays of Robertson, Pinero and Henry Arthur Jones, and the highly pointed dialogue of Wilde and Shaw. Fully controllable illumination of the stage by gaslight was not to come finally until the 1870s, by which time the producer (or stage manager as he was then called) had discovered how to use elaborately varied and atmospheric forms of stage presentation. Before the productions of Macready and Charles Kean plays had been very roughly mounted and, as far as acting was concerned, entirely subject to the hit-and-miss style of the all-powerful actor-manager, whose main concern was to frame his own star performance with so many supernumeraries kept suitably in the background while he stormed his way to victory over his audience. There were virtually no training schools for acting in Britain other than those provided by the stock companies attached to the provincial playhouses, where personable young men and women boldly sought their initial engagements in a profession which was still greatly despised in respectable society. No player, man or woman, could reach the top unless he possessed a flamboyant talent. It was into this kind of theatrical enterprise, still for the most part operating in the harsh conditions surviving from the eighteenth century, that Ellen's parents had launched themselves, and it was in this kind of theatre that she and her sisters were to serve their apprenticeship during childhood and adolescence.

For Ben, the opportunity to play supporting parts in one of the leading London companies was a considerable step forward. He had worked since 1837 in the provincial theatre, and London was virtually unknown to him. But the cost of rearing his family was rising: Benjamin, a youth of fourteen, was at school in London;

though Sarah's second boy, George, was still an infant, Kate, aged ten, was rapidly growing up and needed the clothes suitable for a girl becoming a well-known child actress in a great London theatre; Nellie, the Terrys hoped, would also be on the stage but in the meantime she too, had to be provided for; and Sarah was involved in yet another pregnancy, which resulted in the birth of Polly (Marion) Terry in 1853. Money was short with only two members of the family bringing in a wage, so Sarah, who was rapidly losing the youthful good looks required of an actress, decided she must accept the humble position of wardrobe woman at the Princess's. The family, now seven in number, took rooms at the top of a tall house in Gower Street. Although the stairs were arduous, the place was at least reasonably close to the theatre.

In February 1853 Nellie was six. While Kate was playing small parts in Shakespeare or pantomime, she was absorbed in domestic tasks under the eye of her mother. Ben was playing such parts as the Lord Mayor in *Richard III* and the Surveyor in *Henry VIII*. It was therefore a great moment for the family when on 20 April 1856 Ellen made her début at the age of nine in the part of the child Mamillius in *The Winter's Tale;* Charles Kean played Leontes and Mrs Kean Hermione, while Ben appeared as the Officer of the Court of Judicature and Kate (now twelve) as the Servant to the Old Shepherd. Nellie had more lines and far greater prominence than the two senior members of the family put together.

And now came her chance to develop the lessons in enunciation and deportment which Ben had given her during her early years, for she came under the exacting direction of Mr and Mrs Charles Kean, whose approach to their work was in many respects more academic than it was theatrical. Charles Kean had been sent by his eminent father to Eton, and historical verisimilitude became his passion; the results of the ceaseless research lying behind his designs for sets and properties are revealed in the drawings for a number of his productions which are preserved in the Victoria and Albert Museum.[6] Even *A Midsummer Night's Dream* was developed into an archaeologist's impression of ancient Athens, and he took every opportunity to air his classical erudition. For example, in the workshop of Quince the Carpenter, he informed his audience, 'the Furniture and Tools ... are copied from discoveries at Herculaneum'. The little cart with which Mamillius was bidden to 'go play' was copied by the carpenter from a toy depicted on a Greek vase. At a banquet given in his honour in 1859, Kean said, 'I may safely assert that in no single instance have I ever permitted historical truth to be sacrificed to theatrical effect.' He stood for the idea of pictorial spectacle on the stage which was offered to the public in the guise of historical accuracy, but actually only revealed a romantic elaboration of the places it purported to represent.

Kean applied his schoolmasterly methods to his systematic re-hearsals, which began at ten o'clock in the morning and lasted, with no regard for any children in the cast, the entire day. There was no respite for meals until it was time to prepare for the performance of the current production, which itself, with a curtain-raiser, might well last from seven o'clock to midnight. If there were no production, or if it were Sunday, when rehearsals were also commonly called, the cast might find themselves re-hearsing into the small hours of the night. Nellie, her long legs aching under her body, was often half asleep when she was called to take her place yet again upon the stage. Once the scene was done, she would slip down to the Green Room and drop off to sleep. It was Kean's habit to direct his productions from the auditorium, ringing a handbell when anything went wrong, whereupon Mrs Kean would sweep on to the stage and put matters right with an exactitude of purpose born of long ex-perience and a correct sense of discipline. Nellie had been auditioned for the part of Mamillius by Mrs Kean together with some other children, to each of whom she said in turn, 'That's very nice! Thank you, my dear. That will do.' Later, a thump on the 'fine brass knocker, which mother kept beautifully bright' announced the arrival of the script, bound in green American cloth, and Nellie was 'so proud and pleased and delighted' that she danced a hornpipe for sheer joy.[7] Ben's insistence on clear articulation

had met its reward, and Nellie was contracted to play her first
part in Shakespeare, which to both Ben and Sarah represented the
most desirable thing in the world. Her initial salary was fifteen
shillings a week.

From 1856 to 1859 Ellen appeared regularly in Charles Kean's
productions. She was Puck in *A Midsummer Night's Dream*, Karl
in *Faust and Marguerite* ('a jolly little part with plenty of points in
it'); she carried a basket of doves in *The Merchant of Venice*,
climbed a pole in *Richard II*, was 'top angel' in the vision in
Henry VIII, and was made sick by the heat of the gaslights at
that 'dizzy height', and she was the fairy Goldenstar in a pantomime which was presented on the same night as *A Midsummer
Night's Dream*, thus doing a double production when she was not
yet nine years old.

After the close of their season at the Princess's in 1859, the
Keans left England for America, but the season with them was to
be of the greatest possible value for the child actress. Her training
began at breakfast, when her father insisted on coaching her,
making her put down her fork and recite her lines. He would do
this even in the street or on the horse-drawn bus; he once made
her recite to a chemist in his shop, standing her on a stool to
achieve a finer effect. When she was not doing this Nellie was
minding the younger children, washing and combing their hair,
for Sarah was pregnant yet again; she had already given birth
to Florence in 1855 and she was to have a third son, Charles, in
1857.

Once she had reached the theatre, if she could be spared from
rehearsal Nellie came under the direction of the foppish Oscar
Byrn, Kean's staff dancing master and director of the crowd. He
would pin a blanket round her which came down to the ground
both in front and behind, trailing for inches on the floor, and then
instruct her to walk. This she managed to do, while the other
children in the company jumped and kicked their way along.
'Somehow,' says Ellen, 'I never had any difficulty in moving
gracefully.' Byrn taught the children to dance the minuet to his
violin, and to walk at ever-increasing speed without any deviation

on lengths of planking stretched right across the stage.[8] Certainty of step; uprightness of carriage; chest out; chin in; deportment, always deportment. This is what Mr Byrn declaimed. And if it was not deportment, it was elocution all over again. 'A E I O U, my dear,' Mrs Kean would say emphatically, 'are five distinct vowels, so don't mix them all up together, as if you were making a pudding.' 'No one ever had a sharper tongue or a kinder heart than Mrs Kean,' wrote Ellen. 'Beginning with her I have always loved women with a somewhat hard manner! I have never believed in their hardness, and have proved them tender and generous to the extreme.'[9]

The backstage world of the theatre produced its own nightmares. Up in front were the stage, the lights, the sets, the actors, the music. Behind was a world of shadows and obstructions, brackets to be avoided, props to be watched, unseen actors to be collided with in the wings, stage hands standing ready for the sudden sweep of action the moment the curtain fell. The Green Room window looked down on a courtyard stacked with unwanted scenery and overrun by rats. Nellie, curious and watchful, stared down as the repulsive starving creatures swarmed and waddled between the flats, gnawing the paint off the canvas. She was haunted by the sight of these rats, and once during a storm caught sudden glimpses of them huddled and still crawling as the lightning flashed, the rain swept down and the thunder rumbled and reverberated. The memory of them used to come back to her at the Lyceum during the Brocken scene in *Faust*. What haunted her, she said, was the terrible '*greyness* of the whole thing'.

Excited, impetuous, always straining to be at her best, Nellie one night tore along the twists and turns of the corridors leading down from the stage to the dressing-room and ran slap into the white waistcoat of an elderly gentleman. She all but knocked him down. Speechless with alarm, she looked up at the face towering above her and saw it was the great Mr Macready himself who was regaining his balance. 'Oh, I *beg* your pardon,' she managed to say. He recovered himself and smiled at her. 'Never mind!' he said. 'You are a very polite little girl, and you act very earnestly and speak very nicely.' Nellie, happy again, fled away to change for her next entrance. But she always remembered him from that moment, 'his curling hair, his oddly coloured eyes full of fire, and his beautiful, wavy mouth'.

For all her rigid training and attempts at self-discipline, Nellie tended to make childish mistakes in her work. On her first night as Mamillius, when wearing a little red-and-silver dress of which she was very proud, she tripped over the handle of her toy cart – that ghost of Herculaneum – and fell flat on her back. A terrible sense of humiliation filled her as she heard a titter of laughter stir through the half-visible audience out there in front, and once she was off-stage she wept. This dreadful mistake was all the worse because Her Majesty the Queen and Prince Albert were attending the opening night. So was the Reverend Charles Dodgson, later to become a friend of the Terrys and famous as Lewis Carroll. The triumph of her first appearance on the London stage was ruined for her, though the audience soon forgot the incident; the drama critic in *The Times* next day commended her 'vivacious precocity'. Ben and Sarah praised her, but with circumspection, lest she should become vain. She played the part without a break for 102 nights.

In October 1856 when Kean revived *A Midsummer Night's Dream,* Nellie played Puck, while Kate occasionally took it in turn with Carlotta Leclercq, to whom she was understudy, to play Titania.

Playing Puck, Nellie admits, made her cheeky and vain, and she grew to love herself too much and to identify herself with Puck's mischief. She was gawky now, and her hair was cut short for the part. She looked, she said, 'a sight,' but later on in the evening as the fairy Goldenstar she wore a gorgeous dress and behaved herself beautifully. She was only nine, and one night a bad accident occurred which tested her professional courage. At the end of the play she had to rise on to the stage through a trapdoor to close the evening with the lines beginning: 'If we shadows have offended . . .' The stage hand closed the door too soon and broke her toe, which remained trapped. She was contorted with pain and Kate rushed to help her. Mrs Kean ran on to the stage to release her. 'Finish the play, dear,' she whispered, 'and I'll double your salary.'[10] Thirty shillings a week! Supported by Kate, Nellie managed somehow to bring the curtain down.

On the strength of Nellie's rise in salary (from which, she says, she received sixpence a week pocket money), the family moved to a small house of their own, No 92 Stanhope Street, to the east of Regent's Park, then a new and expanding district in outer London. The house had an iron-railed balcony in front and a small paved courtyard behind it, forming a minute walled garden. The living-room at the back opened on to the courtyard through French windows, later to be seen in one of Lewis Carroll's photographs of the family. This was the first house the family had ever possessed, and soon (in 1857 with the birth of Charles) there would be nine of them to fill it. Money was still very tight, and thrift essential. The main burden, as always, fell on Sarah. Ellen remembers coming home very late from the theatre and finding her mother sewing the dresses in which she and Kate were to go to a Christmas party at some fashionable house in Half Moon Street. Sarah was working by the light of a candle. 'It was no uncommon thing to find her sewing at that time, but if she was tired she never showed it. She was always bright and tender ... I remember when the great evening came our hair, which we still wore down our backs, was done to perfection, and we really looked fit to dance with a king. As things were, I *did* dance with the late Duke of Cambridge.'[11]

Ben was not content to play small parts night after night at the Princess's Theatre. Like all ambitious actors of the period, he was anxious to enter into some kind of management of his own. When the theatres in London closed for the summer recess, from July to September, he conceived the idea of forming a little family troupe – Kate aged twelve, Nellie aged nine and himself – to undertake light entertainment in the Isle of Wight. Accordingly, in 1857 he rented a small theatre at Ryde for the season and the family moved to a cottage provided by Sarah's sister Lizzie, a

lady who in Nellie's infant memories had seemed like an angel –
'she had the softest, sweetest expression and deep-lidded golden
eyes'. The sketches Ben put on with the girls at Ryde originated
on the London stage; they proved very popular, and he took the
theatre for a number of summer seasons.

Nellie's success at Ryde went to her head. It was only to be
expected. Unsophisticated audiences liked to see her showing off
her precocious conception of how adults behaved; her ingenuous
clowning brought the house down and helped Ben to make
much-needed money, and it was the undoubted popularity of the
shows which was to encourage him to form his own small company two years later when the link with the Keans was finally
broken.

But Ben had little more to teach his daughter; his insistence on
endless rehearsals probably sprang more from ambition than
anything else, and it was Mr and Mrs Kean, whom Nellie so
greatly admired, who were to take her a step further in her stage
education.

It was to Mrs Kean that Nellie owed her first glimpse of adult
responsibility to the profession she had entered as a child. It came
with the rehearsals of the part of Arthur in *King John,* the part
Kate had played six years earlier, and which opened on 18
October 1858. Nellie was eleven now, and, as she put it later, she
'began to see the whole thing'.

> My attentive watching of other people began to bear fruit,
> and the labour and perseverance, care and intelligence which
> had gone to make these enormous productions dawned on my
> young mind. One must see things for oneself ... I understood
> that if I did not work, I could not eat. And so I wanted to work.
> I used to get up in the middle of the night and watch my
> gestures in the glass. I used to try my voice and bring it down
> and up in the right places. And all vanity fell away from me.
> At the first rehearsals of *King John* I could not do anything
> right. Mrs Kean stormed at me, slapped me, I broke down and
> cried, and then, with all the mortification and grief in my

voice, managed to express what Mrs Kean wanted and what she could not teach me by doing it herself.

'That's right, that's right!' she cried excitedly. 'You've got it! Now remember what you did with your voice, reproduce it, remember everything, and do it!'[12]

Nellie played Arthur opposite John Ryder, who was Hubert. Ryder had been one of Macready's men, and he was by then an experienced actor in the company who resented Kean's autocratic attitude to his supporting players, certain of whom, like Ryder, were better actors than their managers. 'D'ye suppose he engaged me for my powers as an actor,' he would say to Nellie. 'He engaged me for my damned archaeological figure.' Their scene together earned praise from the critics; Ryder, said Ellen, was 'an admirable actor, and in appearance like an old tree that has been struck by lightning, or a greenless, barren rock'. Once, when the audience was shouting for them to take a curtain after Kean had put up a notice that no calls were to be allowed during the play, Ryder rampaged in the Green Room. 'Never mind,' he muttered furiously to Nellie. 'When other people are rotting in their graves, ducky, you'll be up there!' And he gave a 'terrific gesture' to show the height of the fame.

In 1859, as we have seen, the seven-year period of work with the Keans came to an end. For the girls it had for the most part been a great and rewarding experience. At the ages of fourteen and twelve, they had become well known in the London theatre, and were now sought after for parties and other social engagements.

In spite of his many shortcomings, Charles Kean had produced the most lavish presentations of Shakespeare's plays to be seen at the time, and in a building which was none too large (as he boasted in his farewell speech from the stage) he had given employment to a vast staff of nearly 550 people. Nothing comparable was to take place in the English theatre until the great presentations by Irving at the Lyceum some twenty years later.

For Nellie this was a true start to her professional career. The

critics and other independent observers began to see the actress in
the child. Prince Arthur was perhaps her greatest achievement so
far; the critics spoke of her 'great sweetness, clearness of enunciation, and delicate light and shade', her 'ingenuous grace and art-
less feeling', and her 'heart-touching pathos'. Even the critic of
the *Athenaeum* said she was 'uncommonly excellent'. Writing
more precisely, the contemporary dramatic critic and historian,
Dutton Cook, observed of Kate and Nellie that their talents went
far beyond the usual charm of well-trained child players. They
could, he said:

> ... impart sentiment to their speeches, could identify them-
> selves with the characters they played, could personate and
> portray, could weep themselves that they might surely make
> others weep, could sway the emotions of crowded audiences
> ... They were carried away by the force of their own acting;
> there were tears not only in their voices but in their eyes; their
> mobile faces were quick to reflect the significance of the drama's
> events; they could listen, their looks the while annotating, as it
> were, the discourse they heard; singular animation and alert-
> ness distinguished all their movements, attitudes, and gestures.
> ... I have never seen audiences so agitated and distressed, even
> to the point of anguish, as were the patrons of the Princess's
> Theatre on those bygone nights when little Prince Arthur,
> personated by either of the Terry sisters, clung to Hubert's
> knees as the heated iron cooled in his hands, pleading passion-
> ately for sight, touching eloquent of voice and action; a
> childish simplicity attendant ever upon all the frenzy, and
> terror, the vehemence, and the despair of the speeches and the
> situation.... A peculiar dramatic sensitiveness and susceptibility
> characterized the sisters Terry; their nervous organization,
> their mental impressibility and vivaciousness, not less than their
> personal charms and attractions, may be said to have ordained
> and determined their success upon the stage.[13]

One of the results of their relative fame was that Kate and
Nellie came to the notice of a much wider circle of people who

could be of use and help to them and introduce them to a social life from which the financial status and isolation of their parents would otherwise have debarred them. Clothes were the problem, for Sarah had to go on making these, stitching away alone into the small hours of the night. Among those already drawn to the Terry girls were two men with a deep interest in the drama, Tom Taylor and Charles Reade. Like other Victorian gentlemen, they were accomplished amateurs whose activities in the theatre gradually took on a professional aspect; in 1859 Taylor was forty-three and Reade forty-five. Both were intellectuals and university men, students of literature and law; Reade was a Fellow of Magdalen and had been vice-president of the college in 1851, while Taylor, after being from 1845–7 Professor of Literature at University College, London, had become a civil servant at the Board of Health, where he worked from 1850 to 1871, before editing *Punch* from 1874 until his death in 1880.

As early as 1848 Taylor had written in *The Echo* supporting the foundation of a National Theatre; as a journalist he wrote constantly about the state of the English stage, and composed over seventy plays. Though many of these were domestic dramas of no great significance, by sheer persistence he became one of the best known as well as the most prolific dramatists in a very impoverished period. He was for a time the dramatic critic of *The Times,* and he had collaborated with his friend Reade in writing *Masks and Faces,* a play about David Garrick and Peg Woffington, which proved highly successful, while in 1855 he had written *Still Waters Run Deep,* which dealt more frankly with sexual matters than was at all common on the Victorian stage. He was also an enthusiastic amateur actor and a friend of Charles Dickens, whose Mr Pickwick he somewhat resembled; he was small and fat and clung to breeches and a long coat when they were no longer fashionable; he blinked at his friends through his diminutive spectacles, and regarded the world in general as a place to be kind in. Taylor had a fine house in the crescent of Lavender Sweep, to the north of Clapham Common, and was married to a woman of great force of character. Laura Taylor liked to befriend artists and

actors, and mother them in her home, her fundamentally kind
heart making up for her domineering manner. Among the friends
the Taylors gathered round them were not only the Terry girls
but the painter G. F. Watts.

It was Charles Reade, however, who was to have the decisive
influence on Ellen's later career; she came to regard him as a foster-
parent and even addressed him as 'Daddy'. At this early stage,
however, he got to know their family and was instrumental in
introducing the girls to a wider life than was possible within the
narrow walls of Stanhope Street. He regarded himself primarily
as a dramatist, but he is remembered now for his novels; *It's
Never Too Late To Mend* had appeared in 1856, though *The
Cloister and the Hearth* was not to be published until 1861 and
Hard Cash till 1863. But his ambition was to be successful in the
theatre; according to Ellen, his mother had known Sheridan, 'and
sat on the stage with him while he rehearsed *The School for
Scandal* with Mrs Abingdon, the original Lady Teazle'. His most
famous play, *The Lyons Mail*, which Irving was to present so
frequently, had already been staged as *The Courier of Lyons* in 1854.
Reade, a strange, irascible man who combined the angry instincts
of a social reformer with great kindness of heart, had defied
Victorian convention by living openly with an actress, Laura
Seymour, who kept house for him in London for twenty-five
years and to whom he always claimed to be platonically devoted.
In the discreet two-volume biography of Reade published in
1887 by his relatives, Charles L. Reade and the Reverend Compton
Reade, their relationship is beautifully described. Mrs Seymour,
say the biographers, had 'passed through the dark furnace of
London life, and emerged from it a brave and benevolent woman'.
Reade and Mrs Seymour first met around 1852 when he consulted
her about a play; they were so delighted with each other that they
formed what the biographers call 'a business partnership'. 'The
business partnership with Mrs Seymour,' they wrote, had 'developed into so tender a relationship as is seldom found to gild
the relations of people connected only by the tie of mutual
esteem. . . . Mrs Seymour was not a wife, but she proved herself

a faithful housekeeper to the College Fellow, the compulsory celibate ... her kindly sympathy caused him to forget his loneliness. *Certes,* it became part and parcel of his existence, and when it ceased, his life was wrecked – he died by inches.'[14] In her copy of the biography, Ellen Terry marked this passage with a cross and wrote 'True' in the margin. Charles Reade and Laura Seymour, who was a widow, set up house together initially in Bolton Row, St John's Wood. Mrs Seymour, say the biographers, 'knew the male sex by heart'; she was not a distinguished actress ('though undoubtedly she rose in suitable parts above mediocrity'), but Reade admired 'her *vif* manner, acquaintance with the stage, and physique'. The authors choose to quote the authority of Winwood Reade, Charles's nephew and the author of *The Martyrdom of Man,* that the liaison was indeed platonic, on the grounds that Winwood Reade, one of the most notorious atheists of his day, would undoubtedly have been delighted to have been able to say that Mrs Seymour was his uncle's mistress if he could possibly have found any excuse to do so. 'There was no concealment, no dove-cote in St John's Wood,' they affirm. If there had been any suspicion of this, Sarah, the Wesleyan, would certainly never have let her daughters pass through Charles Reade's door. But she did so, and Ellen started a deep, if much criticized friendship with Reade which lasted until his death in 1884.

With the departure of the Keans, the Terrys were thrown upon their own resources. By now, they were not entirely without means; Ben had inherited a small amount of capital from his mother, the owner of the Fortune of War in Portsmouth, who had recently died.[15] He had decided to develop his experience in management at Ryde and exploit the fame of his daughters by going on the road with a 'Drawing-room Entertainment' – so-called no doubt to catch the public still fearful of the theatre (that 'devil's hot-bed') but curious to see what its performers were like.

The initial tour Ben arranged for his Drawing-room Entertainment was normally made up of one-night stands, but he opened with a season at the Royal Colosseum, Regent's Park. Later the group appeared at the Lecture Hall, Croydon, and at

places as far away as Dublin, Belfast, Plymouth, Exeter and Bristol.
They were assisted by a young pianist called Sydney Naylor, and
Sarah accompanied them when they went on tour and even
appeared in small parts on the stage. Their various engagements,
which included Ryde during the summer, appear to have lasted
until 1861, when Kate was contracted to play supporting parts
under the management of Mr and Mrs Alfred Wigan at the St
James's Theatre.

The opening of the Drawing-room Entertainment in the Royal
Colosseum was most successful, and ran for thirty consecutive
nights, playing to audiences that totalled over 30,000. The
Colosseum was a remarkable centre for Victorian recreation; it
was one of the sights of London, and was famous for what a
contemporary describes as its 'weird, imitation stalactite caves',
which, as we shall see, held a peculiar fascination for Nellie. The
girls enjoyed playing in the comedies which so entertained their
audiences.

But Nellie's ambition demanded sterner stuff than this. It was
the habit of the sisters to imitate grown-up actresses, especially
Mrs Kean, whose mannerisms on the stage they knew so well,
and Nellie, encouraged no doubt by Ben, spent much of her time
studying the 'classic' parts she one day hoped to play. Among
these was Juliet, and she crept into the stalactite caves of the
Colosseum to get the right atmosphere from its 'gloomy horror'.
'Here I could cultivate a creepy, eerie sensation, and get into a
fitting frame of mind for the potion scene. Down in this least
imposing of subterranean abodes I used to tremble and thrill with
passion and terror.'

The tours must have reminded Sarah of her early days with
Ben more than twenty years before. There were five of them on
the road – Ben, combining the functions of front-of-house and
stage manager, Sarah coaching the girls, dressing them, and
making them sleep a little, when she could, in the daytime, and
Sydney Naylor, little more than a boy himself but, apparently,
an entertaining companion. 'We usually journeyed in a carriage,'
Ellen recalled. 'Once we tramped from Bristol to Exeter. Oh,

those delightful journeys on the open road! I tasted the joys of the strolling players' existence, without its miseries. I saw the country for the first time. When they asked me what I was thinking of as we drove along, I remember answering: "Only that I should like to run wild in a wood for ever"!' At night they stopped in whatever local inns they could find. They were comparatively well off, making from £10 to £15 from each performance, at a time when a young supporting actor's wage was about £2 a week.

Sarah, who now had servants in her house, could afford to be away from home, and the boys' school fees could be met. At Stanhope Street were Benjamin, aged twenty-one, George, now about ten, and the younger children, Marion, Florence and Charles. Another child, Tom, was to be born at some time during this period; the date is not known.

Nellie was to have one more brief engagement in London before her transfer to Bristol with the rest of the family, a period which was to be of great moment in her young life. A theatrical agent secured her an audition with the exotic Madame Albina de Rhona, a French dancer and actress who had ventured into management somewhat quixotically after a successful career in Paris, St Petersburg and London. Dressed in Kate's bonnet of pink silk trimmed with black lace, Nellie went for her audition accompanied by her father, who tried to reassure his lanky daughter of fourteen by telling her that pink was her colour, no doubt of it. Madame de Rhona took to her at sight, and Nellie was contracted to join the company in the process of being formed at the Soho Theatre, which Madame had renovated in the French style and renamed the Royalty. The Theatre was to open in November 1861.

Madame de Rhona was a very different woman from Mrs Kean. Her first appearance in London had been at the St James's in a piece from the French called *Smack for Smack,* in which both her agility and vivacity impressed the critics. Ellen remarks how small she was – 'she was a wee thing – like a toy' – but she was fascinated by her, never having met a Frenchwoman before. She

c

thought her dancing, her whole movement exquisite, and it made Nellie feel 'long and gaunt'. In her methods of production Madame was as unlike Charles Kean as could be imagined – 'she really frightened me out of my wits at the first rehearsal by dancing round me on the stage in a perfect frenzy of anger at what she was pleased to call my stupidity. Then something I did suddenly pleased her, and she overwhelmed me with compliments and praise.'

Madame's taste in drama was as odd as her manners; she had chosen to open with a melodrama adapted from a story by Eugene Sue. It was set in Jamaica and called *Atar-Gull;* it showed the vengeance of a Negro on the family of a planter who has had the Negro's father hanged. Nellie, as the planter's daughter Clementine, became one of the Negro's victims when he set a live snake upon her, which was meant to coil itself round her neck and strangle her. In order to extract the right scream from Nellie, Madame finally flew at her 'like a wild-cat' and shook her till she cried; then suddenly the 'wild, agonized scream' emerged from her, and she got a kiss from Madame for her pains. Ellen, looking back on this experience in her training, comments:

> I know perfectly well why I, a mere child of thirteen, was able to give such a realistic display of horror. I had the emotional instinct to start with, no doubt, but if I did it well, it was because I was able to imagine what would be *real* in such a situation. I had never *observed* such terror, but I had previously *realized* it, when as Arthur, I had imagined the terror of having my eyes put out . . . Imagination, industry, and intelligence – 'the three I's – are all indispensible to the actress, but of these three the greatest is, without any doubt, imagination.[16]

In the five weeks between 21 November and 26 December she had to study five new parts, and as she stayed with the company until February 1862, the month of her fourteenth birthday. She had never before had to study so fast, and her memory was never to be her strongest point. On one occasion she had her first experience of stage-fright – that paralysis of the mind and body that leaves an actor speechless and helpless under the intolerable gaze of the audience. Nellie's final reaction was to leave the stage, get hold of the script and conclude her performance by reading the part. She does not remember what Madame de Rhona said about this loss of nerve.

Kate in the meantime had been offered an engagement with James Henry Chute's excellent stock company at the Theatre Royal in Bristol, and had already joined him in 1861, leaving the Wigan company in London where she had only been given small parts. On one glorious night she had understudied for the leading lady, Miss Herbert, in a play by Sardou and won outstanding praise from her friend Tom Taylor and from another eminent critic, Clement Scott, who wrote of her: 'No one knew that we had amongst us a young actress of so much beauty, talent and dramatic power.' It might seem strange that Kate, then a girl of sixteen, did not stay in London after this moment of success. But the pattern of training in the English theatre was to play as full a range of parts as possible in the provinces before finally attempting to achieve stardom in London. Ben and Sarah, so careful of their daughters' talent, must have realized that Kate's experiences as a child actress with the Keans was in fact far too limited to qualify her for a fully-developed career on the London stage. She had simply not fulfilled the range of parts which a provincial stock company would be prepared to offer a talented young actress. So Kate went to Bristol with her father to join one of the finest provincial repertory companies in the country, and was soon followed by her sister and mother in 1862.

II

CHILD ACTRESS AND CHILD WIFE

Kate and Ellen were to stay at the Theatre Royal, Bristol, under Chute's management until early in 1863, and Ellen was to fulfil a further brief engagement in Bath when Chute opened the new theatre there on 4 March 1863 – the earlier historic building having been destroyed by fire in April of the previous year. Many of the players in the Bristol company were later to become famous; they included Madge Robertson (later Mrs Kendal), who was about the same age as Ellen, and her parents, an actor and actress who had twenty-two children, one of them T. W. Robertson, soon to become distinguished as a dramatist. There was also Henrietta Hodson, who had a fine singing voice and who had already played opposite the youthful Henry Irving in Scotland and Manchester, David James, who had begun his career walking on for Charles Kean at the Princess's Theatre in 1857, and Charles Coghlan, the comedian, described by one of his contemporaries as 'handsome, fascinating, selfish and spendthrift'. All these players were young in 1862, the oldest of them still in their early twenties.

Both Kate and Ellen now began a hard year's work which involved continuous appearances in a wide range of popular pieces; Ellen played parts ranging from Alice in *Marriage at any Price* and Marie in *The Noble Heart* to Cupid in a burlesque called *Endymion*.[1] She learned how to play to a local public who followed the work of the individual players in their theatre with personal ardour and devotion. The stock companies of the period put on one-act farces, classical burlesques, comedies, melodramas and tragedies, all of which called for tough and skilful playing, often in several different pieces within a single week. Occasionally there was Shakespeare – Kate played Portia and Beatrice to Ellen's Nerissa

and Hero. Ellen's early biographer Pemberton managed forty
years after this season in the west of England to obtain an anony-
mous account from a young 'general utility' actor who was for a
while attached to Chute's company while the sisters were working
in Bristol. This first-hand description is useful, if lyrical:

Ellen Terry was then a girl of about fourteen, of tall figure,
with a round, dimpled, laughing, mischievous face, a pair of
merry, saucy, grey eyes, and an aureole of golden hair, which
she wore, in the words of a modern ditty, 'hanging down her
back'. Although dwarfed, in a measure, as an actress, by the
more experienced skill and superior *rôles* of her fascinating
sister, Ellen soon became a great favourite in Bristol. Her
popularity was largely due to her performances in two of the
Brough brothers' burlesques – 'Endymion' and 'Perseus and
Andromeda'. In the former Miss Hodson played Endymion,
Kate Terry was Diana, and Ellen, Cupid, and a very arch,
piquant sprite, full of movement and laughter, Miss Ellen was.
She wore a loose short-skirted sort of tunic with a pair of
miniature wings, and of course carried the conventional bow
and quiver. Some of the more prudish of the Bristol theatre-
goers – the same people who had been wont to roar over the
vulgar comicalities of Johnny Rouse – were half inclined to be
shocked at a scantiness of attire that even Mr Chute himself
was disposed to think a little daring. ... But Ellen Terry's
charm, her delightful grace and innate refinement, quite dis-
armed the prudes, and Cupid triumphed in front of the curtain
as well as behind it, and lightly shot his darts in all directions
.... If I had to describe her acting in those days, I should say
its chief characteristic was a vivacious sauciness. Her voice
already had some of the rich sympathetic quality which has
since been one of her most distinctive charms .... Mrs
Terry always accompanied her daughters to and from the
theatre every night, and watched them from the wings during
the whole time they were on the stage. They lodged during
the season in Queen Square, then the recognized quarter for

theatrical folks. . . . Outside the little narrow stage-door, crowds of dazzled Lotharios and stage-struck worshippers used to throng to see the 'Terrys' go home after the performance. Mrs Terry played her part of duenna with uncommon vigilance, and it was little more than a snap-shot of three hurrying and well-wrapped-up figures that rewarded the admirers for their patience.[2]

According to Ellen herself, the great lesson she learned at Bristol was the idea of being 'useful' on the stage. 'Usefulness . . . on the stage it is the first thing to aim at. . . . Not until we have learned to be useful can we afford to do what we like. The Tragedian will always be a limited tragedian if he has not learned how to laugh. The comedian who cannot weep will never touch the highest levels of mirth.'[3] In stock, she adds, there was no question of parts being cast to suit the players; they had to perform what they were told to perform. In a classical burlesque she had to sing and dance, and it was no good her saying that she could do neither. A stock company must be able to turn its hand to everything, from pantomime to Shakespeare. At Bristol Kate was the 'principal lady' and Henrietta Hodson, with her skill at singing and dancing, the principal 'soubrette', featuring especially in popular burlesque. There were rival factions in the audience supporting either one or the other young actress. Ellen's own description of her following complements that quoted above:

> We were petted, spoiled, and applauded to our hearts' content but I don't think it did us any harm. We all had scores of admirers, but their youthful ardour seemed to be satisfied by tracking us when we went to rehearsal in the morning and waiting for us outside the stage-door at night. When Kate and I had a 'benefit' night, they had an opportunity of coming to rather closer quarters, for on these occasions tickets could be bought from members of the company, as well as at the box-office of the theatre.
>
> Our lodgings in Queen Square were besieged by Bristol youths who were anxious to get a glimpse of the Terrys. The

Terrys demurely chatted with them and sold them tickets. My mother was most vigilant in her role of duenna, and from the time I first went on the stage until I was a grown woman I can never remember going home unaccompanied by either her or my father.

Among Ellen's admirers in the audience at the Theatre Royal was a young architect who had a great interest in the theatre. Edwin William Godwin (whom Oscar Wilde was later on to describe in *The Truth of Masks* as 'one of the most astute spirits of this century in England' and whom Max Beerbohm in 1880 called 'that superb architect . . . the greatest aesthete of them all') was destined to become one of the three men whose influence on Ellen was enduring. The first of these men, as we have seen, was her father; the third was to be Henry Irving.

When Ellen first arrived at Bristol in 1862, Godwin was twenty-eight, almost double the age of the fifteen-year-old girl, who eight years later was to become the mother of his illegitimate child. Godwin in 1862 was a young and ambitious architect who three years earlier, on 1 November 1859, had married Sarah Yonge, a highly cultured and beautiful woman some years older than himself. She was a clergyman's daughter from Henley-on-Thames, where the wedding had taken place. Sarah Godwin, during the brief period of her married life, was forced through ill-health to retire into the background of her husband's activities; by 1864 she was to become a chronic invalid, nursed by her sister Ann. She died a year later. But at the time Ellen first met them in 1862, the Godwins had just become the occupants of 21 Portland Square, a fine Georgian house in a fashionable area.

The conventional Bristolians found young Godwin a somewhat disturbing influence. They could not understand why he saw fit to decorate his new town house with a door-knocker of his own design – a ball suspended on a chain. They heard that the walls inside remained entirely undecorated – large areas of plain colour relieved only by an occasional Japanese print. The floors were bare except for Persian rugs, and the furniture instead of being heavily upholstered and monstrously Victorian, consisted of a few carefully selected antiques from the previous century. How poor the young couple must be, they thought, to be unable to afford thick wallpaper and comfortable chairs.

Godwin, in fact, was already establishing his highly individual taste in the face of the *bourgeois* pretensions of his time. As a youth he had been articled by his father, a well-to-do tradesman and builder in Bristol, to a firm of architects and civil engineers, the head of which, William Armstrong, knew nothing of the niceties of architecture and was content to leave such things as design to his brilliant young apprentice. Godwin's father hoped his son would become an engineer in Bristol and follow the genius Brunel had so magnificently demonstrated in the construction of the Clifton suspension bridge. But Godwin's interests lay elsewhere; at the age of only eighteen he helped to illustrate *The Architectural Antiquities of Bristol and Neighbourhood,* a work which was published by subscription in 1851, and revealed his initial interest in a Gothic revival in architecture.

Godwin's passion was for architectural design and in the absence of any formal tuition he had to teach himself. He took his relaxations equally seriously, and these included attendance at Bristol's Theatre Royal and a close study of Shakespeare. Rather spoiled by the success he had achieved in defiance of his elders, Godwin, in 1854, as soon as he reached the age of twenty-one, had resigned from Armstrong's firm, determined to seek his fortune independently. Slim, elegant, brown-eyed, strikingly handsome if somewhat delicate in appearance, he had by now acquired many of the social graces. He was already a good conversationalist; he could talk well about the work of the novelists of the century, especially about Scott, whose medievalism attracted him. He was interested in music and he played the organ. Women found him fascinating, and his unexpected knowledge of costume design only added to this charm.

He had set up his own architect's office in Bristol, and began to receive modest commissions, but the economic crisis in the mid-1850s following the Crimean War to some extent held him back.

With time on his hands, he had persuaded the editor of a local paper to let him write critical notices of the plays produced at the Theatre Royal. This encouraged his already lively interest in the theatre, and gave him a stake in it which was later to become professional.

Next came a period working with his brother, a civil engineer engaged in Ireland, and then Godwin returned to Bristol. He was maturer now, with an increased knowledge of how to design and build in the style he favoured. His articles on the theatre, which he resumed, became as much comments on décor and costume design as they were criticism of acting and production. He made friends with William Burges, a wealthy young architect in London, and studied Ruskin's new book, *The Stones of Venice,* which deflected his taste from Victorian Gothic. When the corporation of Northampton announced a competition for the new town hall, Godwin, now newly married, decided to enter. Forty designs were submitted from all over the country, and in the spring of 1861 Godwin learned that his had been successful. It was a triumph for a young man of twenty-seven; it was also a triumph for the new style he had adopted, that of the Italian Renaissance; 'the building was entirely founded on *The Stones of Venice*', he wrote later, and the furniture and decorations were also placed in his hands. Godwin's reputation was made. The following year he was elected a Fellow of the Bristol Architectural Society.

The work of supervising the building at Northampton and fulfilling subsequent commissions that followed on this success did not lead to Godwin abandoning his other artistic interests. In his fine house in Portland Square he installed an organ, and friends interested in Shakespeare were invited to take part in readings from the plays. Godwin and his wife remained enthusiastic supporters of the Theatre Royal, and he still wrote his 'jottings' about the productions staged there. His criticisms were apparently not always welcome; one actor was so incensed that he called on the unsuspecting critic at his house and, when Godwin entered the room, assaulted him with a horsewhip. The incident was hushed up, all the more so because the actor had discovered Godwin dressed up as Henry V.

It was to one of his Shakespearean readings that Godwin decided to invite the two young actresses he so much admired at the Theatre Royal. He had already made the acquaintance of their parents, and he was, of course, well known to the theatre management. There seemed no harm to Ben and Sarah in letting their girls visit so attractive a household to take part in a reading of *A Midsummer Night's Dream,* in which Godwin had seen Ellen play the part of Puck the previous year at the Princess's Theatre in London. The Godwins represented 'society' to the Terrys, and therefore a desirable outlet for their daughters in contrast to their enclosed lives in the theatre.

Ellen was entranced by the unusual atmosphere in Portman Square:

> This house, with its Persian rugs, beautiful furniture, its organ, which for the first time I learned to love, its sense of design in every detail, was a revelation to me, and the talk of its master and mistress made me *think.* At the theatre I was living in an atmosphere which was developing my powers as an actress and teaching me what work meant, but my mind had begun to grasp dimly and almost unconsciously that I must do something for myself – something that all the education and training I was receiving in my profession could not do for me. I was fourteen years old at Bristol, But I now felt that I had never really lived at all before. For the first time I began to appreciate beauty, to observe, to feel the splendour of things, to *aspire* . . .[4]

She found the decoration of the house beautiful and not the least eccentric. When Godwin revealed that he was the author of the 'very wonderful criticisms' she had cut out of the local paper, she was more than ever excited to meet the author of remarks she felt to be 'very clever, most amusing – and generally right'.

Among the guests at this reading were William Burges from

London, by now a frequent visitor to Bristol, and another architect, Henry Crisp, who lived in a cottage called Cherry Orchard, where Ellen leapt in one bound from top to bottom of the straight cottage staircase opposite the front door. The men were entranced by her charm and vitality. Throughout the rest of the winter of 1862–3, Ellen and Kate were constant visitors to Portman Square, and Godwin took another step towards his involvement in the theatre. He undertook to design Ellen's dress when, in March 1863, she appeared as Titania at the re-opening of the Theatre Royal, Bath, under Chute's management. 'Mr Godwin,' she wrote in her memoirs, 'designed my dress, and we made it at his house in Bristol. He showed me how to damp it and "wring" it while it was wet, tying up the material as the Orientals do in their "tie and dry" process, so that when it was dry and untied, it was all crinkled and clinging. This was the first lovely dress that I ever wore.' After this, the Terrys returned to London and for a while the friendship with Godwin was interrupted. When Ellen met Godwin again in London he was a widower and she was a wife.

The return to Stanhope Street brought new work for Kate and Ellen. Kate was already working in the company of the noted actor from France, Charles Albert Fechter, who had established himself at the Lyceum, while Ellen, announced as 'late of the New Theatre Royal, Bath', appeared at the Haymarket on 19 March 1863 in John Baldwin Buckstone's company, in which the star was the comedian Edward Askew Sothern, famous as the creator of the part of the foppish and imbecile Lord Dundreary, with his elongated side-whiskers and trend-setting clothes.

The play in which Ellen opened was an adaptation from the French of a light comedy called in English *The Little Treasure;* she had already played Gertrude Howard in this play at Bristol, and the opportunity to repeat a familiar part in London was of the greatest help to her. John Oxenford, reviewing the production in *The Times,* wrote, 'it presents Miss Terry in an entirely new light . . . she is matured into one of the happiest specimens of what the French call the *ingénue* that has been seen on any stage'.

The audiences' fascination for Sothern was not reflected backstage; his taste for sadistic practical jokes angered his fellow-players. In spite of 'his wonderful hands and blue eyes', Ellen found him hateful because he teased her – pulling her hair, making her forget her lines, and exposing her to ridicule. Sothern, who was almost forty, became the object of dread to Ellen at sixteen, and this no doubt helps to account for her feeling of distaste for the theatre and her growing interest in adopting the other kind of life which was soon to open to her with what appeared to be magical splendour.

Later she described her experience with Buckstone's company as a 'lost opportunity'. She could have learned much more from the veteran players at the Haymarket. Buckstone, who was over sixty, had played in the time of Edmund Kean, who was said to have known him and admired his work. Another veteran, Henry Howe, who had decided to go on the stage after seeing Kean as Lear, had played with Macready, and was to work at the Haymarket for forty years before joining young Irving at the Lyceum in 1881. The company also included Henry Compton, grandfather of Fay Compton and Compton Mackenzie; he was now nearly sixty; William Farren, also with long connexions with the Haymarket, and the grandson of a distinguished actor who had played in Drury Lane and Covent Garden during the last quarter of the eighteenth century, was a noted member of the company. They were all specialists in performing Sheridan's plays and eighteenth-century comedy, and another of them, W. H. Chippendale, was so old, says Ellen, that, like Charles Reade's mother, he might even have known Sheridan personally. Chippendale taught her how to make a sweeping curtsy. Later she was to write of this company of veterans: 'their bows, their curtseys, their grand manner, the undefinable *style* which they brought to their task, were something to be seen.' As actors they were in the direct line of Sheridan's own exacting style of production, but Ellen, in a mood of blind adolescent intolerance, was either unable or unwilling to appreciate them. For some months she played a succession of 'useful' parts, including Hero, Nerissa, Lady

Touchwood in *The Belle's Stratagem*, Julia Melville in *The Rivals* ('I played ... very ill,' says Ellen), and finally Mary Meredith in *The American Cousin*, in which Sothern appeared as Lord Dundreary. She even appeared in burlesque before the newly-married Prince and Princess of Wales.[5]

A contemporary description of Ellen on the stage in *The Little Treasure* reveals how she appeared at the age of sixteen:

> She is very young, but shows no trace of immaturity either in her style or figure. Tall for her age, of prepossessing appearance, and with expressive features full of vivacity and intelligence, she secured at once the sympathies of her audience, and retained them by the joyous spirit and deep feeling with which she imbued the personation.[6]

The critic Clement Scott foresaw her future in his description of her in *The American Cousin*:

> When Ellen Terry played Georgina she was a young girl of enchanting loveliness. She was the ideal of every pre-Raphaelite painter, and had hair, as De Musset says, *'comme le blé.'* I always sympathized with Dundreary when he, within whispering distance of Ellen Terry's harvest-coloured hair, said: 'It makes a fellow feel awkward when he's talking to the back of a person's head.'

Her year's season at the Haymarket was by far the best opportunity Ellen had yet had to shine, but she was at odds with the world of the theatre for reasons quite outside it. She was repelled by the gossip and scandal-bearing that took place in the theatre Green Room, and on one occasion used her well-practised curtsy to advantage and swept out in a huff, crying as she did so Sheridan's line, 'Ladies and gentlemen, I leave my character behind me!'

'In the middle of the run of *The American Cousin* I left the stage and married.' With this abrupt sentence, Ellen announced in her memoirs the great change that had come into her life to distract her from her profession at the very time when great opportunities were open to her. She was married on 20 February 1864 about a week before she became seventeen. Her husband was the distinguished painter, George Frederick Watts, and his age was three days short of forty-seven.

The extraordinary story of Ellen's first marriage begins with Tom Taylor. We have seen that he and Charles Reade had been instrumental in introducing the Terry girls into those branches of London society with which as dramatists and men of culture they were well acquainted. At some date in 1862, and possibly even earlier, Watts had made the acquaintance of Kate and Ellen through their mutual friend Tom Taylor. According to Ellen's daughter Edy, and her friend Christopher St John, Watts had seen Kate on the stage and had asked Taylor to bring her to his studio; they even go so far as to suggest that Taylor regarded Kate as a prospective wife for the middle-aged painter.[7] However that may be, Taylor had responded to his friend's interest in Kate by introducing him to both sisters, and Watts had eventually come to recognize that Ellen rather than Kate possessed the kind of beauty that Clement Scott characterized as 'the ideal of every pre-Raphaelite painter'. The result of this meeting was the painting by Watts known as *The Sisters,* in which the face of Kate appears shadowy and remote compared with the bold and finely moulded features of Ellen, who is shown to be a strong and magnificent girl with a visionary expression in her eyes. It was painted, it would seem, sometime in 1863.

The sitting took place in Watts's studio at Little Holland House, where he had lived in the most extraordinary circumstances since 1851 as the house-guest of Mr and Mrs Thoby Prinsep. In this arrangement, Mrs Prinsep was, as might be expected, the guiding genius, and her husband, a good-natured man always ready to indulge his formidable wife, the acquiescent partner.

Watts was used to female patronage. Born on 23 February 1817, he had been brought up in Georgian London at a house in Queen Street, off Bryanston Square. His father, an ineffective enthusiast with a passion for inventing rather than manufacturing musical instruments, lived in straitened circumstances, and George Frederic was his first child by his second wife, whom he had married in 1816. He was the only son to survive of four boys born of this marriage, and his mother, who was a consumptive woman obsessed by piety, died when he was nine years old. Her surviving son's adolescence had been spent in the impoverished household of an ageing father and two quarrelling step-sisters almost twenty years older than himself.

As a youth he was asthmatic and suffered from headaches. He lay in a darkened room, watched over by his father, who cherished him as the genius he had failed to be himself. He began very early in life to draw well, and his father apprenticed him at the age of ten to the studio in Soho of the sculptor and draughtsman, William Behnes. William's crippled brother, Charles, taught Watts about literature and science. Watts in his youth became influenced by Haydon, who painted in the Grand Manner, and he soon became obsessed by the need to show himself as a great master. He studied anatomy and spent much time examining the Elgin marbles. He was finally admitted in 1835 at the age of eighteen to the Academy School, while his father was reduced to piano-tuning and music-teaching to earn a meagre living.

Watts was growing up in the period when the so-called High Art and the Grand Manner were still the aspiration of many painters, but portraiture was the stock-in-trade of the Academy. Watts, however, remained the idealist, inspired by the dreams of romantic literature and the genius of Michelangelo. His teachers thought highly of him, and he thought even more highly of himself. In 1837 he set up his own studio, and won his first patron, a Greek merchant called Constantine Ionides.

A self-portrait by Watts at the age of seventeen shows him to have had long and curling black hair, dark eyes and a handsome face with an introvert expression. He might have been a poet of the romantic school with his wide, untidy collar and loosely open jacket. People thought he looked like Shelley, and he began to act the part of the inspired painter. But he was lonely in spite of the growing recognition which his work was bringing him. In 1843 he won a coveted prize of £300 for a drawing of Caractacus, the British chieftain, being led in chains through Rome, a work he had submitted in a competition for a mural to decorate the new Houses of Parliament. His work was exhibited for public criticism in Westminster Hall together with that of other successful competitors.

With the seemingly vast sum of £300 at his disposal, Watts left at once for Italy, the object of his dreams, spending six weeks in Paris on his way to the south. Travelling in turn by river, by coach and by cart, he ended up in Florence, where he had an introduction to Lord Holland, the wealthy British Minister to the Court of Tuscany, whose house, the Casa Feroni, was a centre of culture. Lady Holland, petite, attractive, with pointed features and wide eyes, sat for her portrait in a vast conical hat tied beneath her chin with a large neat bow. She is shown staring out of the picture at the painter with that possessive female stare which was to become only too familiar to Watts throughout the remainder of his life. Before he knew quite where he was, Watts had acquired the first of a succession of zealous patronesses who were to dominate his life.

Lady Holland invited him to join her household as her resident painter-genius. She called him Fra Paolo, after Veronese, and the great Florentine mansion became his home. Lord Holland took him to Rome to see the Sistine Chapel and to Naples to see Vesuvius and Pompeii.

The relationship with Lady Holland was of a kind Watts liked to have with women. On New Year's Day she threw a gold chain over his head and cried, 'We not only bind you to us, we chain you.' This was all very well, but a beautiful Florentine woman whom he was teaching to draw mistook a gift of flowers for a declaration of passion, and Watts in a flutter of embarrassment had to throw the flowers on to the fire and flee the threatened danger. Board was fine, but he was not inclined for bed.

Later Watt's relations with Lord Holland became more strained; he refused the commissions for portraits his patron put in his way. Lord Holland wrote:

I have scolded, and reasoned, and for the time kept him

quiet, but he vows he shall return the money and will not paint portraits for gain. I think this foolish. However, I suspect he is just now in the fervour of historical painting, and will not be so unreasonable when the fit of glory and the visions of Michael Angelo shall subside a little.

Even Lady Holland became to some extent disillusioned with her young genius:

> I have a strong and determined wish to break the spell, and make him feel that he is ever a welcome guest but not a constant and *necessary* inmate. . . . Watts's prolonged *séjour* in our house will not be ascribed to its real cause – good nature and kindness of heart on our side, want of energy, affection and gratitude on his. His idleness will be laid to our door; and we shall be accused of having been the ruin of him, lucky if both of us escape with even so mild a censure.

In spite of this disenchantment, when the Hollands departed from Florence at the close of 1845, they left the villa at Careggi in the hands of Lady Caroline Duff Gordon, who appears to have taken over the patronage of Watts where Lady Holland had laid it down. She was the energetic widow of a baronet, Sir William Duff Gordon, who had died in 1823, and she shared Lady Holland's interest in the arts. She had two attractive daughters, Georgie and Alicia, who were also studiously engaged in the pursuit of culture. Watts at the age of twenty-nine found himself in the care of three admiring women; he was to give Georgie and Alicia, who were of about the same age as himself, instruction in drawing, and it was not long before Georgie felt herself to be in love with this inspired young man of genius who poured his views about High Art into the eager ears of his young pupils.

Watts never mustered the energy to make open love to Georgie. In spite of her artistic leanings she had, like her mother, a common-sense outlook on life. She was well aware that marriage with Watts would be regarded as a misalliance. Lady Duff Gordon saw the danger signals and withdrew with her daughters to enjoy

other, and no doubt higher, society in Rome. At a safe distance,
Watts began a prolonged, self-revealing correspondence with
Georgie which was to last until 1849.

However that may be, the Hollands encouraged him to enter
for another competition in England, that for an oil painting to
adorn the House of Lords. Working against time, he left Italy
by ship in April 1847 with five great canvases in the hold. He won
a prize of £500 with his subject entitled, *Alfred inciting the Saxons
to resist the landing of the Danes by encountering them at sea;* it was,
of course, painted in the Grand Manner and somewhat severely
criticized in the *Athenaeum*. But his success made him dream of
creating his own Sistine Chapel, and he started plans and sketches
for a vast House of Life to be built and adorned by him in London.
Watts felt himself to be England's Michelangelo, destined to
create huge allegorical masterpieces in fresco. That he never
achieved this position, or was even afforded the opportunity to
attempt to do so, only increased the frustrations and inhibitions
of his later life. He became lonely and lacking in self-confidence.
He was forced back on the form of painting he most despised –
the commissioned portrait. Lord Holland suggested that he
should set out to paint all the great personalities of the time in
the hope that one day they would be housed together as his
monument. This was good advice; it is on his portraits that his
considerable reputation now rests.

These decisions were being taken at about the time of Ellen's
birth in 1847. Watts established a studio in Charles Street. With
the English winter approaching, he wrote in 1848 a succession of
letters of self-analysis to Georgie:

> I am not doing anything 'beautiful' nor indeed anything at
> all but indulging my natural indolence and growing melan-
> choly under the depressing influence of the climate.... No
> doubt you are quite right in accusing me of a morbid state
> of feeling but wrong in imputing it to the effect of living
> in an atmosphere of enchantment. I wish I could find one,
> but the world has been my study and I have discovered that

the prizes it offers for competition are not worth contending for. . . .

If you will promise to look out for, and if possible find me a wife, I will promise while I am abroad to work hard, upon my honour I am serious. I must have something to look forward to. You talk of Fame! I am no longer to be taken in by such a pretence, but an agreeable companion in Italy would be an object worth working for. I take a commercial and common-sense view of the subject and therefore should not risk being deceived or disappointed and if I myself felt no violent love at least I am incapable of betraying a trust. You are probably somewhat surprised at such apparently new ideas in me, but they are not new, I have long thrown my romance to the wind. . . .

I would (not neglecting the higher walks of my profession) seek to make money in the hope of some day sharing it with some amiable companion, whose society would give a charm to my life and whose happiness and welfare would form a real and tangible object for my exertions, and I would exert myself, for I am not by nature unjust. Every day I feel more and more the impossibility of living alone. I am becoming subject to frightful fits of melancholy and despondency. But there is no reason why I should bore you with my absurdity excepting that I have always looked upon you, may I say as a sister? . . . I could find it in my heart to wish you were an ill-used or overworked governess.

This was as near a proposal as Watts came in his relations with Georgie Duff Gordon. But she was no longer responsive, and the correspondence ended. Georgie, with her vivacity, her humour, and her downright common sense would have made Watts a good wife and no doubt helped to make a successful career more palatable to him. However, another woman was ready to take him up in such a manner that made the patronage of Lady Holland and Lady Duff Gordon seem like the gentlest of intrusions upon his private life.

He had seen and admired a beautiful young woman, who after
due investigation turned out to be a Miss Virginia Pattle. Watts
was introduced to her and painted her portrait When a lady sat
for an artist, it was normal for her to be chaperoned, and Virginia
Pattle had a married sister who accompanied her to the studio.
This was Mrs Thoby Prinsep, the wife of a former jurist in India
who had retired at the age of fifty and was now a benign and
good-humoured member of Council at the India Office in
London.

The Pattle girls – there were seven of them in all – were remarkable Victorian women of mixed French and Irish descent;
most of them made distinguished marriages, while one of them,
Julia Margaret Cameron, who had also married a former jurist in
India and legal member of the Surpeme Council in Calcutta, took
up amateur photography in the 1860s, when she was approaching
fifty, and became, almost involuntarily, a pioneer in the art. She
started this hobby just in time to make a historic portrait of Ellen
shortly after her marriage to Watts. Julia Cameron and her
husband became close friends of Tennyson while living in the
Isle of Wight. Virginia Pattle, at the time Watts discovered her,
was nicknamed Dash; she was still unmarried and living with her
sister, Mrs Prinsep, in Chesterfield Street; soon she was to marry
Lord Somers.[8] Mrs (later Lady) Sophie Dalrymple and Mrs
Jackson were other sisters. Virginia was the acknowledged beauty
of the family, and Mrs Cameron (nicknamed Talent) its most
accomplished member; she had ceaseless energy that rather overwhelmed her more indolent friends. Mrs Prinsep, inappropriately
nicknamed Beauty, was the lion-hunter of the family. She was
dumpy, untidy, and both socially and culturally voracious. It
was she who told her nieces to read their Bibles before going to
a dance in order that they should acquire 'heavenly expressions'.
She had a son, Val Prinsep, born in 1838, who was to become a
painter, and she had only to look at Watts to want to acquire him
for herself. Lonely and disturbed, he was quite ready to respond
to her cultural advances.

Mrs Prinsep's ambition, to which her husband – tall, fat, genial and acquiescent – found it convenient to concur, was to establish a *salon,* but for this the house in Chesterfield Street was altogether inadequate. Through Watts, they learnt that Lord Holland was prepared to rent them Little Holland House, a property described as a farmhouse adjoining Lord Holland's own residence. The farmhouse had many historic associations, and in 1850 Thoby Prinsep took a lease on it for an initial period of twenty-one years.[9] Meanwhile, Watts's mental state had deteriorated more and more, clouded over with melancholy; 'often I sit among the ruins of my aspirations, watching the tide of time,' he wrote. Mrs Prinsep could not bear it; she invited him to come and live in comfort and seclusion with herself and her husband. She would see to it that he would be well looked after and well supervised. Watts did not need much persuasion to accept, and the enveloping relationship which was to last unbroken for over twenty years began. Indeed, it endured as long as the Prinseps' lease of the house. As Mrs Prinsep used to put it later: 'He came to stay three days; he stayed thirty years.'

Little Holland House, which was demolished in 1875, was a rambling affair. As described by the Hon. Mrs Edward Twisleton (an American married to an Englishman, and for a while a close friend of Mrs Prinsep until they quarrelled and the lady discovered the Pattle sisters to have what she termed 'grave moral defects'), the house with which Ellen was to become only too familiar had had 'another house as it were built on to it, so that the rooms are low and large, and wainscotted, and oddly placed in relation to each other, and then there are long passages, and out you come again into rooms where you don't expect them'. The setting was rural and virtually undeveloped in the mid-nineteenth century; there was open country to the west, and much of Kensington had still to be built. Between Holland Park and the river to the south lay little but fields.

The Hon. Mrs Twisleton also described Mrs Prinsep as 'rather stout and not handsome, but delightful to look at, and the sort of person one would like to live under the shadow of or rather bask in the sunlight of'. Virginia was 'fair, and round and sweet'. Mrs

Prinsep's 'darling'. Her manner – no doubt the manner in which she first welcomed Kate and Ellen – was fulsome; she 'took both my hands in hers, and said she was so glad to see me with her sisters, and that I must learn to call them all by their names, and not Mrs, and they were so sweet with each other, and so sweet to me, and overcame me so, with every kind of loving-kindness, that I was really upset, and fairly cried in Mrs Prinsep's face'. When she entertained, Mrs Prinsep appears to have arranged her meals in extraordinary style, moving her guests from room to room between the courses.

Once Watts was installed, he was given studio space in rooms sheltered behind a door covered with red baize, and he was gradually warmed back to work by Mrs Prinsep's bristling attentions. Mrs Twisleton wrote home in 1853: 'Mrs Prinsep has taken into her house and home a poor forlorn artist, with great talents and weak health, which is just like her, and in consequence her house is full of his pictures.' He painted frescoes for her on the walls, and many allegorical figures and portraits. As she built up her salon of notable visitors and guests, Mrs Prinsep arranged to show off her artist in the guise of a resident lion. He was always known as the Signor, a term a little more playful than Maestro but with something of its implied respect for the artist. Watts fortunately got on well with Thoby Prinsep, who remained un-perturbed by the constant flux of people who invaded his house at his wife's bidding. A regimen was prepared to help Watts overcome the indolence to which he readily gave way. He learned to get up early and work before breakfast as well as after-wards. When lunch was finished, Mrs Prinsep would send her two menfolk, Thoby (whom unkind friends called 'dog Thoby') and Watts, into a dimly-lit room where they lay on couches and listened to the voice of a woman introduced by Mrs Prinsep to read for the good of their nerves. After a little of this recreation, Watts would return to his studio. In the evening, while Thoby perhaps sat transposing Indian stories into verse, Laura Taylor, Tom's wife, might accept an invitation to come and sing for whatever company Mrs Prinsep assembled to listen to her.

There were plenty of enemies to laugh at Mrs Prinsep's bourgeois Bohemianism, but soon enough the greater names began to respond to her enthusiasm, and her guests came to include Tennyson, Browning, Thackeray, Disraeli, Gladstone and, of course, the Tom Taylors, and the proliferation of Pattle sisters. Titled people were always welcome; one of them, Lady Constance Leslie, wrote before her marriage to Sir John Leslie (a cousin of Aubrey de Vere, the poet, who was Watts's friend) with the same kind of enthusiasm that seems to have affected Ellen when she first came into contact with the glories of Little Holland House:

> John took me to what was to me a new world – something I had never imagined before of beauty and kindness. I was a very ignorant little girl, and oh how proud I felt, though rather unworthy of what seemed holy ground. The Signor came out of his studio all spirit and so delicate, and received me very kindly as John's future wife. Thackeray was there with his young daughters ... and Lady Somers, glorious and benevolent. Signor was the whole object of adoration and care in that house. He seemed to sanctify Little Holland House.[10]

Under this spell, Watts assumed more and more the manner of an established maestro. He acquired a beard which covered the mildness of his clean-shaven features; these may be seen in the portrait of him by Cousens before he became Mrs Prinsep's dependant and the object of her devouring admiration and devotion. His health remained poor – his letters of the 1850s are full of allusions to his illness – and he acquired another confidante, a successor to Georgie, in the person of Mrs Jeannie Nassau Senior, the sister of Tom Hughes, author of *Tom Brown's Schooldays,* and a social worker who tried in the teeth of Victorian convention to help unmarried mothers. Watts poured out his heart to her in endless letters which are the accompaniment to his voluntary imprisonment at Little Holland House. His neurosis grew, and the letters to this sympathetic woman became an outlet for his hypochondria:

The misery and despondency that often fall upon me makes my life a burden. I am constantly so nervous that I am afraid almost of mounting the stairs and really quite alarmed at the idea of getting on my horse. Then it is I feel the horror of being alone, yet the dread of seeing anyone. . . . I wish I were strong enough to go where deeds of heroism and daring are done, and privations suffered. The aspirations, even with the violence, of an heroic age would have suited me better. As it is I am sick of life, and desire to rest.[11]

This was the painter to whom Tom Taylor introduced the Terry girls in 1862, more than ten years since Mrs Prinsep had first assumed her domination over Watts as a man if not as an artist. Mrs Prinsep received them; Mrs Prinsep opened the red baize door and led them through to the Signor's studio. There they were received and invited to pose together, and the unfinished picture, *The Sisters,* was the result.

Ellen was apparently enchanted. 'Little Holland House,' she wrote, 'seemed to me a paradise, where only beautiful things were allowed to come. All the women were graceful, and all the men were gifted.' At some time during her subsequent visits Watts began to realize that young Ellen had fallen in love with him and he with her. So he kissed her. Ellen, so strictly brought up in spite of the theatre, had never before been kissed, as she wrote over thirty years later to Bernard Shaw:

I'll never forget my first kiss. I made myself such a donkey over it, and always laugh now when I remember. Mr Watts kissed me in the studio one day, but sweetly and gently, all tenderness and kindness, and then I was what they call 'engaged' to him and all the rest of it, and my people hated it, and I was in Heaven for I knew I was to live with those pictures. 'Always,' I thought, and to sit to that gentle Mr W. and clean his brushes, and play my idiotic piano to him, and sit with him there in wonderland (the studio).[12]

A further passage, suppressed when the Shaw–Terry letters were published, is more significant:

Then I got ill and had to stay at Holland House – and then – he kissed me – *differently* – not much differently but a little, and I told no one for a fortnight, but when I was alone with Mother one day she looked so pretty and sad and kind, I told her – what do you think I told the poor darling? I told her I *must* be married to him *now* because I was going to have a baby ! ! ! ! *and she* believed me ! ! Oh, I tell you I thought I knew everything then, but I was nearly 16 years old then – I was *sure* THAT kiss meant giving me a baby!

A copy of a letter said to have been written at this period by Watts to Lady Constance Leslie includes the remarks that he is 'determined to remove the youngest Miss Terry from the temptations and abominations of the stage, give her an education and if she continues to have the affection she now feels for me, marry her'. These scarcely seem like the words of a lover. It is also claimed that he wrote to Lady Leslie, 'To make the poor child what I wish her to be will take a long time, and most likely cost a great deal of trouble, and I shall want the sympathy of all my friends.'[13]

Since Watts was in no position to remove himself from Little Holland House and to support a wife and possible children, it is evident that the marriage had to meet with the full initial approval of Mrs Prinsep. Nellie, high-spirited, responsive, used to the unrestrained behaviour of the stage and the applause of audiences, successful in her profession but still very much a minor and utterly inexperienced where men were concerned, seems eager to regard this neurotic man, almost three times her own age, as a desirable husband. And, it would appear, Ben and Sarah agreed. From their point of view, the match no doubt seemed advantageous, though the equivocal nature of Nellie's position as the girl-wife of an artist who, however well known, was unable or unwilling to support himself independently and was content to let his wife live with him in a patroness's house could hardly have escaped Sarah's critical notice. Mrs Prinsep had for long shown herself prepared to meet any artistic wish that her beloved Signor expressed. If Ellen had proved to be an ideal model and would in any way help him to come to terms with his distracted genius, then she could scarcely stand in his way when he made it known to her and to his friends that he wanted to marry this young actress. So the marriage was arranged at St Barnabas, Kensington, for 20 February 1864, and the names of the witnesses show quite plainly that neither the Prinseps nor the Terrys were actively opposed to the match. They were Ben Terry, Kate, Tom Taylor, Val Prinsep and Sophie Dalrymple.

Ellen herself, writing some forty years after this unfortunate misalliance, is naturally reticent about its darker side. She admits she was too young to marry while she was but fifteen years old. However, she adds, 'I was delighted, and my parents were delighted . . . It all seemed like a dream – not a clear dream, but a fitful one which in the morning one tries in vain to tell. And even if I could tell it, I would not. I was happy, because my face was the type which the great artist who had married me loved to paint.[14] Life at Stanhope Street was so demanding that even on her wedding day she had first to bath the youngest children and wash their hair. Holman Hunt had designed a wedding dress for her in brown silk, and she wore a white quilted bonnet with a sprig of orange-blossom and a 'beautiful' Indian shawl. She 'went away' in a sealskin jacket trimmed with coral buttons, and on her head she wore a little sealskin cap. When she started to cry, which was only natural, her husband merely told her to stop. 'It makes your nose swell,' he said, no doubt regarding such behaviour as unbecoming in his model.

The marriage, which was to last a bare ten months, has ever since been the cause of rumour and counter-rumour. The inaccuracies, says Ellen, were never contradicted by her because she felt that they were manifestly absurd. She asserts that she never had 'one single pang of regret for the theatre. . . . I wondered at the new life, and worshipped it because of its beauty'. As for the marriage, 'it was in many ways very happy indeed'.

People in a position to watch the couple began to exhibit various forms of prejudice. Edy Craig and Christopher St John, who were always to resent Ellen's relationships with men, claimed that Lady Constance Leslie, who was present at the wedding, remarked on the contrast between the 'atrabilious' bridegroom, walking slowly and heavily up the aisle, and the 'radiant child bride dancing up it on winged feet'. It struck her, she said, as painful.[15]

Ronald Chapman, Watt's most recent biographer, roundly asserts that the marriage was not consummated. There is some unpleasant gossip that on her marriage night Nellie was found crying bitterly on the staircase outside Watts's bedroom. What is certainly true is that her months of marriage were largely spent in modelling for her husband, and that this is what she loved. 'I remember sitting for him in armour for hours,' she writes, 'and never realizing that it was heavy until I fainted!' This was for the picture *Watchman, what of the Night?* Among the finest portraits he painted of her are *The Sisters* and *Choosing* (both now in private collections), *Ellen Terry* (in the National Portrait Gallery), and *Ophelia* (to be seen in the Watts Gallery), based on a purely imaginary conception, since Ellen was not to play this part until 1878 at the Lyceum. In *Choosing*, possibly painted soon after the marriage, Ellen is seen wearing the wedding dress designed by Holman Hunt.[16]

The relationship of the young, high-spirited and frolicsome actress to the disillusioned, middle-aged bachelor to whom she was now tied was by no means unfruitful. It is surely significant that Watts was to enter on a highly productive period of painting at the time of his marriage, and that his best work was to be portraiture and not the allegorical or didactic works, which he nevertheless stubbornly continued to paint. To this period belong the portraits not only of Ellen Terry herself, but of the Countess Somers (Virginia Pattle), of Tennyson (1863), of himself (1864) and of Swinburne (1865). During a long career which was to outlast the century, and to which his second wife, Mary, whom he married in 1886 at the age of sixty-nine, contributed so greatly, many more fine works were to swell this achievement. With Mary, once more he married a woman over thirty years his junior, but this time he gained a wife who was to become a mature and dedicated servant to his welfare and his art. He celebrated his honeymoon with her in Constantinople by painting her portrait – another fine work – but it seems unlikely that this marriage either was ever consummated.

In her life of her husband, published in 1912, Mary Watts all but dismisses his first marriage as scarcely worth any comment. It would perhaps be asking too much of human nature to expect her to be objective in this matter, but David Loshak, a critic who has made a most careful study of the effect of Watts's association with Ellen on the artist's work, is much more positive. 'His portraits of her are charged with a romantic sentiment which, while resembling a little that expressed in some pre-Raphaelite works, is never subjected to the naturalistic embarrassments of Hunt and his followers or overlaid with archaism or *femme fatalism* in the manner of the Rossetti school.' Generalizations of mood were anathema to the pre-Raphaelite. Loshak finds *Choosing* an attempt by Watts to present his wife as 'the loving emblem of his own quest for the "unattainable".' In *Watchman, what of the Night?* (originally called *Joan of Arc*), for which Ellen posed in armour, 'the light of noble endeavour plays about her face . . . there can be little doubt that it was her vitality and devotion that encouraged him to personify [it] with the bloom of a living presence, without resorting to the abstractions of his later years'.

Loshak himself has a small painting in which, he claims, Watts produced his own self-portrait as an armoured Knight, bearded and in middle-life, looking down in sober tenderness on a gentle girl, whom he identifies as Ellen Terry, 'the inclination of her head the very embodiment of yielding tenderness'. The Knight's regard is protective, 'satisfied perhaps at being able to shield her from what he conceived to be the dangers and temptations of her previous life, yet sad because age and long habits of abstinence obliged him to be protector rather than lover. It is a picture full of compassion, a story of two unhappy people who find consolation by ministering to one another's infirmities'. Loshak believes the disillusionment of Watts lay in discovering that Ellen was a girl who was in personality far different from the image of her he had conceived during the period of her initial enchantment with himself, his studio and the 'culture' of Little Holland House. However, Loshak does not agree that the artist was an impotent bachelor incapable of ardent desire, and he instances the various versions of *Paolo and Francesca* which Watts painted as the principal evidence for the seeds of the erotic which lay in his inhibited nature. When he was in Italy and drew initial pencil sketches for the subject, he used as his models the women he knew best – most notably Lady Holland, of whom, according to his biographer Chapman, he had once made 'some rather daring little sketches . . . whether . . . from nature or from imagination is not revealed'. However, the fresco of the period in the Victoria and Albert Museum portrays Lady Holland as a draped Francesca, whereas that of 1865 (owned by David Loshak) represents Ellen, and she is naked. When Watts painted the subject yet again in the version that is best known – that of the early 1870s preserved in the Watts Gallery – Countess Somers was the model, and she is shown as respectably covered. Loshak points out the difference between the version of 1865 and that which followed some seven years later: 'Gone is the gentle lyricism of the earlier version, to be replaced by cold tragedy, classically sculptural and remote.' Paolo no longer looks at his lover 'protectively . . . and with warm regret'. The 'romantic intimacy' is gone. Mainly on the evidence of this picture, David Loshak claims that the marriage must have been consummated, however inadequately, by this man of forty-seven, whose long preserved virginity must, he says, have been ended at last in the arms of Ellen.

Later, Watts was to become fascinated by the image of Ellen as Ophelia. He must have seen her play the part in the Lyceum production which opened in December 1878. He put his original study of Ellen in the guise of Ophelia back on his easel and retouched it; the picture is the very image of his tenderness, and memory of past love. He got hold of an insipid photograph of her in the part (she was aged over thirty) and developed a pencil study of it which gives vitality and distinction to her fully mature face. Most interesting of all, as if utterly rejecting the banality of the stage photograph, he painted round 1880 a haunting study of her in oils which he called *The Madness of Ophelia*.[17]

Only the previous year, in the divorce proceedings of March 1877, Watts had had the unhappy task of recalling his memories of what had led up to the collapse of his marriage in a matter of ten months. Advised by his lawyers, guided possibly by Mrs Prinsep, the painful words had to be found, and they echo a suffering and disappointment which the years had not assuaged:

> That although considerably older than his intended wife he admired her very much and hoped to influence, guide and cultivate a very artistic and peculiar nature and to remove an impulsive young girl from the dangers and temptations of the stage.
>
> That very soon after his marriage he found how great an error he had made. Linked to a most *restless and impetuous* nature accustomed from the very earliest childhood to the stage and forming her ideas of life from the exaggerated romance of sensational plays, from whose acquired habits a quiet life was intolerable and even impossible, demands were made upon him he could not meet without giving up all the professional aims his life had been devoted to.
>
> That he did not impute any immorality at that time but there was an insane excitability indulging in the wildest suspicions, accusations and denunciations driving him to the verge of desperation and separation became absolutely necessary unless he gave up his professional pursuits which was out of the question as he had no independent means and it was arranged by his friends and those of his wife that a separation should take place. That separation took place within a year of his marriage.
>
> That he was willing to take all the blame upon himself (excepting of course charges of immorality if any had been made against him but none were made and there could have been no sort of foundation for them).

That the matter pained him very much and that he refused to go into Society altogether and gave himself up entirely to study and close pursuit of his profession.[18]

There remains certain evidence of what happened at Little Holland House and elsewhere which can be extracted from the gossip of the period. This reveals that Ellen was quite unable to repress her impetuous nature and bring herself to conform to the unnatural pattern of behaviour that Watts seemed to desire and Mrs Prinsep was prepared to demand. There was, for instance, the famous incident which occurred during the summer at Esher, when the household moved out of Little Holland House to stay with yet another of the Pattle sisters, the widow Mrs Sandeman. Ellen suddenly pulled out her hairpins in company and let her long hair fall about her shoulders. No doubt this was a childish gesture of boredom, the expression of an instinctive desire for release from companionship which was too genteel. A less stupid or prejudiced woman than Mrs Prinsep would have let so small a matter pass, but she treated it as shocking behaviour in the wife of her beloved Signor, and reproved her on the spot. These reproofs, whether given in company or in private, became constant; Ellen was treated like a 'naughty child who must be scolded and made obedient, and a high-spirited, unconventional girl naturally resented this treatment'.[19]

Soon after the marriage, the Prinseps took their protegés to Freshwater in the Isle of Wight where they all stayed at Dimbola, the house of the Camerons. Mrs Cameron had by now made photography a serious hobby, and it was during this visit that she took the celebrated portrait of Ellen standing bare-shouldered in her nightdress.[20] It is one of the most beautiful photographs to be taken during the nineteenth century. Near-by was Farringford, the house of the poet Tennyson, who was a close friend of the Pattles and a constant visitor both to Little Holland House and Dimbola. 'At Freshwater,' Ellen wrote later, 'I was still so young that I preferred playing Indians and Knights of the Round Table with Tennyson's sons, Hallam and Lionel, and the young

Camerons . . . jumping gates, climbing trees, and running paper-chases.'[21] Tennyson in 1864 was fifty-five; Hallam and Lionel were still boys of twelve and ten and of an age to enjoy Ellen's high-spirits; Ellen, however, as we shall see, found Tennyson's company congenial, and he soon grew fond of her. Later, of course, she was to appear as a famous actress in his plays at the Lyceum, and meet him on more equal terms.

In London, Ellen was by no means cut off from Stanhope Street. We begin to get glimpses of her at the time of the break-up of her marriage in the diaries of Lewis Carroll who had been attracted by the Terrys ever since seeing Ellen as Mamillius in June 1856 ('a beautiful little creature,' the Reverend Charles Dodgson had written, 'who played with remarkable ease and spirit') and as Puck in December ('very cleverly acted'); he also saw Kate as Titania and Ariel (the latter 'exquisitely, graceful and beautiful'). He had returned constantly to the Princess's Theatre to see the sisters appear in Shakespeare, and later, in December 1864, when he was in his early thirties, he had used his friendship with Tom Taylor to gain an introduction to the family. He finally called on them on 20 December, and although charmed by Kate ('I thought her very ladylike and natural in manner'), was most disappointed to miss seeing Mrs Watts. He found that Mrs Watts, who was there 'on a visit of two or three days', was out when he called, but he used the excuse of showing the family some of his mounted photographs to call the following day, 'when I hope to see Mrs Watts also'. He had been deterred by Tom Taylor from calling on Ellen at Little Holland House. 'I am not going to call, as I had intended,' he wrote. Taylor without doubt had warned him that all was not well. Back he went to Stanhope Street on Wednesday 21 December with the photographs. The entry he made is interesting:

> Polly and Benjamin met me in the hall, and in the drawing-room I found Miss Kate Terry, Florence, and to my delight, the one I have always most wished to meet of the family, Mrs Watts. Mr Tom Taylor called in later to read Miss Terry some

1. Ellen Terry in 1856, aged eight

2. Lewis Carroll's studies of the Terry family:
Sarah and Benjamin Terry

3. Lewis Carroll's studies of the Terry family:
Ellen (in the dark frock) standing with Kate at the window.

4. Lewis Carroll's studies of the Terry family: Ellen Terry

5. Lewis Carroll's studies of the Terry family: Sarah and Ellen Terry

6. Stage portrait of Ellen Terry, *c.* 1866

7. Portrait by Mrs Cameron taken in the bathroom of
Tennyson's house in the Isle of Wight a few days after
Ellen Terry's marriage to Watts. (*By courtesy of the Royal
Photographic Society.*)

8. *Choosing* by G. F. Watts
*(By courtesy of Kerrison
Preston Esq.)*

8a. *Paolo and Francesca*
by G. F. Watts
(By courtesy of D. Loshak Esq.)

9. Self-portrait by G. F. Watts at about
the time of his marriage to Ellen Terry
(*By courtesy of the Tate Gallery.*)

9a. Sketches of Ellen Terry by G. F. Watts
(*By courtesy of D. Loshak Esq.*)

10. *The Sisters* by G. F. Watts
(By courtesy of the Hon. Mrs Hervey Bathurst.)

of her part in a MS play [*Settling Day*], and I remained to listen. I was very much pleased with what I saw of Mrs Watts – lively and pleasant, almost childish in her fun, but perfectly ladylike. Her sister seemed ill and out of spirits. I fancy her gaiety yesterday, and Mrs Watts's today, were both partly assumed. However, both sisters are charming, and I think it a piece of rare good fortune to have made two such acquaintances in two days.[22]

This was the situation at Christmas – Ellen staying at the family home apart from her husband, but nevertheless appearing full of high spirits. Though her fun seemed 'almost childish' to the creator of *Alice in Wonderland* – which was not to be published by Macmillan until the following year, 1865 – it also appeared to be 'partly assumed'. To what extent was Ellen hiding the unhappy circumstances of her life at Little Holland House, of which, it appears, Tom Taylor was already aware? And how much did Sarah know about it? Whatever the situation actually was at Christmas, a deed of separation was signed five weeks later, on 26 January 1865; in it Watts agreed to pay his wife £300 annually 'so long as she shall lead a chaste life'. The cause of separation was formally set down as 'incompatibility of temper', and the Signor was returned to the unsullied care of the Prinseps and the Pattles.

Ellen herself seems to have played no direct part in bringing about the separation:

The whole business was managed by those kind friends whose chief business in life seems to be the care of others. . . . There were no vulgar accusations on either side, and the words I read in the deed of separation, 'incompatibility of temper' a mere legal phrase – *more* than covered the ground. Truer still would have been 'incompatibility of *occupation*', and the inter-ference of well-meaning friends. . . . I was miserable, indignant, unable to understand that there could be any justice in what had happened.[23]

Yet on the whole Ellen gained a great deal from her contact

E

with Little Holland House. Even if she was overawed by the company that was kept by the Prinseps and the Camerons – Gladstone, Disraeli, Browning, Tennyson, Holman Hunt, Sir John Herschel the scientist, and Sir Henry Taylor the poet – the conversation of such men with the brilliant Pattle ladies was a further rich stage in her self-education. She remembered later that Gladstone was 'like a volcano at rest; his face was pale and calm, but the calm was the calm of the grey mist of Etna'. They were to meet again in future years under special and more favourable circumstances behind the scenes at the Lyceum. Disraeli fascinated her so much that after meeting him at the Prinseps' home she crossed Piccadilly in order purposely to bump into him so that she could look at him more closely. He did not recognize her, and merely apologized formally, raising his hat. Yet his image remained in her mind: 'His straggling black curls shake as he walks.' She remembered also 'those quiet, rather indifferent eyes, which didn't open wide'.

Tennyson she found far more approachable; Mrs Tennyson was frail and reminded her of 'a slender-stalked tea-rose'. She met the poet for the first time during the summer visit to Freshwater, and she went for walks with him in the evening. He talked to her of the flight of birds, and taught her to identify the flowers and the trees. 'Always I was quite at ease with him. He was so wonderfully simple.' She remembers the hat she wore at the time, 'brown straw mushroom with a dull red feather round it. It was tied under my chin, and I still had my hair down'. She contrasted Tennyson's direct and simple manner with that of Browning, 'with his carefully brushed hat, smart coat, and fine society manners'. She was proud to be allowed to prepare Tennyson's churchwarden pipe for him, steeping the mouthpiece in a solution of sal volatile to keep it from sticking to his lips. Nevertheless, he seemed at fifty-five to be 'very old'. He read out loud to her and the others; he was best, she thought, reading Browning's 'Ride from Ghent to Aix' [sic], making 'the words come out sharply like hoofs upon a road'.

Whatever unhappiness or disillusionment there had been in

her life with Watts ('I was so ignorant and so young, and he was so impatient,' she wrote to an intimate friend twenty years later),[24] she was shocked, humiliated and broken-hearted at being summarily dismissed from Little Holland House ten months after her marriage. She was sent back to face the family at the crowded house in Stanhope Street, her grand life an utter failure, the vision of beauty destroyed.

She had only fleeting glimpses of Watts after their sudden separation. She came face-to-face with him one day in Brighton; they paused to speak, and he told her how much she had grown! Later, when she was famous and he more reconciled to the kind of fame he too had achieved, they saw each other again through a garden hedge.[25] The sight of her moved him to write asking her to 'shake hands with him in spirit'. 'What success I may have,' he wrote, 'will be very incomplete and unsatisfactory if you cannot do what I have long been hesitating to ask.' He could not rid himself of the pain of feeling that he had spoiled her life, and he begged her forgiveness. 'If you cannot, keep silence. If you can, one word "yes" will be enough.'

'I answered simply "Yes"!' says Ellen.

III

GODWIN

Ellen was back at Stanhope Street, with Ben and Sarah and their whole family from Benjamin to Charles, and the two last babies, Tom born in 1863 and Fred in 1864, just before Ellen's marriage. Ellen wrote of this time:

> I hated going back to live at Home. Mother furnished a room for me, and I thought the furniture hideous. Poor Mother! For years Beethoven always reminded me of mending stockings, because I used to struggle with the large holes in my brothers' stockings upstairs in that ugly room, while downstairs Kate played the 'Moonlight Sonata'. This was the period when, though everyone was kind, I hated my life, hated every one and everything in the world more than at any time before or since.[1]

A number of letters have recently come to light written by Ellen to her friend Mary-Anne Hall between the years 1865 and 1868. Mary-Anne Hall was a young girl who painted, and became a much-needed confidante to whom Ellen could pour out her heart. Ellen, at low ebb, had caught a severe cold, which she only made worse by going out to the Olympic Theatre on 2 February. Kate, her season with Fechter finished, was appearing in 1865 at the Olympic with the romantic actor Henry Neville. Ellen complains that her cough was 'very, very bad', and she wrote to Mary-Anne to explain that her mother would not dream of letting her go out in the foggy weather, but that a kind friend, a Mrs Simon, had invited her and Kate to stay in Blackheath. She ends her letter:

Goodbye dear little Marian my clever little (I hate the word *Artist*) Painter: Believe me always, Your very loving friend, Ellen Alice Watts, N.B. Better known as 'Poor Nell'.

Having signed herself off, she then decides to go on as follows, with an evident reference to her feeling for Mrs Prinsep:

'Ah me I am weary, and I wish that I were dead.' No dear Marian I have much to live for *even now*. 'Nil Desperandum' is my motto. I have youth (I'm not very old rather) and I have *great, great hope* – Oh! so much and I can't believe that *all* is lost yet – I have Faith too dear, for I cannot but think that help *will,* must come to me *some day*. Hope – Faith – Two great things – but Charity! Oh Ellen, Ellen I'm afraid you have not one particle of that, the most beautiful of *all, all,* feelings or you would not feel *as you do* towards a person of flesh and blood and that person a Woman. God forgive her for I *can not* do so – I suppose I'm very, very wicked to feel so but indeed Marian I think, and think what have I done that she should use me so. God knows I'd forgive anyone that even *killed* me if I loved them – but 'Hope up, hope ever' and don't be selfish Nell. You are talking to yourself. Pray forgive me, for this is selfishness. I believe the great business of life is to be merry and wise – and the best way to 'keep up one's self' is to go out, to learn the savours and troubles of others which must make one forget one's own – and still be 'merry and wise' to relax. The ugliness of those furrows, and wrinkles, which sorrow ploughs in the fair forehead of God's creation. Oh! what an 'idiot' I am! God bless you dear, Nelly Watts.[2]

Later in the month she is evidently staying with Mrs Simon. In another undated letter to Mary-Anne, she speaks of seeing Mrs Simon with her hair down (long hair evidently had a fascination for Ellen): 'She looked *charming!*' she writes. 'I wish she could wear it so! Oh, it was so fine too, and soft.' On 25 February she begs Mary-Anne to look after herself (such constant pre-occupation with health was common among women in Victorian

England, where tuberculosis and other serious illnesses were rife),
and then she adds:

> My old face looks like a tallow candle, only there's not so
> much colour in it – and I am in such bad spirits and can't account
> for it.

Ellen was, however, moving about now, and is evidently going
the following Sunday to meet friends at Tom Taylor's house in
Lavender Sweep.

She was not the kind of girl to mope around for long, and the
Taylors evidently tried their best to cheer her. Ellen wrote in her
memoirs:

> Their house in Lavender Sweep was lovely. We are always
> welcome at the Taylors' and every Sunday we heard music and
> met interesting people – Charles Reade among them. Mrs
> Taylor had a rather hard outside . . . and I was often frightened
> out of my life by her; yet I adored her. She was in reality the
> most tender-hearted, sympathetic woman, and what an admir-
> able musician! She composed nearly all the music for her
> husband's plays. Every Sunday there was music at Lavender
> Sweep, quartet playing, and Clara Schumann at the piano.[3]

Kate was now a leading actress, universally admired, and, says
Ellen, the favourite of Tom Taylor, in whose plays she appeared.
Ellen did not have to work; her allowance of £6 a week was
more than adequate to keep her, and she had no immediate plans
for returning to the stage. Apart from a single appearance on 20
June 1866 in support of Kate's benefit performance in *The Hunchback* by Sheridan Knowles,[4] she seems to have taken part in few
professional productions until 8 June 1867, when she opened in a
play by Tom Taylor called *The Antipodes; or the Ups and Downs of
Life* at the Theatre Royal, Holborn. The play was unsuccessful.
Before that, she says, there had only been occasional appearances
with Kate in Bristol and at the Adelphi in London.[5]

Ellen herself says nothing of these intermediate years. She had,
she admits, to be 'practically *driven* back' to the stage by her

mother and father and by Tom Taylor. 'It *was* a good thing,' she writes, 'but at the time I hated it.' But what was there for her to do at home, except help bring up her mother's babies? Again it is Lewis Carroll who gave a brief picture of her at Stanhope Street. On 7 April 1865 he writes: 'Went to call on the Terrys. I stayed for lunch, and also heard Mrs Watts play and sing, and Florence sing two songs, one being "Pretty Polly Perkins".' That night he went to the Olympic to see Tom Taylor's play *The Ticket-of-leave Man,* in which he thought Kate 'as heroine was the making of the piece: very beautiful acting and very real'.

It was on Friday 14 July that, mainly at the invitation of Kate, he brought his camera to Stanhope Street and that day and the following day made the celebrated series of studies of the Terry family. This is his note of the sittings:

> July 14 (F.). Spent the day at the Terrys, and took: Miss Kate Terry, Mr and Mrs Terry, Mrs Watts, a large one of Polly, Polly and Flo, Flo, Charles etc.
>
> July 15 (Sat.). Went to Macmillan's and wrote in twenty or more copies of *Alice* to go as presents to various friends. This took so long that I did not get to the Terrys till 12.30, where I photographed till about 4.30.[6]

After a game of 'Castle Croquet' with Kate, he made 'a sort of dinner of their tea' and took twelve-year-old Polly (Marion) to the theatre to see her sister act. In December he visited them again, and in January the following year he took Polly, Flo and Charlie to the pantomime *Little King Pippin.*

We next hear of him with the Terrys on Saturday 11 May 1867, when he came to London from Oxford to see the exhibition at the Royal Academy and to attend an amateur performance for charity at the Adelphi, a series of plays and musical items (including the operetta *Cox and Box,*[7] with music by Arthur Sullivan) and *A Sheep in Wolf's Clothing.* In the latter, a domestic one-act play by Taylor, Ellen appeared alongside her sister, Tom Taylor himself, Mark Lemon, the part-founder and first editor of *Punch,* and Tenniel, the illustrator of *Alice in Wonderland,* all of whom were on the staff of *Punch*. Kate's acting was so good that she made Polly cry, as Carroll observed when he joined the Terry family party in the stage-box. Here, sitting alongside Kate, was her fiancé, the wealthy Arthur Lewis, whom she was to marry later the same year, retiring from the stage and leaving the field open to her sister to re-establish her career and maintain the name of Terry in the London theatre. Kate's acting, says her sister shrewdly, was 'scientific. She knew what she was about. There was more ideality than passionate womanliness in her interpretations. For this reason, perhaps, her Cordelia was finer than her Portia or her Beatrice'. Her marriage was as socially successful as her stage career had been brilliant; after a brief engagement, on 18 October 1867, at the age of twenty-three she married Arthur Lewis and became mistress of Moray Lodge, a fine house with a garden and stables on Campden Hill which, like Little Holland House, adjoined the estate of Holland House. It was a curious coincidence which could scarcely have been lost on Ellen, who had been banished from the same grand territory two and a half years before.

Campden Hill, as described by Kate's daughter Kate Terry Gielgud (the mother of Sir John Gielgud) was 'as remote as a country village'. The three-mile drive to Piccadilly was taken every morning by Arthur Lewis, starting at 9.30 sharp, in a Stanhope drawn by a 'well-groomed chestnut cob'; he drove himself each day to town, where he was a partner in the prosperous business of Lewis and Allenby of Conduit Street and Regent Street, 'by royal warrant silk mercers to Her Majesty Queen Victoria'. His mother, Jane Lewis, an autocratic and puritanical widow, had been deeply opposed to her son's marriage to an actress; to her the stage was a monstrous and immoral institution. But Arthur Lewis was a cultured man who was interested in music and the arts and had become the friend of many musicians, artists and painters. Moray Lodge, which he had bought for himself in 1862, became the centre of gatherings which included Frederick Leighton, John Everett Millais, Fred Walker the landscape artist, and the enthusiastic group that had founded and contributed to *Punch:* Mark Lemon, Tom Taylor, John Tenniel, F. C. Burnand, and George du Maurier. In 1863 Arthur Lewis had also founded the Arts Club, with its headquarters at 7 Hanover Square; founder members of the club included Dickens, Tom Hughes, Lord Houghton and James Whistler. Soon they were to be joined by a newcomer to London, Edward Godwin.

The year 1867 was also the one that Ellen was finally 'driven' back to the theatre by her parents and Tom Taylor. It was by far the best thing for her; she had no ties except her mother's children, but the surviving letters to Mary-Anne Hall show that returning to the stage put a great strain upon her. Even the single performance of *The Hunchback* in June 1866 worried her greatly. In an undated letter enclosing two tickets for the stalls, she writes:

> I am so nervous about this affair, that I get quite feverish about it. . . . You must *please* not mix me up, in yr thoughts, with the character I am playing! for she ('Mistress Helen Heartwell') is not a very desirable person to *be*! *I* think! *although no harm in her.*

In her memoirs she says she was 'feeling wretchedly ill, and angry too, because they insisted on putting my married name on the bills'. During the performance itself she appears to have become almost hysterical, to judge from a further letter to Mary-Anne Hall dated 22 June:

> I was so very nervous, and oh wretchedly unwell – on the stage I *laughed* as you know, but when I reached my dressing-room I cried with pain in my side. I am however very much better now.

'I was *quite* an amateur,' she adds, in comparison with Kate, who was 'an acknowledged favourite with the public'.

She returned to the professional stage, as we have seen, on 8 June 1867, and played a succession of parts, none of them really notable, at the new Queen's Theatre, Long Acre, between June 1867 and spring the following year. On 4 and 5 October she appeared at the Prince's Theatre, Manchester, with Charles

Wyndham in a supporting play, *The Little Savage*, when Kate in
the main three-act drama, *Plot and Passion*, made 'her two last
appearances on any stage' two weeks before her marriage; during
the interval between the two plays the 'Kate Terry Valse' was
'performed by command before the Sultan, Viceroy and His
Royal Highness the Prince of Wales, by the Band of the 1st Life
Guards'.[8]

The company at the Queen's, a fine new theatre and one of the
largest in London, was under the management of Alfred Wigan,
the veteran actor-manager who had worked with Vestris, Kean
and Macready, and many fine actors were assembled, including
John Ryder, Charles Wyndham, John Lawrence Toole, and
Ellen's former colleague from Bristol, Henrietta Hodson, who
was soon to be married to Henry Labouchère, the wealthy
proprietor of the *Daily News* and lessee of the theatre. Charles
Reade was also connected with the project, one of the most
ambitious stage enterprises of its time. The play chosen to open
the season on 24 October was Reade's *The Double Marriage*, a
new work in which Ellen in the part of the younger sister of the
heroine had to step forward to the footlights at a tense moment of
the play with the heroine's baby in her arms, nobly claiming it
to be her own. Ellen had the usual cold in the head from which
she always seemed to be suffering. 'It's bine,' she cried, and her
passionate utterance did nothing to help a play already past saving
from inevitable failure. On Boxing Day she appeared in the
supporting section of the evening's presentation; this was *Katherine
and Petruchio*, Garrick's shortened stage version of *The Taming of
the Shrew*, and her leading man was a young and ambitious actor
of twenty-nine, Henry Irving. This was her first fleeting appearance with him and their performance, though receiving mixed
notices, enabled them to meet for the first time. It is evident that
Ellen 'humanized' Katherine, who was usually played as a terma-
gant; according to the critic in *The Times*, she played her more as
a spoilt child than as a vixen, while her concluding speech of
capitulation, he wrote, was 'a model of quiet elocution, so sensibly,
so feelingly, and with so unequivocal an appearance of moral

conviction is it delivered'. Irving's Petruchio, however, appeared to him more like 'a brigand chief who has secured a female captive than an honest gentleman engaged in the task of moral reform.'[9]

There has naturally been much speculation concerning their reaction to each other during the short period they played together in this mutilated version of Shakespeare. It appears to have been slight enough; later Ellen remembered his grave courtesy as he gave up his place to her in the queue on 'Treasury Day', the weekly occasion when the actors received their salaries. She adds that he thought her 'hoydenish' as an actress, but 'charming and individual' as a woman. They both played badly, she claimed, for different reasons – she because at this time she no longer cared for the theatre, he because of his stiffness on the stage and his self-consciousness: 'his eyes were dull and his face was heavy'. Yet she was impressed by 'his fierce and indomitable will' which showed itself in his application to his work. 'Quite unconsciously I learned from watching him that to do work well, the artist must spend his lifetime in incessant labour and deny himself everything for that purpose.' But when the piece, which opened on a foggy night, failed to find a public, it was withdrawn, and Ellen was not to appear on the stage with Irving until she joined him at the Lyceum in 1878.

Alfred Wigan's wife, like Mrs Kean before her, struggled to make Ellen take the theatre seriously. She criticized her lack of repose on the stage. 'Stand still!' she would shout from the stalls. She reproved her for 'fooling' on the stage; Ellen had seen the funny side of 'It's bine!' in *The Double Marriage* just as much as the audience, and thereafter could not refrain from giggling when the line came up. Off-stage, the very thought of it 'used to send us off with fits of laughter. We hung on to chairs, helpless, limp, incapable'. When she laughed on stage, Mrs Wigan very properly went in front and hissed her! But Ellen no longer cared whether she acted or not. Her last appearance during this brief interlude in the theatre was in a 'comedietta' by Francis Talfourd called *The Household Fairy* in which, according to her Victorian admirer and biographer, Edgar P. Pemberton, her performance as Kitty 'added lustre to the author's meaning, and was, as he intended her to be, a veritable fairy of the fireside'.

The reason for Ellen's complete lack of interest in the theatre is that she is in love. She was, she admits, 'a woman who was at this time caring more about love and life than the theatre'. The man with whom she was in love was Edward Godwin, the architect whom she had so admired during the time she had lived in Bristol.

No date can be given to this renewal of their acquaintance.[10] It seems to have occurred at Little Holland House before she had been driven from its doors. Godwin, as we have seen, was a constant visitor to London, and he had no difficulty in being introduced into the two more or less distinct artistic circles in which Ellen moved before and after her separation from Watts. It could be that he was the 'friend' who took her to Paris at some period before June 1866, when she was back in London appearing in *The Hunchback*. However, by the summer of 1868 she had decided to abandon the career in which she was no longer interested, desert her family and friends, and without word or warning to anyone set up house with Godwin in the country.

She could not have done this before May 1868. On 2 April she wrote to Mary-Anne Hall from Moray Lodge; 'I'm quite idle now – doing no work at the theatre and staying with Kate.' She adds that she has not seen 'our sweet Mrs Simon', their mutual friend in Blackheath, 'for ever so long'. She was apparently still appearing spasmodically at the Queen's Theatre, for on 6 May she is writing to Mary-Anne that she 'hopes she will keep her promise not to be disgusted at the shrewish part' she is playing, adding that she hardly coughed at *all* last night, I'm happy to say'. Both letters are signed Nelly Watts. It must have been very soon after this that she disappeared. 'I left the stage quietly and secretly,' she wrote later, 'and I was cut off from my family and friends.'

When this new association in London actually began may be doubtful, but Ellen soon learned what had been happening to Godwin since she had seen him last in Bristol. By now he regarded himself as an artist rather than simply an architect. His interest lay in the integration of all the arts that combined to provide man with his environment; he wanted to encompass total design – architecture, decoration, furnishing, utensils, costume. He shared the attitude of William Morris, though not his tastes; Godwin used to say that he 'did not wish to eat his dinner in a chair suited for Edward the Confessor'. He had formed a partnership with his friend Crisp in January 1864; Godwin's share in this was to inspire the designs for competitions. The entry for Congleton town hall was chosen in 1864, the year his building in Northampton was completed. He was also interested himself in the training of young architects, and this, together with his growing friendship with Burges, took him frequently to London. When Godwin's wife died in May 1864, he increasingly left the work in Bristol in the hands of Crisp, and in October that year he opened an office in London at 23 Baker Street, Portman Square.

His creative activities took a toll on his health, which remained delicate, and he was not without certain additional worries. He exercised little control over his financial affairs, not caring whether he had money in the bank or not, and came to know well what it was to be in debt and to have trouble with the bailiffs. In 1866 he and Crisp had been grievously disappointed that one of Godwin's finest designs, that for the Bristol assize court, though winning the initial competition, had not been finally adopted; meanwhile Burges had asked him to act as his partner in submitting designs for the New Law Courts in London. The resulting design, though considered subsequently to be outstanding, was not successful in winning the open competition. He and Burges had spent many enjoyable weeks together during the creative period for this design. Godwin undertook architectural research at the British Museum, and relieved the tensions of the time by constant visits to the theatre. He also went for long walks to keep his body active during the prolonged bouts of reading and draughtsmanship.

This was the young man, now in his early thirties, alert, handsome, bearded, an entertaining talker with an extensive knowledge of the arts and a passion for Shakespeare and the theatre, who renewed his friendship with Nellie Watts. His conversation no doubt relieved the tedium of her life in Stanhope Street. Because of his ready response to women, he could give this lively, beautiful girl who was still in her teens what she most needed – sympathy and an understanding of the things in which she was most interested. He offered her the love and companionship she had been denied during the brief months of her marriage, and during the period of suffering and isolation that followed when she felt herself unwanted by anyone. She fell deeply in love with him, and gave him her sympathy, which was always generous and unrestrained, when she realized that he, too, had his difficulties and frustrations.

Ellen in her memoirs wrote that at about Easter 1866, she paid her first trip to Paris with an unidentified 'friend'.[11] The friend who was possibly Godwin, 'took her everywhere'. 'I often went to parties at night,' she writes. She saw Sarah Bernhardt for the first time – 'thin as a harrow' – and the actress Croisette, 'a superb animal'. She saw the Empress Eugénie driving in the Bois 'looking like an exquisite waxwork'. She found the newly asphalted boulevards of Paris wonderfully quiet after the rattle of London's cobblestones; above all, she found Paris supremely elegant and luxurious: 'Oh, the beautiful *slope* of women at this period! They looked like lovely half-moons, lying back in their carriages.' And she liked the men too because, she says, 'they liked me', though she did not admire them; she saw instances of their cruelty which she did not like, including the spectacle of a girl – 'a strong, splendid creature of the peasant class' clinging in a passion of resentment to a gentleman's *fiacre* which he set in motion, dragging her along the street. But she was happy in Paris, though she did not know a word of French. She was with her friend – drinking coffee at Tortoni's, visiting Meissonier's studio, growing weary tramping the 'endless galleries' of the Louvre, fainting away out of sheer ecstasy in the Madeleine when the Host was raised. The only things she remembers missing while she was away were the serial numbers of Dickens's *Household Words* which the paper-boys sold on the London streets, 'pursued by an eager crowd'.

During the summer of 1867 Godwin and Burges began what was to prove a most difficult assignment in Ireland. At first everything appeared to be most congenial; the Earl of Limerick, who was an enthusiastic medievalist with a taste for Chaucer, wanted to build himself a castle on his estate at Dromore near the Atlantic coast. Godwin had to spend much time on research among the ruins of medieval castles in Ireland, and he produced a design which seemed to him to fulfil perfectly what the earl had in mind. The structure took two years to build, and seemed to suit the site admirably from every aspect. Godwin, who was usually critical of his work as he was of the work of others, nevertheless pronounced it 'about as charming a thing as ever he saw in his life'. He designed the furniture and other decorations, including frescoes for the walls. While he was occupied with building this castle in a remote part of Ireland, he undertook to design another mansion in Glenbegh, County Kerry, and to restore Castle Ashby for the Marquis of Northampton. This was the period during which he and Ellen decided to discard Victorian convention and live together in a cottage on Gustard Wood Common near Wheathamstead in Hertfordshire. Ellen apparently assumed the title locally of Mrs Godwin.

Ellen's disappearance led to a macabre incident, of which she has left her own account:

A dreadful thing happened. A body was found in the river – the dead body of a young woman, very fair and slight and tall. Every one thought it was my body.

I had gone away without a word. No one knew where I was. My own father identified the corpse, and Floss and Marion, at their boarding-school, were put into mourning. Then mother went. She kept her head under the shock of the likeness, and bethought her of 'a strawberry mark upon my left arm'. (*Really* it was on my left knee.) That settled it, for there was no such mark to be found upon the poor corpse. It was just at this moment that the news came to me in my country retreat that I had been found dead, and I flew up to London to give ocular proof to my poor distracted parents that I was still alive. Mother, who had been the only one not to identify the drowned girl, confessed to me that she was so like me that just for a second she, too, was deceived. You see, they knew I had not been very happy since my return to the stage, and when I went away without a word, they were terribly anxious, and prepared to believe the first bad tidings that came to hand. It came in the shape of that most extraordinary likeness between me and that poor soul who threw herself into the river.[12]

There is no record now of the exact nature of the rift between Ellen and her parents which led to this scene, which might have been devised by Dickens himself. But that Ellen should have left her mother and father without news of where she had gone shows how complete the break between them had been. We do not know when Ben and Sarah were told about the liaison with Godwin, whom they had, of course, met in Bristol. We do not know if he moved in Kate's circle; it seems he visited Little Holland House. But if Ben and Sarah did not know about Ellen at the time the body was discovered, it is evident Kate did not know either. It would seem that Ellen left no knowledge of her whereabouts simply because she did not want her parents to discover that she was living 'in sin' with her lover, and that she did not wish them to know this because of the grave shock it would be to them. But to judge from this story in her memoirs, when she heard they were distraught at the thought she might have committed suicide, she was forced to tell them where she was, and presumably with whom she was living. There is also a curious reference to Ellen in Lewis Carroll's diary, dated 6 April 1869: 'I also visited the Terrys and had a long chat with Mrs Terry; Mrs Watts is still staying in lodgings, but had called at the house that day.' Ellen was certainly at this period living with Godwin in Hertfordshire, and was already pregnant, her daughter Edith being born on 9 December that year. The reference to 'lodgings' may have been Mrs Terry's method of explaining her daughter's absence to a man of such correctness as the Reverend C. L. Dodgson. There seems little doubt that Ellen had continued to live at the family home until she took it in her head to leave, but the entry does show that she was in touch with her mother and was not altogether cut off from the family. One wonders if Sarah knew yet about the baby.[13]

All Ellen tells us herself is that she was blissfully happy. By the spring of 1868 she was twenty-one and she gave herself up to love, irrevocably and completely. To the end of her days, Godwin remained the one unforgettable, unforgotten love in her life whose memory she cherished most dearly, and he was the father of the only children she had. She had no regrets at leaving the theatre; for the first time, she says, she was able to devote all her energies to living. Looking back on this period, she wrote:

> If it is the mark of the artist to love art before everything, to renounce everything for its sake, to think all the sweet human things of life well lost if only he may attain something, do some good, great work – then I was never an artist. I admire those impersonal people who care for nothing outside their own ambition, yet I detest them at the same time, and I have the simplest faith that absolute devotion to another human being means the greatest *happiness*. That happiness for a time was now mine.[14]

For a while she was in love with the sheer novelty of being in love. She also experienced 'exquisite delight from the mere fact of being in the country'. She took up gardening, she learned to cook ('I had a wonderful hand for pastry'), she walked in the countryside, she drove a pony and trap. Mrs Beaton replaced Shakespeare as the book to study. She acquired she admits, 'a perfect mania for washing'. She had poultry to look after; she maintained two hundred ducks and fowls. And soon she had her first baby to tend. After her daughter was born the family moved to the large house Godwin had designed and built for them at Fallows Green, near Harpenden.[15] Here on 16 January 1872 she gave birth to her second child, Teddy (later to become famous as Edward Gordon Craig). When Teddy was born, Godwin registered the birth and cocked snooks at local authority (and Watts) by entering Ellen as 'Eleanor Alice Godwin, formerly Watkins'. There was no baptism. ('I was born a Pagan,' said Gordon Craig.)

From their earliest days these children, born of Ellen's great love of Godwin, were utterly spoiled. Godwin, of course, had his own ideas about their upbringing. Everything commonplace and 'Victorian' was as far as possible kept from their sight. Japanese prints hung in the nursery; the children were brought up on Walter Crane's prints and picture books. Anything unsuitable that was given them by 'injudicious friends' was promptly burned – picture-books, toys and all. In fact only wooden toys were allowed. 'Vulgar!' cried out little Edy, aged two, when someone gave her a doll clothed in a silk dress of violent pink.

But during the period of his intimacy with Ellen, Godwin's fortunes as artist and architect fluctuated wildly. He travelled by train to his London office, now at 197 Albany Street, but inevitably brought back work to complete in the country. He was fully established and indeed well known, though he was not universally popular on account of his uncompromising opinions which he expressed freely and at times arrogantly. He was involved in the affairs of both the Architectural Association and the Archaeological Association, and he was made a Fellow of the Royal Institute of British Architects and a member of the Council. In 1871 he won the initial competition for the town hall of Leicester, but once more this proved abortive when the Corporation decided to hold a further competition, in which Godwin's design came only second. It was a case of the Bristol assize court over again and a matter for acute disappointment to this ambitious and overworked man. Though the professional assessors chose Godwin's design, the lay judges from the local authority voiced their doubts concerning his work. His public designs remained in the Victorian Gothic tradition, which was by now beginning to be challenged by the advocates of a return to the simpler style. Godwin's private taste was for something quite different, a style more Japanese or Oriental – an interest which he shared with the artist Whistler, with whom he had by now become friendly and whose paintings he championed when they were most unpopular with the critics and the public. He even criticized his own work in an article for *The Building News*. As he wrote at this time, 'we are the slaves of those who will employ us, and not their leaders.' He turned to the design of wallpaper, introducing oriental motifs of sunflowers, birds in flight and interlaced bamboo, and in addition to the furnishings required in the buildings he created, he had since 1868 began to design furniture quite independently. Godwin was often grossly overworked, maintaining his professional partnership with Crisp until 1871 and his friendly collaboration with Burges, who frequently visited the couple in their cottage, and even drew on Ellen's services to help him with his tracings.[16]

Problems had arisen which were to lead eventually to the dissolution of Godwin's partnership with Crisp in January 1871, when the original agreement was due for renewal. A serious and prolonged dispute developed, partly concerning conditions of damp which had appeared in the thick stone walls at Dromore – a fault causing Crisp rather than Godwin deep concern – and partly because it emerged that Godwin, without consulting his partner, had accepted £600 from the building contractor for the 'royalty' on certain of his furniture designs, the sum being passed on by the contractor to Lord Limerick's account. The dispute between Godwin and Crisp dragged on and was eventually put to arbitration. The matter is somewhat obscure but it appears that Godwin, who at this period mortgaged Fallows Green, may have done so in order to find money to meet his obligations. In any case, Godwin was beginning to suffer even more acute difficulties over money than he had experienced hitherto. By 1873 his affairs were in so poor a state that the brokers appeared at Harpenden and took possession of the furniture. Though he secured the commission to design the town hall for Sunderland, the owner of Glenbegh had since 1871 been threatening to sue Godwin and Crisp because the building costs had exceeded the estimate. He also alleged that the walls had a defect in their construction which

let in water, and that the roof was faulty. While Godwin remained
quite indifferent to these threats of legal redress, Crisp, who had
carried the main burden of the dispute for two years, suffered
prolonged anxiety. He was a man whose honesty was impeccable,
and these wearisome contentions wore him out. The affair was
finally settled in 1874, when Crisp undertook to work on the
house himself. Godwin, it must be presumed, had at least to
share in meeting the considerable legal costs involved in this
affair.

By this time Ellen had herself taken the matter in hand. She
was still deeply in love with Godwin, but had come to understand his shortcomings and to realize that if the children were to
enjoy a stable upbringing it would have to be as a result of her
endeavours rather than their father's. Godwin, desperately overworked and preoccupied, was often careless of Ellen's feelings;
the journeys to and from the country in bad weather were tiring,
and he grew worried and irritable. Ellen's loyalty to him permits
few of her troubles to become visible through the protective
screen with which she surrounded the six years of her life with
Godwin in the country and finally in London, to which she had
to return in 1874 in order to earn a living in the theatre for herself
and her children. In a letter to Bernard Shaw she admitted that
she had had to live on £3 a week for 'some number of years in
the days gone by with Edward'.

To her intimate friend Graham Robertson she lifted a little of
the curtain, as the following passage in his autobiography *Time
Was* shows:

> During these six years, which I have often heard called the
> lost years of Ellen Terry, she lived through those emotions
> which she was to portray later on; she knew great happiness
> and keen suffering, glad tranquillity, fear, loneliness, and even
> actual want; she learned in her sorrow to creep close to the
> heart of Nature and to draw from it help and comfort, in her
> joy to turn to Nature for an answering smile.
>
> That quiet but eventful time was very sacred to her. She

spoke of it seldom, but to me not at all during the first years of
our friendship, but I know that it was often in her thoughts, and
later on, especially when we were together in the country,
perhaps jogging along the lanes in a donkey-cart or sitting in
the spring copses among the bluebells, she would often say,
'This is like Harpenden days,' and would tell me tales of
those hidden years which had so developed her character and
her art. Most of the tales were sad, yet like Sophie Arnould,
she held in loving memory '*les Beaux jours quand j'étais si
malheureuse*'.

Often during that period, she had felt the pinch of poverty
and had not known where to look for supplies. She had sat up
many a night doing copies of elaborate architectural drawings
for which, when finished, she would get a guinea, and this fine
work, done by very insufficient light, strained her eyes and
produced a weakness in them which ever afterwards troubled
her.

One dismal evening, she told me, everything had looked
unusually black. She had been alone for many days, funds
were very low, she was ill and anxious. She had harnessed the
little rough pony and driven to meet the last train hoping that
someone, half expected, would come by it and put an end to
the fears and the loneliness.

But the last train played her false as it had often done before,
and she drove back through the dark lanes wearied out in body
and brain. She would not trouble about supper, she would
creep into bed and rest – rest was all she could think of. She
would go straight to bed – but there was the pony. The pony
must be unharnessed and rubbed down, and though she wanted
no supper, the pony must have his. So the weary girl led the
weary pony into his stall and made him comfortable; shook
up his bed, gave him his drink of water, and finally, raising herself on tiptoe, began to pull down his supper of hay into the
manger from the rack above her head. As she did so, out of
the hay and straight down her back fell a mouse. . . . Never
had she been so tired, never so unhappy, never so utterly alone;

here was the darkest hour of her life – and she had a mouse
down her back. It was her nadir. Never, before or after, did
she touch the misery of that moment.[17]

On another night, driving back in the dark, she was assaulted
by a drunken labourer and had to fight him off unseen with the
butt of her whip. Another encounter in the dark had a strange
outcome. She was

> . . . returning home through a wood, late on a dark night, ill
> and nervous, starting at the snapping of a twig or at the tall
> shadows cast by her lantern. As she reached the middle of the
> wood a shining object in her way attracted her attention. She
> lowered the lantern and found herself looking into the bright
> eyes of a large frog. Behind him sat another frog, also solemnly
> staring, beyond him still more; she was in the midst of a circle
> of frogs which swarmed over the path in all directions. When
> she had thoroughly taken in these details she dropped the
> lantern, which immediately went out, leaving her in pitch
> darkness.
>
> Even afterwards, in broad daylight, she was never able to
> make up her mind as to what she ought to have done. If she
> stepped forward – no, that did not bear thinking of. But the way
> back presented equal difficulties. What she finally did was to
> feel about for a clear space and then to sit down and wait
> shiveringly through the long hours of darkness until dawn
> began to steal between the branches.

Ellen told Graham Robertson another singular story. Godwin
had heard her pass some trivial remark and had said such expressions were unworthy of her; her thoughts, he said should
reflect greatness of mind, and he told her to lie out in the fields
alone throughout one whole night, watching the sky from dusk
to dawn. Inspired by this, she told Robertson that she lay in the
short grass of the common 'looking up into the great mystery of
the night'. 'No sleep came to her,' wrote Robertson, recounting
what she said, 'but the stillness and the awe and the beauty sank

into her and brought rest and knowledge.' Only in the grey of
the early morning did she creep to her room and sleep, and the
memory stayed with her for the rest of her life. Robertson understood what this experience had meant to her:

> What she had learnt that night she could not tell; she could
> not remember, but she *knew,* and the knowledge remained with
> her. What she had learnt was something of proportion, some-
> thing of rhythm, of reverence, of melody – she could not
> formulate, only feel, but the memory never faded, and all
> through her life she found courage and peace in a vision of
> stars passing across the sky above Fallows Green.... Ellen
> Terry was a daughter of the night, happy in its shadow and
> mystery and loving the moon with a strange ecstasy which I
> have never met with in another.

The recollection of Fallows Green always came back to her in
later years, with the memory of the days and nights spent with
Godwin while they were still in love. But by 1873 they were
beginning to grow apart. There were no telephones by means of
which he could have warned her in advance of the occasions when
his preoccupations in London prevented him from coming home,
where she was dying for his company. He just failed to come,
and she would return disconsolate from the station where she had
gone to meet him.

But the love affair constantly rallied. She herself, she says,
seldom went to London. But they spent one 'blissful quiet'
holiday in Normandy, visiting Lisieux, Nantes, Bayeux. 'Long
afterwards,' wrote Ellen, 'when I was feeling as dry as sandpaper
on the stage, I had only to recall some of the divine music I had
heard in those great churches abroad to become soft, melted, able
to act.' Godwin was exploring the churches and cathedrals. 'I
remember in some cathedral we left little Edy sitting down below
while we climbed up into the clerestory.... The choir was
practising, and suddenly there rose a boy's voice, pure, effortless
and clear.... When we came down to fetch Edy, she said: "Ssh!
ssh! Miss Edy has seen the angels!"'[18]

At home, the money ceased to come in; the house was mortgaged and the bailiffs were threatening to take away the furniture.
By the winter of 1873–4, Ellen knew that something had to be
done, and that she would be the one to do it. She was twenty-seven
now, and Godwin was forty. Edy was four and Teddy two, and
their future, as well as the stability of her relationship with Godwin,
which was continually undermined by persistent disputes over the
unpaid bills, had unhappily to be faced.

Then, at the psychological moment, she ran into one of her old
friends – Charles Reade. Reade, clad in a pink coat, was out hunting in the Harpenden area when his horse jumped over a hedge
into a country lane. He pulled up when he saw a young woman
in trouble with her pony-trap; a wheel had just come off, and she
was standing there alone considering what to do. Reade came up
to offer assistance, and then stared hard at her. 'Good God, it's
Nelly,' he cried. 'Where have you been all these years?' Ellen
equally astonished, replied that she had been having a very happy
time. 'Well, you've had it long enough. Come back to the stage!'
Ellen's first reaction was to exclaim that she would never go back
to the theatre, and then she remembered the threats of the bailiffs.
So she said the first extravagant thing that came into her mind.

'Perhaps I would think of it if someone would give me £40 a
week!'

'Done!' said Reade. 'I'll give you that, and more, if you'll come
and play Philippa Chester in *The Wandering Heir*.'[19]

So England's greatest actress since Sarah Siddons returned to
the stage, very unwillingly, and through a chance meeting with
an old friend in a country lane. For six years she had been in
voluntary retirement, living only a few miles from London, and
yet so completely cut off that her closest friends and admirers
had no idea where she was. Presumably they had some inkling of
what had happened, and had been discreet enough not to press
their inquiries. The circumstances of Ellen's relationship with
Godwin, and the fact that she now had two illegitimate children,
enforced her almost complete seclusion in Victorian England.
Now for the sake of her lover and their two children, she was

forced to come out of this seclusion and face the limelight of the theatre in London. It was a hard and courageous decision.

The entry in Lewis Carroll's diary, to which I have referred, shows that she had been in touch with her mother for a while at least in the months before Edy was born. To a woman of Sarah's strict outlook, the fact that her daughter possessed illegitimate children must have come as the most terrible shock. Benjamin, who had always been something of a trouble to his parents, was now in Australia; Kate, with her growing family of small daughters, was moving in higher society than that open to Ben and Sarah, though she had money enough to help them through the lean years when the family had no one on the stage; Ellen was 'lost', and the little ones, Polly and Flo, only at the start of their careers as young actresses. George, after serving an industrious apprenticeship as a cabinet-maker at Maples, was twenty; soon he was to marry and become a Catholic to please his wife, which was another shock to Sarah, the Wesleyan. His only link with the theatre was formed much later, when he was appointed master carpenter at the Lyceum under Irving. The remaining brothers, Charles, Tom and Fred, were still at school. Apart from Fred, their sons were to prove a grave disappointment to the Terrys.

During this difficult period Ellen's chief friend and confidante was 'Boo'. What domestic help Ellen could afford had been limited to inexperienced local girls until good fortune brought Boo into the household, where she was to outlast the century. Boo was Mrs Rumball, wife of the doctor who had delivered Edy; she had tried unsuccessfully to maintain her husband's private asylum near Harpenden after his death. The lunatics in her charge tended to escape and disturb the neighbourhood. So she gave up, and accepted Ellen's invitation to join her household as a 'companion'. 'For the next thirty years I was her only lunatic,' says Ellen.

The wealth of her affection being slowly starved through Godwin's neglect, Ellen turned to the children as the great outlet for her love. Without any question she spoiled them from the moment they were born; in her eyes they were utterly adorable, and their most casual wish was her command. They were, she says, 'educating their mother'. Edy at four was dressed in a kimono in which, according to Ellen, 'she looked as Japanese as everything that surrounded her', while Teddy would appear in a 'minute white piqué suit'. Teddy was 'a greedy little thing' who was always drawing when he was not eating; he is described by his mother as 'fat and fair and angelic-looking', and the maid Essie called him 'the feather of England'. Edy, who did not speak until she was two, 'seemed to notice everything with her grave dark eyes'; when she was old enough to do so, she hammered clothes on to her wooden dolls with nails, and she would hit her little brother on the head with a wooden spoon. She always referred to herself as 'Miss Edy', but she had a certain charm as well as a fierce, childish determination; she would bring her mother little sprigs of flowers from the garden with the news that there were lots more, and when she first dug up a turnip she rushed in crying 'Miss Edy found a radish. It's as big as – as big as *God!'* Ellen's heart had responded to this wonderful life with her children in the country; she had scrubbed the floors, laid the fires, cooked, gardened, harnessed the pony to the trap, and chased the goat away if it butted at the children – until one day when she seized it by the horns and found its eyes were exactly like her own. But the idyll had to end with the tramp of the bailiffs up the garden path, and Ellen went to London by herself, leaving the children at Fallows Green in the charge of Boo.[20]

We get a glimpse of Ellen in 1873 (probably while on a visit to London) from Alice Comyns-Carr, who was to become a close friend and to design many of Ellen's dresses when she went to the Lyceum. She was enjoying a brief hectic courtship with Joe Comyns-Carr (later director of the Grosvenor Art Gallery and one of Irving's dramatists) and at the same time trying to nerve herself to go on the stage by playing in amateur theatricals. Suddenly Ellen appeared one day at the rooms of her friend the architect Fred Jameson, where rehearsals for *The Hunchback* were being held. 'She was wearing the black Matador hat which she always affected at that time,' writes Alice, 'and to me she looked the very incarnation of spring as she stood there smiling half-hesitatingly.' Ellen was not sure whether or not she should intrude on the rehearsals, but she was invited in to be introduced to Fred's friends, and so met the young girl who was to become one of her closest confidantes.

On 28 February 1874 Ellen returned to the stage in the 'kind of Rosalind part' of Philippa in Reade's play *The Wandering Heir* at the Queen's Theatre, which was under his own management. Reade, careful of his publicity with £40 a week at stake, had only just released her name to the Press; he had announced at first that the new Philippa would be played by an 'eminent' actress who was returning to the stage after a long period of retirement. *The Wandering Heir* and its successor in April, *It's Never too late to Mend,* the melodrama which Reade had adapted from his own novel, and which was always good for a revival, served to re-establish Ellen as a popular actress with the London public. Lewis Carroll notes in his diary that he went to see her in *The Wandering Heir* on 15 April, and that 'her acting is simply *wonderful*'. She had returned now for good, and, what was more, she felt enthusiastic about the work. Her friends seemed prepared to welcome her back – the six years seemed dispelled like six days

and she had a sympathetic manager. He sat out in front night after night watching over her work, and sending her written notes about her performance between each act. When he was angry with her, he addressed her severely as 'Madam!'; when he was pleased, he called her his 'dearest child'.

Reade, the Fellow of Magdalen who liked playing blind-man's-buff with Ellen at his home and who could stand up at Tom Taylor's house on a Sunday and make himself weep by singing 'The Girl I Left Behind Me', loved the theatre passionately. On tour, after the London season, Ellen used to watch him working the stage set for his play *Hard Cash,* standing side by side with one of the stage hands. She knew he was losing money on the tour, yet he insisted on paying her £25 a week. 'Your Nelly!' cried Reade to Boo, when she had reproached him over some remark or other, 'I love her a thousand times better than you do, or any

puling woman.' They quarrelled – the young actress of twenty-
six and the veteran author of sixty – and then enjoyed themselves
hugely making it up; a lunch out, or a present would follow. He
called her 'Eleanore Delicia' (after her baptismal name of Ellen
Alicia), and at the foot of one of his innumerable notes to her
(letters and written messages being the normal form of exchange
at this period) he printed in large letters the words: 'THERE DO
EXIST SUCH THINGS AS HONEST MISUNDERSTAND-
INGS.' Get these words into your head, he told her, and it will
save you 'a world of unhappiness'.

This happy, stormy relationship with Charles Reade was another stage in Ellen's self-realization as an actress. He poured out
his criticisms of her, just and unjust alike, in a ceaseless flow of
words, spoken or written. He refreshed her, renewed her, making
both rehearsal and performance a necessary development in her
advanced training. Her voice was good, but her prolonged absence
from the stage had restricted her breathing and made her tired.
He told her to vary her pace ('pace is the soul of comedy' as Ellen
came to realize) and put more bite into her words. He trounced
her for 'limpness' without realizing she was limp through lack of
breath-control, and he ordered her to make her exits 'ardent'.
'That word set me on the track of learning the value of moving
off the stage with a swift rush,' she wrote when she looked back
over a long and valuable letter he wrote her about her playing of
Philippa. He made her examine every detail in her performance,
line by line. The letter, which she quotes, is packed with valuable
advice, though written virtually a century ago about a play long
outmoded, and it shows in some detail the quality of Ellen's work
when she returned to the stage, a highly experienced young
actress once more on her mettle:

> I prefer you for my Philippa to any other actress, and shall
> do so still, even if you will not, or cannot throw more vigour
> into the lines that need it. I do not pretend to be as good a
> writer of plays as you are an actress, but I do pretend to be a
> great judge of acting in general. And I know how my own

lines and business ought to be rendered infinitely better than any one else, except the Omniscient. It is only on this narrow ground I presume to teach a woman of your gifts. If I teach you Philippa, you will teach me Juliet; for I am very sure that when I have seen you act her, I shall know a vast deal more about her than I do at present.

No great quality of an actress is absent from your perform-ance. Very often you have *vigour*. But in other places where it is as much required, or even more, you turn *limp*. You have limp lines, limp business, and in Act III limp exits instead of ardent exits.

The swift rush of the words, the personal rush, should carry you off the stage. It is in reality as easy as shelling peas, if you will only go by the right method instead of by the wrong. You have overcome far greater difficulties than this, yet night after night you go on suffering ignoble defeat at this point. Come, courage! You took a leaf out of Reade's dictionary at Man-chester, and trampled on two difficulties – impossibilities, you called them. That was on Saturday. Monday you knocked the poor impossibilities down. Tuesday you kicked them where they lay. Wednesday you walked placidly over their prostrate bodies.

You don't seem quite to realize that uniformity of pace leads inevitably to langour. You should deliver a pistol-shot or two. Remember Philippa is a fiery girl; she can snap. If only for variety, she should snap James's head off when she says, 'Do I *speak* as if I loved them!'

After the beating, wait at least ten seconds longer than you do – to rouse expectation – and when you do come on make a little more of it. You ought to be very pale, indeed – even to enter with a slight totter, done moderately, of course; and be-fore you say a single word, you ought to stand shaking and with your brows knitting, looking almost terrible. Of course, I do not expect or desire to make a melo-dramatic actress of you, but still I think you capable of any effect, provided *it is not sustained too long.*

Climax is reached not only by rush but by increasing pace. Your exit speech is a failure at present, because you do not vary the pace of its delivery. Get by yourself for one half-hour – if you can! Get by the seaside, if you can, since there it was Demosthenes studied eloquence and overcame mountains – not mole-hills like this. Being by the seaside, study those lines by themselves: 'And then let them find their young gentleman, and find him quickly, for London shall not hold me long – no, nor England either.' Study to speak these lines with great volubility and fire, and settle the exact syllable to run at.[21]

After Ellen's death, her daughter found a scrap of paper on which as an old woman nearly finished with life she had scribbled some names under the heading 'My Friends'. The first name on the list was Charles Reade, the second, Bernard Shaw. She called Reade 'dear papa' in her letters to him. That Reade, who had no children of his own, loved her like a wilful daughter is true to his nature, and in his notebooks he wrote his own, private judgement of her at this time:

Ellen Terry, a character such as neither Molière nor Balzac, I believe, had the luck to fall in with. Soft and yielding on the surface, egotistical below. *Varia et mutabilis,* always wanting something 'dreadful bad' today, which she does not want tomorrow, especially if you are weak enough to give it her, or get it her. Hysterical, sentimental, hard as a nail in money matters, but velvet on the surface.

Later, he amended his view of her, adding in his notebook:

This was written while she was under the influence of —. Since then greatly improved: the hardness below is melting away. In good hands a very amiable creature but dangerous to the young. Downright fascinating. Even I, who look coldly on from the senile heights, am delighted by her. . . . A young lady highly gifted with what Voltaire justly calls *le grand art de plaire* . . . Ellen Terry is an enigma. Her eyes are pale, her nose rather long, her mouth nothing particular. Complexion a delicate brickdust, her hair rather like tow. Yet somehow she is *beautiful*. Her expression *kills* any pretty face you see beside her. Her figure is lean and boney; her hand masculine in size and form. Yet she is a pattern of fawn-like grace. Whether in movement or repose, grace pervades the hussy. In character impulsive, intelligent, weak, hysterical – in short, all that is abominable and charming in women. . . . Ellen Terry is a very charming actress. I see through and through her. Yet she pleases me all the same. Little duck!

Ellen also set down her view of Reade as she looked back thirty years later at their relationship:

Dear, kind, unjust, generous, cautious, impulsive, passionate, gentle Charles Reade. Never have I known any one who combined so many qualities, far asunder as the poles, in one single disposition. He was placid and turbulent, yet always majestic. He was inexplicable and entirely lovable – a stupid old dear, and as wise as Solomon! He seemed guileless, and yet had moments of suspicion and craftiness worthy of the wisdom of the serpent.

In her personal copy of the two-volume biography of Reade that appeared in 1887, three years after Reade's death and thirteen after his reintroduction of her to the theatre, many passages are scored with marginal notes written much nearer the period of their association: 'so like him! the dear thing – Touchy'; 'Sympathy'; 'Cynic'; 'He was a cautious silly-billy!!'; 'Dear sweet'; 'Oh, Lord, how lifelike. How like *himself* he wrote.'

While Ellen was on tour with *The Wandering Heir,* two events of some importance happened to Godwin in London. First, after writing an article for *Woman and Work* in support of women entering the profession of architecture (he referred to women possessing 'That equipoise which is indispensable for the creation of beauty' and their likely proficiency as designers for interior decoration), he accepted a girl (probably Beatrice Phillips, his future wife) in his office as a pupil. Secondly, he occupied his growing free time by completing a series of thirty-three articles on the *Architecture and Costume of Shakespeare's Plays,* in effect a considerable work of research. The many evenings spent in reading and discussing Shakespeare bore fruit, and this detailed series of studies included not only Shakespeare's references to the subject but the results of Godwin's own examination of costumes and decoration in painting and sculpture contemporary with the action of the plays – sets, furniture, costumes, the background needed for a full realization of the life of the period involved. By the time Ellen returned to London, her contract finished, she found that though Godwin had undoubtedly been hard at work the brokers were once again confiscating the furniture.

The winter 1874–5 was one of great difficulty. She and Godwin were living in a house in Taviton Street, off Gordon Square. Charles Reade sent a young actor, Johnston Forbes-Robertson, who had been educated at Charterhouse and had also studied art, to pay his respects to Ellen at Taviton Street before he joined her in the cast of *The Wandering Heir.* Forbes-Robertson, highly impressionable at the age of twenty-one, was to describe his reception in the drawing-room, the décor of which had just been entirely recreated by Godwin:

The floor was covered with straw-coloured matting, and there was a dado of the same material. Above the dado were white walls, and the hangings were of cretonne, with a fine Japanese pattern in delicate grey-blue. The chairs were of wicker work cushions like the hangings, and in the centre of the room was a full-sized cast of the Venus of Milo, before which was a small pedestal, holding a little censer from which rose, curling round the Venus, ribbons of blue smoke. The whole effect was what art students of my time would have called 'awfully jolly'.

Presently the door opened, and in floated a vision of loveliness! In the blue Kimono and with that wonderful golden hair, she seemed to melt into the surroundings and appeared almost intangible. This was my first sight of Miss Terry. I was undergoing a sort of inspection, but her manner was so gracious that it soon cleared away my embarrassment. I was afterwards shown

Master Gordon Craig in his cradle and Miss Craig, a lively little girl, black-haired, with great inquiring eyes.[22]

From this moment Forbes-Robertson fell in love with Ellen, and there is a hint in Gordon Craig's reminiscences that he haunted Taviton Street, and even Harpenden, and may have annoyed Godwin by his presence. 'He seems to me to have been melancholy-eyed, long thin face – a real aesthete as *Punch* drew him and W. S. Gilbert wrote him down. All slow wiggles,' wrote Craig.

Of this period following her work with Reade Ellen says little enough, except: 'My interest in the theatre again declined. It has always been my fate or my nature – perhaps they are really the same thing – to be very happy or very miserable. At this time I was very miserable. The house in which I first lived in London, after I left Hertfordshire, had been stripped of some of the most beautiful treasures by the brokers. Pressure was being put on me by well-meaning friends to leave this house and make a great change in my life.' Undoubtedly Reade among others was urging her to abandon Godwin, whom he detested.[23] But however badly Godwin treated her, she remained in love with him, and for the rest of her days the recollection of their life together remained the most treasured of her memories.

It was into this Cinderella-like situation that Mrs Bancroft (who appeared on the stage as Marie Wilton, famous for her performances in burlesque) stepped like some beneficent fairy-godmother. Her stout little figure dressed in elegant black, she arrived at Taviton Street to find the front door open and much of the furniture gone. She went in and found Ellen alone in the drawing-room, its floor still covered with Japanese matting and the plaster cast of the Venus de Milo still in place. Apart from this there was nothing. Ellen, 'painfully thin', stood there in a Voillet-le-Duc tabard costume made of yellow material speckled with brown, like frog's skin. Ellen felt Mrs Bancroft's grey eyes taking in herself, her costume and the bare room. When she saw the Venus de Milo, she put her hand to her eyes in her best stage

manner and said, 'Dear me!' Then she explained the reason for
her visit – to ask Ellen to play Portia in the production of *The
Merchant of Venice* she and her husband Squire Bancroft planned
to put on in the spring at the old Prince of Wales's Theatre, which
occupied the site of the present Scala Theatre in Charlotte Street,
off Tottenham Court Road. She also went on to suggest that Mr
Godwin might like to take over the archaeological supervision of
the production design. Ellen, incoherent with joy, agreed on the
spot. Did she not know Portia by heart already? Had not she and
Godwin pored over the works of Titian to study the architecture
and furnishing of Venice at the height of its grandeur? When the
contract followed this fortuitous visit, Ellen sent the Bancrofts a
characteristic letter of thanks: 'My work will, I feel certain, be
joyful work, and joyful work *should* turn out good work,' she
wrote.[24] Her starting salary was to be £20 a week, which was
not excessive, but Godwin would be working as well.

The production of *The Merchant of Venice* was the last work
Ellen and Godwin were to undertake together. The Bancrofts
believed in production value, and Godwin, acknowledged in the
programme as archaeological consultant, now had his first professional engagement in the theatre. Gordon, the principal painter,
with his assistant Harford, were dispatched to Venice to make
initial drawings from which the scenery, comprising seven
elaborate set-pieces, was finally derived.[25]

Because of Godwin's link with the production, the artists, poets
and men of letters who either belonged to the new, so-called
aesthetic movement or were associated with some other faction
opposed to established convention in the arts, leavened the scanty
audiences. The play attracted a small but distinguished public.
It led to the first meeting of Godwin and Oscar Wilde. Ellen
wrote:

> The aesthetic movement, with all its faults, was responsible
> for a great deal of true enthusiasm for anything beautiful. . . .
> A more gorgeous and complete little spectacle had never been
> seen on the English stage. Veronese's *Marriage in Cana* had

inspired many of the stage pictures, and the expenditure in carrying them out had been lavish.

In the casket scene I wore a dress like almond-blossom. I was very thin, but Portia and all the ideal *young* heroines of Shakespeare ought to be thin.... I moved and spoke slowly. The clothes seemed to demand it, and the setting of the play developed the Italian feeling in it, and let the English Elizabethan element take care of itself.

Mrs Bancroft remembers that 'elaborate capitals of enormous weight cast in plaster were incorporated into the sets, which were designed in the diagonal scheme favoured by Godwin and originated, it was believed, by Charles Kean.

In spite of all these splendid preparations, the Bancrofts opened with what they later admitted to be a heavy heart. 'Exquisite as we could see the Portia would be – beautiful, beyond our hopes, as were the scenery and dresses – we felt, alas! that the version of Shylock which Coghlan proposed to offer would fail, at the time, at any rate, to be acceptable.' On the opening night the production raised little real enthusiasm. 'I think surprise had much to do with this,' wrote Squire Bancroft. 'It all looked so unlike a theatre, and so much more like old Italian pictures than anything that had been previously shown upon the stage. Some of the dresses seemed to puzzle many among the audience, noticeably those worn by Bassanio and the Venetian nobles who accompanied him to Belmont in their velvet robes of state; the gorgeous attendants on the prince of Morocco; and the Spaniards who accompanied the Prince of Arragon. It may be that it all came a little before the proper time, and that we saw things too far in advance.... I count it a failure to be proud of.' And he adds uxoriously: 'nor should it be forgotten that the absence of Mrs Bancroft was another serious drawback to the attraction, for Miss Terry had still, in those days, to earn the brilliant position she now owns, and of which her acting in this production was, without doubt, the foundation-stone'. The losses were too great to carry, and the play was withdrawn after only three weeks;

it was, no doubt appropriately, replaced by Lord Lytton's comedy *Money,* which ran successfully until the end of the season in August.

Nevertheless, three weeks was enough to show what Ellen could do in Shakespeare. Bancroft was right in claiming it as the foundation-stone of her mature career. While damning Charles Coghlan – a highly respected actor of considerable power who unaccountably failed to establish the dramatic strength of the character of Shylock and merely recited the lines – the Press united to praise Ellen: 'the very poetry of acting', said the critic of the *Telegraph,* 'graceful and commanding', said the *News,* and spoke of 'the bold innocence, the lively wit and quick intelligence, the grace and elegance of manner, and all the youth and freshness of this exquisite creation'; Joseph Knight particularizing, said:

> More adequate expression has seldom been given to the light-heartedness of maidenhood, the perplexities and hesitations of love. . . . The famous speech on mercy assumed new beauties from a correct and exquisite delivery. A very noteworthy point in the performance was the womanly interest in Shylock – the endeavour to win him for his own sake, from the pursuit of his firm resolve. The delivery of the lines —
> 'Shylock, there's thrice the money offered thee,'
> and
> 'Have by some surgeon, Shylock, on our charge
> To stop his wounds, lest he do bleed to death,'
> were dictated by sublime compassion.[26]

Alice Comyns-Carr was at the theatre with her husband and describes the effect of Ellen's performance on the audience:

> As the curtain rose upon Nell's tall and slender figure in a china-blue and white brocade dress, with one crimson rose at her breast, the whole house burst forth in rapturous applause. But her greatest effect was when she walked into the court in her black robes of justice, and I remember my young husband, who had rushed out between the acts to buy the last bouquet in

Covent Garden, throwing his floral tribute at her feet amidst the enthusiasm of the audience. [27]

What Ellen established as the characteristic of her performance in an age when pompous, rhetorical, windy and monotonous acting was still the rule, was an utter naturalness of manner which came directly from her own essential nature. As soon as she put her foot on the stage she did not assume artificial limbs and an artificial voice – she intensified by careful study and the thoughtful invention of 'business' her own natural reaction to whatever part she was playing. Her high spirits led her to find her fullest realization in comedy; her own suffering led her to understand the human aspect of pathos and compassion. To this she added the faultless enunciation which Ben had been the first to teach her; her mature voice possessed a fine control and range which allowed her to bring a resonant intensity to everything she said, and helped her to succeed in tragedy, which otherwise might have been beyond her full capacity as an actress. She was quick and graceful in all her movements; her tall, lithe figure, her beautifully moulded face, clear and open in its expression, and the impulsive warmth of her personality, which was communicated to the audience the moment she appeared on the stage, all combined to build up the attribute of 'charm', the word too invariably used to describe her. 'There is more to my acting than charm,' she used to insist. She knew the self-discipline she had to impose on herself in case her high spirits ran away with her, betraying instead of illuminating her art.

The effect on Ellen of her three-week success was profound. She experienced a new emotion on the stage, an emotion which mattered deeply to her both as a woman and as an actress. Later she attempted to evaluate the nature and extent of her gifts:

I had had some success in other parts, and had tasted the delight of knowing that audiences like me, and had liked them back again. But never until I appeared as Portia at the Prince of Wales's had I experienced that more than once in a lifetime - the feeling of the conqueror. I knew that I had 'got them' at the

moment when I spoke the speech beginning, 'you see me, Lord
Bassanio, where I stand'.

'What can this be?' I thought. '*Quite* this thing has never
come to me before! *This is different.* It has never been quite the
same before.'

It was never quite the same again.

Elation, triumph, being lifted on high by a single stroke of
the mighty wing of glory – call it by any name, think of it as
you like – it was as Portia that I had my first and last sense of it.[28]

Coghlan was to wipe out some of the bitter memory of his
ineffectual performance as Shylock with his later successes in the
Bancrofts' season. Ellen, though she could not account for his
failure, bore him no resentment; he was an old friend from
Bristol days, and they worked together throughout the rest of the
year, and for a single night in August she played opposite to him
in Lytton's celebrated *Lady of Lyons,* he as the cad Melnotte and
she as Pauline, the 'proud beauty' who respects him. She disliked this
part because she could find no root of humanity in it which she
could combine with her own warm personality on the stage.
She had to entertain her public with lines such as these, which
she quotes in her memoirs:

Go! (*White to the lips.*) Sir, leave this house! It is humble; but
a husband's roof, however lowly, is, in the eyes of God and
Man, the temple of a wife's honour. (*Tumultuous applause.*)
Know that I would rather starve – aye, *starve* – with him who
has betrayed me than accept *your* lawful hand, even were you
the prince whose name he bore. (*Hurrying on quickly to prevent
applause before the finish.*) Go![29]

Nevertheless, the critic Joseph Knight chose this single performance as sufficient evidence to declare that he was witnessing during
the Bancrofts' season 'the advent of genius' to the British theatre.

From now on, Ellen was to look increasingly for the human
side of the character she was called upon to portray, and she
found some satisfaction in Lytton's other play, *Money*. Taylor

wrote to her after the first night advising her, as a friend, to study to be 'quiet and composed', and not to show 'too evident feeling' in the early scene. The Press was again complimentary; the *Telegraph* said, except for Aimée Desclée 'we can recall no actress in modern times who has possessed the gift of so absorbing herself in the creation that the actress is lost entirely, or who so thoroughly compels her audience to follow the workings and anxiety of her mind.... It is not acting, it is nature itself.' The *Standard* agreed: 'Miss Terry has the rare gift of identifying herself with the personage she presents.' Lewis Carroll went to see the play three times in June and July, and thought her 'a perfect treat'.

It was said that by now the nature of Ellen's success was not altogether to the personal liking of Mrs Bancroft, who took over the leading roles for the rest of the season. Ellen played a small, supporting part in Reade's and Taylor's *Masks and Faces,* which opened on 6 November with Mrs Bancroft as Peg Woffington, and she had no part at all in J. H. Byron's comedy *Wrinkles,* though Bancroft claimed he had asked the author to include good parts for both Ellen and Coghlan. When this play failed, Ellen was invited to play another subsidiary role in a revival of Robertson's comedy *Ours.* 'Ellen Terry at once consented to play Blanche Haye, adding with great good nature, that she would even have taken part in *Wrinkles* had we asked her,' writes Bancroft. *Ours* opened on 6 May 1876, but was dogged by ill luck through sickness; Mrs Bancroft withdrew through a serious illness on Saturday 17 June, while the following Monday Ellen telegraphed her inability to act also through illness, and the season finished without her. In the autumn she was already booked by John Hare to appear with his company at the original Court Theatre, Sloane Square. Before she withdrew from the Bancrofts, however, a young newcomer to London, George Bernard Shaw, went to see *Ours,* this Cup and Saucer drama, as he called it. He remembered that she left on him an 'impression of waywardness; of not quite fitting into her part, and not wanting to'. He had hoped to find her 'interesting and singular', but was disappointed.[30]

Meanwhile Ellen's life at home had been unhappy, except for

the companionship of Boo and the children; in the summer of 1876, Edy was six and Teddy four. According to Gordon Craig, whose recollections reach back to those days, Ellen and Godwin finally parted in November 1875 ('E. T. worked on. Brave,' he writes. 'Strange to realize now that she did not kill herself'),[31] and the following January Godwin married Beatrice Phillips, the twenty-one-year-old girl who was, nominally at any rate, his student. He signed the marriage certificate Edwin Godwin, since Edwin was the name his wife preferred to use, but apparently went off to dine at his club after the ceremony. (Later after Godwin's death in 1886, Beatrice Godwin, who was the daughter of the sculptor, John Bernie Phillips, married their mutual friend, the painter Whistler.)

The effect of this loss on Ellen can only now be imagined. Godwin had been, and was always to remain in her memory, the single love of her life. But he had tired of her and of the children, or at any rate had come to associate them all with ceaseless trouble and financial difficulty. He was increasingly preoccupied with the affairs and discussions of the Arts Club, where he met Whistler and other artists whose views, like his own, differed from the conventional academic view. He wrote about Japanese art, and became closely identified with the newer manifestations in painting of which Whistler was the pioneer. He wrote regularly for *The Building News* and *The Architect,* and began to design houses for people of moderate means in the new Victorian–Queen Anne style. But life with Ellen was at an end, and she moved the family to rooms in Camden Town – at 221 Camden Road. From here she travelled to and from the theatre by omnibus.

Gordon Craig's comment is characteristic, though necessarily subjective: 'I knew that when they separated it was by mutual misunderstanding.' They had lived together on equal terms, he asserts, for some years without either seeking to bind the other with legal ties. 'Then by mutual disagreement they parted. Sad: but there was no unkindness, no dissension – they were neither of them desertable people.' Now, in Camden Town, there was just money enough from the theatre to maintain a manless household –

with Boo as housekeeper, Bo, her niece, as nursemaid, and servants to look after them all. But, at present, there was still no communication between Ellen and her parents in Stanhope Street. Ellen and her children were a disgrace in the eyes of Ben and Sarah, whose hopes, turning away from the boys, centred on Polly, who used her real name of Marion on the stage, and Floss, who professionally was called Florence. Marion, now twenty-three, after doing well in comedy at the Strand went in September 1876 to the Haymarket and starred with Johnston Forbes-Robertson in a new play by W. S. Gilbert, *Dan'l Druce, Blacksmith*, while Florence, aged twenty-one, was on tour in another play by the indefatigable Tom Taylor.

Ellen's children continued to be brought up in the manner prescribed by Godwin and fervently endorsed by Ellen. Gordon Craig himself describes it: verses by such poets as Herrick and Blake repeated 'at lunch . . . whenever E.T. took a fancy to torture me'; the picture-books of Crane and Caldecott; the tittle-tattle of Boo and the servants, and the 'lovely Dream of good'. Ellen, with memories of Ben and her own childhood, was insisting on exact enunciation, and Teddy, already learning to resist his mother's more dangerous blandishments, found he could not at the age of four pronounce the word 'sheep' in a poem by Blake which she had told him to learn. In the end she frightened him by the scene she made, which in her memoirs she described as a prolonged wrestling match with his 'obstinacy', which ended in mutual tears. She became actressy, he says. He was already beginning to taste the exigencies of his lifelong struggle with women; they were out to get you, he discovered, even at the age of four.

From now on, Ellen was never to be short of men who were in love with her. She enjoyed loving them back, but without any real personal or physical involvement. There were many reasons for this. From now on she lived exactly as she herself wanted to live, with no desire ever to be made to suffer again, if that were possible. Life now should be something un-intense, unwounding. Her Portia prompted a flood of letters from men expressing their admiration for her. 'Everyone seemed to be in love with me!' she writes. 'I had sweethearts by the dozen, known and unknown. Most of the letters written to me I destroyed long ago, but the feeling of sweetness and light with which some of them filled me can never be destroyed.' This helped her, no doubt, to recover her composure and face her audiences night after night when Godwin had left her. But after him she had to remain somehow invulnerable.

Over twenty years later, she was to express this in a letter written to one of her more intimate women friends:

> The times of which you were part were my *best* times, my happiest times. I can never think of him *but at his best,* and when he died he thought only so of me. I could never suffer again I think as I have suffered, but I joy in the remembrance of him, and the thought of him is my strongest incentive to the right. I have had too much happiness – too many blessings and have deserved none of them. Thank God *Mother* is alive (and so fond of me) that I can atone a little to her for all my unintentional paining of her. He loved me – and I *loved* him – and that I suppose is the reason we so cruelly hurt each other. He went away and shut the door after him – it seems like that to me! but *he knows.*[32]

But beyond this harbouring of past love she had another duty; to give her children a name so that they might live a normal life in the Victorian society of the 1870s, and establish a proper relationship with their grandparents, whom they had not yet seen. At some period between the marriage of Godwin in January 1876 and 13 March 1877, when Watts, as we have seen, instituted divorce proceedings on the grounds of her adultery with Godwin, some approach must have been made to encourage her first husband to free her so that she could, when she wanted, marry again.[33] Watts was by now in a better position to afford the comparatively heavy costs of a divorce and, to judge from his later communication with Ellen, he was in a frame of mind to be helpful, since he came to accept some part at least of the blame for the breakdown of their marriage. Could it be that Tom Taylor, the friend who had helped to bring about the marriage in the first place, stepped in now to help dissolve it? If so, it would account for the association in Ellen Terry's mind which guided her, some thirty years later, to insert several pages of tribute to Taylor's friendship precisely at this period in her memoirs. In any case, whoever made representation to Watts to start proceedings must have done so at some time during 1876, or the case itself would not have reached the courts by March. Watts who was not himself to marry again until 1886 (the year of Godwin's death) presumably had no need to go to all this trouble on his own account. He must have done it out of compassion for her situation. A decree absolute was granted him in September 1877.

Meanwhile, in November 1876, she had begun her season at the Court Theatre under the management of John Hare, the last engagement she was to have before joining Irving at the Lyceum in 1878.[34] At the Court she appeared for over eighteen months in a succession of plays, the first of which, a comedy called *Brothers* by her ill-fated friend Charles Coghlan, lasted barely a month. It was followed by Tom Taylor's *New Men and Old Acres,* which had a part specially written for her, Lilian Vavasour, though when the play was first put on at the Haymarket Mrs Kendal had taken it. It was in this play that she 'completely conquered' Bernard Shaw, and convinced him that 'here was the woman for the new drama which was still in the womb of Time, waiting for Ibsen to impregnate it'.[35] Lewis Carroll, who saw it on 16 January 1877, thought her 'unsurpassable', but lamented her lost girlhood – 'the gush of animal spirits of a light-hearted girl is beyond her now, poor thing! She can give a very clever imitation of it, but that is all'.

Hare commissioned W. G. Wills to adapt *The Vicar of Wake-field* for the stage, and the result was *Olivia,* which was finally ready for presentation on 30 March 1878. In this modest senti-mental piece Ellen, who played the title-role, had an undemanding part, but one that exactly suited her particular talent to charm her audiences. On 5 March, during the initial rehearsals, Ellen wrote

to Wills from the theatre: 'I can't tell you how *much* I was delighted with the play, and with my part, but I *was* delighted.'
The critics were equally entranced by her performance: 'natural
and touching ... when she repelled the further advances of the
man who had wronged her, it touched absolute greatness,' wrote
Joseph Knight. 'A memory that will never die ... her indescribable charm ... it went on from perfection to perfection,' declared
Clement Scott. Ellen's photographs were on sale everywhere, and
the milliners' windows filled with Olivia hats and kerchiefs.
Lewis Carroll went to see her on 22 April and was much moved:
'the gem of the piece is Olivia herself, acted ... with a sweetness
and pathos that moved some of the audience (nearly including
myself) to tears.' Henry Irving managed to visit the Court after
the play had opened, and determined on the strength of what he
saw to make Ellen his leading lady at the Lyceum.

Then, as if on an impulse, Ellen decided to marry again. According to Gordon Craig, this happened on 21 November 1877, some
two months after the divorce was completed. Ellen, on the other
hand, says that she married 'secretly' during the run of *Olivia*
which, as we have seen, did not open until 30 March the following
year. In any case, she moved her household to 33 Longridge
Road, Earls Court. Previously, they had been living in various
localities – Gordon Craig records the address of 221 Camden
Road in Camden Town for 1876, and Edy claimed number 44
Finborough Road (off the Fulham Road, near Brompton
Cemetery) for 1877. But it was to Longridge Road that she
brought her new husband to live with her and the children. He
was Charles Wardell, one of the actors in the company at the
Court; his stage name was Charles Kelly.

The advent of Kelly into Ellen's life illuminates another, and
new, aspect of her complex nature. She had, as we have seen, a
host of suitors, serious and not so serious, and it is likely during
this period that she was prepared to behave more frivolously than
that at any stage in her life. She admitted her delight in receiving
love letters and other forms of attention. Among the more serious
of her devotees was Johnston Forbes-Robertson, already a success-

ful young actor working with her sister Marion. However, he was much younger than she – in February 1877 she entered her thirty-first year – but, probably far worse in her sight, he was an aesthete, a man who might prove as unreliable domestically as Godwin. What she evidently felt she needed, now that she was no longer a girl and was the mother of two growing children who had no 'name', was the kind of stability acknowledged in Victorian society – a solid and presentable husband who would act as a good father should to Edy and, above all, to young Teddy. However, once more she made an unfortunate choice.

As she saw it, the advantage of marrying a man like Kelly lay in the fact that he was not by background so much an actor as a soldier. This she stresses in her memoirs. He had fought in the Crimean War, when Ellen was less than ten years old. His father was a clergyman who lived in Northumberland and who still possessed many relics of Sir Walter Scott, whose friend he had been during his youth in the earlier years of the century. Kelly had gone on the stage with none of the prolonged training which Ellen, the true professional, had received, and he had to be type-cast. 'Charles, a manly bulldog sort of man, possessed as an actor great tenderness and humour,' wrote Ellen years afterwards. He was plainly the antithesis of Godwin.

Edy, his step-daughter, who was around eight at the time of the marriage, made this rather cold comment in 1933 on her mother's affections: 'All through her life the man of brains competed for her affections with the man of brawn,' and she added that he proved to have 'a violent and jealous temper which Ellen Terry eventually found intolerable'.[36] However, in later years Edy resented her mother having any close friendship with men, and was hardly likely to look back with much favour on Kelly, who was in any case addicted to drink. According to Edy, he was to become jealous of Irving because he fancied himself as his wife's permanent leading man. As we shall see, the marriage finally broke up in 1881, and a judicial separation ensued.

Gordon Craig, who did not share his sister's particular prejudices against men, contents himself by regarding this marriage

as 'a curious notion', admitting that Kelly at least taught him
how to read the clock. Later he adds ironically (since he was
always proud of being Godwin's son) that when his mother
married Kelly it was probably the result of admiration for him,
but never love. She needed, it seemed to him, a 'hefty protector
for herself', and he believed that the marriage was undertaken to
please everyone. It certainly pleased her parents, who emerged
out of their long retirement from her life and called at Longridge
Road. For Teddy the first appearance of his grandmother late in
1877 is mingled with the images of sleep – the silvery voice
murmuring by his bedside the names of strange women, Kate
and Marion and Flossie. Later Sarah came to tea, a respectable
Victorian tea, with Ellen saying in advance that Granny was gay
and merry, and Edy intoning tragically, 'That's Gran'mama' when
the front-door bell rang. Teddy, aged five, tried to help the
'sweet, white-haired' lady with a nose like his mother's into her
chair by moving it politely to one side; whereupon, Granny sat
down, quietly and gracefully, on to the floor. But Sarah was
equal to the moment, 'That *was* fun!' she said, smiling at Teddy,
who in any case had burst out laughing.[37]

For Ellen, this reconciliation with her mother was no doubt
the greatest benefit to come from her marriage. As if by magic.
the children were suddenly 'acknowledged' – they became over-
night Edith Wardell, Edward Wardell. They did not care, but
the Terrys did, and the vacuum in the family relationship caused
by the scandal of the past was now filled; there was granny,
grandpa, aunts and uncles. Uncle Fred was only thirteen, and
still at school. After a further respectable interval, even the Rev.
C. L. Dodgson ventured, in June 1879, to renew a friendship he
had allowed to lapse for twelve years – 'called on the Wardells. . . .
She was charming as ever, and I was much pleased with her
husband. I also liked her two children, Edith and Eddie'. Lewis
Carroll, however, made no such favourable impression on little
'Eddie', though he tried to entertain him with a story, illustrated
by means of matches, of how five sheep were taken across a river
in one boat. 'I was not amused,' comments Gordon Craig, who

at this time was being looked after by a newcomer to the family, Miss Harries, who had a shrill voice, a scraggy neck, and was kind to animals and very religious. She took him to church, which he hated.

On 20 July 1878, a letter arrived for Ellen with the address 15a, Grafton Street, at the head:

> Dear Miss Terry, I look forward to the pleasure of calling upon you on Tuesday next at two o'clock. With every good wish, believe me,
>
> Yours sincerely, Henry Irving.[38]

It was Ellen's first letter from the new manager at the Lyceum. The greatest partnership in the history of the English Theatre was about to begin.

BRITISH THEATRICAL LINEAGE

From Shakespeare to Irving and Ellen Terry

William Shakespeare 1564–1616
Richard Burbage c. 1567–1619
  Shakespeare's principal actor
William Davenant 1606–68
  Shakespeare's godson and putative natural son
  Director of one of the two royal patent companies established in London after the Restoration, 1660.
Professional actresses appear in English theatres from this time.
Thomas Betterton c. 1635–1710
  Trained by Davenant and head of the company by 1671
  Married to *Mary Sanderson* (d. 1712), also trained by Betterton
  Leading ladies include:
    Elizabeth Barry 1658–1713
    Anne Bracegirdle c. 1663–1748. Trained by Betterton
    Anne (Nance) Oldfield 1663–1748
  Later exponents of Betterton's declamatory style at the Patent theatres (Drury Lane and Covent Garden):
    Barton Booth 1681–1733
    James Quin 1693–1766
  Reacting against this style:
David Garrick 1717–79
  Main career spent at Drury Lane. Leading ladies include:
    Susanna Maria Cibber 1714–66
    Hannah Pritchard 1711–68
    George Anne Bellamy 1727–88
    Frances Abingdon 1737–1815
  Roger Kemble (1721–1802), strolling player, marries the d. of one of Betterton's actors, and becomes the father of:
Sarah Siddons 1755–1831, England's greatest tragic actress, and
John Philip Kemble 1757–1823
  Tragedian, and manager successively of Drury Lane and Covent Garden
  Marries *Priscilla Hopkins* 1755–1845, a member of Garrick's company
William Charles Macready 1793–1873
  Tragedian, and manager successively of Covent Garden and Drury Lane
  Assists towards abolition of royal patents in 1843. Rival actor to:
Edmund Kean 1787–1833
  One of England's greatest tragedians. Father of:
Charles Kean 1811–68
  Ben Terry 1818–96, strolling player, works with Macready
  Father of:
Ellen Terry 1847–1928
  England's greatest comedy actress; worked with Charles Kean. In 1878 entered into partnership with:
Henry Irving 1838–1905
  One of England's greatest actors and stage producers in whose company appeared many veteran actors who had worked with Macready and Edmund Kean.

THE LYCEUM

For over twenty years Henry Irving had been shaping a career for himself in the theatre. He had lacked Ellen's good fortune in having devoted parents already on the stage and in enjoying a career which, however interrupted, had shown from the first a steady progress towards popular success. As a young actor he had possessed neither the voice nor the appearance to excite immediate unthinking admiration, and he had to learn the technique of holding an audience in the teeth of what sometimes proved to be cruel opposition in the hard school of the provincial playhouse.

In July 1878, when he called at Longridge Road to invite Ellen to join his company, Irving was already forty years of age. He had been born on 6 February 1838 in Somerset, and christened John Henry Brodribb; his mother was Cornish, and he had been for a while reared in Cornwall by his aunt. His adolescence had been spent in the city of London, where his father had minor employment, possibly as a caretaker; here Irving had studied elocution at the City Commercial School. At the age of twelve he had seen Phelps play Hamlet at Sadler's Wells. At thirteen he had become clerk to a firm of lawyers, but developed his interest in the theatre through continuing his study of elocution and taking part in amateur productions. Eventually, to his mother's horror, since she was a strict Methodist, he had gone on the stage in 1856, beginning his professional career at the age of eighteen in Sunderland. He assumed the stage name of Irving, since it was obvious that 'Brodribb' would lack attraction for the playgoer.[1]

Irving's long career in the provinces, like that of Sarah Siddons, enabled him to hammer out his experience until there was no branch of performance with which he was not familiar (burlesque,

H

comedy, melodrama, tragedy), and no aspect of his weakness as a performer to which attention had not been drawn by rough and ruthless audiences. From Sunderland he went to Edinburgh, where he held the rank of 'first walking gentleman'; now and then he even appeared in London. In Edinburgh he attracted attention as the villain in burlesque, and his sardonic sense of humour began to develop. He became passionately interested in the details of costume and make-up. Convinced of his talent, and prepared to temper it like steel against any opposition, he began giving individual recitals at the age of twenty-one. Well liked on the Scottish circuit, he was barracked in Dublin, but he got used to the irreverent kind of provincial audiences who would respond from the 'gods' to Lady Macbeth's 'To bed – to bed – to bed' with, 'Go along, ninnie, and I'll be after yez.' His weekly salary in these hard days was seldom more than £2.

In his private life Irving was respectable, God-fearing and affectionate to his father, to whom he wrote regularly and for whom he always spared a few shillings from his scanty wage. He had no contact with his mother, whose sympathy he had forfeited by going on the stage. He could be boisterous in his humour, and he liked joining in a noisy party with his friends. As an actor he learned burlesque from John Toole, and expanded his idea of tragic acting when he saw the American actor Edwin Booth perform in Manchester in 1861. In 1864 he travelled specially from Manchester to Birmingham to inquire from the veteran actor W. H. Chippendale how Edmund Kean had played in *Hamlet;* he announced on his return that he would play the Prince on the occasion of his 'benefit', which he did adequately. He was beginning to acquire the *persona* of a true actor.

His first success in London had not come until 1866, in a play by Dion Boucicault. It was at a party given by Clement Scott, the civil servant and drama critic, that he met Florence O'Callaghan, the tall and handsome girl who later became his wife. His relation with his first love, the actress Nellie Moore, failed to lead to an engagement. Florence O'Callaghan's father was a surgeon-general in the army, and his wife disapproved of her daughter's growing attachment to the actor. There seems little doubt that this opposition offended Irving's pride at the same time as it roused a certain stubbornness in his future wife. It was at this period of his expanding fortunes that Irving was engaged by Wigan to play Petruchio to Ellen's Katherine at the Queen's Theatre. Later he played Sykes opposite Nellie Moore as Nancy in an adaptation of *Oliver Twist*. 'If he some day doesn't come out as a great actor I know nothing of the art,' said Charles Dickens of Irving's work in 1868.

In January 1869 Nellie Moore died in tragic circumstances, a grief Irving was never to forget;[2] the following July he married Florence O'Callaghan. His salary by this time, when he was favoured with work, was some £10 a week. His two sons, Henry Brodribb and Laurence, were born in 1870 and 1871. His aim now was to lose his stage image as a grim comedian and assume the status of a tragic actor, but he did not achieve this until his phenomenal performance in *The Bells* (Leopold Lewis's adaptation of a French play, *Le Juif Polanais*) which he insisted his new manager, H. L. Bateman, should introduce into the repertoire at the Lyceum in 1871. This play offered a *tour de force* to an actor who could sustain its mounting tension in a form which developed virtually into a monologue at the climax of the play, when a murderer who has escaped from justice is arraigned by the vision conjured up in his own imagination. He first played the part in November 1871 at the age of thirty-three; *The Bells* was a curtain-raiser to *Pickwick,* in which, following within minutes this most demanding performance, he had to reappear as Jingle. Clement Scott said afterwards, 'Tonight I have seen a great actor.' From this moment he became the mainstay of the Bateman company, and in 1878 he finally achieved his great ambition and took over the management of the Lyceum for himself.

Throughout this period of tension in the development of Irving's art, his wife Florence had grown resentful and even callous in the face of his increasing self-absorption. 'Are you going on making a fool of yourself like this all your life?' was all she could say after his triumph in *The Bells*. He left her on the

spot and never spoke to her again. They were crossing Hyde
Park at the time; Irving told the driver to stop, and got down
without a further word. This was the last she ever saw of him in
private, but he always maintained the ritual of sending her reser-
vations for a box on his opening nights, and she as regularly
attended them. The two pregnancies through which she had
passed had not helped the situation, and she had begun to find the
company of Irving's colleagues intolerable to her genteel taste.
Gradually Irving had begun to avoid his wife's company; he
turned to the Bateman family, where warmth and sympathy were
always uppermost. Two months after the birth of his second son,
whose christening he did not attend, he wrote Florence a final
letter severing their relationship; he allowed her eight pounds a
week out of his salary of fifteen and it was paid punctiliously.
The emotional strain of this period was so great that it took all the
influence of the Batemans to keep him from excessive drinking
once the night's hard work was done.

Irving's story between 1872 and 1878 – when he was able with
the help of borrowed money to take over the management of the
Lyceum from Mrs Bateman, whose husband had died in 1875 –
reveals his ascendancy as the star performer of the Lyceum. He
appeared in such leading parts as the title-roles in Wills's plays,
Charles I (1872) and *Eugene Aram* (1873), as the Cardinal in Lytton's
Richelieu (1873), as Hamlet in 1874, and with indifferent success,
as Macbeth (1875) and Othello (1876). He retrieved his reputation
in Shakespeare with his commanding performance as Gloucester
in his production of *Richard III* (1877), scored a double triumph in
the contrasting parts of Lesurques and Dubosc in a revival *The
Lyons Mail* (his retitling of Reade's play, *The Courier of Lyons*),
and capped this in 1878 as the mad king in Boucicault's adaptation
of Casimar Delavigne's *Louis XI*. Throughout this time, of course,
he repeated his phenomenal *tour de force* in *The Bells,* performing
it on tour as well as at his theatrical headquarters at the Lyceum in
London. His staple repertoire of star parts, many of which he
was to revive during the next quarter century, was now gradually
being built up. But Irving chafed under Mrs Bateman's sym-

pathetically maternal management, which was wholly dependent for its success upon him, and he was all the more uneasy because Mrs Bateman's daughter Isabel had fallen uncontrollably in love with him.

In 1872 he moved to 15a Grafton Street, where he was to remain for nearly thirty years, even though his rooms were little more than lodgings to him. He came to live a bachelor existence and grew into an inveterate clubman; at this time he only felt completely at home in his office, his dressing-room, or on the stage at the Lyceum. He was deeply embarrassed by the adoration of Isabel, and acutely aware that she and her sister Virginia were actresses entirely below his own calibre. But he knew that so long as he worked for Mrs Bateman he would be forced to accept them as his leading ladies. When in 1878 he sought to free himself from Isabel, Mrs Bateman, though deeply hurt at this affront to her daughter, offered to surrender the lease of the Lyceum to him if he could raise the money to purchase it. She had previously made it clear that she was even willing to encourage her daughter to live with him until such time as he could free himself to marry her. In spite of her disappointment, Mrs Bateman behaved with the utmost generosity throughout the negotiations. 'Perhaps he had to be a little cruel,' wrote Ellen later of Irving, 'not for the last time in a career devoted unremittingly and unrelentingly to his art and his ambition.' Yet Irving's only freedom now was his freedom as an artist; his wife would never entertain the idea of divorcing him, and he was to remain tied to her for life.

This was the man who arrived on the doorstep of Ellen's house in Longridge Road in July 1878. He brought his dog with him. She looked at him, noticing the great change that had taken place in his manner and appearance. When they had last met in 1867, he had had a moustache and he had seemed to her nervous, uneasily sensitive, stiffly self-conscious and, as she put it, 'conceited'. The only thing she found sympathetic was his air of melancholy, which was natural to him, quite unassumed, and she had noted his sigh ('the deepest, profoundest, sincerest sigh I have ever heard from any human being') when he had discovered her playing the piano in the Green Room at the Queen's. He had asked her to play the music for him once more. Now, ten years later, she found herself facing a confident man who had realized his stature, and combined now a certain 'massive' strength with a great gentleness of manner.

Ellen, as women will, was taking Irving's measure while he was searching for the right words with which to broach the subject he had come to discuss. Then the ice was broken by his dog, which 'misbehaved' itself on the carpet. Nevertheless Irving, for all his maturity, suffered from some diffidence, for while he left Longridge Road quite sure he had invited Ellen to join him at the Lyceum ('I have engaged Ellen Terry – not a bad start – eh?' he wrote a few days later to his old headmaster and friend, Dr Pinches), Ellen herself felt it necessary to write while on tour in Liverpool the following month asking for more precise terms:

> The Fly is waiting at the door to take us out of this *most horrible place*. My husband will be in London all next week . . . if you will write to me there . . . making me some definite proposition, I will answer you definitely. So far, I think I understand, you wd like me to be with you at the Lyceum next season and will you be good enough to understand that I on my part most earnestly desire to be with you. I hope we shall be able to arrange.[3]

Terms were then settled at forty guineas a week and 'a half clear benefit'. She was never to know poverty again.

Irving's hesitation may have been due in part to his desire to see Ellen once again on the stage before clinching a matter of such great importance to him. He had not had the opportunity to see her in her current success at the Court Theatre, and had in fact relied on the advice of one of his woman friends, Lady Pollack, who had shrewdly recommended that here was the kind of actress he needed. Ellen herself was in no two minds about the advantages of working with Irving; she had seen him on the stage on several occasions since the time they had worked together. In 1874 Tom Taylor had taken her to the first night of Irving's

Hamlet at the Lyceum – 'by far the greatest part that he had ever played, or was ever to play', she says; in 1876 Coghlan, who 'was always raving about Irving at this time', had gone with her to see him play King Philip in Tennyson's *Queen Mary;* now, at Irving's invitation, she went in mid-December to Birmingham to see the production in which he was asking her to play Ophelia. In 1878, she felt, he was 'far more wonderful' than in 1874:

> He knew I was there. He played – I say it without vanity – for me. We players are not above that weakness, if it be a weakness. If ever anything inspires us to do our best it is the presence in the audience of some fellow-artist who must in the nature of things know more completely than any one what we intend, what we do, what we feel. The response from such a member of the audience flies across the footlights to us like a flame.[4]

In the part of Philip she had already marvelled at his work in the scene when Mary pours out her heart to the King – 'the horrid dead look, the cruel unresponsiveness, the indifference of the creature' standing there polishing his ring, 'the perfection of quiet malignity and cruelty'. Irving drew from the part far more than Tennyson had put in, she thought, and understood well why Whistler wanted to create a Velasquez-like image of Irving in the part, and why Irving had never liked the picture when it was done – probably 'not nearly showy enough', she thought. And then his Hamlet, so 'absolutely right', his make-up pale, his face haggard but beautiful, his hair blue-black, like the plumage of a crow, his eyes 'two fires veiled by melancholy' a melancholy 'as simple as it was profound'. His distinction was the capacity to keep three qualities alive always in perfect combination: 'the antic madness, the sanity, the sense of the theatre.' His first entrance was meticulously contrived, the climax of a procession set to music with Hamlet as the last, solitary figure, tall and thin, his cloak trailing the ground while the lights dimmed at his approach.

She also recognized another quality in Irving's performance, a

certain extravagance, a 'bizarrerie' as she calls it. She approved it.
Yet she knew it invited derision, and mocking imitation from the
deriders. She saw it, in the words of Socrates, as 'a divine release',
a pitch that lifted performance beyond a common realism towards
a special revelation. His speech rose above nature, becoming the
articulation of passion, an illumination of thought. He imbued
his interjections, his exclamations, his words with their own
emotional intensity. Yet Irving's peculiarities of speech were
universally discussed.[5] Henry James, who was always highly
critical of Irving, wrote of him in 1880:

> The opinion flourishes on the one side that Mr Irving is a
> great and admirable artist, and on the other the impression
> prevails that his defects outnumber his qualities. He has at least
> the power of inspiring violent enthusiasms, and this faculty is
> almost always accompanied by a liability to excite protests.
> Those that it has been Mr Irving's destiny to call forth have
> been very downright, and many of them are sufficiently intell-
> igible. He is what is called a picturesque actor; that is, he
> depends for his effects upon the art with which he presents a
> certain figure to the eye, rather than upon the manner in which
> he speaks his part. He is a thoroughly serious actor, and evidently
> bestows an immense deal of care and conscience upon his work;
> he meditates, elaborates, and, upon the line on which he moves,
> carries the part to a very high degree of finish. But it must be
> affirmed that this is a line with which the especial art of the
> actor, the art of utterance, of saying the thing, has almost
> nothing to do. Mr Irving's peculiarities and eccentricities of
> speech are so strange, so numerous, so personal to himself, his
> vices of pronunciation, of modulation, of elocution so highly
> developed, the tricks he plays with the divine mother-tongue
> so audacious and fantastic, that the spectator who desires to be
> in sympathy with him finds himself confronted with a bristling
> hedge of difficulties.[6]

Ellen came to know every part, every particle, of Irving's
greater performances, and with a detailed memory of his work

she could set it all down; recalling the moments of his 'infinite variety' she wrote of his Hamlet:

During the first scene with Horatio, Marcellus and Bernardo, he began by being very absent and distant. He exchanged greetings sweetly and gently, but he was the visionary. His feet might be on the ground, but his head was towards the stars.... Bit by bit as Horatio talks, Hamlet comes back into the world. He is still out of it when he says:
My father! Methinks I see my father.
But the dreamer becomes attentive, sharp as a needle, with the words:
For God's love, let me hear.
Irving's face as he listened to Horatio's tale, blazed with intelligence. He cross-examined the men with keenness and authority. His mental deductions as they answered were clearly shown. With 'I would I had been there' the cloud of unseen witnesses with whom he had been communing again descended. For a second or two Horatio and the rest did not exist for him.... So onward to the crowning couplet:
... foul deeds will rise
Though all the earth o'erwhelm them to men's eyes.
After having been very quiet and rapid, very discreet, he pronounced these lines in a loud, clear voice, dragged out every syllable as if there never could be an end to his horror and his rage.[7]

Although Ellen was pleased to feel he dedicated his performance of Hamlet in Birmingham to her especially because he had asked her to witness it, she was to become aware that this master-artist of the stage was 'always quite independent of the people with whom he acted'. Though he could drill his supporting players until 'he became livid with fatigue' and 'the skin grew tight over his face', he was but preparing the paints in order to achieve a perfect canvas in which his own performance would be the highlight of a total masterpiece. Perhaps the conflagration of his genius drew her towards him, for this intensity was something she had scarcely experienced before, though she had touched a fringe of it both in Watts and Edward Godwin in another branch of art:

He was an egotist – an egotist of the great type, *never* 'a mean egotist', as he was once slanderously described – and all his faults sprang from egotism, which is in one sense, after all, only another name for greatness. So much absorbed was he in his own achievements that he was unable or unwilling to appreciate the achievements of others. I never heard him speak in high terms of the great foreign actors and actresses who from time to time visited England. It would be easy to attribute this to jealousy, but the easy explanation is not the true one. He simply would not give himself up to appreciation. Perhaps appreciation is a *wasting* though a generous quality of the mind and heart, and best left to lookers-on, who have plenty of time to develop it.

Ellen realized that she did not herself possess this involved and devouring genius. She knew that she was highly talented, and wanted always to make the best of her gifts upon the stage. She asserts repeatedly that her object was to become a '*useful* actress – ever the height of my ambition', a modest aim, perhaps deliberately so, as if to shield herself from the unwanted consequences of genius as she had seen them manifest in men. 'I have always been more woman than artist,' she adds. But her instinct was a sure one. By joining Irving she was to supply a foil to his art; she was the perfect complement to his particular genius. His capacities lay at the darker end of the dramatic spectrum, in tragedy and melo-drama; even his humour on the stage was either sardonic or malevolent, seldom merely gay. Her strength lay in the lighter forms, in comedy and in pathos, in the expression of delicacy of feeling and in creating the release of laughter. Yet this delicacy was no genteel refinement: in acting one must possess great strength before one can be delicate in the right way. Too often weakness is mistaken for delicacy, wrote Ellen. Irving's instinct was also sure; he recognized the strength beneath the charm, and claimed it for himself. In a period of fustian, Ellen on the stage remained above all a woman of flesh and blood, not a mask. Off-stage too, she had the preoccupations of a woman, spilling out her forty guineas a week on her children and her household and adjusting herself to the problem of an unfortunate marriage. During the autumn preceding the start of her season with Irving, she toured with her husband as her leading man. They included in their repertoire a two-part comedietta by Alfred Thompson called *All is Vanity: or the Cynic's Defeat* (in which Ellen played Iris and Kelly Diogenes of the tub) and *Dora,* the play by Tenny-son and Reade. *Dora,* the part originally created by Kate, was only played by Ellen in the provinces. Ellen's brother George was brought in to act as business manager for the tour, which lasted from August to October, and was to be repeated in 1879 and 1880. Rehearsals at the Lyceum began in mid-December, and Kelly lost his leading lady. He was not invited by Irving to join the Lyceum company.

As soon as Ellen stepped inside Irving's theatre, she entered a temple dedicated to the drama. Irving would allow nothing to stand between himself and the realization of his art. He took from the great traditions of the stage (the traditions of Garrick, Mrs Siddons, Kean and Macready) such elements as he needed – for he respected these traditions deeply – and then heightened them for his own purpose. In his productions, every detail was designed to contribute to the whole: setting, lighting,[8] costume, music, movement, grouping, mime, gesture, rhetoric. This was total theatre. To achieve this end, Irving drove his team of artists and technicians with a grave and merciless courtesy through the end-less hours of preparation. The system, as described by Ellen her-self, began with Irving's private study of the play extended over months: he would then soak himself in the current dramatic subject to the exclusion of any other interest:

When there was a question of his playing Napoleon, his room in Grafton Street was filled with Napoleonic literature. Busts of Napoleon, pictures of Napoleon, relics of Napoleon were everywhere. Then when another play was being prepared, the busts, however fine, would probably go down to the cellar. It was not *Napoleon* who interested Henry Irving, but *Napoleon for his purpose* – two very different things.[9]

Rehearsals for the actors began with a reading, perhaps in the Green Room at the theatre, perhaps at Grafton Street. Irving, sure now of his intentions in the handling of each part, would realize his interpretation by reading the entire play aloud, enacting each part, including his own, as he intended it should be done, and pausing every so often to comment on grouping and movement. Then he gave out the scripts to the players; they were either handwritten or printed, never typed. The handwritten scripts never gave more than each player's individual lines, together with his cues.

After this reading a rehearsal was held on the stage; there was a second reading by the actors, seated, to check the accuracy of the copying up of their scripts. These two rehearsals normally succeeded each other on a Thursday and a Friday, and the weekend that followed was free, unless there was a production already active in the theatre. Then 'stand-up' rehearsals began the ensuing Monday and the long task of coaching commenced, one act of the play each day initially, with Irving in absolute control. He was assisted by H. J. Loveday, his stage manager, who helped in the marshalling and positioning of the players, and J. H. Allen, his staff prompter. He was insistent on the minutest detail, working without any break for lunch, the actors snatching what food they could when they were off the stage. Only when Irving arrived for rehearsal wearing a silk hat did they know he had a social engagement which might allow them some respite.

Irving's despotic methods – to use Ellen's description – achieved their ends. Gradually the detail was built up through succeeding days of rehearsal; sometimes only half an act would be composed in a full day's work. All the action, including such stage spectacles as processions, were rehearsed with equal care; Irving knew exactly what timing he wanted. And the rehearsals did not take place on

a bare stage; sets, or substitute sets, were used to 'dress the rehearsals' and give the players an 'environment' in which to
develop their work. For some private reason of his own, Ellen
soon noticed, he drilled his actresses far less than his actors;
once they knew their positions and movements, Irving was
content to leave the nature of their performance largely in their
control.

Many distinguished actors were to learn their craft initially
from Irving, but they were induced by the Guv'nor (as Irving was
always called in the theatre) to render pale copies of the master's
particular theatrical style and not to develop a style of their own.
Irving did not surround himself with pleasant nonentities, as
many theatrical managers were content to do. In his company,
at one time or another, were many young men who were to
make a name in the theatre: Sir Johnston Forbes-Robertson, Sir
Frank Benson, Sir John Martin-Harvey, as well as the dramatist
Sir Arthur Wing Pinero, were all men of the Lyceum. So was
Ellen's son, Edward Gordon Craig, who was to appear in Irving's
company for many years. In addition, Irving sought out old-
timers in the theatre, supporting players of tried merit and personality, who brought with them established traditions from the
past to leaven the style of his productions.

Irving made his actors, therefore, part of the pattern of his
genius; they were peripheral to his performance, or, as Gordon
Craig put it, the legs to his table. They were not required to shine;
they were required to be good, to be reliable, to be trustworthy, to
be, in fact, what they were called – supporting players. Everyone,
that is, except Ellen Terry. Occasionally, Irving would associate
himself on the stage with actors whose status approached his own:
with Booth or Bancroft. But this was exceptional. For the most
part his supporting actors were either veterans or young men at
first profoundly excited to be working with Irving or exasperated
when, season after season, their allocation of minor roles allowed
them no chance to promote their talents. In order to do this, they
had one by one to break away and make their own careers before
the public. Meanwhile, they were well paid compared with other

actors at this time; their salaries ranged from £5 to £50 a week when the Lyceum was at the height of its success in the 1880s and 1890s.

Irving extended his art to include spectacular scenic effects and carefully integrated musical scores, specially written for him by such distinguished composers as Sullivan, German and Stanford. The head of the scene-painting rooms was Hawes Craven, who worked with Irving from his original production of *The Bells* in 1872; later he was assisted by William Telbin, a devotee of Claude and Turner. The design of sets was sometimes entrusted to famous painters of the day, such as Burne-Jones for *King Arthur* (1895) and Alma-Tadema for *Henry VIII* (1892) and *Coriolanus* (1901). The sets created by Hawes Craven and Telbin were masterpieces of scenic craftsmanship, and offered to the Victorian theatre-goer something of the same pleasure as the spectacular period film of today. Irving was prepared to spend thousands of pounds on the décor and costumes for a single production, even though the Lyceum was a comparatively small theatre, bringing in no more than some £230 capacity at each performance up to 1881, when the auditorium was enlarged to increase the theatre's business capacity to some £350. According to Bram Stoker, his manager, Irving spent some £200,000 on his productions during the period of his management, but his total box-office takings exceeded £2 million.

Gordon Craig has succeeded better than anyone else in creating on paper a living image of Irving at work upon the stage. In the days before sound film the memory of players, however great, has remained entirely dependent on accurate depiction of their styles by critics and observers who saw them at the peak of their art. These descriptions usually record the general *effect* of a performance on the observer rather than its actual nature and conduct, but Gordon Craig has left us a detailed record of what Irving actually did on the stage in such extraordinary feats of performance as he achieved as Mathias in *The Bells*. This is Irving as Craig described him a few moments after Mathias's first entrance, which was usually the cue to the audience for prolonged applause during which Irving stood, as if becalmed, waiting to leap into the winds of action. He sat down and began the business of changing his outdoor boots for shoes:

Now you might think that the act of taking off some boots could be done in one way only – but the way Irving did it had never been thought of till he did it, and has never been done since.

It was, in every gesture, every half move, in the play of his shoulders, legs, head, and arms, mesmeric in the highest degree – slowly we were drawn to watch every inch of his work as we are drawn to read and linger on every syllable of a strangely fine writer.

It was the perfection of craftsmanship.

While he is taking off the boots and pulling on the shoes the men at the table, who are smoking and drinking lazily, are telling in drawling tones that just before he came in they were saying that they did not remember a night like this since what was called the Polish Jew's winter.

By the time the speaker had got this slowly out – and it was dragged purposely – Irving was buckling his second shoe, seated, and leaning over it with his two long hands stretched down over the buckles. We suddenly saw these fingers stop their work; the crown of the head suddenly seemed to glitter and become frozen – and then, at the pace of the slowest and most terrified snail, the two hands, still motionless and dead, were seen to be coming up the side of the leg ... the whole torso of the man, also seeming frozen, was gradually, and by an almost imperceptible movement, seen to be drawing up and back, as it would straighten a little, and to lean a little against the back of the chair on which he was seated.

Once in that position – motionless – eyes fixed ahead of him and fixed on us all – there he sat for the space of ten to twelve seconds, which, I can assure you, seemed to us all like a lifetime, and then said – and said in a voice deep and overwhelmingly beautiful: 'Oh, you were talking of that – were you?' And as the last syllable was uttered, there came afar off the regular throbbing of sledge-bells.

There he sat looking at us, and there sat the others, smoking and musing and comfortably motionless, except for the smoke from their pipes – and on and on went the sound of these bells, on and on and on – nothing else. Again, I assure you, that time seemed out of joint, and moved as it moves to us who suffer, when we wish it would move on and does not stir.

And the next step of his dance began.

He moves his head slowly from us – the eyes still somehow with us – and moves it to the right – taking as long as a long journey to discover a truth takes. He looks to the faces on the right – nothing. Slowly the head revolves back again, down, and along the tunnels of thought and sorrow, and at the end the face and eyes are bent upon those to the left of him . . . utter stillness . . . nothing there either – every one is concerned with his or her little doings – smoking or knitting or unravelling wool or scraping a plate slowly and silently. A long pause, endless, breaking our hearts, comes down over everything, and on and on go these bells. Puzzled, motionless . . . he glides up to a standing position: never has any one seen another rising figure which slid slowly up like that. With one arm slightly raised, with sensitive hand speaking of far-off apprehended sounds, he asks, in the voice of some woman who is frightened yet does not wish to frighten those with her: 'Don't you . . . don't you hear the sound of sledge-bells on the road?' 'Sledge-bells?' grumbles the smoking man; 'Sledge-bells?' pipes his companion; 'Sledge-bells?' says the wife – all of them seemingly too sleepy and comfortable to apprehend anything . . . see anything . . . or understand . . . and, as they grumble a negative, suddenly he staggers, and shivers from his toes to his neck; his jaws begin to chatter; the hair on his forehead, falling over a little, writhes as though it were a nest of little snakes. Every one is on his feet at once to help: 'Caught a chill' . . . 'let's get him to bed' . . . and *one* of the moments of the immense and touching dance closes – only one – and the next one begins, and the next after – figure after figure of exquisite pattern and purpose is unfolded, and then closed, and ever a new one unfolded in its wake.[10]

Irving's voice and gestures were designed to give theatrical illumination to the part, and his walk itself became another deliberate act of artistry. Then there was his facial expression. As Craig put it Irving's face became on the stage 'the really agile portion of his body', a 'mask' which he created to define the essentials of the role. According to Gordon Craig, he deliberately cultivated the powers of hypnosis in order to exercise control over his audience and his fellow-actors. Be that as it may, his face epitomized on the stage the mime to which his whole bodily expression was devoted.

Irving was ready to apply this intense art daily to a variety of characters in his repertoire, to Mathias or to Hamlet, to Charles I or to Richelieu, to Becket or to Corporal Brewster. Yet he could also be Jingle or Mephistopheles, Benedick or Shylock. He was the master of a single style, yet of a style expressed through the widest range of parts. But he shone best as a villain. His was a style which many able critics could not accept – such men as Henry James, William Archer and Bernard Shaw. But Ellen, like the great Victorian public who filled the Lyceum for some thirty years in order to see Irving perform, responded to him completely though she was never to adopt anything approaching his style herself, nor did he ever try to impose it on her.

Ellen discovered Irving's diffidence about giving direction to women as soon as she first arrived at the theatre to rehearse for Ophelia. She looked in some awe at her new manager, who began work as usual by reading the whole play aloud, omitting nothing but the part of Ophelia. The reading became a performance in itself. For the rehearsals that followed, in spite of his familiarity with the part, he always wore a cloak and carried a rapier. As the opening night drew nearer Ellen became more anxious and miserable because Irving rehearsed everything in the play except the scenes with Ophelia. Apart from these he attended to every

I

detail, rehearsing the lighting, and after this the music with his music director and staff composer, Hamilton Clarke. Nervously she approached him; could they not, please, rehearse her scenes. 'We shall be all right,' replied Irving, quite simply.[11] Ellen, who had never played Ophelia before, could only feel frustrated and utterly unprepared for the great challenge of appearing for the first time as Irving's leading lady.

Like many actresses in search of an image for mental derangement, Ellen admits that she visited a madhouse 'to study wits astray'. Yet she found the pathetic creatures with whom she was allowed to mingle far too theatrical for her purpose; their behaviour seemed to her to have neither beauty nor 'nature' in it. Then she saw a girl, very young and thin, sitting quite still, gazing into a wall. She looked her in the face, and found her eyes quite vacant, as if the girl were waiting endlessly without hope or expectations. Then suddenly, 'she threw up her hands and sped across the room like a swallow . . . the movement was as poignant as it was beautiful'. Ellen left the place convinced that unless the actor has first imagined the part he has to play and so created its image in his mind, no amount of extraneous observation will bring about an artistic solution for his difficulties. Observation of this kind must follow after the art of creation.

When the opening night came, Ellen felt she had played badly, and she fled from the theatre as soon as her part was done; 'I have failed; I have failed,' she is said to have cried out before leaving the theatre.[12] She drove up and down the Embankment in a cab before she felt she had the strength to go home. She was only to be comforted when she read the good press she had received the following morning: '. . . picturesque, tender, and womanly throughout,' wrote Joseph Knight. 'The support she afforded Irving was of the utmost importance.' Dutton Cook, after using almost the same adjectives in her praise, thought she had made the finest Ophelia since the days of Macready, and commented upon her 'singular power of depicting intensity of feeling'. In this view she was 'exquisite'.

There is no doubt that Irving thought the same. He said to

Bram Stoker at supper after the third performance: 'How Shakespeare must have dreamed when he was able to write a part like Ophelia, knowing that it would have to be played by a boy! Conceive his delight and gratitude if he could but have seen Ellen Terry in it!' He had introduced her to Stoker a few days before the play had opened: 'not even the darkness of that December day could shut out the radiant beauty of the woman,' Stoker wrote. 'Her face was full of colour and animation, either of which would have made her beautiful. In addition was the fine form, the easy rhythmic swing, the large, graceful, goddess-like way in which she moved.' Stoker already knew Kelly, and was grateful for Ellen's quick and friendly response the moment she was introduced. Stoker, too, needed reassurance. He had just thrown up his post in the Civil Service in Dublin to become Irving's business manager. He noted the effect of her presence on Irving: 'From the moment . . . she began to rehearse at the Lyceum his admiration for her became unbounded.' Irving said that her pathos was 'nature helped by genius'. So the partnership had begun auspiciously. According to Marguerite Steen, Irving, worried by Ellen's disappearance from the theatre on the first night, had hurried round to her house. Ellen, she says, told her that this midnight meeting at Longridge Road was the beginning of an 'attachment' that lasted twenty years. To this we must return later.

The years 1879 and 1889 were each broken by Ellen's provincial tours in the summer with Kelly which she felt bound to undertake, perhaps as much for her neglected husband's sake as for any contractual obligation undertaken before her partnership with Irving.[13] At the Lyceum during these same two years she played eight new parts. On tour, working on her own account and starting in Birmingham on 18 August 1879, her repertoire, already including *New Men and Old Acres* and *All is Vanity*, was extended to include *Butterfly* (opening in Glasgow on 12 September, and adapted for Ellen by Alice Comyns-Carr from the French play *Frou-Frou*), *Dora* (played in Liverpool), and scenes from *Hamlet, The Merchant of Venice* and *The School for Scandal*, the last two revived during the autumn of 1880, when Ellen, appearing in Leeds, played Beatrice in *Much Ado about Nothing* for the first time.

During one of these provincial tours, Ellen introduced her young brother Fred Terry in the part of Bertie Fitzurse in *New Men and Old Acres*, and when his voice cracked (he was about sixteen) improvised an imitation of him in order to extract some extra comedy from the moment. Fred, embarrassed and unhappy, did not see the point. While Ellen was at the Lyceum, Kelly did what other work he could; he went on tour with his sister-in-law, Florence (Floss) Terry, now aged about twenty-five, in the inevitable *New Men and Old Acres,* and Fred appeared with him briefly in *A Pair of Wings*, which was a failure. Ellen's good-natured friend Alice Comyns-Carr, whose energetic and volatile husband had almost deserted the law and the stock exchange for an English 'Bohemia', as she called it, reports that Kelly 'was given to reinforcing himself with stimulants' even when on the stage. Nevertheless, she admired his work, even calling him 'a clever actor'.

At the Lyceum, Ellen's position became stronger with each season. Irving was able to test their partnership, and its growing importance with the public, in a variety of parts. During their first two seasons together they appeared in romance and melodrama, *The Lady of Lyons* and *Eugene Aram*, in Wills's so-called historical play, *Charles I,* and, more important, they tested themselves in Shakespeare, with *Hamlet* and *The Merchant of Venice*.[14] Ellen's passionate desire to be considered a 'useful' actress was clearly exploited when Irving cast her for the minor part of Ruth Meadows in *Eugene Aram*; her gift for pathos was only momentarily required in this play compared with the more demanding part of Henrietta Maria in *Charles I.* Only in *The Lady of Lyons,* which opened in April, and *The Merchant of Venice,* which followed in November, were Ellen's capacities as an actress given an opportunity to fill the stage on two very different levels. Irving, it must be remembered, was in management for the first time on his own, and it was imperative he should confirm his leadership of the London stage with a series of successes. He played safe during this testing year, for the most part reviving his major successes during his first season in 1879, and only gradually introducing new productions, such as *The Merchant of Venice*, as the strength of his position became assured.

In this situation he had to feel his way in his exploitation of his leading lady. Only in the case of *The Lady of Lyons* could it be said that he put on a play as much for her sake as for his own. He knew that Ellen had given an effective performance in this now much dated play, and it was always effective 'theatre' he was looking for, never literary merit. On the first occasion she had played the part of Pauline (on 7 August 1875 at the Princess's Theatre), Ellen had won, as we have seen, the highest praise from Joseph Knight in one special article which proclaimed 'the advent of genius' while at the same time claiming that she deliberately sunk the pride of Pauline in her desire to achieve a study in pathos and tenderness. Ellen claims she never felt really happy in the part. Later, however, she had appeared in the play again outside the West End, and now that she was with Irving she found he was attracted by the idea of playing the part of Claude Melnotte opposite her, and so wanted to include *The Lady of Lyons* among the revivals during his first season. 'Henry was always attracted by fustian,' she admits. 'He simply revelled in the big speeches.' So on 17 April the play went on, presented magnificently. The production costs amounted to £1,700. When, in the fourth act, Melnotte joins the army departing for the wars ('Place me wherever a foe is most dreaded,' cries Melnotte, 'wherever France most needs a life!'), the Brigade of Guards supplied 150 'supers' at double the standing rate for stage mercenaries, which was at this period only sixpence a night for each man. A sergeant of the Guards was added to the Lyceum staff to keep the men in order. They marched four abreast across the back of the stage, seen through the windows and the open door of the set. Once out of sight of the audience, they doubled back behind the scenes, running to make up the column once more in what appeared to be an endless march past. Irving as Claude ran out to join them amid cheers from the men and massive applause from the audience,

the curtain rising and falling, the men marching and re-marching.
'A superb effect,' says Ellen.

Irving changed the established nature of Claude Melnotte from
gay to grave, and the dramatic characterization, such as it was,
scarcely made much sense by the time he and Ellen had shifted
the hero and heroine into the theatrical slots that proved most
convenient to themselves. No one took the old chestnut very
seriously with so much spectacle to excite their eyes. Clement
Scott accused Ellen of trying to be a French Olivia, tender and
tearful, not resentful and proud; she substituted a girl of charm
who 'in pale amber, moved gracefully about her settees and
spinettes, or lolled upon mossy banks in the garden of an old
château, or trembled with emotion in white satin and primrose
ribbons'. The revival was a great box-office success. But one
dissident voice at least was raised in criticism of Ellen's command
of what seemed to him to be her over-appreciative public. This
belonged to Henry James, who was living now in London; he
found all the British efforts at acting distinctly inferior to those of
the French, and said so in an article written for the *Nation* of
New York in July 1879:

> She is greatly the fashion at present, and she belongs properly
> to a period which takes a strong interest in aesthetic furniture,
> archaeological attire, and blue china. Miss Ellen Terry is
> 'aesthetic'; not only her garments but her features themselves
> bear a stamp of the new enthusiasm. She has charm, a great
> deal of a certain amateurish, angular grace, a total want of
> what the French call *chic*, and a countenance very happily
> adapted to the expression of pathetic emotion. To this last
> effect her voice also contributes; it has a sort of monotonous
> husky thickness which is extremely touching, though it gravely
> interferes with the modulation of many of her speeches. Miss
> Terry, however, to my sense, is far from having the large
> manner, the style and finish, of a *comédienne*. She is the most
> pleasing and picturesque figure upon the English stage.[15]

The Fate of Eugene Aram was a play dedicated to Irving's

particular talent. 'I had very little to do,' wrote Ellen, 'but what there was, was worth doing.' Irving introduced an overhanging tree, which he called the Fate tree, into the graveyard set, and when the curtain rose on the last act, he was discovered stretched out on a gravestone, though only when a moonbeam came through was he revealed, wrapped in a black cloak. In this part, Irving performed a small feat of acting which normally drew applause from the audience. Harried by a blackmailer who knows his past crime, Eugene's passion is brought up to a pitch of momentary desperation. Bram Stoker describes the effect that followed:

> As Irving played it the hunted man at bay was transformed from his gentleness to a ravening tiger; he looked the spirit of murder incarnate as he answered threat by threat. Just at that moment the door opened and in walked Ruth Meadows, bright and cheery as a ray of spring sunshine. In a second – less than a second, for the change was like lightning – the sentence begun in one way went on in another without a quaver or pause. The mind and powers of the remorse-haunted man who had for weary years trained himself for just such an emergency worked true. Unfailingly a sudden and marked burst of applause rewarded on each occasion this remarkable artistic *tour de force*.[16]

At this stage in his career, says Ellen, Irving was obsessed by the desire to present either melancholy or macabre pieces. In *Charles I* he played a part in which he had already distinguished himself, his make-up closely modelled on the portrait by Van Dyke. 'His make-up in this, as in other parts,' wrote Ellen, 'was the process of *assisting subtly and surely the expression from within*.' He never adopted a make-up which would hamper the movements of his face. He was, she adds, also assisted by nature, since he possessed 'the most beautiful Stuart hands'. Each costume he wore represented exactly the clothes shown in the original painting of the King. His wig in the last act, in the emotional farewell scene that he played with Ellen, was not only dressed for age, but carefully thinned as well. As for Ellen, she was, says her contemporary biographer Hiatt, at once 'exquisitely feminine' and 'austerely regal'; what always caused controversy about the play was the representation of Cromwell as a mean, debased and sinister villain of melodrama. However, Irving's Charles became one of the classic performances in his repertoire, and, as Pemberton put it, 'the public forgave the slanders for the sake of the prettiness and the pathos of the domestic scenes'. The last scene may seem utterly deficient in poetry now, but for Ellen it was to become a favourite part which she was to play with Irving until the end of their partnership. In her bound copy of the play, Ellen wrote a private note of her reaction to performing with Irving in *Charles I*:

> His stateliness – gentleness – *his atmosphere of dignity* could never be told of. Every inch a King. So pure – so un-asserting – so lofty, simple – Holy = I mean H. I. – as the King = I have lost myself looking at him and half doubted its being Henry. It surely was the best Van Dyke portrait – moving and speaking – alive. His hands – his face – his bearing – Nothing – nobody cd describe and do any justice to the subject – but thank God I've seen the noble bit of work.[17]

Ellen later wrote about this scene to the author W. G. Wills:

> I'm just returned from our last rehearsal of *Charles I.* and, coming home in my carriage, have been reading the last act, and I can't help writing to thank you and bless you for having written those *five last pages*. Never, *never* has anything more beautiful been written in English – I know no other language. They are perfection – and I – often as I've acted with Henry Irving in the play, am *all melted* at reading it again. An immortality for you for this alone.[18]

Let us grant this represents the emotional response of an actress aware that she has been given a part by an author which stirs her as much as she can stir her audience whilst playing it. But a young Irishman just down from Oxford came to see her performance, and was so moved by it that he wrote the first of three sonnets he was to address to her. This poet was Oscar Wilde, soon to

become a friend, and the scene to which he refers was the one
preceding the final act of parting:

> In the lone tent, waiting for victory,
> She stands with eyes marred by the mists of pain,
> Like some wan lily overdrenched with rain;
> The clamorous clang of arms, the ensanguined sky,
> War's ruin, and the wreck of chivalry
> To her proud soul no common fear can bring;
> Bravely she tarrieth for her Lord, the King,
> Her soul aflame with passionate ecstasy.
> O, hair of gold! O, crimson lips! O, face
> Made for the luring and the love of man!
> With thee I do forget the toil and stress,
> The loveless road that knows no resting place,
> Time's straitened pulse, the soul's dread weariness,
> My freedom, and my life republican!

Ellen liked the sonnet. 'Wan lily', she says, exactly expressed what
she was aiming to achieve not only in this part, but in Ophelia.
The sonnet also shows what her mature beauty inspired in the mind
of the young and ambitious poet seven years younger than herself.

When the season closed in July, Ellen went off on her summer
tour with her husband, while Irving left for a six-week Mediter-
ranean cruise with his friend and patroness, the Baroness Burdett
Coutts and her future husband, Ashmead Bartlett. During the
cruise Irving visited Venice, and brought back a collection of
prints and pictures for Hawes Craven to use, should he decide to
produce *Othello*. In the first new production of the autumn season,
The Iron Chest (another sombre play originally written for Edmund
Kean), Floss was called in to deputize for her sister. But the play
was a failure, and Ellen returned from her tour in October just in
time to take over in a revival of *Hamlet*. Irving had determined
by now to produce not *Othello*, but *The Merchant of Venice*. He
became increasingly fascinated by the possibilities that lay in
playing Shylock not as the traditional grotesque villain, but
sympathetically, as a man of racial pride and fine temperament, an

isolated alien living in the rich Venetian setting. The Levantine
Jews he had seen during his summer cruise became his models.
But the failure of *The Iron Chest* meant that time was short. The
new production was scheduled for 1 November, and it had to be
rehearsed and mounted in under four weeks. For Ellen this presented no great problem; it was an opportunity to revive the
performance in which she had enriched her reputation in 1875.

In addition to the presentation of the current productions,
work never ceased now at the Lyceum, either by day or night.
Hawes Craven, Telbin and their assistants designed and painted
seven distinct scenes. Hawes Craven when hard-pressed wore a
red handkerchief round his head like a turban instead of his
customary brown bowler. The combined forces of the company,
extras, artists and technicians alike, mounted the play between 9
October and 1 November. The production costs exceeded £2,000.
The play was an immediate success, and ran unbroken for 250
nights, some seven months, and on the 100th performance Irving
presented each member of the audience with a copy of his acting
edition of the play, printed by the Chiswick Press and bound in
white vellum.

The production commanded universal interest, not so much for
its settings – though these recalled the Venetian masters – but for
its interpretation, especially of Shylock and Portia.[19] Joseph
Knight said Ellen looked as if she had been painted by Veronese
and praised the subtlety and purity of her playing; William
Winter said that an 'essential womanhood' was revealed for the
first time in the modern theatre; his phrases included 'incessant
sparkle' and 'impetuous ardour'; gone was the didactic Portia of
the past, and in her place appeared 'an enchanting woman'. Even
the Lord Chief Justice was pleased to express his astonishment at
her forensic style in the Trial Scene, which Lewis Carroll described
when he saw the play in January 1880 as 'about the best thing I
ever saw'.

Even the younger generation, children still, were enraptured.
Graham Robertson, later to be one of Ellen's closest friends, saw
her in 1879 when he was only thirteen, and the memory of her

stayed in his mature mind though he was never to see her in the part again. He wrote of her later:

Pale eyes, rather small and narrow, a broad nose slightly tilted at the tip, a wide mouth, a firm, large chin, pale hair, not decidedly golden, yet not brown – by no means a dazzling inventory of charms, yet out of these was evolved Ellen Terry, the most beautiful woman of her time. . . . Her charm held everyone, but I think pre-eminently those who loved pictures. She was *par excellence* the Painter's Actress and appealed to the eye before the ear; her gesture and pose were eloquence itself. . . .

She had learnt to create Beauty, not the stage beauty of whitewash and lip salve, but the painter's beauty of line, harmony and rhythm.[20]

Another childhood memory, by a girl this time, lingered on in the mind of Kate Terry Gielgud, Ellen's niece, Kate's daughter, later to be the mother of Sir John Gielgud. She was eleven when she was taken to the Lyceum in 1879 to see her aunt in Shakespeare, and this is how she described it later:

The open gallery at Belmont where the sunlight seemed to focus on, and radiate from, a golden-haired Portia, welcoming her guests, gay, mocking, resourceful, her bright eyes relieved suddenly of anxiety and opened wide in love; the jesting manner of a great lady forgone for the staid air of the young doctor-of-law, only to bubble up again as, the session ended and the case won, she and Nerissa wheedled the incriminating rings from Bassanio and Gratiano; the moonlit bank of the final scene, the soft music, the veiled figures stealing out of the shadow, home again to joy and gaiety.[21]

In spite of the loud protests of the Shakespearean scholar, Dr F. J. Furnivall, founder of the New Shakespeare Society and a great admirer of the production, Irving cut the last act of the play during its final weeks from 20 May (when Ellen's 'benefit' performance took place) and substituted the one-act piece, *Iolanthe*.

This meant that Ellen was able to offer two contrasting performances in a single evening, the 'strong' part of Portia and the
'pathetic' part of Iolanthe, the blind daughter of a Danish King
whose sight is miraculously restored to her, while Irving once
more made love to her in the romantic part of Count Tristan.

Not everyone, however, was so enraptured. Henry James was
again writing at length about the British theatre for the American
intelligentsia, and in 1880 he wrote in some detail about *The
Merchant of Venice* for *Scribner's Monthly.* After attacking Irving
for his eccentricities of speech while acknowledging the ingenuity
of his 'by-play', James describes his 'pathetic' Shylock as utterly
ineffective, and then turns to consider his 'constant coadjutor',
Ellen Terry:

> Her manner of dealing with the delightful speeches of Portia,
> with all their play of irony, of wit and temper, savours, to put
> it harshly of the schoolgirlish. We have ventured to say that
> her comprehension of a character is sometimes weak, and we
> may illustrate it by a reference to her whole handling of this
> same rich opportunity. Miss Terry's mistress of Belmont giggles
> too much, plays too much with her fingers, is too free and
> familiar, too osculatory, in her relations with Bassanio. The
> mistress of Belmont was a great lady, as well as a tender and a
> clever woman; but this side of the part quite eludes the actress,
> whose deportment is not such as we should expect in the splendid
> spinster who has princes for wooers. When Bassanio has chosen
> the casket which contains the key of her heart, she approaches
> him, and begins to pat and stroke him. This seems to us an
> appallingly false note. 'Good heavens, she's touching him!' a
> person sitting next to us exclaimed – a person whose judgment
> in such matters is always unerring. But in truth there would be
> a great deal to say upon this whole question of demonstration
> of tenderness on the English stage, and an adequate treatment of
> it would carry us far. The amount of kissing and hugging that
> goes on in London in the interest of the drama is quite in-
> calculable, and to spectators who find their ideal of taste more

nearly fulfilled in the French theatre, it has the drollest, and often the most displeasing effect.[22]

Ellen was, indeed, in trouble over the demonstrativeness of her attitude to her lover on the stage. Long before James delivered his longer-term verdict to America, she had been assailed in her own country on precisely the same point. An article in Blackwood's magazine attacked her for her actions with Bassanio before the casket is chosen:

> Throughout all this fine speech she holds him caressingly by the hand, nay, almost in an embrace, with all the unrestrained fondness which is conceivable only after he had actually won her. This, too, when all eyes are fixed upon her, and when her demeanour would have made her secret known to all the world in the last way a lady would court under any circumstances, but especially when, had her lover chosen wrong, she must have parted from him once and for ever. There is altogether too much of what Rosalind calls 'a coming-on disposition' in Miss Terry's bearing towards her lover.[23]

'This affected me for years, and made me self-conscious and uncomfortable,' wrote Ellen subsequently. 'Any suggestion of *indelicacy* in my treatment of a part always blighted me.' Because of Irving's quiet playing of Shylock, Ellen had developed the robustness of her own performance, making Portia stronger and more demonstrative. In doing so she unquestionably offended Victorian prudery. John Ruskin, for example, then aged sixty, sent his particular comment to Irving in a letter written on 30 November 1879:

> Though Miss Terry's Portia has obtained so much applause, it greatly surprised me that you have not taught her a grander reading of the part. Portia is chiefly great in her majestic humility (the main sign of her splendid intellect) and – to take only one instance of what I do not doubt to be misinterpretation – the speech, 'You see me Lord Bassanio ...', she would, I am certain, produce its true effect on the audience only if spoken

with at least half a dozen yards between her and Bassanio – and with her eyes on the ground through most of her lines.[24]

Criticism of such a kind concerning her performance, and the controversy about Irving's romanticized interpretation of Shylock, only served to fire public curiosity and fill the theatre. On the hundredth performance on 4 February 1880, Irving invited some 350 guests to a reception and supper-party on the stage after the play was finished. This event cost him some £600. Peers, judges, admirals and Members of Parliament jostled with artists, writers, dramatists and critics. With the showmanship required of London's leading producer, the Belmont set was struck in a matter of minutes and the stage reset in the form of a pavilion of scarlet and white. A five-course supper was served by Gunter's after those invited had been introduced to this transformation scene only minutes, as it seemed, after the close of the play. Among the guests was the youthful Oscar Wilde in hot pursuit of literary fame and London society. He had written a new sonnet to the beautiful actress who stood ready to receive him alongside his host, Henry Irving:

> I marvel not Bassanio was so bold
> To peril all he had upon the lead,
> Or that proud Aragon bent low his head,
> Or that Morocco's fiery heart grew cold;
> For in that gorgeous dress of beaten gold,
> Which is more golden than the golden sun,
> No woman Veronese looked upon
> Was half so fair as thou whom I behold.
> Yet fairer when with wisdom as your shield
> The sober-suited lawyer's gown you donned,
> And would not let the laws of Venice yield
> Antonio's heart to that accursed Jew –
> O, Portia! take my heart; it is thy due:
> I think I will not quarrel with the Bond.

V

THE NEW LIFE

During the period of her engagement at the Court Theatre, probably during the season before she joined Irving at the Lyceum, Ellen had been able to afford to indulge her longing to live once more in the country. She had taken a cottage – 'a wee place' in Hampton Court Road. This 'wee place', called Rose Cottage, was soon bright with new paint and whitewash. It had four or five rooms and a kitchen; and was one of a short row of small houses looking out at the back on Bushey Park, where stags and deer roamed, treading delicately, and lifting their heads to listen, poised and still. Teddy, his legs straddling the window-sill, watched the stags engage each other with locked antlers; he and Edy would search afterwards for fragments of broken horn in the grass, or run off to help make ice-cream at the confectioner's near the main gates of the Palace.

Miss Terry's children – 'little Miss Edy', thin and dark, 'Master Teddy', fat and fair – soon became the spoilt pets of the district and of Hampton Court itself. Dressed, according to Ellen, in blue and white check pinafores, they ran around in the Palace gardens christening the trees after the parts their mother was playing – Mabel Vane, and later, Portia and Iolanthe. Life was easier, less formal in its arrangements, than at Longridge Road. 'Come along, Teddy, don't be a coward,' Edy would shout as she assailed the old soldier who stood guard at the Palace gates; soon they were helping him sell ginger-beer, sweets and postcards to the visitors. Inside, they made friends again and soon they had the freedom of the famous Maze, climbing up to the crow's nest which acted as an observation post from which the Keeper could direct the lost souls below, some laughing, some frightened, all

of them floundering in their efforts to reach the wooden benches
in the centre. It was fun for the children to shout down mis-
directions just to watch them flounder more. Inside the Palace
Teddy would calm down as he wandered round, staring at the
'impossible, grand, motionless' beds in which nobody ever slept.

Life with Ellen could never be quite stable. Sometime after
1880, when Teddy was eight and Edy ten, Rose Cottage was given
up, and the house in Longridge Road, ruled by Boo and the
beloved, shrill-voiced Miss Harries, became the only domestic
centre. Ellen – in her early thirties – became more and more the
great actress, her way of life a pattern established partly by the
demanding nature of her work, and partly by the energetic
response she gave to everything that came to her immediate
attention: her work, her domestic decisions, her friends, her
children, her husband. Boo, as Ellen herself has said, was used to
lunatics, but was old now and tended to shut herself away from
the turmoil of the house. Everything came to depend on Miss
Harries, as Gordon Craig recalled, the memories of Longridge
Road coming back to him nearly seventy years later:

> Miss Harries, who, now I come to think of it, looked certainly
> very crazy – eccentric, to say the very least of it – Miss Harries
> had everything to see to. She would be upstairs and down-
> stairs – passing along my mother's orders to the kitchen, to
> Boo, to the children, to the maids, ordering everything from
> the tradesmen – going out rapidly and back again in the house
> within twenty minutes, and dozens of things accomplished in
> that time.
>
> My mother remained in her bedroom until lunchtime, some-
> times later, unless she had a rehearsal at the Theatre – for she
> would return late at night to the house, tired after her performance
> of an exhausting part, and might not get to bed until one-
> thirty or even two. She pottered at night. Some actresses,
> singers, dancers, return home, and prefer to go out to suppers
> and receptions and keep things going until three in the morning
> – not so E. T. Back she came, tired out, but unable to turn in

immediately. Supper was spread and waiting for her – her letters, and someone of the house waiting up for her – she would potter, all things had some interest for her – she never idled, but at night she looked at this or that and gradually drifted upstairs to bed – but not hurriedly: slowly she moved from one room to another and from one interest to another, talking or alone and humming, and so off to sleep.[1]

The neighbours in Longridge Road could not be unaware of the lady in their midst. D. S. MacColl, the art critic, was a student at the time in the house directly opposite. He remembered the excitement when Ellen moved in, and he caught sight of her 'dazzling shape' at the window when she was moving about handling a broom. He and his visitors called her the Greek Lady, not knowing at first quite who she was. They soon found out.

Each morning when the Greek Lady went off to rehearsal, there was a scene as pretty as anything she played upon the stage. She appeared upon the steps like April morning, lifting wide eloquent lips, hooded eyes and breathless face to the light. She raised and kissed two little tots who were to be known as Edith and Gordon Craig. She greeted the next-door neighbours, family of a Rabbinical scholar, who had promptly become slaves of her apparition, and stood ready on the pavement. Her cushions were brought out, placed and patted in the open carriage; herself installed; the air became tender and gay with wavings and blown kisses; the wheels revolved and greyness descended once more on Longridge Road.[2]

Other neighbours in Longridge Road at the time beside the 'Rabbinical scholar' (Dr Kalisch from Germany) included Marie Corelli and her half-brother, Eric Mackey, 'bright as enamel in face and dress', and the bearded Scottish novelist, George MacDonald, a former minister of the Kirk in his ulster and deerstalker.

Ellen's individualism was now fully matured. After years of

K

expansive living in the theatre, subject to its disciplines, its excitements, its climax of work at night when others are at leisure, its
uninhibited social life that separated it from formalized society,
Ellen's waking hours were all aspects of her personal self-expression.
She lived on the spur of her emotions, loving almost everything,
but experienced also in desperation and in sorrow. She had lived
in free association with a lover, had borne children without a
legal name, had been rejected by her beloved parents, had known
the anxiety of debt, and had endured the agonizing loss of the
only man she had ever really loved. 'She loved once, and that
without criticism – only once,'[3] says Gordon Craig. Now, it
seemed to her she had a fortune in the bank and all London at her
feet.[4] The past, though not forgotten, was a storm outridden and
dispelled. She believed in happiness not sorrow. 'It was to E.T.
rather a sin to grieve,' wrote Gordon Craig. Her instinct was
usually sound; she was, her son once said, like a ship that always
righted itself and never foundered. She could afford now the
luxury of indulgence in the benefits that came to her as a result of
her celebrated charm. Though far from sentimental, she lived on
top of her emotions, for ever laughing, sometimes crying – 'but
only because the heart was too full were the eyes called in to help
things out', as Gordon Craig puts it.

In later life, her son attempted to reach an understanding of her
complex and volatile Irish nature. She was 'all imagination, all
feeling, and all in a dream', he says. 'She was always a good deal
at the mercy of her imagination.' Like many accomplished women,
she had a fixed image of herself which was often far from true.
She believed herself to be 'wretchedly weak' when she was really
very strong, and sometimes quite ruthless; but her gravest fault,
he thought, was a ceaseless desire to be liked. For him, she combined two women: Ellen Terry, the famous actress and public
figure, and Nellie, the little girl, a tender secret spirit visible only
to himself, her beloved son. It is true that she saw herself in
various guises, pouring out letters with varying signatures that
echoed the mood in which they were conceived – some signed
Ellen Terry or E.T., others signed simply Nellie or the name of

the part uppermost in her mind – Ophelia, Ellaline, Beatrice, or even to her special friend, Stephen Coleridge, anything from E.T. to Nell, Livie and Cecily. She came to play different parts both on stage and off, as some actresses do who are very much themselves whether they are acting or the centre of attention outside the theatre. The image works, so they play it, enjoying life immensely as people mill admiringly around them. Ellen loved her home, making it another stage, her own private stage. This is not to imply Ellen was merely artificial. It means rather that she lived to the top of her bent, desiring the maximum from every moment, whether it was a scene on the stage or a domestic situation in her home. And it could mean that she lived so energetically she did not always give the others in her circle the chance to do the same.

Yet there was an ambivalence in her nature. At one breath she did not care a toss for social convention, and at the next her woman's desire for security, for harbouring her life, craved for it, for convention offers permanency, security, social acceptance. 'You have to remember that if you are a public person you cannot afford to offend the public,' she once said. Yet she hated convention, because it destroyed freedom of the spirit. As Gordon Craig saw it:

> E.T. was certainly rebellious – she scorned respectability, despised all sorts of sensible things, rode life like one of the wildest of Amazons – always taking leaps in the dark – surmounting difficulties rapidly and easily – but for ever preaching what she did not practise ... a conundrum, a success and a glory of the English stage.
>
> She hated the conventional, and what a blessing that she did so. It wasn't that she couldn't be conventional – it was that she hated being so, because it seemed that being so would be to her all a sham.[5]

It was as a concession to respectability rather than to love that Ellen entered into her second marriage to Charles Kelly. Edy later accepted that this must have been so.[6] As we have seen, it gave

the children a legal 'name' (which in any case was later abandoned),
and restored her to her parents in Stanhope Street. Yet according
to Gordon Craig at least, she was, like many great actresses (he
lists Bernhardt, Duse, Rachel among others), 'not a marriageable
person'. And he adds, 'How could anyone in his kind senses ask
such a dear madwoman in marriage?' Her marriage, he declares,
now Godwin was gone and the children were born, was to the
stage. Yet every so often Ellen Terry tried, for everyone's sake,
to live by the rules. So, for two years or so, she remained with
Charles Kelly.

Gordon Craig wrote that Kelly had disappeared by the time he
was six years old. He remembered him as 'something large and
heavy-footed', growling and clumping along the passages of the
house, whereas Ellen seemed 'to sing or whisper her way'. He
had a memory of Kelly flourishing a hunting-crop after the style
of a lord of the Manor when he and Edy made too much noise;
nevertheless in some ways he regretted the departure of the only
man in the house. Kelly at least braced him with his male attention;
the women relaxed him with mere petting, or exasperated him
with their ridiculous demands: 'I fell once more into the hands of
a house of women – who, lovely as women are, are utterly un-
suited to be of the very service they would most like to render.'
He felt deprived once more of a father, and Edy had not helped
when one day in 1878 she had asked him if he would like to see
what the father whom he could not remember was like. Yes, he
had said, filled with curiosity. And she had whipped out a terrifying
drawing of a fiend with long teeth and claws and thrust it under
his frightened eyes. 'There – that's him!' she had said.

Gordon Craig felt that Ellen was certainly torn between being
Nellie, loving, carefree, devoted to the children, and E.T., the
actress, the woman living under the public gaze. She even told
him so in later years, contrasting herself with Elena, the mother
of his two children, little Teddy and little Nellie Craig. To some
extent it preyed on her mind that she was never entirely just a
mother, never entirely that other kind of woman. Sometimes
Gordon Craig would run in to find Nellie, his mother, and find

only E.T., his mother-in-art, which, as he puts it, is only one remove from a mother-in-law. In the end, with no man in the house to stop her, she utterly spoiled him with the excesses of kindness, an indulgence both of them had to pay for in later years. For example, she herself wrote:

> I have always been 'cracked' on pretty mouths! I remember I used to say 'Naughty Teddy!' to my own little boy just for the pleasure of seeing him put out his under-lip, when his mouth looked lovely![7]

By eighteen, Gordon Craig says, 'I was as helpless as a penny toy in a shop window. The blessed lady, my mother, no more knew how to bring up a boy than she knew how to swim.' As for Edy, everything this wilful young lady did was marvellous in her mother's prejudiced eyes. She spoiled her children not only because they were the abiding symbol of her love for Godwin, but also because she was terrified that the preoccupations of her profession might make her seem to be neglecting them. Teddy, a sensitive as well as an over-indulged child, was subject to night fears and other horrors his mother could not, or thought she should not, understand; he was forced to take long walks although he was by nature fat and lazy; above all, he was far too often banished from her to Rose Cottage, while this was still Ellen's property, to Brancaster, or to Brighton. So E.T. decreed, he thought, never Nellie.

It can only be presumed now what effect life with Ellen had on her second husband. 'A good fellow in some ways,' concedes Edy coldly, 'he had a genuine affection for his wife's children.' Once, while Ellen and Kelly were playing in *Butterfly*, he, as her husband in the play, opened a locket in which she was supposed to see the portrait of her child. When she looked she saw it was a new silver locket, in which he had put the picture of Edy and Teddy, and her stage tears suddenly became real. He knew by now why she had married him. 'I did it for her [Edy] and for Ted,' she confessed to Shaw years later, 'A mistake I know now.'[8] Edy's allegations that he was subject to fits of jealousy and ill-temper have already been mentioned, but she refrained from adding that he also drank. She does admit that his subordinate position in relation to his wife 'mortified' him. He lost his position as her leading man – the role in which he fancied himself – except for the provincial tours of 1879 and 1880. Edy, however, makes a further comment: 'It is known that he resented the friendship with Henry Irving which was the sequel to the engagement.' More serious still, it also appears that she was never willing to consummate the marriage. At all events they parted and there was a judicial separation in 1881. 'I should have died had I lived one more month with him,' wrote Ellen to Shaw. 'I gave him three-quarters of all the money I made weekly, and prayed him to go.'

With the loss of Kelly, who was soon to die in 1885, E.T., now an eminent Victorian, had to decide what to do about Nellie, an impulsive and affectionate woman who wanted to be liked, admired, and loved. There was no shortage of men to give her lasting devotion and happy to come round to her house to say so. Soon D. S. MacColl, watching from the windows of 36 Longridge Road, noticed a new caller. The 'manly bulldog sort of man', Charles Kelly – so utterly unsuitable, he thought – disappeared, and another visitor took his place, 'spare, and grim-jaunty in close-fitting short jacket, and tilted wide-a-wake'. This was Henry Irving.

Gordon Craig puts the year of these appearances at 1880, and says that Irving, who was later to have so great an influence upon him, 'proved as kind as a father'. There is a glimpse of Ellen and Irving at this time (and some indication of Ellen's waywardness) in this passage by Gordon Craig:

E.T. was persuadable – especially on Mondays – less so on Tuesdays. On Wednesday, people around her found it difficult to make her understand what they were trying to say – but by the time Thursday arrived she could be counted on to do the very thing they didn't expect. Friday she devoted to telling them that it didn't hurt, and that they must be brave and not cry – Saturday was always a half-holiday, spent in promising her advisers that she would be good next week – and on Sunday she generally drove away to Hampton Court with Irving, waving her lily white hand.[9]

Since 1880 appears to be the year Rose Cottage was given up, Ellen may have anticipated her break with Kelly, which was formalized the following year.

Ellen enjoyed the company of men, but her relations with them must be seen in the light of the period in which she was living and the public position she now occupied. She was, all her life, a prolific letter-writer.[10] There was still no telephone to pick up, and it was never to be an instrument which she used happily. But she had only to think of a person she liked to snatch paper and pen (or pencil) and pour out her immediate thoughts, loading the recipient, whether man or woman, with every term of endearment. Men and women of the theatre seldom fall short in their use of endearing expressions – at least since the nineteenth century – and Ellen was no exception. In 1879, for example, she wrote to Stephen Coleridge who was travelling in the Middle East, from her father-in-law's rectory in Winlaton, County Durham: 'Pretty boy, I'm very happy, even without you. Still you see you are in my thoughts, or how should I be talking to you in pencil at this moment . . . little dear, take care of yourself. . . . Think how dear you are to *very many,* and if the knowledge will only make you *more prudent,* know that you are dear in a guise to "Livie" too.' Coleridge was twenty-four at this time, and Ellen thirty-two. Later that year she wrote to him: 'It's not easy to put from one's thoughts such a bright, affectionate boy.' When he came back to England in the autumn, she wrote, 'Praise be blest you're safe. Oh! I *am* glad you're safe.' He always sent her gifts and flowers, which she came to expect; once at least she offered him a private box at the Lyceum, and wrote complaining that he rejected the offer and sent no flowers. It is evident that he was familiar with Rose Cottage. When he sent her later some amber beads, she wrote. 'Oh! my pretty beads!! . . . Did you expect to hear from me before. . . . I've nothing to tell you, and

I thought only *lovers* wrote when they'd nothing to tell and we are not lovers – though I am very loving. I could find it in my heart to love every *pretty* thing I meet.'

Ellen was utterly without shyness. She was free from any economic dependence on men, and had been so for most of her working life; even as a child and adolescent she had helped support the family. Her affection for men, therefore, was the affection of an equal, even (though she would not think this consciously) of a superior, or at least of a senior spirit. Nearly all the men she liked were just sufficiently younger than she was for her to enjoy showing a lightly protective attitude to them and their welfare, and when they were on the stage her professional position alone put her far ahead of them. In return they gave her the kind of devotion that she felt she most needed, a devotion that made her feel happy, admired, wanted, loved. It would have been quite out of keeping for them to expect to sleep with her. On neither side would such an outcome have been contemplated.

Graham Robertson, another man younger than herself to whom she was devoted throughout the whole of her life, described her demonstrative affection, which could burst out at any moment, even to some child in the street whom she had never seen before. The demonstration over, she would soon forget it in the all-absorbing duties of her home and her theatre. As Graham Robertson saw it:

One thing strikes me in reading her letters and looking back – that *people* had less influence in her life than might be imagined. Things, thoughts, dreams, memories seemed to affect her more. She would write often and lovingly of her friends with that playful affection that was especially her own, but the note of deep feeling is absent with which she would write or speak of things that really moved her. She once wrote to me – *One's work is the best of us all – don't you think so? With most folks I've met, I've loved their work better than them.*

Every now and again in her letters would come a little litany of names that were dear to her. They varied very slightly and might, I think, easily have been cut down to three [Edward, Edy and Ted] which never failed to turn up. Here is a long-ago specimen written on an American tour. (About 1907):

> *Do you love me very much now I am far away from you? I do you*
> *– 'and twenty such!' – only – only there aren't twenty. I'm thinking*
> *about you – and your mother – and Edward (and Edward) – and*
> *Henry – and Ted and Edy – and the work – and the moon – and I*
> *just love all and every and can't help it.*[11]

In this gaily expansive innocent love of all mankind – provided they were from her point of view lovable – there was to be one exceptional case – that of Henry Irving. Her love for him was to acquire a far greater depth; he was older than she was, more eminent in the profession than anyone else, and she was dependent on him for her security and her livelihood, as virtually all women of that period were on a husband. In spite of her unconstrained nature, she welcomed this dependence in her heart, and treasured the comfort it brought and the absence of anxiety for her children. No man before had given her this. But her devotion to Irving was never to supplant her absolute and unquestioned love for Godwin.

With Irving, in a sense, she achieved and enjoyed a professional marriage which began in the theatre, but soon extended into their private lives. There would never be any doubt for either of them that it was the theatre which came first in their regard. Their great reputation was a power they could share together, enjoying the wealth it was for a while to bring them. Irving would in any case have won his unassailable position; but she could never have reached similar heights without him. She knew this and was grateful.

But Ellen did not have a blind admiration for Irving. In her memoirs she is wholehearted about what she liked in his work, but she analyses his failings. Their taste in plays was by no means the same, though it often coincided. She was as responsive to 'good theatre' as he was, and she enjoyed performing pathos as well as comedy. But her ideal of being the 'useful' actress came

uppermost at the Lyceum, and her unswerving loyalty to Irving
was such that she was ready to play (not without the occasional
protest) subordinate parts in plays he had chosen because they
afforded him the particular opportunities for 'picturesque' acting
which his genius craved. But her complementary talents were
always in his mind, and he never doubted she was the most perfect
actress on the English stage. In this the English critics and the
public wholeheartedly concurred.

That she was seldom satisfied with her achievements on the
stage was partly her nature, partly the outcome of her particular
training. In spite of her constant reference to self-discipline and
her patient study of her parts, she had been given no formal
framework of technical performance in a school of acting to
which she could turn to counteract the ups and downs of her
temperament. This was precisely what the actors in the Théâtre
National in Paris had been given, until their acting shone with a
clean bright polish whatever their private feelings might be when
they were on the stage. But Ellen had only her intuition on which
to rely. As Gordon Craig puts it:

> Ellen Terry met almost every one, and everyone certainly
> had a good chance of meeting her, for they had but to go to
> the Lyceum Theatre, and there she was – now Ellen Ophelia,
> now Nelly Oldfield or Nell Beatrice. She played but one part
> – herself; and when not herself, she couldn't play it.[12]

Such an attitude as this in a leading actress was (and still is)
peculiar to the English genius for the stage, and gave it its distinction from those countries with long-established national
schools of acting, where a recognized style of performance can
be acquired to which the player adds the qualities of his personality and his genius. For Ellen, there was no half-way performance in which the rules could be effectively observed when her
genius was feeling out of sorts. If she failed, she failed quite
completely, in her own estimation at the least. 'I'm so unsatisfactory to myself as Ophelia,' she wrote to Coleridge soon after
the play had opened. 'I imagine her so delicate, and feel myself

old and frumpish in the part.' When he went to her in her dressing-room, he found her with her dress all wet with tears. Ellen did not give a technical performance. It was time she knew her business on the stage, but what really mattered was that she knew that art of holding audiences in her personal spell. As far as technique went, she had learnt her art for the most part in bad plays from actors who, like herself, were virtually self-taught. Behind her lay such tutors as Ben Terry, Charles Kean, Madame de Rhona, Charles Reade, Squire Bancroft and John Hare. Now she had to measure up to Irving, who was equally self-taught, and whose skills were equally reliant on the hypnosis engendered by his performance.[13]

Her father still watched over her with pride. She had re-discovered him as a fine-looking man of sixty with a square white beard and all the old enthusiasm for his favourite, if errant, daughter. 'Duchess' he still called her, and 'Duchess, you might have been anything' was what he still believed. He liked everything 'rotten perfect', as the theatrical slang of the times had it, and his definition of rotten perfect was quite simple: 'If you get out of bed in the middle of the night and do your best, you're perfect. If you can't, you don't really know it!' Although he worshipped the boards on which Macready had stood in earlier years, he put Irving above him for his originality. Ben's mind was by no means closed to innovations. But he grumbled because his daughter did not get adequate opportunities as the result of her triumphs at the Lyceum. 'We must have no more of these Ophelias and Desdemonas,' he said after Irving's production of *Othello*. When Ellen protested, he only went on, 'They're second fiddle parts – not the parts for you, Duchess.' But Ellen rejected this argument completely, claiming that the parts she had in many Lyceum productions – *Hamlet, The Merchant of Venice, Olivia,* and *Charles I* among them – were equal to Henry's in their way. At first, she admits, she was overawed by Irving, whose melancholy worried her during the run of *Hamlet*. Once he caught her sliding down the banisters of the stairs leading from her dressing-room. It was as if she had been caught laughing in church.

However, as she and Irving grew close together, he even expected her to drill the actresses for him in the same way as he drilled the men. Ellen, however wisely and kindly she might speak to apprentice players, was not a born producer, as Irving undoubtedly was. She knew her limitations, and was content to follow the master. In only one matter did she feel her advice was useful, in costume, sets and lighting. Here she was the disciple of Godwin, whom Irving had never met. She believed herself to be a specialist in lighting, and deplored the experimental use of electricity in the theatre:

> We never had electricity installed at the Lyceum until Daly took the theatre. When I saw the effect on the faces of the electric footlights, I entreated Henry to have the gas restored, and he did. We used gas footlights and gas limes there until we left the theatre for good in 1902. To this I attribute much of the beauty of our lighting. I say 'our' because this was a branch of Henry's work in which I was always his chief helper. Until electricity has been greatly improved and developed, it can never be to the stage what gas was. The thick softness of gaslight, with the lovely specks and motes in it, so like *natural* light, gave illusion to many a scene which is now revealed in all its naked trashiness by electricity.[14]

After she had become established at the Lyceum, Irving always consulted her about the sets and costumes he commissioned.

During 1879, the first full year Ellen was playing at the Lyceum, the Comédie Française paid its first visit to London, and revealed during a six-week season at the Gaiety Theatre the results of quite another tradition of performance. As Henry James chose to put it, it had made the English barbarians stare. The season was highly successful and became a talking-point in London. The tradition of the Comédie Française so greatly admired by Henry James seemed to him to demonstrate what professionalism really meant to the theatre, and showed the British players to be mere amateurs. Though the kings of England, as we have seen, had expressed

their patronage of the theatre in the form of restricting the performances of the 'legitimate' drama in London to the licensed
patent houses of Drury Lane and Covent Garden, they did not
establish a school of dramatic art. So effective British acting became a survival of the fittest, those men and women with the
stamina, the spirit, the bombast or the art to secure the attention
of the crowd. If Garrick, Sarah Siddons, Edmund Kean and James
Macready were indeed great performers, they had to be so in
such theatrical conditions as they discovered and moulded to their
purposes.

The initial patronage of the kings of France enabled a quite
different institution to grow up out of the Maison du Molière,
the Théâtre Français or Comédie Française. A tradition of training
and employment had been developed by this company since the
seventeenth century which allowed performers of acceptable
quality to join a theatrical fraternity dedicated to the performance
of the best in French dramatic literature. It offered young actors
a life career in a single, established company where the virtues of
ensemble acting and the niceties of declamation were studied to
perfection and followed with avidity by audiences who understood the *finesse* of the game. If the faults of the British theatre
lay in its crude dramas and its dependence on the cult of stage
personality, the faults of the French system soon developed
cultural inbreeding and sterility of invention. Nevertheless, it was
recognized that great acting in both countries could survive these
divergent limitations – the philistinism of the British and the cold
perfectionism of the French.

In spite of his admiration for French culture, Henry James
finally deserted Paris and became resident in England. In his article
of 1880 already mentioned he exposed what he held to be the
insufficiencies of the actor and the actress whom he acknowledged
to be the greatest the London theatre could produce. He found
Irving inadequate in Shakespeare: he was 'picturesque but diffuse'
and 'inordinately slow', missing the 'heat, rapidity, passion, magic'
of Shakespeare's dramatic verse, and at his best in contemporary
drama, as Louis XI, for example, and Charles I, or as Mathias,

because 'the part of the distracted burgomaster is so largely pantomimic'. Of Ellen herself he wrote:

> The difficulty is that Miss Terry has charm – remarkable charm; and this beguiles people into thinking her an accomplished actress. There is a natural quality about her that is extremely pleasing – something wholesome and English and womanly which often touches easily where art, to touch, has to be finer than we often see it. The writer of these lines once heard her highly commended by one of the most distinguished members of the Comédie Française, who had not understood a word she spoke.
> *Ah Miss Terry, for instance; I liked her extremely,*
> *And why did you like her?*
> Mon Dieu ⌐ *I found her very natural.* ⌐ truth

This seemed to us an interesting impression, and a proof the more of the truism that we enjoy things in proportion to their rarity. To our own English vision Miss Terry has too much nature, and we should like a little more art. On the other side, when a French actress is eminent she is eminent by her finish, by what she has acquired, by the perfection of her art, and the critic I have just quoted, who had had this sort of merit before his eyes all his life, was refreshed by seeing what could be achieved in lieu of it by a sort of sympathetic spontaneity. Miss Terry has that excellent thing, a quality; she gives one the sense of something fine. Add to this that though she is not regularly beautiful, she has a face altogether in the taste of the period, a face that Burne-Jones might have drawn, and that she arranges herself (always in the taste of the period) wonderfully well for the stage. She makes an admirable picture, and it would be difficult to imagine a more striking embodiment of sumptuous sweetness than her Ophelia, her Portia, her Pauline, or her Olivia, in a version of Goldsmith's immortal novel prepared for the Court Theatre a couple of years ago by the indefatigable Mr Wills. Her Ophelia, in particular, was lovely, and of a type altogether different from the young lady in white muslin, bristling with strange grasses, whom we are accustomed to see in the part. In Miss Terry's hands the bewildered daughter of Polonius became a somewhat angular maiden of the Gothic ages, with her hair cropped short, like a boy's, and a straight and clinging robe, wrought over with contemporary needle-work. As for her acting, she has happy impulses; but this seems to us to be the limit of it.[15]

The French tradition of training was based on developing the talents of a player within his chosen *emploi,* or type of part; in this he perfected his performance over the years, studying every appropriate role within the classical range of drama. He acquired the poise of body thought to be correct and above all exactness in the declamation of the Alexandrine, the French dramatic verse-form which has nothing of Shakespeare's rhythmic virtuosity or sensitive response to individual characterization. Thus, the whole approach to stage performance in France and Britain was entirely different, though both were totally demanding. In French playing, a studied control was everything, involving the greatest concentration on achievement of effect by the conscious exercise of art. In British playing, attack was everything, and the actor with the necessary powers was most admired when he really let himself go. Coquelin *aîné,* Irving's contemporary and a great exponent of French tradition more especially in comedy, would despise such exhibitionism or, if he saw that it succeeded in holding an audience, regard it as merely 'picturesque'. He was horrified by the thought of real tears being shed upon the stage. Perhaps it was inevitable, he allowed, when one had to perform in bad plays the only aim of which was to make such picturesque effects. All that mattered to him was the self-discipline which enabled him to triumph in declamatory drama: 'The actor must in all circumstances remain the absolute master of himself,' he wrote, 'and leave nothing to chance.'

Coquelin's principles are firmly established in his approach to his art:

The arts differ according to the nature of their medium; well, the actor's medium is – himself. His own face, his body, his life is the material of his art; the thing he works and moulds to draw out from it his creation. From this it follows the existence of the comedian must be dual; one part of him is the performer, the instrumentalist; another, the instrument to be played on.[16]

Coquelin was well aware of the distinction between the French and British genius in the theatre and said as much:

> When Garrick came to France he admired our actors very much, but he did not consider them natural enough. I shall be told that that is because they were acting in tragedy; but when Talma appeared he made tragedy natural, and to that he owed his success and his influence. Was his naturalness that of Garrick? I cannot tell. The genius of the two races is too different; the love of originality is too strong with our neighbours for them always to remain within the true measure of things; in any case, today it is we who when we go to see Irving no longer find him near enough to nature. The truth is his nature does not correspond to ours.

Coquelin, indeed, with some of his colleagues, was the guest of Irving at the Lyceum. Watching Ellen through his opera glasses, Coquelin whispered to a neighbour from the Théâtre, 'Angelique, très sympathique, très tendre. Mais c'est charmant; elle a des vrais larmes aux yeux.' Francesque Sarcey, the distinguished French critic who came from France to watch the experimental spectacle of his National Theatre performing before the ill-trained London audiences, could not appreciate Irving, in whom he could only see 'a wilful tendency to exaggeration'. This he ascribed to Irving's need to follow the tastes of his public. It could not, he felt, be that proper to London's leading actor.

Since Ellen's supremacy in the English theatre was to remain unchallenged throughout the remaining years of the nineteenth century, it was inevitable that she should face comparison with leading actresses elsewhere. Of those, only Sarah Bernhardt, Ellen's strict contemporary, and Eleanora Duse, some ten years her junior, were to challenge her both in England and the United

11. Kate Terry

12. Godwin at the time of his association
with Ellen Terry

13. Portrait of Ellen Terry, age unknown

13a. Charles Reade
By courtesy of Radio Times Hulton Picture Library.)

13b. Lewis Carroll
(*By courtesy of Radio Times Hulton Picture Library.*)

14. Portrait of Ellen Terry, age unknown

15. Portrait of Ellen Terry, age unknown

16. Stage portrait of Kelly

17. Portrait of Ellen Terry, *c.* 1878, at about
the time she joined Irving at the Lyceum

17a. Edy, aged eleven

17b. Edward Gordon Craig in 1886

18. Ellen Terry, c. 1878

19. Henry Irving in *The Bells*
(*By courtesy of Pamela Hansford Johnson.*)

States. Though Duse did not come to London until 1895, Bernhardt arrived in 1879, the very year in which Ellen was establishing
her reign in London. In his amusing account of the excursion of
the Comédie Française to London – an event somewhat disapproved of by the more censorious French – Henry James leaves
us in no doubt that it was the flamboyant reputation of Sarah
Bernhardt that gave the visit its *réclame* in London society.
Although the prices for seats were doubled, the support for the
season from fashionable playgoers was unquestioned, especially on
the nights when Bernhardt was playing. There was, as James puts
it, a 'vogue' for this lady; she became a 'topic'.

James puts the matter succinctly, and in a form which could
have given Ellen some cause to ponder her own position in the
London theatre:

> Mlle Sarah Bernhardt is not, to my sense, a celebrity because
> she is an artist. She is a celebrity because, apparently, she desires
> with an intensity that has rarely been equalled to be one, and
> because for this end all means are alike to her. She may flatter
> herself that, as regards the London public, she has compassed
> her end with a completeness which makes of her a sort of
> fantastically impertinent *victrix* poised upon a perfect pyramid
> of ruins – the ruins of a hundred British prejudices and prop-
> rieties. Mlle Sarah Bernhardt has remarkable gifts; her success
> is something quite apart as the woman herself is something
> quite apart; but her triumph has little to do with the proper
> lines of the Comédie Française. She is a child of her age – of
> her moment – and she has known how to profit by the idio-
> syncrasies of the time.[17]

It would be an obvious understatement to say that Sarah
Bernhardt's career had been in marked contrast to that of Ellen.
She was the illegitimate daughter of a cocotte and as a child had
been brought to the pitch of chronic hysteria by the alternate
excesses of love and desertion by her mother, who was only
sixteen when her daughter was born in 1845. Put to school in a
convent, where she showed further symptoms of hysteria, she

L

nevertheless distinguished herself in the school plays. One of her mother's lovers, the Duc de Moray, sent her at the age of fifteen to the Conservatoire Dramatique, the official training ground for the Théâtre Français operating under the State. When she had completed her training, she worked for a while at the Comédie Française, but by her early twenties it was clear she could be bounded by no set tradition either of art or personal behaviour. Her philosophy – *'Je ferai toute ma vie ce que je veux faire'* – was soon expanded to include a voracious capacity for lovers. As she put it herself, *'J'ai été une des plus grandes amoureuses de mon temps.'*

After leaving the Comédie, she had become pregnant by a prince, and by the age of twenty-five had settled for a life of *amour* and exhibitionist acting, which she coupled with a flair for personal eccentricity which she was careful to make known. By 1874 she was back at the Comédie Française; there she realized the height of her headlong fame in the part of Phèdre, in which even James allows she had 'a chance to give the measure of her great talent', though in the last act he felt she was 'painfully shrill and modern'. 'Charming as are some of her gifts,' wrote James in London in 1879, 'peculiar and picturesque as is her whole artistic personality, it cannot in the least be said that she is a consummate actress.' She had already made it known that she was about to leave the Comédie Française, and had her eye on new conquests in the United States. 'I strongly suspect that she will find a triumphant career in the Western world,' wrote James for his American readers. 'She is too American not to succeed in America.'

Ellen, as we have said, had already seen this actress in Paris, where she noted at once that she was 'as thin as a harrow' and that she 'was not a bit conventional'. Ellen, true to British empiricism in the matter of tradition in acting, had admired everyone she saw, then added, 'Old school – new school? What does it matter which, so long as it is *good enough.*' As for Irving, he saw Bernhardt for the first time in 1879, and was left quite unmoved – but, as Ellen put it (in italics), *'It was never any pleasure to him to see the acting of other actors.'* Irving and Bernhardt were to become acquainted, but he always admired her as an actor-manager rather than as an actress. Bernhardt returned to London again, but the outstanding occasion was to be in June 1895 when London had Ellen at the Lyceum, Bernhardt at Drury Lane and Duse at Daly's, with Bernard Shaw present to make the critic's judgment between the three goddesses of the theatre.[18]

The arrival of the Comédie Française in 1879 did not affect Irving's receipts adversely during his first season as manager. In addition to her salary, Ellen received £233 from a 'benefit' performance; during the second season, that of 1880, the profits at the Lyceum alone amounted to £10,000.

On her return from her last provincial tour with Kelly, during which, as we have seen, she had played Beatrice in *Much Ado about Nothing* for the first time, Ellen was needed at once at the Lyceum, where Irving was anxious to put Tennyson's new play, *The Cup,* a two-act tragedy derived from Plutarch, into rehearsal. Irving took his two principals, Ellen and William Terriss, to hear Tennyson read his short play at Eaton Place; Ellen took Edy, who began to laugh when Tennyson, who had turned seventy and normally read poetry in a low-pitched monotone, suddenly raised his voice to a falsetto he was unable to sustain when reading the women's parts. Edy began to giggle at young Hallam Tennyson, and then Irving himself grinned. Ellen was very embarrassed when Edy made uncalled-for comments on how confusing the men were, but Irving condoned her bad behaviour. Irving accepted the fact that the play was far too short, and would have to be put on with *The Corsican Brothers;* but he spent a small fortune (£2,370) on the elaborate production, particularly on the sets and costumes for the Temple of Artemis, where Camma, the Galatian heroine, whom Ellen played, avenges the death of her husband by giving a poisoned cup to his murderer, who has persecuted her with his love. A huge figure of the many-breasted Artemis was set at the rear of the stage, bathed in misty blue light, while a crowd of women in the foreground performed rhythmical movements in unison. During rehearsals one dancer attracted Ellen's attention; she found out the girl only possessed

one dress of black velveteen, and that she had little to wear under-
neath. She disappeared shortly after the opening of the play on 3
January 1881, and Ellen traced her to a hospital ward. She visited
the ward where the dancer lay looking at her with her 'great eyes,
black, with weary white lids'. Ellen gave her the amber and
coral beads she was wearing. The girl died sending her love
to 'dear Miss Terry', and was buried with the lilies Ellen had
brought for her. She had asked that the beads be returned after
her death.

Irving, who could never look like a Roman, aimed to create in
the part of Synorix an impression of barbarous cruelty and
lechery. Tennyson disliked the interpretation, but Ellen admired it:
'With a pale, pale face, bright red hair, gold armour and a tiger-
skin, a diabolical expression and very thin crimson lips, Henry
looked handsome and sickening at the same time. *Lechery* was
written across his forehead.' With what might seem an incredible
generosity in any other woman than Ellen, she asked for her
dresses to be designed for her by Godwin. The cup used in the
second act was also designed by Godwin, and on the hundredth
night Ellen sent a silver replica of it to Tennyson as a gift. Ellen
admired *The Cup*, which she called 'a great little play', but always
felt herself unequal to the demands of the second act. On 16 April,
The Corsican Brothers was replaced by the light comedy, *The
Belle's Stratagem*, which was put on before *The Cup*; so now, on
a single night Ellen had to change the mood of performance from
that of the gay Letitia Hardy to that of the High Priestess of
Artemis.

During May and June 1881 Irving made a most generous gesture
to Edwin Booth, the distinguished tragedian from the United
States, who was having an unsuccessful season at the Princess's
Theatre. Booth, who was almost fifty, was at the height of
his powers. He was the son of the English actor Junius Brutus
Booth, who had at one time both rivalled and played with
Edmund Kean in Britain before deserting his wife and going
off to America with a flower-girl called Mary-Ann, who was
Edwin Booth's mother. There was both tragedy and insanity in

the Booth family, and father and son were alike afflicted with
melancholia. Irving knew that Edwin Booth had brought his
second wife with him to London, and that she was seriously ill
and mentally deranged, an unhappy circumstance made all the
worse for Booth because his first wife had died in 1863 following
a visit to London, where he had been playing at the Haymarket.
Booth was a much travelled performer, appearing in Australia,
England and Germany, and touring widely in the United States;
he was a man of courage and tenacity. His youngest brother,
John Wilkins Booth, a less successful actor, had assassinated
President Lincoln in 1865.

Like his father, Edwin Booth was a great instinctual actor,
tireless and strong, hampered only by the element of despair
which fastened on his temperament and threatened his extraordinary talent. Irving, who admired him, made him a handsome
offer after the conclusion of his season at the Princess's Theatre –
to alternate with him the roles of Othello and Iago for a series of
performances at the Lyceum, with Ellen in the part of Desdemona.
Booth accepted the offer.

Ellen found Booth courteous but apathetic, for his wife lay
dying while he worked. 'I have never in any face, in any country,
seen such wonderful eyes,' wrote Ellen. 'There was mystery
about his appearance and his manner.' But she sensed in him an
air of defeat, a lack of any ambition; his Othello was melancholy
and dignified, with none of the huge passion Salvini gave to the
part. 'I shall never make you black,' he said to her. 'When I take
your hand I shall have a corner of my drapery in my hand. That
will protect you.' When Irving played Othello, however, the
stain he used was soon passed on to her. However, her pathos as
Desdemona was so great that she even made Irving's eyes 'soft
and full of tears' when he played Iago. However genuinely moved
he was, he turned his own tears to account and wiped them away
as a mark of Iago's cynical hypocrisy. He played Iago like some
Borgia, full of devilish charm. Booth's Iago, like Irving's was
better than his Othello. Apart from the speech to the Senate,
Irving turned Othello into a ranter; it was a performance Ellen

could not bear. In the end he could not bear it himself, and after
the six weeks were over he said to her, 'Never again.' Ellen, however, enjoyed playing Desdemona. 'Some nights I played it
beautifully. My appearance was right – I was such a poor wraith
of a thing.'

The curtain down on the last performance of Othello, Booth
departed with his dying wife for New York. After a brief holiday
Ellen accompanied Irving on the first provincial tour they had
undertaken together. It was a royal progress by special train
loaded with the scenery and other equipment for nine different
productions and transporting a company of fifty-four actors and
actresses as well as Irving's key stage staff. The tour included
Glasgow and Edinburgh, and the profits accruing from sixteen
weeks' exacting work was over £6,000.

By now, with Kelly gone, Ellen's future, both in public and in
private, was closely bound up with that of Irving. There was no
question that she had become an essential part of the Lyceum
company, second only to Irving himself as the principal attraction
for audiences that returned again and again to see the Lyceum
repertoire. She had become 'our lady of the Lyceum'.[19] New
presentations at the theatre were events in the social life of London.
Cartoons of Irving appeared in *Punch,* while photographs of both
Irving and Ellen in their more celebrated roles were sold by the
thousand.

During the fourth and fifth seasons at the Lyceum, spanning
the years 1882–3, Ellen was able to play Juliet to Irving's Romeo
and Beatrice to his Benedick. Irving's ambition was to present
every 'actable' play of Shakespeare. As far as *Romeo and Juliet* was
concerned, it was now or never, with Irving already forty-four
and Ellen thirty-six – both of them more than double the ages of
the parts they were playing. The production opened on 8 March
1882 and ran for twenty-four weeks. Knowing that he was miscast
as Romeo, Irving made this production more elaborately pictorial
than anything he had so far done; the sets became a spectacular
effort to bring the colour and warmth of Italy to the London
stage, and the cost was the phenomenal sum of £7,500. As Irving

said to Ellen, *Romeo and Juliet* as a play proceeds from picture to picture. He was never to create a more spacious production with the organized use of large crowds. The atmosphere at the beginning was bitter and threatening; the rival factions fought venomously in the street. At the close, with its reconciliation of the rival families united in mourning the deaths of Romeo and Juliet, the stage was filled with figures carrying torches. As Clement Scott said:

> The play glows and burns with the picturesqueness and fantastic beauty of old Verona. The stage, with its crowds, its conflicts, its cabals, its maskers and mummers, its balls and revels, is as animated and sunny as any artist would desire, and as instinct with life as any picture that ever came from the Court of Meiningen.[20]

Irving restored the full action of the play, which up till then had suffered from being performed in Garrick's version. Mrs Stirling, who had worked with Macready, was invited by Irving to come out of retirement to play the Nurse and, although Ellen admired the seriousness of her performance, she had to struggle now and then to get the old lady to break with tradition and let her give a new reality to her conception of Juliet. Tradition, for example, decreed that Juliet should play the coquette in order to extract the news of Romeo which the Nurse withholds. Ellen was to make Juliet impatient to the point of anger. Ellen, in fact, withdrew to the country to study Juliet, reading everything she could about her and her environment – researching the girl in fact, instead of *imagining* her. It would have been better, she says, if she had gone to Verona and let her instinct be fired by what she saw. In any case, she realized the part was a supremely difficult one, needing the knowledge of a mature woman in the body of a child. Ellen felt she had come to understand Juliet only when she had reached sixty.

Irving knew the critics would dislike his Romeo but he was convinced of Ellen's excellence. In one of the rare letters to have survived among the immense number that were to pass between

them, Irving expresses his feeling following the dress rehearsal.
Ellen quotes it in her book.

Beautiful as Portia was, Juliet leaves her far, far behind.
Never anybody acted more exquisitely the part of the performance which I saw from the front. 'Hie to high fortune,' and
'Where spirits resort' were simply incomparable ... Your
mother looked very radiant last night. I told her how proud she
should be, and she was.... The play will be, I believe, a
mighty 'go' for the beauty of it is bewildering. I am sure of
this, for it dumbfounded them all last night. Now you – we –
must make our task a delightful one by doing everything possible
to make our acting easy and comfortable. We are in for a long
run.... I have determined not to see a paper for a week – I
know they'll cut me up, and I don't like it.[21]

Irving was right; the critics, while praising his production, did
not praise his performance. As for Ellen, although the usual
tributes to her charm took up the usual space, her Juliet was said
to be 'far below her Portia' (Clement Scott), lacking in tragic
passion (*The Saturday Review*), and 'wanting in the imagination
of tragedy' (*The Academy*). Henry James, writing for the *Atlantic
Monthly*, was more caustic. He speculated on what Mr Henry
Irving might have been prevented from doing on the stage had
he been to a training-school in acting and learnt to suppress 'some
of his extraordinary peculiarities' which 'blossomed and flowered
at such a prodigious rate'. He simply could not understand how
such a performance as Irving's Romeo could attract the public,
still less since he entrusted 'the girlish Juliet to the large, the long,
the mature Miss Terry'. The production, he says, 'converts the
play from a splendid and delicate poem into a gorgeous and war-
weighted spectacle', full of 'glowing and deceptive pictures'. As
for Ellen, he allows that 'she is what the French call ... a "Nature"';
she is almost always interesting, and she is often a delightful
presence: but she is not Juliet; on the contrary! She is too vol-
uminous, too deliberate, too prosaic, too English, too unversed in

the utterance of poetry.' Only Mrs Stirling, 'a rich and accomplished actress', stirred him. The play, he felt, had been 'sacrificed to the machinist and to the gas-man'. As if to atone for this, Ellen tells us how touched she was when the gas-men of the Lyceum sent her a bouquet on the hundredth night of the play with a note inscribed, 'To Juliet, as a mark of respect and esteem'. She was also touched because Sarah Bernhardt came to see her and praised the *vraies larmes* which so invariably astonished the French.

During the run of *Romeo and Juliet* Ellen acquired yet another faithful servant, her dresser Sarah Holland, who stayed with her throughout the rest of her career at the Lyceum, and accompanied her to America. She was, says Ellen, 'a dear character', orderly when Ellen was disorderly, controller of her dressing-rooms from their permanent quarters at the Lyceum to the horrific places assigned them in the provinces and, worst of all, during the one-night stands in America. When Ellen was upset by her thinness she would tell her she was 'beautiful and fat', and later, when for a while she filled out too much, Sarah would say, 'Beautiful and thin tonight, dear.' Sarah's children walked on in *Romeo and Juliet,* and one night Irving, who always loved children, found Flo, one of Sarah's girls, waiting for her mother. He asked her – the great man peering down very kindly – what exactly she did in the play. 'Please, sir, first I'm a water-carrier, then I'm a little page, and then I'm a virgin,' she said. 'Henry and I sat down on the stairs and laughed until we cried!' says Ellen.

Interesting new names began now to appear in the cast-list of the Lyceum. For example, a young actor, Arthur Wing Pinero, who had been in the original Lyceum company, played Roderigo in *Othello,* though he had left the theatre again before the production of *Romeo and Juliet.* In 1897 Irving incorporated one of Pinero's one-act plays, *Daisy's Escape* into a triple bill which included *The Bells,* and permitted the author to play the lead in it. But not everyone thought Irving's supporting company a sufficiently good one. 'Many of the parts were poorly filled, as is the way at the Lyceum,' wrote Lewis Carroll in April 1881, when Ellen gave him two stalls one night for *The Cup* and *The Belle's Stratagem.* In *Romeo and Juliet,* the handsome romantic actor William Terriss played Mercutio; he had joined the company in 1880. Terriss came of a good family, but had run away from school and, after a brief appearance in the Bancrofts' company, had departed with his wife for the Falkland Islands. Later he returned to England and joined Hare's company at the Court, where he had played with Ellen in *Olivia.* He had been a tea-planter, a sheep-farmer, even an engineer now and then. He was known as Breezy Bill and, at the Lyceum, he tended to treat Irving with a respectful lack of tact which the Guv'nor came to relish. Ellen, naturally, was fond of Terriss; he was male and jolly, and had the kind of humour she appreciated; she would dance burlesque quadrilles with him. Often, it seems, he had little grasp of what he was actually doing on the stage, but being a 'heaven-born' actor got it right by instinct, though he was often nervous, shaking like a leaf in spite of his dare-devil courage. He was good with horses, and used to do cowboy stunts in Richmond Park. He was, says Ellen, a kind of Adonis, rather like Lord Byron, who always looked young and 'had a beautiful mouth'. He arrived one night at the Lyceum wet through because he had jumped into the Thames to save a drowning girl. Many people thought he should have played Romeo to Irving's Mercutio. Late in 1897, he was stabbed to death at the stage-door of the Adelphi Theatre.

George Alexander was also in the Lyceum company for a while, and his part of Paris was taken over in the autumn by a newcomer from Oxford, Frank Benson, whom Irving and Ellen had seen in a student production of the *Agamemnon* in Greek, in which he had played Clytemnestra to sufficient effect for Ellen to think him a beautiful girl.[22] The following year he was invited to the Lyceum by Irving and met Ellen: 'a presence rustled round us, an atmosphere of joyous, vibrant vitality ... alert, erect in her radiant beauty,' he says. She told him he ought to join them at the Lyceum, to 'help in the great work'. He did, for part of one production, arriving over-confident, and finding his feet in the

particular professionalism of the Lyceum with some awkwardness
and difficulty. Ellen sent him a typical note after his first night:
'Well done, for first done.' Later she warned him he was not
really as good as she had thought after she had seen him in the
Greek play; she suggested he should study and watch old Howe,
who was seventy-eight, and, as Benson remarked, 'could tell you
first-hand traditions of Garrick, and had seen and acted with the
Keans and Macready'. Ellen added: 'We are the only artists who
never see the art work we are producing. I would give ten years
of my life to see myself act, that I might learn what to avoid.'
She told him that the hardest thing she was required to do on the
stage was to make an exit across its whole width. Even Benson's
expert fencing was to no avail at the Lyceum; Irving had his
stage presence pat, and before Benson knew where he was, he
heard the famous voice hiss in his ear: 'Die, my boy, die; down,
down.' Ellen, seeing how keen and earnest he was about succeeding on the stage, persuaded Irving to let him sit in the wings and
watch the company at work. She told him she had never had any
education except what she had picked up for herself. He found
her 'very live, very human, very lovable'; he noticed the range of
her sympathies and 'her gift of acquiring the inner meaning of all
the arts of expression'. He felt it was she who made it natural for
the leading artists, composers, poets and sculptors to draw closer
to the theatre and even to work in it.

Another recruit to the Lyceum during the run of *Romeo and
Juliet* was John Martin-Harvey, who became a 'Lyceum Gentleman' earning twenty-five shillings a week. He was to stay for
fourteen years, by which time his weekly salary had risen to £10.
He had seen Ellen originally as Ophelia, and found her physically
irresistible: 'Her long, virginal limbs, her husky voice, her crown
of short flaxen hair, her great red mouth, her inability to stand
still for a moment ... a poise so frail that one trembled for her
security, a physical attractiveness which gave one ample excuse for
Hamlet's "Get thee to a nunnery".'

Martin-Harvey noticed the strong line of demarcation that
existed between the company and its two leading players. Irving

saw to it that the Green Room was comfortable, well furnished and well decorated with fine prints of famous actors and actresses or with historic playbills. A fire always burned there when the weather was cold. Yet Ellen, for all her friendliness to individuals, was never to be seen there, and Irving but seldom, and then only to cause a hush to fall on the assembly of principals, supporting actors and small-part players. 'Humph!' Irving would give a friendly grunt, and ask, 'All right? Quite comfortable here?' 'Oh, quite, sir; very comfortable,' everyone would hasten to reply. Irving had his office and dressing-room separate from those of the rest of the company, with his private entrance shared only by Ellen, but even she only approached the office when the coast was clear and business would not make her feminine presence ill-timed. Irving, served in the front of the house by Bram Stoker and on the stage by Loveday, lived in a remote empyrean, like some High Master in a public school. The theatre belonged wholly to the Guv'nor.

But Irving himself liked to be convivial, and in order to play the part within the walls of his own theatre revived in new form the past tradition of the Sublime Society of Beefsteaks, a distinguished group of men, which had included Sheridan, who had formed a social circle to eat steaks and drink porter. These gatherings were said to have dated back originally to the early eighteenth century, in association with the Covent Garden playhouse. The apartments later dedicated to these celebrations had deteriorated into lumber-rooms attached to the Lyceum, but they were now redecorated and provided Irving with a fine dining-room where he could entertain distinguished guests after the play. He employed his own chef, established his own cellar of champagne, wines and brandy, and created a new tradition – the lavish hospitality of the Beefsteak Room. The way through to it led past the company's dressing-rooms, and the actors preparing to go home after the play always knew when the Guv'nor was going to entertain. Their mouths would water as the aroma of cooking reached the back-stage corridors. Martin-Harvey, the walking gentleman, stole one night into this sacred room to see for himself what kind of place it was and to imagine the scene once Irving and the guests had arrived:

I tiptoed into these mysterious and hallowed haunts one night when preparations for a midnight feast were in progress. Through an ante-room, decorated with the armour and weapons used in various productions, I passed into a fine old Gothic hall – the Gothic of Pugin, no doubt.... I liked to picture the great man here, seated at the head of the long table, lighted with candles and loaded with good things supplied by Gunter, a great fire crackling in the broad Baronial hearth, his clear-cut alabaster profile outlined against the sombre oaken panelling.... But I must fly these hallowed precincts before I am caught by the ubiquitous Stoker. I can only catch a glimpse of a remarkable full-length portrait of Irving hanging in the ante-room. This is Whistler's picture of him in the character of Philip the Second in Tennyson's *Queen Mary*, which he had produced in 1876.[23]

These pictures were later to include Sargent's portrait of Ellen as Lady Macbeth, and Bastien-Lepage's famous picture, now in the National Portrait Gallery, originated from one of these Beefsteak gatherings and reflected Irving's geniality as a host. Though some of the dinners were confined to men, women were frequently invited, and Ellen on these occasions became Irving's hostess. She saw how 'raffish and mischievous' he could become in the right company. He was in the course of time to entertain at the Lyceum hundreds of people in society and in the academic and artistic worlds, as well as members of the Royal Family.

When the next Lyceum production, *Much Ado about Nothing*, began on 11 October 1882, Ellen was happy to be able to welcome her old admirer Johnston Forbes-Robertson back on to the stage alongside her. He joined the Lyceum to play Claudio; at the same time, he undertook several drawings of members of the company and of the stage sets. Irving commissioned him to paint the scene of Claudio's marriage to Hero, a magnificent set of the interior of a church.

Beatrice became one of Ellen's most effective parts. She played the 'witty strife' between Beatrice and Benedick in such a way as to leave no doubt from the first that she half-liked if not half-loved him. The critics, for once, were unanimous in praise of this production.

In 1882, during a speech after a midnight banquet on the Lyceum stage following the hundredth performance of *Romeo and Juliet*, Irving declared his intention of taking his company to the United States in the autumn of the following year. *Much Ado about Nothing* enjoyed an unbroken run from October 1882 until June 1883, and it was then time to put into repertory revivals of the plays he intended to present on his first tour in North America. Irving had conquered London; it remained now to test his strength in the great territory of the New World.

VI

❦

NORTH AMERICA

Ellen was to spend in all some five years in the United States, and her great reputation there was built up through a series of triumphal progresses with the Lyceum company that began in October 1883 and lasted until her final tour with Irving in 1901. After this she visited the States independently, primarily to give her lecture-recitals. 'I often feel that I am half-American,' she said. Her third husband, the actor James Carew, was American.[1]

Quick in her response to impressions, excited by the vociferous receptions she received everywhere she went, Ellen found America easy to like. Nevertheless, like many English people of the period, she approached the New World with some trepidation. The United States had the reputation in Europe of being a 'strange barbarous land'. She was convinced she would 'never, never return'. If she ever did, Boo would be dead (or so Boo herself said), and the children would undoubtedly be lost, let alone the bullfinches and the parrot. For weeks the word America brought tears to Ellen's eyes. Acting at the Lyceum during the farewell performance made her weep as if she faced some impending doom.

When the curtain fell on 28 July, their last night at the Lyceum, Irving asked the audience to give a lead in supporting the American actor, Laurence Barrett, who was to take over the theatre in the winter during his absence. The applause went on, and the cast was called back again and again; even actors from other theatres, their work done, gathered in the aisles to join in the cheering, the applause and the tears of enthusiasm that filled the theatre when the whole company, including the stage staff, surrounded Irving and Ellen during the singing of *Auld Lang Syne*.

The whole Lyceum company and staff embarked on 11 October on the *Britannic*, a liner of the Cunard fleet, for the week's voyage to New York. Oscar Wilde and Mrs Langtry were among those who came to see them off. The ship was laden with pig-iron and rolled endlessly, to the delight of Ellen, who loved the sea whatever it did: 'The sudden leap from home into the wilderness of the waves does not give me any sensation of melancholy.' It was certainly not the Atlantic crossing which worried Ellen. It was the great distance set between herself and her home, her children, her friends, the theatres and the audiences she knew and loved. As companions, she had brought her dog, Fussy, and Miss Harries.

The British theatre was no stranger to North America. Companies of varying merit had been visiting the United States and Canada since the colonial period in the eighteenth century. After the Revolution America had developed her own companies of players to attract audiences to the theatres which had been or were being built in cities such as New York, Washington, Philadelphia and Baltimore. By the turn of the nineteenth century, actors were frequently crossing the Atlantic in both directions to appear in British and North American theatres. Among the great actors from Britain who had preceded Irving to the United States were Edmund Kean, Junius Brutus Booth (the father of Edwin Booth), William Charles Macready, Charles Kean and Charles Kemble. All of these actors made their first appearances in America between 1820 and 1832. By the time Irving arrived in 1883 New York had become the capital of the American theatre, with many fine playhouses, such as Daly's, Wallack's, the Union Square Theatre, the then Lyceum, the Park, the Bijou and the Star. Throughout the United States, in fact, the presentation of plays was developing at a phenomenal rate. By the 1880s there were some 5,000 theatres of every kind from the grand to the inglorious spread across the Continent, in addition to those in New York. There were audiences eager to welcome Irving in Philadelphia, Boston, Baltimore, Chicago, St Louis, Cincinnati, Columbus and Washington. Irving's visit was sponsored by the impresario Henry E. Abbey, who had begun his theatrical career as a cornet-player. He had been present at the midnight banquet Irving had given after the hundredth performance of *Romeo and Juliet*. Abbey was to make the vast profit of £50,000 out of the first tour of the Lyceum company in the United States.

Irving knew that he had to face a keenly critical public, where standards had been set high by the work of actors such as Booth and by the theatrical genius of Augustin Daly, whose own company was to appear in London the following year. The Comédie Française had also preceded him; the work of Coquelin and of Sarah Bernhardt was known in America. But he was conscious that he had something new to offer, his innovations in production and presentation, and his own unique approach to the parts he played. Or, as Ellen put it, 'we were pioneers, and we were *new*; to be new is everything in America'.

In one matter only did Irving feel it necessary to take precautions in advance; the handling of the American press. In addition to being a great artist, Irving was always a careful showman, and in many ways he anticipated public relations in the twentieth century in his conception of publicity and the handling of the Press. He had for some while been the friend of Joseph Hatton, the British correspondent in London of the New York *Tribune*, who, with the permission of his paper, agreed to accompany him throughout the tour not only to act as his adviser but to keep a record of the tour which would be published the following year as a book, *Henry Irving's Impression of America*. Irving also took the personal advice of William Winter, the leading dramatic critic in New York, who had visited London in 1882 and advised him to open with *The Bells*, in order that the 'agitation' of the first night should be matched by the 'agitation' on the stage. Having secured Winter's undying allegiance, Irving sent a young journalist, Austin Brereton, to represent him in New York and make all the arrangements necessary for publicity and the Press. This, coupled with Abbey's own arrangements, was the reason why the *Britannic* on her arrival off Staten Island was intercepted

M

at dawn on the morning of 21 October by the *Blackbird,* a river steamer on which Abbey had invited a formidable gathering of reporters to 'grill' Irving and Ellen. Abbey had also hired thirty Italian musicians from the Metropolitan Opera House to play 'God Save the Queen' as the ship drew alongside, while the crowd of pressmen, who had spent what was left of the night in the ladies' saloon eating breakfast, clambered up to measure their competitive wits on these latest victims of their columns. The band, having finished with 'God Save the Queen', played 'Hail the Chief' while Irving was shaving. At the same time, in another craft, a handsome yacht called the *Yosemite,* Irving's friend, the actor Laurence Barrett, was racing to meet the *Britannic,* and he became the first to greet his English fellow-artists.

Eventually, amid the confusion caused by the arrival of this second vessel, the original press conference took place. Ellen appeared excited and brought near to tears by the beauty of the crowded harbour and the wooded shores of Staten Island brown with the tints of autumn. Here she was at last in America; Hatton describes her looking across 'the broad river, the gay wooden villas ashore, the brown hills, the bright steam-craft on the river, the fast rig of the trading schooners, and above all the stars and stripes of the many flags that flutter in the breeze'. Meanwhile, the pressmen stared at Ellen, and Hatton's pen hastens to catch this historic moment:

> Escorted by Mr Barrett, and introduced by Mr Irving, she is deeply moved, as well she may be, by the novel scene. *Britannic* passengers crowd about her to say good-bye; the band is playing 'Rule Britannia'; many a gay river-boat and steamer is navigating the dancing waters; the sun is shining, flags fluttering, and a score of hands are held out to help Portia down the gangway on board the *Yosemite.*[2]

The reporter of the *Tribune* was equally busy with his notebook:

> As she stepped with a pretty little shudder over the swaying plank upon the yacht she showed herself possessed of a marked

individuality. Her dress consisted of a dark greenish-brown cloth wrap, lined inside with a peculiar shade of red; the inner dress, girt at the waist with a red, loosely-folded sash, seemed a reminiscence of some eighteenth-century portrait, while the delicate complexion caught a rosy reflection from the loose flame-coloured red scarf tied in a bow at the neck. The face itself is a peculiar one. Though not by ordinary canons beautiful it is nevertheless one to be remembered and seems to have been modelled on that of some pre-Raphaelitish saint – an effect heightened by the aureole of soft golden hair escaping from under the plain brown straw and brown velvet hat.

Irving got on famously with the interviewers. He took their measure in an instant and, according to Ellen, adopted his best Jingle manner ('refinement, bonhomie, elegance and geniality') putting both himself and them at ease by offering cigars all round. Then he told them of the enterprise that lay ahead – to presen, the whole Lyceum company in the authentic Lyceum productions, for which some seventy actors and stage staff had been brought to the United States. When Ellen's turn came, Irving whispered to her to say something pleasant, moving and bright. The first reporter asked her if he could send any message for her to her friends in England. 'Tell them I never loved 'em so much as now,' cried Ellen, and burst into tears. The reporter described her later as 'a woman of extreme nervous sensibility,' while another noted for his readers that her 'figure was spare almost to attenuation'. They questioned her about the parts she played:

'What are your favourite characters?'
'Oh, I hardly know,' she says, now fairly interested in the conversation, and turning easily towards her questioners for the first time. 'I love nearly all I play; but I don't like to cry, and I cannot help it in "Charles I". I like comedy best – Portia, Beatrice, and Letitia Hardy' ...
'You prefer to cast your fortunes with the Lyceum company?'
'Yes, certainly. ... There is no chance of my ever desiring to change. I am devoted to the Lyceum, and to Mr Irving. No

one admires him more than I do; no one knows better, I think, how much he has done for our art; no one dreams of how much more he will yet do if he is spared.'[3]

The first season at the Star Theatre in New York (the company was to return for a second season in April 1884) meant the re-hearsal and preparation of seven plays (*The Bells, Charles I, The Belle's Stratagem, Richard III, The Lyons Mail, Louis XI* and *The Merchant of Venice*) with only a single week between the company's arrival and the opening night on 29 October. The Star, originally built by James Wallack at Broadway and 13th Street in 1861, was leased to Abbey by his son, Lester Wallack, and was already a dated building in the not-too-fashionable down-town quarter of the rapidly developing island of Manhattan. This was the period when the shifting sands of 'up-town' and 'down-town' were rapidly changing. But the tickets for the first night were already in the hands of a ruthless speculator, who sold them for over five times their face value to the annoyance of genuine theatre-goers whose places in the box-office queues were occupied by well-paid touts.

Meanwhile Ellen interspersed demanding rehearsals with essen-tial social visits and sightseeing. Hatton and his wife took her with Irving to dinner at Delmonico's, where the ice-creams were a feature: 'Artistic in construction, they were triumphs of delicate colour. I think they were the *chef's* tributes to Miss Terry's supposed aesthetic taste,' wrote Ellen's host. Invitations of every kind poured in, and had to be resisted. Irving was offered the loan of a carriage, a horse, even a steam launch for the period of his stay; but he put up resolutely at Brevoort House. Flowers arrived ceaselessly for Ellen at the Hotel Dam, where she stayed in the care of Miss Harries. She cried again, but Irving took her on the first night of their stay to see a minstrel show playing at the Star; she enjoyed their 'dry, cool' humour without understanding a word of it.

New York in 1883 fascinated her immediately. She missed the hansom cabs of London and its 'poetry of the past', but responded in New York to the poetry of the present – 'gigantic, colossal, enormous'. The age of the skyscraper ('what a brutal name,' said Ellen later) had not begun, but the Statue of Liberty, 'dominating all the racket and bustle of the sea traffic of the world' was there, and so was Brooklyn Bridge, 'hung up high in the air like a vast spider's web'. She noticed also 'the dilapidated carriages in which one drives from the dock, the muddy sidewalks, the cavernous holes in the cobble-paved streets', the horse-drawn tramcars and 'the El' (New York's celebrated overhead railway), 'the first sign of *power* that one notices after leaving the boat', thundering over the streets. She was not impressed then, as she was to be on subsequent visits, by the way the women dressed: 'some of them wore Indian shawls and diamond ear-rings. They dressed too grandly in the street and too dowdily in the theatre'. But at any rate, the legends were dispelled. 'I had a vague idea that American women wore red flannel shirts and carried bowie knives, and that I might be sandbagged in the street!' Her reactions, at once naïve and shrewd, were decisively in favour of the new country. 'Was it terribly vulgar?' asked a friend when she got back to England. Ellen records her reply:

'Oh yes, if you mean by that a wonderful land – a land of sunshine and light, of happiness, of faith in the future!' I answered. I saw no misery or poverty there. Every one looked happy. What hurts me on coming back to England is the *hopeless* look on so many faces; the dejection and apathy of the people standing about in the streets. Of course there is poverty in New York, but not among the Americans. The Italians, the Russians, the Poles – all the host of immigrants washed in daily on the bosom of the Hudson – these are poor, but you can't help feeling that in their sufferings there is always hope. The barrow man of today is the millionaire of tomorrow! Vulgarity? I saw little of it. I thought that the people who had amassed large fortunes used their wealth beautifully.[4]

London, she felt on her return, seemed in comparison with New York like 'an ill-lighted village, strangely tame, peaceful and backward'. She missed 'the sunlight of America, and the clear blue skies of an evening'.

Irving also liked New York. He had brought his old dog, Charlie, with him, and to the astonishment of the regular users of the train took him for a ride on the El; Irving thought the El 'a marvellous piece of work'. He loved animals, and regarded the trotting-horse as the most characteristic thing about America that he found during his first few days there.

Tickets on the first night, which was marred by torrential rainfall, had cost many of the audience dear. Latecomers were many. Ellen was not playing, and saw the opening play, *The Bells,* from a box. Irving was nervous, and the company, according to Ellen, played too slowly. But the audience was, she says, 'a splendid one – discriminating and appreciative. We felt that the Americans *wanted* to like us. We felt in a few days so extraordinarily at home. The first sensation of entering a foreign city was quickly wiped out. The difference in atmosphere disappears directly one understands it. . . . We had transported the Lyceum three thousand miles – that was all'. As in London, the Press was not entirely unanimous in its praise of Irving. But, as he put it himself, 'It needs a little hostility here and there in the Press at home and on this side to give a wholesome flavour to the sweets.'

On the second night, when *Charles I* was played, Ellen felt overwrought and played badly, crying too much in the last act. But the audience was again responsive: 'The Americans are passionately fond of history,' she observed. The Press covered the opening night extensively. According to Hatton, 'long telegraphic dispatches were wired to the leading cities of the Union: the Associated Press sent out special messages, the London journals were wired in evidence . . . Since the Forrest-Macready riot no theatrical event had created so general an interest as the first appearance of Irving in America'. So delighted was Ellen with the first-night audience that she danced her way along the streets to her hotel, arm-in-arm with Irving and their friend, Gilbert Coleridge, son of Lord Coleridge, the Lord Chief Justice, who was on a visit to the United States.

In spite of her own dissatisfaction with herself, Ellen had excellent notices. The *New York Herald* wrote:

> Miss Terry made the impression of a charming actress. There was something very captivating in the sweetness of her manner, the grace of her movements, and the musical quality of her tones. In acting her points were made with remarkable ease and naturalness.[5]

The company played in New York for four weeks, taking for Abbey over $75,000. Allowing for the speculators' profits, the public had paid some $200,000 to see Irving. The next stage of the tour was to be in Philadelphia, where they opened in November at the Chestnut Street Theatre.

During the five weeks in New York, Irving and Ellen were fêted whenever they could spare time from the theatre. They spent a Sunday at the church of the celebrated revivalist, Henry Ward Beecher, in Brooklyn. After the service Ellen walked away arm-in-arm with Beecher and his wife; Beecher who was normally opposed to the theatre, had broken his sacred rule and gone to see Irving as Louis XI. Irving was careful to note, and pass on to Hatton, the reaction of the Beechers to Ellen. They discovered Beecher had an unexpected taste for jewels.

> He brought out from a cabinet a handful of rings, and asked me which I thought Miss Terry would like best. Then he took them to her, and she selected an *aqua marina,* which he placed upon her finger, and begged her to accept as a souvenir of her visit to Brooklyn. 'May I?' said Miss Terry to Mrs Beecher. 'Yes, my dear, take it,' said Mrs Beecher, and she did. It was quite touching to see the two women together, so different in their stations, their years, their occupations. Miss Terry was the first actress Mrs Beecher had ever known. To begin with, she was very courteous; her greeting was hospitable, but not cordial. The suggestion of coldness in her demeanour gradually thawed, and at the close of the visit she took Miss Terry into her arms, and the two women cried.[6]

Beecher had the stone set for her in the Venetian style to wear in
The Merchant of Venice. Like almost everyone within Ellen's
reach, Mrs Beecher became her friend, breaking her strict reserve
to do so. As Ellen described her:

> Mrs Beecher was very remarkable. She had a way of lower-
> ing her head and looking at you with a strange intentness,
> gravely, kindly, and quietly. At her husband she looked a
> world of love, of faith, of undying devotion. She was fond
> of me, although I was told she disliked women generally
> and had been brought up to think all actresses children of
> Satan.[7]

After commenting on the strictness with which Mrs Beecher had
been brought up (her father, she told Ellen had once thrown hot
soup all over her neck because her dress was cut to reveal it),
Ellen added: 'That a woman who had been brought up like this
should form a friendship with me naturally caused a good deal of
talk. But what did she care! She remained my true friend until
her death.'

The journey to Philadelphia was undertaken by private train,
the company's first taste of American rail travel; according to
Ellen, they normally filled eight cars, including those set aside
for the freight. Irving had his own parlour car. Ellen, used to the
English conception of privacy, soon discovered the American
aversion to this curious British taste for what was regarded as
concealment. Everyone seemed to walk freely through the coaches,
however private they were supposed to be. The journey to
Philadelphia was by American standards a short one, and they
faced in this city what were reputed to be the severest audiences
and critics in the United States. Broadly the Press was overwhelmingly enthusiastic, though opinion in Britain which was
hostile to Irving was already known to journalists on this side of
the Atlantic. The *Press*, referring to drawings which had appeared
in *Punch* satirizing the aesthetic movement in England, said of
Ellen's Ophelia, 'It is unfortunate that Du Maurier has taken Miss
Terry as the model of the aesthetic set. The curly blonde hair,

delicate face, and soft, clinging robes remind one so often of *Punch's* caricature, that it was difficult to take it seriously.'

During the second week in December the company moved to Boston, travelling in sleeping cars, the comfort of which delighted them. They played in the Boston Theatre, claimed to be the largest in the United States and seating 3,000. Irving thought it magnificent, but, as at the Star, the dressing-room accommodation proved to be poor. Once more, audiences were enthusiastic and the critics somewhat divided over Irving's Hamlet and Shylock. In Boston the first snows fell, transforming the brown of autumn into a sea of white; the snow was a foot thick and the sleighs appeared in the streets, the bells on the horses sharp and clear. Irving went for a sleigh ride with Hatton, admiring the cleanliness of the wooden houses across the river, where anthracite was burnt instead of coal, no smoke appearing from the chimneys. On 15 December Ellen, free from the theatre, was guest of honour at the Papyrus Club, where 120 members of Boston's society came to meet her to the strains of the Germania Orchestra. Hatton noticed specially the different reactions to Ellen's success shown by American women in contrast to the English:

She captivated the women, all of them. It is easier for a clever woman to excite the admiration of her sex in America than in England. A woman who adorns and lifts the feminine intellect into notice in America excites the admiration rather than the jealousy of her sisters. American women seem to make a higher claim upon the respect and attention of men than belongs to the ambitious English women, and when one of them rises to distinction they all go up with her. They share in her fame; they do not try to dispossess her of the lofty place upon which she stands. There is a sort of trades-unionism among the women of America in this respect. They hold together in a ring against the so-called lords of creation, and the men are content to accept what appears to be a happy form of petticoat government. So the women of Boston took Ellen Terry to their arms and made much of her.[8]

Christmas was spent in Baltimore, where they opened on Christmas Day itself. Many of the company, wary of Christmas festivities in the States, had brought their own Christmas puddings with them. Among these was Ellen, who brought a pudding made for her by her mother. The journey was a fearful one; the eight coaches of the private train, coming from Boston to New Jersey on the first lap of the journey, had to be transported several miles down the Harlem river, hauled by a tug-boat.

The ploughs eventually got them through to Baltimore after a journey lasting forty-two hours, and the Christmas Day audience at the Academy of Music, where they were playing only a few hours after their arrival, was small owing to the fearful conditions of mud and slush in the streets. Nevertheless, Irving had insisted on an afternoon rehearsal of *Louis XI*. Loveday employed extra coloured labour to unload the scenery from the train. After the play the following night, Irving, Ellen and a small party sat down in the hotel to Christmas dinner and ate up Sarah's pudding. 'Well done; bless her heart,' cried Irving. The coloured servants were delighted with the flames when Stoker poured brandy over the pudding and lit it up. When Hatton left for his hotel the slush had iced over, and the city lay dead and encrusted around him.

After a few nights in Baltimore, the company moved to Brooklyn, a journey of some 500 miles; then on 5 January they went on to Chicago, over 1,000 miles farther. Fussy, Ellen's terrier, insisted on running through the streets by her carriage in the middle of the night when they went to join the Brooklyn ferry, which took them to their train. Fussy, who went with Ellen everywhere in America, had his own strip of carpet to lie on, and dragged it with him everywhere if no one took it for him. Hatton gives a description of the Lyceum principals gathered on the ferry:

Mr Terriss looks like a dashing Capt Hawksley on his travels – fur coat, cap, self-possessed air, and all. Mr Tyars wears a 'Tam O'Shanter' and ulster. He might be the laird of a Scotch county, just come down from the hills. The grey-haired, pale-faced gentleman, muffled to the eyes in fur cap and comforter, is Mr Mead, whose imperial stride as 'the buried majesty of Denmark' is repeated here in response to the call of a friend in the cabin. Mr Howe carries his years and experience with an elastic gait, and a fresh, pleasant face. He is a notable figure in the group, dressed in every respect like an English gentleman – overcoat, hat, gloves. He has a breezy, country manner, and, if one did not know him, one might say 'this is a Yorkshire man, who farms his own land, going West to have a look at Kansas, and perhaps at Manitoba'. Mr Ball, the musical conductor, wears his fur collar and spectacles with quite a professional air. Norman Forbes brings with him ideas of Bond Street, and Robertson, who sings 'Hey, Nonnie', to the swells in Leonato's garden, is wrapped up as a tenor should be, though he has the carriage of an athlete. The American winter lends itself to artistic considerations in the matter of cloaks, coats, leggings, scarfs, and 'head-gear'. The ladies of the company have sought the hot shelter of the spacious saloon. Miss Terry pushes the swinging-door. 'I shall be stifled in there,' she says, retreating before a blast of hot air.[9]

Although Irving had resisted undertaking the one-night stands customary for touring companies, the immense journeys had none the less to be undertaken at what seemed now to be ever-increasing intervals. Irving had decided in Philadelphia to abandon a considerable part of the elaborate scenery he had hoped to take on tour with him. It was left in store at New York, and the productions were drastically simplified to make lading for the journeys and stage management more feasible. In a number of cases he divided his season at the larger cities into two separate stages. Though this gave him the opportunity to present a wider range of plays, it added greatly to the exhaustion of constant travel during the height of the American winter.

After Brooklyn the company moved to Chicago, where they were to appear at Haverly's Theatre for a longer stay of two weeks. The city was snowbound, though the sun was bright and clear.

The year 1884 began with the worst winter in the United States for over twenty years, and the storms were devastating. Lake Michigan was frozen over for twenty miles from the land; the shores were barricaded with ice. Hogs for Chicago's notorious stockyards were frozen to death on the freight trains. Ellen, however, was taken with Irving for sleigh-rides along the lakeside, and shown something of the prospects for expansion planned for the great city, which had been twice burned down, and twice rebuilt.

Far from being a 'barbarous' city, Chicago proved immensely responsive to the Lyceum productions, and Ellen, who had expected the people to be 'a rough, murderous, sandbagging crew', found them instead to be wonderful audiences. She claimed she never played Ophelia better in the whole of her career than she did on this visit to Chicago, and that in the mad scene she had never 'felt such sympathy'. The box-office yielded over $36,000 for the two-week season. Outside the theatre endless hospitality was pressed upon both Irving and Ellen. Then, on 20 January, they went to St Louis through snowdrifts which flanked the line, arriving finally at three o'clock in the morning. When daylight came they found the Mississippi ice-locked. After St Louis, all within the space of two weeks, came Cincinnati, Indianapolis, and Columbus. Everywhere Irving made speeches from the stage, and usually made gallant references to Ellen as his most valued partner. A return visit to Chicago was followed by two nights in Detroit; after this the company were given a brief holiday so that they could visit Niagara on 20 February.

Ellen's own reaction to Niagara is interesting, for she was always drawn to visit the Falls whenever she went to the States:

The first time I saw the great falls I thought it all more wonderful than beautiful. I got away by myself from my party, and looked and looked at it, and I listened – and at last it became dreadful and I was *frightened* at it. I would not go alone again, for I felt queer and wanted to follow the great flow of it. But at twelve o'clock, with the 'sun upon the topmost height of the day's journey', most of Nature's sights appear to me to be at their plainest. In the evening, when the shadows grow long and all hard lines are blurred, how soft, how different, everything is! It was noontide, that garish cruel time of day, when I first came in sight of the falls. I'm glad I went again in other lights – but one should live by the side of all this great-ness to learn to love it. Only once did I catch Niagara in *beauty*, with pits of colour in its waters, no one colour definite. All was wonderment, allurement, fascination. The last time I was there it was wonderful, but not beautiful any more. The merely stupendous, the merely marvellous, has always repelled me. The great canons give me unrest, just as the long low lines of my Sussex marshland near Winchelsea give me rest.[10]

While she was in Canada Ellen went tobogganning at the invitation of the Toronto Toboggan Club; it was a new sensation, like flying. She was escorted by a 'nice' Canadian who insisted on helping her up the hill afterwards. 'I didn't like *that* part of the affair quite so much,' she says; none the less, according to Hatton, she skimmed down the mountainside once again.

Much of the final part of the tour after Toronto (where the company appeared at the Opera House), consisted of return visits to cities in the States. They went from Toronto to Boston for a further week, and then on to Washington where Irving met President Arthur – 'well-read', he thought, and a 'gentleman'. After a week in Washington, the company briefly toured the cities of New England, leaving Ellen behind to enjoy a week's holiday in the capital in the meantime. This was followed by return visits to Philadelphia, Brooklyn and New York. Ellen found Philadelphia a unique American city:

Philadelphia, as I first knew it, was the most old-world place I saw in America, except perhaps Salem. Its red-brick side-walks, the trees in the streets, the low houses with their white marble cuffs and collars, the pretty design of the place, all give it a character of its own. The people, too, have a character of their own. They dress, or at least *did* dress, very quietly. This was the only sign of their Quaker origin, except a very fastidious taste – in plays as in other things.[11]

While playing in Brooklyn they stayed in New York, crossing the bridge at night after the performance was over. 'I shall never forget how it looked in winter,' wrote Ellen, 'a gigantic trellis of dazzling white, as incredible as a dream ... It looks as if it had been built by some power, not by men at all.' It was at Brooklyn that a reception was given on 29 March to Irving and Ellen by the Hamilton Club, and the *Brooklyn Times* reported Ellen's appearance in detail:

> Miss Terry, over whom some of the younger ladies were mad with curiosity, was completely hemmed in, and was given no opportunity to move about, as Irving did. She sat during intervals in an old arm-chair covered with red plush. She wore an artistic gown, with a Watteau plait. Her fair hair curled from beneath a round French hat, covered with brown velvet, and with a dark feather. At her neck was an eccentric scarf of orange-coloured satin.[12]

The final month of the tour was spent in New York at the Star Theatre. Her *Much Ado about Nothing* was staged with its full settings, and the Press had nothing but praise for Ellen's Beatrice; it was called 'her greatest triumph'. 'She permeates the railling of Beatrice with an indescribable charm of mischievous sweetness,' said the *Tribune,* and spoke of her 'pliant, effortless power, and absolute simplicity'. So the tour ended, and the company returned to London in time to see the may-blossom after the snows of America. The profits gained by the Lyceum from the tour were £11,700. Irving's management was now not merely secure but free to undertake the most ambitious projects.

So successful had the tour been that for some time before it was finished Irving and his colleagues were poring over a map of the United States planning a second visit the following autumn. Their London season did not begin until 31 May, but with the agreement reached to return in September for a tour (due to start this time in Quebec), barely three months were left in which to present plays at the Lyceum. Nevertheless, Irving managed to launch one new production in July, *Twelfth Night*, which had a poor reception from both audience and critics, and gave Ellen some initial trouble. She had to appear as Viola on the first and succeeding nights with a poisoned thumb; her arm was only saved from possible amputation by the prompt action of Bram Stoker's brother, a doctor from Ireland, who lanced the swelling one night when Ellen was half-way through the play. She had been in such pain that she had had to play the part sitting down, and the poison in her system resulted in the worst illness she was to experience while working at the Lyceum. She had still not fully recovered when the company travelled to Quebec, and her illness made it plain that Ellen needed a responsible understudy.

Before the second American tour (1884–5), Winifred Emery, daughter of the actor Sam Emery, was engaged for this purpose, and was soon to be given the opportunity to show her competence in spite of her youth. She was only twenty-two. Ellen, who was to play Viola better in America than she was in a position to do in London, was saddened to see how unpopular Irving was as Malvolio. The production had cost some £4,000, and the brief summer season at the Lyceum ended with a loss. Ellen, far from well, sailed with the company from Liverpool in September in the *Parisian*. Again, it was a rough crossing. According to L. F. Austin, Irving's secretary, who accompanied him on this second tour, Ellen suffered a 'terrible weariness' which 'nearly quenched the light in her eyes'. Though she seemed to recover once they had reached Quebec, she collapsed when they reached Montreal, and Winifred Emery had to take her place in both London and Hamilton, Ontario; she only rejoined them for Toronto. In the United States, where *Twelfth Night* proved more popular, they toured Boston, Pittsburg, Philadelphia, Chicago, Brooklyn and

New York. They spent Christmas Day in Pittsburg, and Christmas dinner was marred because the pudding Ellen had so carefully brought was discovered to reek of camphor through having been packed in one of the theatrical baskets. Nevertheless, the gentlemen of the company subscribed to give Ellen a silver tea-service to show how much they felt for her at this time.

Ellen, sick at heart for the children from whom she had been parted for nearly ten months out of the past fifteen, suddenly demanded that either Teddy or Edy be brought to her. She had, apparently, cabled Stephen Coleridge: 'Bring over one of the children.' The Hon. Stephen Coleridge, Ellen's close friend and the brother of Gilbert, was Teddy's guardian ('chosen by my mother – why I have never known') and was about to sail to New York. Teddy, now aged twelve, was sick on the voyage and took to sleepwalking on the ship during the daytime. Austin was dispatched to New York to bring him to Pittsburg; according to Austin, Teddy 'looked like a peach. . . . He is a perfect little gentleman and his love for his mother is delightful'. Apparently the little girls in the hotel wanted to date him. 'They wear captivating pinafores,' noted Austin, 'but he is not "mashed".' When they moved to Chicago in January, Teddy got his first speaking part in an Irving production – the gardener's boy, Joey, in Act I of *Eugene Aram* – and walked on in many of the other plays.

According to Austin's letters home, Ellen enjoyed herself on the journey from Chicago to Boston:

> In Henry's car seven of us had eaten an excellent lunch. Ellen *would* act as waitress and when I stole Loveday's pie and hid it, she pursued me with a fork. Teddy (Craig) has a little sledge, so when we stopped I took this out in the snow and gave him a ride. Then Ellen came and I pulled her about. Then she would make me sit on the sledge while she acted as a horse! I wonder what the Lyceum stalls would have thought if they could have seen the sight. We couldn't persuade Henry

to compromise his dignity by taking a ride. He stood on the steps of the car and gazed at us with a tragic air. Ellen was just like a schoolgirl, every bit as young in feeling as her boy.[13]

In Boston, Irving, who was never ill, developed a painful swelling on his leg which forced him to retire for three days at the end of February and let the company work without him. The result, said Austin, was near-panic. George Alexander, who had replaced Terriss, went on as Benedick with an imperfect knowledge of the lines, and in Irving's absence the reputation of the company rested squarely on Ellen. On 26 February, Austin wrote:

Last night Alexander played Benedick at very short notice and, except for a few slips, played it very well. Ellen had most of the burden on her shoulders and she rose to the occasion magnificently, rousing the audience to positive enthusiasm. I never saw her play the scene in the cathedral when Beatrice tells Benedick to kill Claudio with such fire and energy. We in the audience were all very nervous at first. Mrs Alexander ruined her fan by biting it in her excitement, and once or twice she tried to prompt her husband from a box near the stage. It was one of the most interesting evenings of the whole tour, for we sat on tenter-hooks, wondering what surprising improvement in the text would come next.[14]

The profits of this second American tour brought Irving £15,000, but work was resumed in London almost immediately on the company's return. On 2 May they reopened at the Lyceum with *Hamlet*, and were not to return to the United States until the autumn of 1887. But these two tours, amounting between October 1883 and April 1885 to some 14 months' continuous performance and a profit of £23,000, had added to the prestige of Irving as a great, if not the greatest, tragedian in the English-speaking theatre. It also proved to him beyond a doubt that the production of Shakespeare should become his prime responsibility.

It had shown him that, if London audiences and critics could at times become hostile, he could rely on his North American tours and the British provinces to bring him both popular and financial support. His confidence in himself as an actor and stage-director was confirmed, and he was determined to make Ellen Terry a permanent partner in his life upon the stage, and, he hoped, his partner in private life as well.

VII

SHAKESPEARE, MY SWEETHEART

Irving realized that Shakespeare alone could not sustain him at the Lyceum. His most urgent problem, therefore, was to obtain new plays with the right theatrical potentialities to suit his particular genius both as actor and stage-director. These plays must have pictorial possibilities to stretch the talents of his designers and scene painters, and the development of situations which were charged with the kind of emotion, either comic, pathetic, melodramatic or tragic, to which he responded as an interpretative artist. He was, of course, aware of the literary values in Shakespeare, but if Shakespeare, the dramatist, had not himself possessed such a profound sense of theatrical showmanship, Irving would never have been drawn to produce his work. It was the theatrical aspect of Shakespeare's plays rather than the poetic to which he responded, and this was the reason why he was prepared to enjoy fustian dialogue in the contemporary drama provided always that it sprang from some richly theatrical setting.

His taste was undoubtedly shared by his audiences both in Britain and America. They went to the Lyceum or to the theatres in which he appeared when on tour to share the same theatrical excitements and visual spectacles. Irving's approach in many respects anticipated that of certain film producers of today, who care little for subtleties or refinements of dialogue provided their basic theatrical instinct and their love for spectacle are fulfilled. Within the limits of this approach to the production of Shakespeare, Irving has never had an equal in the history of theatrical enterprise in Britain. But so far as contemporary plays were concerned, he was always prepared to rely on the revival of old

nineteenth-century favourites rather than venture on the production of new plays that did not stir his imagination. Nevertheless, he invested some £3,000 in commissioning new plays during
the first four years of his management at the Lyceum. Undoubtedly
the failure of the dramatists to supply the kind of script he wanted
encouraged him to concentrate during this period on touring and
to hire the Lyceum to other companies. In any case, the leading
provincial centres were of first importance in consolidating an
actor-manager's national reputation.

So the 1885 season at the Lyceum opened with revivals of
Hamlet, in which Irving naturally was the star player, and of
Olivia, which featured Ellen's performance. In *Olivia,* Terriss
played Squire Thornhill, as he had done at the Court Theatre,
and even Edy and Teddy were allowed upon the stage. Irving at
first played the Vicar so stiltedly at rehearsal that Edy, now aged
fifteen could stand his manner no longer and cried out, 'Don't
go on like that, Henry. Why don't you talk as you do to me and
Teddy? At home you *are* the Vicar.' Irving was not the least
affronted by this outburst; in fact he found the point enlightening.
'A terrible child *and* a wonderful critic,' wrote Ellen, bursting
with pride. At the opening night on 27 May, he played the part
quite simply, and gave what she called a 'lovable performance'.
However, he found this continual sweetness of manner trying,
and was heard one night on leaving the stage to mutter 'Ba – a –
a – a – a' in the wings.

But the time had come when a new play must be prepared for
the repertoire. Wills, who had revised *Olivia* for the Lyceum
production, had also been working on a much-simplified adaptation of Goethe's *Faust.* He wrote his play in verse, and with
every accommodation to Irving's needs, the result, as Laurence
Irving has remarked, was naturally much closer to Gounod than
it was to Goethe. When the script had reached a form which was
acceptable to Irving, he invited Ellen, the children and Alice and
Joe Comyns-Carr to join him in a working holiday in Germany,
where he hoped to gather local atmosphere and buy furnishings
for the production.

Joe Comyns-Carr was by 1885 a member of the 'aesthetic movement'. He had become editor of the *English Illustrated Weekly* as well as director of the Grosvenor Gallery, the first centre at which the new styles in painting were exhibited. He was also beginning to establish himself as a playwright. The circle to which he and his wife belonged included Burne-Jones and Browning as well as the painter John Sargent and Henry James, who was now devoting his attention to writing novels. Alice's particular interest was in costume design, and she was soon to take charge of all Ellen's dresses at the Lyceum. The purpose of the expedition to Nuremberg was in effect to find 'locations' from which ideas for stage sets could be developed by Hawes Craven. Irving was anxious, too, for Alice's help in devising the best results from the library of books he acquired on costume and furnishings for the period of *Faust,* which was set in the fifteenth century.

With all the exactitude of Godwin, Alice and Ellen set about their research. The men, meanwhile, soon discovered Rothenburg, the picturesque medievalism of which made it appear to be in itself a composite stage set; Hawes Craven was at once summoned by telegraph from London. Meanwhile, Ellen and Alice toured the shops of Nuremberg searching for antique jewellery and other accessories useful on the stage. Alice, who knew German, also acted as interpreter. The whole thing developed into a glorious spending spree, and the prices asked were so low that Irving often insisted on giving more than the shopkeepers suggested. Crates of everything transportable, from furnishings to costume materials, were shipped back to London. Houses opened up when the local people learned that the great English actor and actress were planning a production of *Faust;* Irving was even serenaded by the local band, and he gave them a staggeringly large present, ostensibly to spend on beer. Hawes Craven was invited inside private houses to make sketches, and Ellen, knocking with her umbrella on the great door of Nuremberg Castle, used her charm to get herself shown round the building by the small daughter of the caretaker when it was officially shut. Typical of

Ellen's informality is the way Irving was rushed into Alice's bedroom when she was only half dressed in order that Ellen should give him a better view from Alice's window of a fire that had broken out in the distance. 'What a scene if only one could get it,' cried Irving.

Alice was invited to attend the rehearsals for *Faust* to help supervise the costumes – her first experience of seeing Irving at work as a stage-director:

> Gone was the debonair, cheery holiday companion and in his place was a ruthless autocrat, who brooked no interference from anyone, and was more than a little rough in his handling of everyone in the theatre – except Nell. Irving allowed no one to watch him at work, and was ever ready with a flood of bitter satire if anyone accidentally strayed within his vision.[1]

The audience took note of Ellen's costumes, which were correctly 'period' as distinct from the draperies long established by stage convention as suitable for the character of Margaret. In one scene, considered somewhat daring, Ellen had to begin to undress on the stage. Alice wrote:

> A pair of tight sleeves and the fact that Gretchen did not have a lady's maid on the stage almost wrecked one gown. Finally Nell peeled them off inside out, but the next trouble was what garment was to be revealed underneath, for in those days we considered such things. At last we settled on a soft white petti-coat. . . . On the first night there was a buzz of admiration and much whispered comment in the stalls, which I knew spelt success, when Nell appeared.

Margaret in *Faust* called for all the pathos at Ellen's command, and became one of her favourite parts. She was trained to use a real spinning-wheel on the stage. The production, which opened on 11 December 1885, featured great set-piece scenes, such as Nuremberg Cathedral, which reached their climax in the re-markable spectacle of the Brocken scene with its infernal para-phernalia lit by a combination of electricity, gas and calcium arcs.

Irving himself, naturally, appeared as Mephistopheles, clad from head to foot in scarlet. George Alexander played Faust. Of the critics neither William Archer nor Henry James could abide the show; the production, according to James, suffered from 'an abuse of pantomimic effects'. The kind of verses into which Ellen had to infuse her pathos were of this order:

> To-morrow I must die,
> And I must tell thee how to range the graves.
> My mother the best place – next her my brother,
> Me well apart, but, dearest, not too far,
> And by my side my little one shall lie.[2]

According to Hiatt, the part of Margaret was occasionally taken over by Winifred Emery during the phenomenal run, spanning two seasons, which *Faust* achieved. Although it had cost £8,000 to produce, it ended by producing a profit for Irving of over £24,000 by 1887.

A brief interlude in the flow of production was another piece of fustian verse, *The Amber Heart* by A. C. Calmour, the rights of which Irving acquired specially for Ellen. She played the part of Ellaline for a single matinee on 7 June at the Lyceum, and with a youthful Herbert Beerbohm Tree making his initial appearance with her, Irving was for the first time able to see Ellen act from the front of the house. He was entranced, and wrote to her, 'I wish I could tell you of the dream of beauty that you realized.'[3] He regarded the piece as sufficiently successful to be revived from time to time, both in Britain and America, but whatever its short-comings it gave Ellen the chance formally to put the design of her future costumes into the hands of Alice Comyns-Carr. Until this time, they had been supervised by Patience Harris, whose brother was manager of Drury Lane Theatre; but Patience Harris favoured elaborate dresses. Ellen's taste, ever influenced by Godwin, was all for simplicity. One evening she went to dine with Alice and became excited by a plain, unstarched muslin frock she was wearing. 'I'm going to have a dress exactly like that,' she said in what Alice calls 'her usual direct manner'. 'You tell Pattie Harris just how to get that crinkly effect,' she said, 'and let her make me up one at once. It's just the thing I want for Ellaline.' 'Well,' replied Alice, 'I twisted the stuff up into a ball and boiled it in a potato steamer to get the crinkles, but I don't quite see myself suggesting that idea to Patience Harris.'

Ellen insisted, and this finally led to the loss of Pattie Harris. From 1887, Alice took over the design of all Ellen's costumes, and she secured the help of Mrs Nettleship, the wife of the painter of animals, as her dressmaker. 'In the early days, when the range of material was still very limited, I resorted more than once to methods quite as unprofessional as boiling a frock in a potato steamer,' wrote Alice.

The winter of 1887-8 saw a provincial tour of Britain (Edinburgh, Glasgow, Manchester and Liverpool) and the third American tour, which included prolonged seasons in New York, Philadelphia, Chicago and Boston, as well as a special visit on 19 March to the Military Academy at West Point, where *The Merchant of Venice* was put on after another train journey hampered by the formidable blizzards. The play was staged at West Point without scenery, just as it had been in Shakespeare's time. At the end of March the company returned to London having scored another triumph in America with the presentation of *Faust*.

No new productions were undertaken until the close of 1888. Irving, fresh from his tour of Paris with his friend Joe Comyns-Carr, returned to prepare his production of *Macbeth,* with which he planned to open on 29 December.[4] *Macbeth,* according to Ellen, 'made a turning point in the history of the Lyceum'. The discussions before the decision to produce the play was finally reached had been taking place since 1887. Ellen had wanted to play Rosalind before she grew too old, but *As You Like It* had no obvious, prominent part for Irving. *Julius Caesar* had been rejected because Irving had only wanted to play Brutus, while Antony, the part which dominates the play, was usually considered to be the actor-manager's star-turn. So, with *Macbeth* in mind, Ellen and he had gone together to Scotland in August 1887 to search for 'local colour'. Ellen later found an entry in her diary:

'Visited the "Blasted Heath". Behold a flourishing potato-field! A smooth softness everywhere. We must blast our own heath when we do *Macbeth*.'[5]

Ellen had good reason to be nervous about playing Lady Macbeth. Her two strongest qualities on the stage were charm and vivacity in comedy and command of feeling in pathos. Not that she lacked attack. She had claimed often enough that charm by itself was insufficient in an actress; to back it and make it effective across the footlights strength was needed. Had not the single line 'Kill Claudio', made her audiences freeze when she spoke it as Beatrice? But Ellen's reason for favouring plays, however indifferent, which gave her the opportunity to exercise her virtuosity for exciting laughter and tears in her audiences, and for that matter in herself, was little different from Irving's pursuit of the macabre, the sardonic and the melodramatic. These performances were their stock-in-trade. While Macbeth was a part Irving had already played (indifferently it seemed) in 1885, and wanted now to attempt once again, there appeared at first little in the character of Lady Macbeth to suit Ellen's talents. All that sustained her, once she had accepted that she must undertake the part, was Irving's complete faith in her powers. However, she also knew that he was in love with her, and thought her perfect every moment she trod the stage. Could his judgment, therefore, be fallible?

Lady Macbeth was a part with a strong tradition of interpretation. A notable succession of actresses had imposed their dramatic image on the character and made her, it seemed irrevocably, a 'fiendlike queen' after the style of Clytemnestra. But, Irving in the course of his researches had come upon a lengthy essay on the play, signed G. Fletcher, in the *Westminster Review* of 12 August 1843. This scrutinized the traditional conception of the relationship of Lady Macbeth to her husband and produced an altogether different interpretation which appealed greatly to Irving's desire for innovation. The essay in the *Westminster Review* is concerned with the character of Macbeth and Lady Macbeth, and discusses at length the tradition associated with the overwhelming performance of the part by Sarah Siddons, which drove the more susceptible ladies of the 1780s and 1790s into hysterics. Hazlitt's celebrated commendation describes Mrs Siddons at work: 'We can conceive of nothing grander,' he wrote. 'It seemed almost as if a being of a superior order had dropped from a higher sphere to awe the world with the majesty of her appearance. Power was seated on her brow, passion emanated from her breast as from a shrine; she was tragedy personified.' Though Sarah Siddons, for temperamental reasons, played Lady Macbeth in the style of a fiendish woman driven by evil motives to destroy her virtuous and yielding husband by forcing him to commit murder, her own personal notes on Lady Macbeth have fortunately survived and show that her private view of the character differed greatly from the way in which she played her. She describes Lady Macbeth as 'fair, feminine, nay, perhaps, even fragile', a woman 'captivating in feminine loveliness' and possessing 'a charm of such potency as to fascinate the mind of a hero so dauntless, a character so amiable, so honourable as Macbeth'. At the end of the play, she writes, Lady Macbeth's 'feminine nature, her delicate structure, it is too evident, are soon overwhelmed by the enormous pressure of her crimes'.[6] The essay goes on to argue that the plot to murder Duncan and seize the crown sprang originally from Macbeth, and that his wife, far from conceiving the idea, exceeded her own strength in her ceaseless efforts to give him the courage to complete the killing he had himself suggested.

If Mrs Siddons, England's greatest tragic actress, was capable of remoulding the celebrated character in order to suit her peculiar talents on the stage, even against her better judgment of the part, why should not Ellen abandon this seemingly false tradition and play the part in *her* own way? Ellen, who had a habit of arguing with herself on paper, pursued these thoughts to their logical conclusion!

Yes, Shakespeare's Lady Macbeth and Mrs Siddons's Lady Macbeth are two *distinct* persons and totally different ... of course as part of a *whole* Shakespeare's is the one which it *wd* be right to try and enact, but as a single, forceful dramatic figure, I believe Mrs Siddons's was far the most *effective* . . . far finer and probably beyond imitation. I cannot understand why Mrs Siddons shd write *down one* set of ideas upon the subject and carry out a totally different plan. Why? . . . because *one* way is well within her methods and physical presentation.

Now which of 3 courses – for and against?

1. Make up in every way. In spite of thin lips – build **up** thick ones. In spite of Roman nose and flashing black eyes – build a nez retroussé and weak, gentle, irresolute eyes – in place of nature's loud voice – low and soft, seductive. Be in fact (I'm afraid) a great actor – deceive audience into at least *thinking* all this.

2nd Method. Play to the best of one's powers – one's own possibilities. Adapt the part to my own personality with the *knowledge* that sometimes nature *does* freak and put an honest eye into a villain's head.

3rd Method. Don't play at all.[7]

Irving, preoccupied once more with another embodiment of evil, made Macbeth, in the words of his grandson Laurence Irving, 'a barbaric chieftain entirely lacking moral fibre and the courage of his dark convictions'. Having prepared his customary acting edition of the play, Irving had it printed and bound with inter-leaved blank pages for use by his players and production helpers. Still with grave misgivings about her capacity to fulfil a bold new conception of Lady Macbeth, Ellen settled down with the leather-bound Lyceum text and started to make a remarkable series of annotations. These scribbled notes represent in part a search for confirmation of anything which is essentially feminine in the character, and in part suggestions to herself as to how best to realize this on the stage. Her notes are a kind of conversation with herself – words are heavily underlined, written large or small for emphasis, decorated with exclamation marks. There is nothing academic about them – they are the immediate personal reactions of one woman, an actress, to another woman, Shake-speare's lady. On the flyleaves to her working scripts Ellen Terry began to sketch her approach, first to Macbeth himself. 'A man of great *physical* courage frightened at a *mouse,*' she writes. 'A man who talks and talks and works himself up, rather in the style of an early Victorian hysterical heroine. His was a *bad* Nature and he became reflected in his wife. M. must have had a neglectful mother – who never taught him the importance of self-control. He has *none*! and he is obsessed by the one thought *Himself.*' Then she considers Lady Macbeth in relation to her husband: 'A woman (all over a *woman*) who *believed in Macbeth,* with a lurking knowledge of his weakness but who never *found him out* to be nothing but a brave soldier *and a weakling,* until that damned party in a parlour – "Banquet Scene" as it is called. Then, "some-thing too much of this" she says and gives it up – her mistakable softening of the brain occurs – she turns quite gentle – and so we are prepared for the last scene madness and death.' Later Ellen adds: 'Yes, Lady M. was ambitious. Her husband's letters aroused intensely the desire to be a Queen – true to woman's nature, even more than to a man's to crave power – and power's display.'

Her conception of Lady Macbeth, taken scene by scene, is humane and penetrating. Her controversial interpretation broke the hitherto inflexible mould in which the part had been confined, that of the cruel and bitter-tongued virago. The new Lady Macbeth was a scheming and ambitious but very feminine woman who does not know her husband well enough to realize the profound evil that lies in him. She realizes her own limitations, as the great 'unsexing' speech reveals. Ellen knew that this speech would be the first exacting test of her capacities as a tragic actress. Beside the speech she notes: 'I *must* try to do this: 2 years ago I could not *even* have tried.' This Lady Macbeth is as afraid of her own weakness as she is of her husband's lack of nerve to under-take the action. So she beguiles him into murder in order to fulfil their secret longing for the throne, and uses every feminine device at her command to goad him into the single, necessary action. But Ellen cannot help her sense of humour breaking out:

'Be damned *charming*,' she writes, no doubt with an irony in the underlining. 'Now see – here is a beautiful plan which your wife has thought all out (the hellcat).' After the murder, she must show that Lady Macbeth does not know what to do with her husband except save him by taking the dagger back herself, and she sees the celebrated faint as perfectly genuine once Lady Macbeth realizes that they are saved by Macbeth's 'masterly explanation'. From now on, it is Macbeth who takes the lead, his true nature no longer inhibited; Lady Macbeth has only one further supreme moment in the relationship – when she has to save her husband from disaster in the banqueting scene. However, even during the murder scene, Ellen cannot help expressing some sympathy for Macbeth; against the line, 'Methought I heard a voice cry "Sleep no more . . ."' she writes: 'The most awful line in the play, if one realizes what it means to his guilt-burdened mind. Poor wretch, he does not sleep after this.' After the banquet, which Ellen calls the 'royal tea-party', Lady Macbeth collapses, leaving all initiative to her husband. She is finished, and the sleepwalking scene is her finale.

In the flyleaves at the end of her copies, Ellen Terry once more summed up the results of her study of the play. Of Macbeth she says:

'With all his rant and bombast he had "Lucidity" – and never belittled his crime – *he* never said, "a little water clears us of this deed". He was far-seeing – therefore he had less excuse – for his crime was more deliberate – the witches turned his head (as witches will do!). His aim was kingdom.'

But Lady Macbeth, she says,

'is full of womanliness' and 'is capable of *affection* – she *loves her husband* – Ergo – *she is a woman* [doubly underlined] – and she knows it, and is half the time *afraid* whilst urging Macbeth not to be afraid as she loves a *man*. Women love *men* [doubly underlined].

On 6 November, she wrote to her friend Calmour, author of

The Amber Heart, from Margate, where she had retired to con-
tinue her study of Lady Macbeth. 'I have seen *very few* people, and
I have been absorbed by Lady Mac, who is *quite unlike* her portrait
by Mrs Siddons! She is *most feminine,* and altogether, now that I
have come to *know the lady well,* I think the *portrait is much the
grander of the two!* But I mean to try at a true *likeness,* as it is more
within my means.'

Yet Ellen remained uncertain of herself. Irving wrote to encourage her while in the throes of the crowd rehearsals:

> Tonight, if possible, the last act. I want to get these great
> multitudinous scenes over and then we can attack *our* scenes. . . .
> Your sensitiveness is so acute that you must suffer sometimes.
> You are not like anybody else. You see things with such
> lightning quickness and unerring instinct that dull fools like
> myself grow irritable and impatient sometimes. I feel confused
> when I'm thinking of one thing, and disturbed by another.
> That's all. But I do feel very sorry afterwards when I don't
> seem to heed what I so much value. . . . I think things are going
> well, considering the time we've been at it, but I see so much
> that is wanting that it seems almost impossible to get through
> properly.[8]

After the dress rehearsal he wrote again:

> You will be splendid in this part. The first time it has been
> *acted* for many years.
>   The sleeping scene will be beautiful too – the moment you
> are in it – *but* Lady M should certainly have the appearance of
> having got out of bed, to which she is returning when she
> goes off. The hair to my mind should be wild and disturbed,
> and the whole appearance as distraught as possible, and dis-
> ordered. . . .

Macbeth opened at the Lyceum on 29 December 1888: 'Mother
was in agony over it,' remarked Gordon Craig. It was, as had
been forecast, an immediate cause of controversy in the press,
but this only encouraged audiences to crowd out the theatre for

150 nights. As always with Irving, the spectacle was tremendous; a popular Scottish landscape painter, Keeley Halsewell, had designed the sets which Hawes Craven and his men had carried out; Sir Arthur Sullivan had composed the incidental score. The crowd scenes were magnificently dressed: 'Henry brought his manipulation of crowds to perfection,' wrote Ellen.

By the opening night, curiosity was at its height. The *Pall Mall Gazette* had even published a mock interview with Shakespeare, who was represented as saying:

> I think of her as a handsome woman, no doubt, and 'feminine' most certainly; Semiramis and Messaline were intensely feminine. If you come to that, who was ever more feminine than Mrs Siddons herself? . . . A fragile Lady Macbeth may be conceivable, for genius can do anything – it made Pritchard genteel and Garrick six feet high – but other things being equal, I'd back a thirteen-stone woman against a seven-stone sylph in the part.[9]

The *St James' Gazette* had an article on the day itself attempting to forecast how she might interpret the part, for this was, of course, a carefully kept secret. Comyns-Carr, however, wrote a pamphlet discussing the character along the same lines as the long-forgotten piece in *The Westminster Review*. Ellen, with Alice to design her dresses for her, was determined to present a striking picture to the eye; she was discovered, in the words of Hiatt, 'with blanched face and copper-coloured hair, clad in magnificent draperies which glowed with the metallic lustre of the wings of green beetles'. Alice herself describes how she conceived Ellen's most celebrated costume:

> The dress which was most talked about was that which Nell wore as Lady Macbeth in the first scene, and it was in this costume that Sargent painted her. The designing of this dress had cost me many anxious hours of thought, for in those times there was not such a wealth of material to choose from as is the case today, and more often than not the exact colours I

needed to get my effects could not be obtained in England at all. I was anxious to make this particular dress look as much like soft chain armour as I could, and yet have something that would give the appearance of the scales of a serpent. Suddenly I had an inspiration. I had just crocheted a little shawl in soft woollen tinsel for my mother, and, seeing it hanging on the back of a chair, I said to myself, 'That's how I'll get my effect.' Mrs Nettleship brought the fine yarn for me in Bohemia – a twist of soft green silk and blue tinsel. I then cut out the patterns from the diagrams in the wonderful costume book of Voillet le Duc, and the yarn was crocheted to match them. When the straight thirteenth-century dress with sweeping sleeves was finished it hung beautifully, but we did not think that it was brilliant enough, so it was sewn all over with real green beetle-wings, and a narrow border in Celtic designs, worked out in rubies and diamonds, hemmed all the edges. To this was added a cloak of shot velvet in heather tones, upon which great griffins were embroidered in flame-coloured tinsel. The wimple, or veil, was held in place by a circlet of rubies, and two long plaits twisted with gold hung to her knees.[10]

This dress, which so excited Sargent, made Oscar Wilde remark:

'Judging from the banquet, Lady Macbeth seems an economical housekeeper, and evidently patronizes local industries for her husband's clothes and the servant's liveries; but she takes care to do all her own shopping in Byzantium.' Sargent's reaction is described by Alice Comyns-Carr:

When Ellen Terry came on in the first scene reading the letter, in the green and blue gown like chain armour, studded with real beetle-wings, he said: 'I say!' But it was during the next scene, when Nell in the same dress but wearing over it the heather velvet cloak embroidered with fiery griffins, swept out of the castle keep to greet the old King that Sargent first conceived the original idea for his famous picture of Ellen

Terry as Lady Macbeth. He made a study in oils of her descending between lines of bowing Court ladies, but then, deciding that a portrait of Ellen alone would be more effective, he forsook his first idea, and painted the picture now in the Tate Gallery, which shows her, a simple, exultant figure, with her arms stretched up holding the crown triumphantly over her head, and the sweeping sleeves of her gown hanging on each side to the ground.[11]

The critics were by no means convinced by this new interpretation of Macbeth and Lady Macbeth, although Irving, according to Ellen, himself preferred his performance in this part even to his Hamlet. Ellen felt his conception was right ('clear as daylight'), but his carrying out of the conception unequal. 'He was tempted by his imagination to do more than any actor can do.' How she wished that he, and not herself, could have undertaken the sleepwalking scene: 'Henry's imagination was always stirred by the queer and the uncanny. This was a great advantage in *Macbeth* in which the atmosphere is charged with strange forces. How marvellously he could have played Lady Macbeth in the sleepwalking scene, which ought above all things to be uncanny.' There were even rumours that she wanted to resign from the part, and these were mentioned in *Punch,* in which two articles on the production appeared. Irving at once scotched the rumour in a letter to Burnand, the dramatic critic; 'Ellen Terry has made the hit of her life. She really begins to like her Ladyship and plays it wonderfully.' But Labouchère had written of Irving in *Truth:*

> Clever as ever, alert to catch the shifting straws of public opinion, knowing full well that Miss Ellen Terry is, perhaps, the most popular actress on the stage at the present time, he has persuaded himself that the Lady Macbeth who, thirteen years ago, was a shrew of the most determined type ... is in reality, the sweetest, most affectionate character that ever drew breath ... A *Macbeth* based on recollection of *Eugene Aram,* is now accompanied by an aesthetic Burne Jonesy, Grosvenor Gallery version of Lady Macbeth, who roars as gently as any

sucking dove. . . . At the same time it should be stated, in all
fairness, that such a magnificent show as the new *Macbeth* has
never been seen before. Mr Irving has proved that he is the
first of living stage-managers, a man with a mind to conceive
and a head to direct, for all the boasted Shakespearian revivals
of Macready, Phelps, and Charles Kean pale before the new
Lyceum splendours.[12]

Two critics have left us their exact impressions of Ellen's performance. Here is part of the notice in the *Daily Chronicle*:

> Without such an affectionate yet determined woman as Miss
> Ellen Terry makes Lady Macbeth, the newly-invested Thane of
> Cawdor, as illustrated by Mr Irving, would never have laid
> violent hands on Duncan. After being the confidant she becomes
> the guide, and urges him forward to ruin whilst she believes it
> will bring him peace. . . . The masterful spirit of Miss Ellen
> Terry's Lady Macbeth when employed upon her husband's
> advancement is still more noticeable in the second act. With
> her homely dress of sober hue, and with bright auburn tresses
> that are sometimes allowed to fall in two long plaits almost to
> her feet, the Lady Macbeth of Miss Terry has no outward re-
> semblance to any other character she has played. The voice is
> the same, her movements are as eloquent as the words she has
> to speak, but all else is different. The new Lady Macbeth feels
> that her husband may fail at the very last, so she nerves herself
> to give him renewed courage.[13]

And here, part of the review in the *Morning Post*:

> The woman who, in a quaint and indescribably beautiful
> costume, read by the light of the fire the letter of her husband,
> pausing to re-read the passages that most impressed or astonished
> her, and that then threw herself back in the long oaken chair
> to dream of the arrival and the fortunes of her king and lover,
> might have stood in the Court at Camelot. . . . No less wonder-
> ful was the creature who, with hair blanched with sorrow and
> eyes steeped in a slumber that was not rest, stood like a spirit at

the foot of the stairs, as she came to visit the scenes of past suffering and crime, and sought in vain to cleanse her hands from the imaginary stain. A creature so spiritual, so ineffable, has never perhaps been put on the stage. Is this Lady Macbeth? Who shall decide? That it is not the Lady Macbeth of tradition or of Mrs Siddons we know. It is scarcely a Lady Macbeth we realize. It is, perhaps, one of which we have dreamed. Shakespeare, at least, it may be said, would have hailed it with delight as revelation, if not as interpretation. In the great murder scene, very powerfully played, this was not the woman to fill Macbeth with her own resolution. It might, however, be the woman to madden him to things beyond his customary reach.

What Ellen treasured most was, perhaps, a letter she had from her father: 'Nelly dear your performance of Lady Macbeth was *fine* ... Don't allow the critics to interfere with your own view of the part ... There will be thousands who will think otherwise, and, who knows, but that the experts may, before the end of the run of the piece, be converted ... I had no opportunity to tell you on Saturday how beautiful you looked, how exquisite were your dresses ... It was a grand performance of a most intellectual conception. ... My joy was prodigious: Always your loving Daddy.'[14]

'There was much diversity of opinion about my Lady Macbeth,' wrote Ellen. 'It was a satisfaction to me that some people saw what I was aiming at. Sargent saw it, and in his picture is all that I meant to do.' Sargent's portrait was exhibited at the New Gallery in Regent Street, where there were, according to Ellen, 'dense crowds round it day after day'. Oscar Wilde, who had moved with his wife Constance to a house in Tite Street, decorated for him by Godwin and Whistler, was delighted to find Sargent's studio near by. He wrote: 'The street that on a wet and dreary morning has vouchsafed the vision of Lady Macbeth in full regalia magnificently seated in a four-wheeler can never again be as other streets: it must always be full of wonderful possibilities.'[15]

Ellen liked the portrait. 'It is a splendid picture,' she wrote to her friend Amy Dickens. 'Oh dear, oh dear, if I were *paid* for all this sitting, my face would be my fortune.' And in another letter: 'The carriage is at the door to take me to Mr Sargent's – I'm dressed up as Lady Mac (and looking 'a sight' in the daytime!).' In her memoirs she writes:

> I have always loved the picture, and think it is far more like me than any other. Mr Sargent first of all thought that he would paint me at the moment when Lady Macbeth comes out of the castle to welcome Duncan. He liked the swirl of the dress, and the torches, and the women bowing down on either side. He used to make me walk up and down his studio until I nearly dropped in my heavy dress, saying suddenly as I got the swirl: 'That's it, that's it!' and rushing off to his canvas to throw on some paint in his wonderful inimitable fashion! But he had to give up *that* idea of the Lady Macbeth picture all the same. I was the gainer, for he gave me the unfinished sketch, and it is certainly very beautiful.[16]

Ellen's humanizing treatment of Shakespeare's women characters was to be seen in four plays at the Lyceum, all of them in the range of tragedy – Katherine in *Henry VIII* (1891), Cordelia in *King Lear* (1892), Imogen in *Cymbeline* (1895) and Volumnia in *Coriolanus* (1901). Her only opportunity for comedy lay in the revivals which Irving constantly introduced, more especially while on tour, but Ellen during the 1890s had to reckon with the hard fact that she was no longer young. She was already forty-six when she first played Cordelia, and forty-nine when she first played Imogen. But her embodiment of these parts remained youthful and imaginative. In all she played eleven Shakespearean characters with Irving;[17] after his death she composed a series of lecture-recitals in which she discussed not only the characters she had played, such as Beatrice, Portia, Lady Macbeth, Desdemona and Juliet, but some of the women she never played, such as Rosalind and Cleopatra.

Shakespeare, she once said to Irving, was the only man she had ever really loved. She implied that she had turned to Shakespeare's

works for comfort in the days of her misery after the parting
from Watts when, as she put it, she had forsworn the society of
men, yet wanted the sympathetic attention of a lover. She discovered then, if not before, the fascination of Shakespeare's
women, whom she came to regard almost as if they were real
people. 'Wonderful women!' she said to the audiences at the
lectures she was to give in later years. 'Have you ever thought how
much we all, and women especially, owe to Shakespeare for his
vindication of women in those fearless, high-spirited, resolute and
intelligent heroines?' She believed Shakespeare had liberal ideas
about women which long pre-dated the 'Women's Movement' of
Victorian times. Shakespeare obviously had a predilection for
'women of strong character, high-spirited, quick-witted and
resourceful'. These were the women Ellen liked to interpret.
'Shakespeare,' says Ellen, after praising the magnificent stand of
Emilia against the half-mad Othello, 'is one of the very few
dramatists who seem to have observed that women have more
moral courage than men.'

In her lectures Ellen grouped the women in Shakespeare's plays
separately as 'triumphant' and 'pathetic', though this was for
convenience only, because, as she says, 'Shakespeare's characters
are far too idiosyncratic to fit this or that mould.' She likes Don
Pedro's description of Beatrice – one of the triumphant women
– as a 'pleasant-spirited lady' and quotes a French medieval description of Margaret of France as the image in which she played
Beatrice: 'Her eyes are clear, and full of fire; her mouth is fine –
intellectual with something of irony, of benevolence, and of
reserve. A singular countenance where the mind and the heart
both rule.' 'Beatrice's repartee in her encounters with Benedick,'
said Ellen in her lectures on triumphant women, 'can easily be
made to sound malicious and vulgar. It should be spoken as the
lightest raillery, with mirth in the voice, and charm in the manner.'
Although she tends, as Lucentio says, to be over-shrewd of tongue,
'yet when her heart speaks seriously, Beatrice listens seriously'.

It is from these lectures, as well as from her notes in the privately-
printed interleaved copies of the plays which Irving prepared,

that we learn most about Ellen's response to the principal characters she played. Portia, of course, is another triumphant woman,
and another high-spirited Renaissance lady. 'There are', she says,
'several ways in which Portia can be played – I have tried five or
six ways myself, but I have always come back to the Italian way,
the Renaissance way.' She hated the German tradition of playing
Portia for low comedy – wearing a fierce moustache in the trial
scene, for instance. She saw Portia as a great and wealthy lady,
used to a fine and very independent way of life, and to wearing
beautiful clothes. Her speech of submission to Bassanio, who is
'so manifestly inferior to her', is a courteous gesture which in no
way threatens her independence of character. She ended her
lecture on the triumphant women (Beatrice, Rosalind, Volumnia,
the Merry Wives and Portia) with a recital of the mercy speech,
which, she says, she regarded as 'a thing "ensky'd and sainted"',
like the Lord's Prayer, with "the same beautiful simplicity and
the same beautiful ideal of justice".'

By using the term 'pathetic' for the other group of Shakespeare's women, Ellen points out that she does not mean they
lacked character or courage. Rather, she sees them as 'small and
slim, of rather frail physique'. The pathetic group include,
notably, Lady Macbeth; 'I don't conceive of Lady Macbeth as a
robust muscular woman, but as a delicate little creature, with
hyper-sensitive nerves.' She regards her, as we have seen, as
sustaining her husband to the point of his own self-destruction.
'In plain prose,' says Ellen, 'she has a nervous breakdown' and dies
of remorse. The other pathetic women she considers to be Viola,
Desdemona, Juliet, Cordelia, Cleopatra, Katherine, Hermione and
Imogen. She had played all of these except Cleopatra, whom she
believes should be played in an ebullient, shallow manner. Her
passion is neither great nor sincere, yet that is how she is mostly
played. 'Shakespeare,' says Ellen, 'has done what no other writer,
novelist, dramatist or poet has done – told the truth about the
wanton.'

With the exception of Ophelia, Ellen is against the 'pathetic'
women being presented as if they were weak. Desdemona, in

particular, is a strong-minded girl, with 'something of the potential nun in her'. She has rejected all suitors except Othello, and to him she 'consecrates' her love, overthrowing convention for his sake. Perhaps Ellen for the moment conceives Desdemona in her own image:

> I have said she is a woman of strong character. Once she has consecrated herself to Othello, she is capable even of 'downright violence' of all the conventions for his sake. But I think by nature she is unconventional. Othello's doubts that she is chaste are usually made to seem absolutely monstrous in the theatre, because Desdemona's unconventionality is ignored. She is not at all prim or demure; on the contary, she is genially expressive, the kind of woman who being devoid of coquetry behaves as she feels. Her manner to Cassio might easily fertilize the poisonous seed of suspicion Iago has sown in Othello's mind. The pertinacity with which she begs Othello to reinstate Cassio does not strike me as evidence that she is a rather foolish woman, lacking in insight. Let an actress give a charming 'I'm really not asking much of you' tone to Desdemona's suit to her husband, and a very different impression will be produced. Her purity of heart and her charity (charity 'thinketh no evil') are sufficient explanation of her being slow to grasp the situation. It is not until she has been grossly insulted and brutally assaulted that she understands. Her behaviour from that dreadful moment should surely convince us that she is not a simpleton, but a saint.[18]

Hence the marvellous contrast devised by Shakespeare of opposing Emilia's sexual cynicism to Desdemona's pure faith in love which is expressed in the scene between them shortly before Othello murders his wife.

Juliet, she says, also possesses this 'inward freedom' which produces the moral courage Shakespeare valued in women. Juliet – 'this passionate young Italian' – achieves a maturity well beyond her fourteen years; and Ellen supports the traditional saying that 'an actress cannot play Juliet until she is too old to look like

Juliet'. Like Desdemona, once she loves she is fearless in love, and her spirit is never broken, even by the worst terrors of her situation; the contrast Shakespeare makes here is between the worldliness and depravity of the Nurse and the pure fire of Juliet's unalterable love. The greatness of Juliet's final speech must test the most experienced actress. 'An actress must be in a state of grace to make that speech hers! She must be on the summit of her art where alone complete abandonment to passion is possible!'

Ellen was to play the younger women of Shakespeare until she was herself nearly fifty. She first appeared as Cordelia in the Lyceum production of *King Lear* in 1892. 'Cordelia is a most difficult part,' she said, 'so little to say, so much to feel.' Still waters run deep, thought Ellen. 'Rarely does an actress fathom the depths of those still waters.' Yet the continuity of the Lyceum productions demanded that Ellen encompass the mature Queen Katherine of Aragon in the same year as she played the youngest of Lear's daughters. 'Perhaps some of you,' she said to the audience who came to her lectures, 'have a daughter, who like Cordelia is extremely reticent, loves you dearly, but never gushes. Perhaps there is a daughter here who knows exactly what Cordelia means when she says her love is "more richer than her tongue".'

Imogen was another of the much-wronged, much-loving women Ellen was called upon to play comparatively late in life. Though then forty-eight, Imogen was a part she loved. 'When I am asked which is my favourite part, her name rises spontaneously to my lips. She enchants me, and so I can find no fault in her.' Again, there seems an unconscious affinity between this Shakespearean character and Ellen herself. 'Imogen is impulsive above all things. Her impulses are always wholehearted ones too. She never does anything by halves! . . . So swift are Imogen's changes of mood that the actress who plays her has hard work to make her a consistent character. Her heart has reasons that reason cannot understand.' Ophelia alone of all the 'pathetic' women seemed to Ellen weak and fearful: 'Her brain, her soul and her body are all pathetically weak.' Frightened of her father, above all frightened of Hamlet, whom she is incapable of understanding, madness is incipient in her nature, and, 'poor derelict', she is left alone, and unguarded, to fall away in death. Ellen, in her old age, always concluded her lecture on the 'pathetic' women by re-enacting for her audience the madness scene from *Hamlet*.

Of the older women in Shakespeare, Ellen first played Katherine in 1892 and Volumnia in 1901. She was convinced that, however many collaborators Shakespeare had for *Henry VIII*, he wrote every line of Queen Katherine. 'Who but Shakespeare could have shown in a few deft touches how the elements are mixed up in her nature, pride and humility, rebelliousness and resignation, hardness and softness? She reminds her of Imogen and of Hermione in *The Winter's Tale*. 'The loyalty Hermione shows to the husband who has slandered her, without abating a jot of her dignity, reminds us of Katherine's to Henry. Hermione has been cruelly and falsely accused. Yet she has more pity for her accuser than for herself.' Katherine, thought Ellen, is very Spanish, and showed 'Shakespeare's sensitivity to racial characteristics', like the Italian quality of Juliet and the Roman quality of Volumnia, who was not a 'pathetic' woman, of course, but 'triumphant'. Shakespeare's love of contrast leads him to place this 'lion-hearted, patriotic mother' against Virgilia, Coriolanus's timid, sensitive wife. Volumnia is a noble Roman. When Ellen played her, she knew she was miscast.

Irving's golden successes of the 1880s were rarely equalled during the succeeding decade, which proved for him a costly and at times even a disastrous period. In spite of his unflagging energy, his age began to tell during the later 1890s, when he was approaching sixty. The costs of his productions rose steadily without the assurance of an equal rise in the box-office returns. Above all, newer, alien forms of drama were emerging – the realistic, contemporary writing of Pinero and Henry Arthur Jones, the wit of Wilde, the theatrical tornado led by Ibsen as well as the critical revolution represented by Bernard Shaw, whose pitiless attacks on Irving and whose adulation of Ellen added to the excitement of dramatic criticism in the 1890s.

Of the Shakespearean productions, *King Lear* (1892), *Cymbeline* (1896) and *Coriolanus* (1901) between them barely accounted for six months, and could not recover their production costs. *Henry VIII* (1892) on which Irving spent £12,000, ran eight months – 203 performances – but even so the season resulted in a loss. Only by undertaking long and arduous tours, more especially in the United States, could Irving hope to sustain the lavish quality of his productions. Apart from *Coriolanus,* in which both he and Ellen were miscast, Irving's performances in the other plays were interesting, to say the least. As Wolsey in *Henry VIII* he found himself compared to Cardinal Manning, who died a few days after the opening performance on 5 January 1892. According to Hiatt, Ellen played the part of Katherine with great tenderness; indeed, he wondered if she were not 'too winning, too graceful, too obviously attractive'. There was, he says, 'no hint of the matron', though in the trial scene she showed dignity and a 'fiery scorn' of a surprising strength. Again she performed in the shadow of Sarah Siddons, but the result, according to Percy Fitzgerald, was an 'astonishing' achievement. 'She let us see the woman's heart,' writes Pemberton. Yet she herself says, 'The production was magnificent, but I was not keenly interested in it, or in my part.'[19]

Ellen's warmth and tenderness as Cordelia, according to Clement Scott, saved Irving's production of *King Lear.* Irving miscalculated his performance on the opening night, and grew inaudible in his efforts to create a study in imbecility. Ellen herself was forced to admit to him that she could not distinguish what he was saying. Ellen wrote to her friend Stephen Coleridge:

It was the nervousness of a first night: he is perfectly in-telligible *now.*

I have told him the 'whole truth', but no number of people 'telling him the truth' could make him articulate on the first night of a great part.

It was *not* perversity with him oddly enough it is a want of knowledge of *where he does it!*

I told him last night of 3 separate examples, and he went on the stage and spoke those three bits as clearly as they could be spoken by anyone. It's strange that *such* an actor as he shd fail to understand *how to convey to a crowd*. He understands himself and thinks everybody else does![20]

With a brilliant act of readjustment, Irving changed the manner of his speech, discarding the assumed voice and returning to his own. The result, according to Graham Robertson, who went back to the Lyceum within a week, was 'magnificent, its pathos terrible'. But the damage had been done, and the audiences fell away. But, Graham Robertson adds, Ellen's Cordelia was 'lovely and gracious, she *was* Cordelia, as she had been Portia, though I regret to say that, when studying the character, she wrote "Fool" in large letters against the young lady's refusal to admit her love for her old father'.

As Imogen, Ellen at the age of forty-nine, according to Graham Robertson, achieved:

Such a radiant embodiment of youth that when she first appeared the audience gasped – there was a silence, then thunders of applause. In the 'Milford Haven' scene her outburst of almost delirious happiness dazzled and amazed: she seemed a creature of fire and air, she hovered over the stage without appearing to touch it. And as a companion picture was Irving's 'Iachimo', no scowling sinister villain, but a fascinating Italian gentleman, entirely without morals but with exquisite manners and a compelling charm which explained his successes as a liar and scoundrel.[21]

A. B. Walkley wrote that Imogen would

rank amongst her first-rate achievements. Sweet and tender, the soul of trust and innocence, full of girlish spirits in the few moments when cruel fate ceases to vex her, piteous beyond measure in her grief, radiant in her joy – hers is a figure that dwells in the memory as one of absolute beauty.

Ellen's Imogen was a wonderful conclusion to over thirty years of achievements in the youthful parts of Shakespeare.[22]

Of the new plays by contemporary authors produced by Irving during the 1890s, Ellen appeared in eight between 1889 and 1899. In many of them her parts were nominal appearances in order to keep her before the public. The contemporary plays were increasingly chosen as vehicles for Irving's overwhelming talent. For Ellen, conscious of her increasing age and never vain of her achievements, such parts as Lucy Ashton in *Ravenswood* (1890), Rosamund in *Becket* (1893), Catherine in *Peter the Great* (1898), Sylvia Wynford in *The Medicine Man* (1898) and Clarice in *Robespierre* (1899) were saddening revelations that the great days of the Lyceum partnership were gradually declining. Once more she was becoming the 'useful' actress, but her complaints were rare. Of Rosamund in *Becket* she said to Graham Robertson: 'I don't know what to do with her. She is not there. She does not exist. I don't think that Tennyson ever knew very much about women, and now he is old and has forgotten the little that he knew. She is not a woman at all.' Yet she made the most of everything she was given to do. One night Robertson was standing with her behind the scenes before her entrance from a gallery after Rosamund has witnessed the murder of Becket in the cathedral. He became aware of her complete identification with the woman she was playing:

> I looked round and found Rosamund de Clifford beside me, pale and breathless, her eyes fixed and full of a gradually growing horror, deaf and blind to everything but the mimic murder on the dark stage below. The dying words of Becket floated up – 'Into Thy hands, O Lord, into Thy hands' – she clutched my shoulder tightly, seeming to struggle for speech which would not come, until at last a long gasping cry broke from her lips as she tottered forward and began to run down the steps. Even as she ran the moment of identity with Rosamund passed, and Ellen Terry whispered back, 'Missed it again! I never can *time* that cry right.'[23]

As Rosamund, he thought, 'she looked her loveliest, especially in the rich gown of her first entrance, a wonderful, Rossettian effect of dim gold and glowing colour veiled in black, her masses of bright hair in a net of gold and gold hearts embroidered on her robe'. Nevertheless the part was supernumerary.

As Lucy Ashton in *Ravenswood* she enjoyed her mad death scene, and one night after it was finished, she hid on the stage with Graham Robertson beside what appeared to be an immobile rock. But during the transformation scene at the close of the play, the rock began to move in the fading light, and it was only by a swift and dexterous crawl that the audience did not see them as the scenery disappeared. Ellen, says Robertson, was 'full of a youthful desire to be where she ought not to be and to see what was not intended for inspection'. Irving saw nothing of this escapade; he had gone to his dressing-room.

Ellen always took an interest in what she wore. She delighted in the ingenuity exercised by Alice to get just the right effects for the stage – regardless of the unusual origin of the cloths she used. For Katherine of Aragon Ellen wore black satin the wrong side out – producing just the *right* steely silver 'because it was the *wrong* side!' The search for the right gold for another dress ended up with the purchase of seven gold lace antimacassars at Whiteleys; the result was magnificent on the stage, but excessively heavy to wear. Mrs Nettleship made her a bejewelled cloak for *King Arthur* which was so heavy she could scarcely breathe; 'Nettle's' seamstresses had to stand off-stage snipping away jewels to lighten the cloak while Ellen stood in the wings. What Ellen wore on the stage often affected women's fashions: for example the riding costumes in *Ravenswood* set the seasonal style in ladies' coats.

The Dead Heart (1889) was an indifferent play, but it gave Ellen the great pleasure of appearing as the mother to her own son for 185 performances. Teddy looked 'a lovely little gentleman', wrote Edward Burne-Jones to Ellen after seeing him play the Count St Valéry. Teddy also supported his mother as Alexander Oldworthy in *Nance Oldfield*, Charles Reade's play about a

popular actress of the eighteenth century, which Ellen bought
for herself, and even directed in a 'great hurry' to act as a curtain-
raiser to Irving's revival of *The Corsican Brothers* in May 1890.
Ellen's memory was becoming increasingly unreliable, and she
and Teddy had to have their parts written out and pinned all over
the furniture on the stage. Ellen was to revive *Nance Oldfield*
constantly in succeeding years, and when Teddy was no longer
with her to play his part, Martin-Harvey, Harcourt Williams, and
Irving's son Laurence were among the actors who followed him.
Irving thought highly of Teddy's talents, and wrote to Ellen in
June 1891: 'He'll be a splendid comedian in time and a genial one.'
After walking on and playing small speaking parts, Gordon Craig
became a prominent supporting player in the Lyceum company
from 1889 to 1897, though he frequently broke away to join
touring companies and to direct plays on his own account. At the
Lyceum he was paid £5 a week, rising to £7 in 1891; he was later
to play, among other parts, Moses in *Olivia*, which he enjoyed,
Henry Ashton in *Ravenswood*, and Cromwell in *Henry VIII* – all
before he was twenty. Later he played Oswald in *King Lear*, and
Edward IV in *Richard III* – 'a really great performance' writes
Ellen. In 1894 he married and, to Ellen's initial regret, gradually
withdrew from acting in favour of the graphic arts of stage
design and direction. In small touring companies, or companies
performing short seasons in provincial theatres, he was to play
Hamlet, Macbeth and Romeo. Edy also joined the Lyceum
company in 1887, playing small parts, but she too turned finally
to stage direction and, in particular, to costume design as her
principal occupation in the theatre. She was responsible for
making the costumes for Irving's production of *Robespierre* in
1899. In a letter written in November 1891, Ellen is obviously
distressed about the lack of direction in Edy's undoubted talents;
she was then twenty-two:

> Edy walks in some of our plays and now and then has a line
> or so given her to speak, but although I *never* should be sur-
> prised if she did something great some day, either as a writer,

or an actress or a musician, the fact remains at present a hard fact that she does *nothing whatever* well.[24]

There remained, therefore, less and less for Ellen to do at the Lyceum, where she continued to receive £200 a week, a salary which exceeded what many humble professional people received in a year. In her final ten years as a member of the Lyceum company, starting in 1893, her major appearances in London were confined to only four new productions: *King Arthur* (1895), *Cymbeline* (1896), *Madame Sans-Gêne* (1897; Queen Victoria's Jubilee year) and *Coriolanus* (1901, the year of the Queen's death). Neither of the Shakespearean productions, as we have seen, sustained long runs – *Coriolanus* ran only 34 and *Cymbeline* 72 performances. But occasional revivals of *The Merchant of Venice* kept Ellen's performance as Portia alive for the public of the 1890s.

King Arthur, written for Irving in prosaic verse by Joe Comyns-Carr (since Wills's own efforts on the subject had failed) gave Ellen certain opportunities as Guinevere. It opened in January 1895, with Irving, of course, as Arthur and Johnston Forbes-Robertson as Lancelot. Already old-fashioned in its presentation of a romantic triangle in a setting of pageant-like medievalism, this play was a field-day to Hawes Craven and his assistants in their realization on the stage of the pictorial vision of Burne-Jones, whom Irving commissioned as production designer. Arthur Sullivan, now at the height of his fame, composed and conducted the music. Both critics and public applauded the piece – all but one, the recently appointed critic of Frank Harris's *Saturday Review,* Bernard Shaw. Irving and his whole policy at the Lyceum were to become the pivot of Shaw's attack on the British theatre of the 1890s; Ellen, however, was the object of his adoration, an actress of genius to be wooed from Irving's Svengali-clutches.

While other critics, including the waspish Archer, remained loyal to Irving, Bernard Shaw had another and very different objective in the theatre. He wrote:

Irving's thirty years at the Lyceum, though a most imposing

episode in the history of the English theatre, were an exasperating waste of the talent of the two artists who had seemed to me peculiarly fitted to lift the theatre out of its old ruts and head it towards unexplored regions of drama. With Lyceum Shakesspear I had no patience. Shakespear, even in his integrity, could not satisfy the hungry minds whose spiritual and intellectual appetites had been whetted and even created by Ibsen. . . . Irving wasting his possibilities in costly Bardicide, was wasting Ellen Terry's as well.[25]

Madame Sans-Gêne, which Irving produced largely for Ellen's benefit, gave her the opportunity to excite the London critics and playgoers into making comparisons between her performance and that of Réjane, who had played this historical piece in French in London and New York during 1895. Shaw thought it ludicrous to compare two actresses playing a part well below their strength; it was like, he said, comparing two athletes throwing the hammer two feet. What Ellen enjoyed was the chance to play the so-called vulgar comedy of the Parisian–Cockney washerwoman,[26] who is later translated into the grand lady; Irving in the part of a stage Napoleon subordinated his massive talents to suggesting rather than playing the Emperor. What he enjoyed was creating his make-up for the part, though he was far too tall, thin and ascetic for Napoleon.[27] As Ellen put it, it was as if she 'were watching Napoleon trying to imitate H.I.' Even the Prince of Wales told him it was not the part for him: 'Wellington perhaps – but not Napoleon,' he said. But the Emperor had always held a fascination for Irving, who had both a bust and a portrait of him in his library, as well as a collection of biographical studies. He even pondered for a long while, whether or not to produce Shaw's one-act play *The Man of Destiny,* which featured the youthful Napoleon. The relation between Shaw and Irving became so strained that no one, not even Ellen, would induce him to adopt a play written by so ferocious a critic.

Although Ellen was out of sorts during rehearsal, she was satisfied with the opening night; as she said, she 'acted courageously and fairly well', and the result was a modest success for her, if not for Irving. An attempt was made to keep Shaw out of the theatre on the grounds that it was by now notorious that he only came to see Miss Terry. The play grew in popularity with the public – the rival attraction at the time being the Jubilee celebrations themselves – and *Madame Sans-Gêne* became the principal piece put on during Irving's provincial tour in the autumn of 1897. But by now, as we shall see, the personal bonds between Irving and Ellen were slackening, and it was during the summer of this year that Irving began his close friendship with Mrs Eliza Aria which came to mean so much to him during his last years.

But, in spite of his many reverses, Irving during the 1890s was still the acknowledged leader of his profession. He was knighted in 1895, during the run of *King Arthur*, and since 1889 had given with Ellen two Royal Command performances at Sandringham and Windsor.[28] No management rivalled his own, though Beerbohm Tree, some fifteen years younger, started his celebrated management at his new theatre, Her Majesty's, in 1897, the year of the Jubilee. This was the year before Irving's financial position became so insecure at the Lyceum that he was forced to allow the theatre to be taken over by a syndicate made up of Joe Comyns-Carr and his brothers, who launched a public company in 1899 for this purpose. Irving, who was ill at the time, did this against the urgent advice of Stoker. Ellen's position changed as a result; she became once more a member of a touring company which no longer controlled its own theatre in London, and this contributed to the final dissolution of her full-time partnership with Irving.

This melancholy decline in Irving's fortunes, if not in his actual reputation with the public, was due to a series of reverses. As we have seen, the mounting costs of his productions were by no means always met by the box-office returns, and as early as 1891 he was forced to bolster falling receipts by abandoning new plays in favour of including revivals of the old favourites in the repertoire. As the public response to the seasons at the Lyceum fluctuated, he undertook long and wearying provincial tours to make the money necessary to mount new plays in London.[29] His health,

P

and that of Ellen, suffered from these prolonged absences from home during the winter months, which had to be spent in the indifferent comforts of hotels. During December 1896 when he was playing *Richard III* (and Ellen, who was ill, was convalescing in Germany), he slipped and suffered an injury to his knee, which forced Stoker temporarily to close the theatre. Even when Ellen returned and appeared in a revival of *Olivia,* Irving's two-month absence from the stage led to a serious decline in the Lyceum's fortunes. In 1898, not only did two plays fail (*Peter the Great* by his son Laurence, and *The Medicine Man* achieved a total of only 62 performances), but he also suffered the almost overwhelming disaster of losing some £30,000-worth of sets and properties when his scene store in Southwark was gutted by fire during the small hours on 18 February. The contents of this store, representing all the magnificence of forty-four productions, were reduced to ashes, and the sum due from their insurance was only £6,000. Now sixty, Irving had relied on the productions, for which these settings were the framework, to support him during his final years. Now he was left with nothing but the sets for the productions currently in the repertoire at the theatre; he still retained the means of staging *Louis XI, The Bells, The Merchant of Venice* and *Madame Sans-Gêne.* The 1898 season saw a loss of a further £6,000. During the provincial tour that followed in the winter he con- tracted pneumonia and pleurisy. It was in these adverse circum- stances that Comyns-Carr made the proposals which led to the formation of the Lyceum syndicate. It is true, however, that substantial profits were made during the American tours of 1893–4, 1895–6, 1899–1900 and 1901–1902. In fact, without these lengthy tours, it seems unlikely that Irving could have stayed in business on his own during the later 1890s.[30]

Irving finally lost the Lyceum as his London centre in 1902. When he returned from his tour in that year, he was faced not only with the fact that the company formed for his benefit was bankrupt, but also the news that the structure of the Lyceum had been condemned by the London County Council as unsafe. It was threatened with closure at the end of the 1902 season unless some £30,000 could be found to renovate it and meet the fire-precaution requirements of the local authorities. Ellen, anxious to be fair in this time of difficulty, wrote on 18 May to Bram Stoker:

1. The present season for *me* please begins when I *begin to act*, on the 7th June and not on the 31st May. (I don't want salary when I don't give services! Many thanks all the same.)

2. I will join Sir Henry on the twelve weeks tour (beginning in Birmingham 22nd September) acting two or six times a week (as Sir Henry may desire) at half my usual touring salary – that is to say at £100 per week.

3. I cannot decide at present about the further ahead tour (January 1903). What you call my '*own repertoire parts*' seem to have dwindled down to 2. Portia and Henrietta Maria – haven't they, unless we played *Macbeth*, *Much Ado*, *The Cup*, or a few things of the kind. However, there is no particular hurry about 1903 and I shall see H.I. soon. Yes thanks, I'm having a good rest, but oh . . . the cold.[31]

Just before the closure of the Lyceum, Irving gave his last grand reception on the stage to the distinguished visitors from the territories of the Empire who thronged London to attend the Coronation of Edward VII on 26 June, an event which had to be postponed owing to the King's illness. On 3 July, Irving played both *A Story of Waterloo* (another *tour de force* performance, this time an aged war veteran), and *The Bells,* and then opened the stage for one of his transformation-scene banquets. Rajahs sultans, ranees, resplendent in their national dress filled the stage together with Irving's friends from the theatrical, artistic and social world. Two weeks later, the theatre was closed, and Ellen and he were faced with another of the wearisome, if money-making provincial tours. They played together for the last time under his management in *The Merchant of Venice* at the Prince's Theatre Bristol on 13 December 1902. Their last appearance together on any stage was also as Portia and Shylock on 14 July 1903 at Drury Lane for the benefit of the Actors' Association.

They had appeared together in twenty-seven plays during a partnership which had lasted unbroken for nearly a quarter of a century. After the fire of 1898, the number of productions in which, at their age, they could effectively appear had dwindled to three: *Charles I, Madame Sans-Gêne* and *The Merchant of Venice*.[32] Of these only *The Merchant of Venice* enjoyed an unabated success; it had lasted them over twenty years. It alone survived from their lost youth, while the settings for the triumphs that had been *Hamlet, Much Ado about Nothing, Macbeth* and the spectacles of *King Arthur*, of *Becket, Faust* and *Henry VIII* had been devoured by the flames.

So ended the greatest association of actor and actress in the history of the English theatre. It ended naturally and without acrimony. If there was any feeling at all on Ellen's side it was her consciousness that Irving, whom she still loved, had ceased to regard her as a 'useful' actress, and, in his sorrow and old age, had sought companionship with another. But she was still live and strong. There was a world elsewhere.

VIII

QUEEN OF EVERY WOMAN

In bringing up her children, Ellen was always conscious that they had no father in the house, and that therefore she should try to become both father and mother to them, and especially to Teddy. She was also very conscious that, as she had received no formal education in her childhood, her children should be as well 'educated' as possible, whether they liked it or not. During the 1880s Edy, who was twelve in December 1881 and Teddy, who was ten in January 1882, were sent to a private school in Earls Court run by a Mrs Cole, who had a reputation for holding advanced ideas; she favoured co-education and the 'new' woman, which meant, among other things, that girls had the right to as good an education as boys, an unusual outlook even in the late Victorian period. Among the other children at this school were three young members of Walter Sickert's family – Sickert was one of Godwin's friends. In 1883, when Ellen first went to America, Edy became a boarder at the school, while Teddy was sent on to a school in Tunbridge Wells. He sent pathetic letters back; 'poor kid' scribbled Ellen on one of them, initialling this E.T., but soon he was writing saying the school, after all, was 'rare jolly'. He was still there at the moment when, in a fit of loneliness around Christmas 1884, Ellen cabled Dr Stephen Coleridge, his guardian (who looked, he thought, 'like a moral but rather sick young vulture'), to bring one of the children over to her. So his education was interrupted and, as we have seen, within two days of his thirteenth birthday he found himself appearing on the stage in Chicago in Irving's *Eugene Aram*.

Teddy was already entranced by the theatre, and seems to have shared some of his mother's privilege in enjoying the freedom of the Lyceum. Irving, separated from his own sons, became a guiding figure in the life of Teddy, who both loved him and held him in a kind of reverence. Teddy was very conscious of having no recognized father, for he says the women in the house were at pains to keep the name of Godwin from him: 'Never a word from them of my father,' he records. 'Not having mine, not hearing of mine, this grave sensation of *something being wrong* grew and grew into a fixed sort of small terror with me.' But at the Lyceum all was well; as he grew a little older he went to the theatre regularly with his mother, seeing the plays and meeting the players behind the scenes. He was 'Miss Terry's boy'; he remembers on the first night of *Much Ado about Nothing* in 1882 sitting in the stage box and seeing his mother sweeping towards him in the dance which brought down the rapturous final curtain. He went to the matinées at other theatres sometimes with Ellen at his side. He was ready for the theatre, and was later to complain that he was not, like his mother, brought up inside it as his particular form of education. But in 1885 he was allowed to stay with the company in America, his schooldays almost forgotten in the delight of acting in the plays.

However, once back in England, there was another school to be faced, a public school, Bradfield College, while Edy was sent to a private school in Gloucestershire. Here he stayed until the summer of 1887, when Ellen sent him to study German at a small college in Heidelberg run by a German and two Englishmen. Edy was also sent to Germany to complete her education. Later, in 1888, she studied music under Hollander in Berlin, but she was prevented from fulfilling her early promise as a pianist because she developed rheumatism in her hands. Ellen, the inveterate letter-writer, wrote to her in 1887, urging her, like Teddy, to work at her German – 'work at your German, and *speak* it'. Edy above all things wanted to go with Ellen to America, as Teddy had been fortunate enough to do. 'I shall not be able to gratify this wish of your heart, which is for your own pleasure, if you don't gratify the wish of *my* heart (which is for your own benefit) and make use of the present time, and work.' Ellen was being mother with a vengeance. 'By the way, I've asked the doctors, and you must on no account drink beer, even of the *smallest* kind! claret, or any wine of the country, but no beer. (A glass once a moon would not hurt just to *feel German*!). . . . Oh, you bad girl writing that letter to the German actor. . . . I would be vexed if some fool or other thought you vulgar.'[1]

A letter written on 9 January 1890, when Edy was twenty, to the 'dear friends' who had charge of her daughter at this time reveals something of the nature of her concern for Edy's welfare: 'I am pleased to hear Edy is improving in her music and vexed – *angry* – to hear she does not take her physic. That she *must* do. . . . I have written to Edy and told her, that as she has spent all her money she must now do *without*, until Feb! . . . I gave her much more money this last quarter, and just as she was going away Mr Irving gave her ten pounds, so do NOT give her any more – but please just pay her *Trams* for her, and that is all.'[2]

There can be no doubt that one side at least of Ellen's nature craved the comforts of respectability. According to her son, if Ellen had a fault it was her 'inability to take a side and stick to it. She was all for Peace – and so would try to pacify two opposed people and ideas'. If pressure were put upon her, she tended to yield to it, and the pressure now was for ease, respectability, acceptance, the luxury of her high success. Up to this time, the children had born the name of Wardell, but events had taken place which guided Ellen to give them entirely new names. During the tour in September 1883, Ellen with Irving, Teddy and Bram Stoker, had after a Saturday night performance in Glasgow travelled to Greenock, and they had then been rowed across the water in the middle of a storm to reach Sir William Pearce's luxurious yacht. It was from this yacht next day that Ellen had been shown the rock called Ailsa Craig, and hearing the words pronounced, she had exclaimed what magnificent names they would make for any actress. So, in 1887, the children were formally christened and confirmed; Edy became Edith Geraldene Ailsa Craig; Ailsa became the name she used when she appeared upon the stage. Teddy became Edward Henry Gordon Craig; Henry was in tribute to Irving, who was godfather to both children, and Gordon derived from Lady Gordon, Ellen's friend, who became Teddy's godmother. Edy's confirmation took place in Exeter Cathedral on 11 January 1887 at a private ceremony performed by the Bishop of Exeter. 'Strange,' wrote Ellen in her diary, 'over thirty years ago Father and Mother (with Kate and me) *walked* (necessity!) from Bristol to Exeter, and now my child is given half an hour's private talk with the Bishop before her confirmation. Praise God from whom *all* blessings flow.'³ But Ellen, who, later at least, always kept a Bible by her bedside and accepted the need for christening and confirmation, was never to become a churchgoer.

On 17 April 1885 Charles Kelly had died at the age of forty-six, leaving Ellen as a widow of thirty-nine. That Ellen felt some kind of debt to this husband whom she had taken to suit her convenience is born out by the fact that she paid all the debts he left, and for some years supported his first wife's sisters. She was in fact brought to his bedside by the girl with whom he was then living, but even at this solemn moment she could not help feeling she was playing Juliet. Charles Reade, the man whom she had once considered like a second father, also died in the spring. Then, the following year, news reached her that Godwin had died at the age of fifty-three on 6 October 1886; the only mourners at his funeral at Norleigh in Oxfordshire were Whistler, Lady Archibald Campbell, and Beatrice, his widow, who was later to marry Whistler.⁴ Whistler was also one of Ellen's friends. Ellen, in her Memoirs, lifts the curtain momentarily when she speaks of Whistler being with 'the dearest of [her] friends, Edward Godwin, when he died'. On 27 November she wrote to a friend, commenting on the irony of Godwin's death coming as it did only a few weeks before Watts's remarriage:

The last two months have been very cruel to me, full of disaster – and I seem to be fighting for power to *use* my life, not to enjoy it. People have a way of dying which makes 'all the difference' to some others – 'to me' – I sometimes sit down and just wonder what it all means – this life of ours – Yes, it

was strange poor Signor marrying – *now* – he should have done
so 20 years ago.[5]

With the death of Wardell, Ellen was independent once again,
but her position was very different from what it had been when
she had hastened into marriage less than ten years before. She was
now eminent in her profession, and her future was as assured as
ever it could possibly be in the theatre. Irving, regarded as the
greatest actor of the age, was her devoted companion, and
her two children, growing up now, were showing every sign
that they would soon join her in the theatre. She was loved,
admired and courted by the most distinguished people of her
time, and she had become as well known and well liked in North
America as she was in her own country. Her life was incessantly
preoccupied with the theatre, where she was often kept from
morning until the small hours of the night, for after the evening
performance was over Henry would frequently expect her to act
as hostess at the elaborate supper-parties held in the Lyceum
Beefsteak Room.

These suppers, together with his constant visits to the Garrick
Club, became the core of Irving's more public social life. For
twenty years the Beefsteak Room was where he relaxed, as well
as a private place for far more formal entertainment. Here he
would discuss things with Bram Stoker and Harry Loveday,
with his collaborators and fellow artists, with his friends and with
the theatre-loving nobility, with financiers and politicians, with
great actors and actresses from other countries during their visits
to his theatre. Large receptions, as we have seen, were given upon
the stage, and it was here that the Prince of Wales and a party
of fifty were received on 7 May 1886. Ellen's own memories of
the Beefsteak Room (which could seat over thirty people) included receiving, with Irving, the Princess May of Teck (later
Queen Mary) and her mother, Lord Randolph Churchill and his
'beautiful wife' (who on one occasion wore a dress embroidered
with green beetles' wings – the origin of the idea for Lady Macbeth's robe), the singers Patti and Melba, the players Coquelin,

Bernhardt, Salvini, Booth and Duse. Many became their friends, whom they met again in London and elsewhere. Once, standing behind the scenes at the Metropolitan Opera House in New York, Ellen watched Patti sing:

> My impression from that point of view was that she was actually a *bird*! She could not help singing! Her head, flattened on top, her nose tilted downwards like a lovely little beak, her throat swelling and swelling as it poured out that extraordinary volume of sound, all made me think that she must have been a nightingale before she was a human being![6]

Melba became a close friend, whom she was eventually to visit in Australia.

In Stoker's description, guests to the Beefsteak Room included 'statesmen, travellers, explorers, ambassadors, foreign princes and potentates, poets, novelists, historians – writers of every style, shade and quality. Representatives of all the learned professions: of all the official worlds: of all the great industries. Sportsmen, landlords, agriculturalists. Men and women of leisure and fashion. Scientists, thinkers, inventors, philanthropists, divines'. When Stoker tried to draw up a list of everyone who rightfully should be asked to a garden party late in the 1880s, his list exceeded 5,000 and the project was abandoned. But in his book he lists more than 1,000 names of eminent or notable people who enjoyed Irving's hospitality at the Lyceum. To read the list of Irving's guests is like scanning the name-index to a social history of the nineteenth century. Irving's smaller parties were often limited to men, and Ellen by no means attended every social reception he gave. But she alone could act as his hostess, and her position at the Lyceum gave her the right of introduction to anyone she cared to meet from this great cross-section of Victorian culture and society. This more convivial aspect of Henry Irving was that depicted in the famous portrait by Bastien-Lepage in the National Portrait Gallery, and in Sir Bernard Partridge's many drawings.

Alice Comyns-Carr gives an amusing account of a Beefsteak supper party after Sarah Bernhardt had been present at a dress rehearsal for *Henry VIII*. Bernhardt had been invited to comment on Alice's costumes for Katherine of Aragon:

> The two had a heated discussion over the gown which Queen Catherine was to wear in the trial scene. It was of rich metal cloth, and had a front panel of very heavy embroidery in fleur-de-lis design.
>
> Nell and I had already had a controversy over this dress, she complaining bitterly that it was far too heavy to wear, and now she tried to enlist Sarah's sympathies.
>
> 'I've told Alice how uncomfortable it is,' she explained; 'just like a tea-tray on my stomach – one of our grandmother's, you know, inlaid with mother-of-pearl.' But although Sarah laughed heartily at Nell's mournful voice, she stood by me. 'Ah, but it is just what it should be. The Tudor touch. So you must not think of your stomach.' Over the supper-table in the Beefsteak Room that night talk turned on age, and the effect it had upon acting. Irving remarked sadly that old age must come to us all, but Sarah, leaning over the table to Nell, said, 'My darling, there are two people who shall never be old – you and I.'[7]

It was from the preoccupation of such a life that Ellen turned towards her home and friends for simpler pleasures. Her personal friends were many, among them Graham Robertson, Alice Comyns-Carr, Sir Albert Seymour, Tom Heslewood and Stephen Coleridge, the 'tight-lipped piece of leather' whom Teddy, now Gordon Craig, later accused of incompetence as an adviser on the placing of his mother's investments. It was Ellen who had first introduced Graham Robertson to the Beefsteak Room in a party which included the Bancrofts. He 'remembered the picture of that first supper at the Lyceum – the bright, candle-lit table among the shadows of the old Beefsteak Room – the beautiful, ivory face of the host against the dark panelling ... that pale face, which seemed to absorb and give out light'. He remembered also that the room was hot and stuffy, and that Ellen insisted on opening the window to let in the fresh air. Ellen, naturally, was in constant demand with hostesses in London. It was at a dance in the winter of 1887 that Graham Robertson first met her:

> I was at a dance, and I remember that it was a dull dance, and I was making preparations to leave it when there was a sudden stir at the door – something was happening – something in the nature of a sunrise.
>
> At the entry stood a golden figure which seemed actually to diffuse light, the golden figure which I had first beheld in the palace of Belmont. A fairer vision than Ellen Terry, then at the zenith of her loveliness, cannot be imagined: she shone with no shallow sparkle or glitter, but with a steady radiance that filled the room and had the peculiar quality of making everybody else invisible. From after experience I feel sure that she was in the act of whispering to her hostess, 'Now don't you bother about me and I'll just slip in without being noticed and sit down somewhere' – a feat which might have been performed with equal ease by the sun at noonday.[8]

Ellen went rarely to these occasions, preferring more intimate social gatherings. But she was always ready to accompany Irving on any of the more important public engagements that he undertook.

Ellen never lost touch with the countryside, even returning now and then with Teddy to Harpenden by pony trap to see the house that had once been hers and Godwin's. In January 1889 she moved her London house to 22 Barkston Gardens, Earls Court, but she always enjoyed owning a succession of properties in the country. After Rose Cottage, the next was the Audrey Arms, a little public house on the outskirts of Uxbridge; it stood in a row of cottages next door to a second inn, and she was obliged by her lease to keep the bar open. However, she served such poor quality beer that she rapidly drove the local custom from her doors. Graham Robertson, who stayed there with her, remembers serving only a single customer appearing throughout his visit. In 1893, Teddy took over the Audrey Arms at a rent of five shilling a week, and Ellen had a little cottage in Kingston Vales. Later again, in 1896,

Ellen acquired from the Comyns-Carrs their Tower Cottage in Winchelsea ('a house built on to the ivied wall of the ancient Town Gate,' says Graham Robertson), and then finally, in 1900, she bought the fifteenth-century farmhouse of Smallhythe, near Tenterden in Kent, which she owned until her death, and which is now a National Trust property and a permanent museum dedicated to her memory.

In these various cottages, and at her home in Barkston Gardens, where she stayed until 1902, she loved to entertain her close friends in the most informal style. Here life was lived freely and naturally. Before buying Tower Cottage from the Comyns-Carrs, Ellen had rented the house next door. She loved, says Alice, 'going out in the early morning and dancing on the lawn in front of the house with bare feet, and clad only in the flimsiest of long white night-dresses'. When Joe became concerned as to what the neighbours might think, Ellen's reply was that they were still in bed and therefore only farm labourers might see her. 'I don't mind amusing them,' said Ellen. 'It's so good for the poor dears.' Irving would come for weekends with her, and, says Alice, 'we often caught glimpses of him in rather queer get-ups as he sat taking his ease in Nell's garden'.

To all her friends and helpers, Ellen poured out her letters in profusion. She had only to think of someone to start writing. Her bold and joyful handwriting filled page after page of notepaper. How many hundreds or even thousands of these letters now survive it is difficult to assess, but there are many in private hands as well as in public collections. Most of them are the small change of daily arrangements – visiting her friends, sending them theatre seats, giving instructions to her dressmaker, giving help or offering advice, settling her domestic affairs. All are characterized by her immediate spontaneity of expression.

Among the surviving letters which form a delightful running commentary are those sent to Mrs Nettleship about the costumes she needed both on and off-stage.[9] 'As I *think* of things I'll write them to you,' she says, expressing her whole approach to letter-writing when sending instructions on 10 November 1892 about

the costumes for *King Lear*. 'No wimples for anyone,' she adds.
Here are remarks from other letters to Mrs Nettleship, the first
concerning the dresses for *Charles I*:

> March 4 1891 – By the way the *yellow* dress must not be *too*
> correct remind Mrs Carr *about the length* – it *must* be too long
> behind for Grace must not be left out for all the archaeology
> in the world – the *breadth* of the dress is great, and so it must be
> kept LONG – especially as I hold it over my arm a good deal
> July 12 1892 – I hear you are making a new Cardinal's dress
> for Mr Irving. Have you still some left to make one more cape?
> If so please send me enough silk for one to No 22. I will suffer
> the wrath of Mr Irving.
> July 15 1895 – Was at rehearsal till past 3 on Sat evening –
> Am half dead . . . I want a Cheap Cloak for Wednesday, look-
> ing like Ermine, but *really* the innocent Bunny-rabbit.

In the latter years, constant reference to her declining health,
and Irving's, occur in many of her letters. She began to suffer
from Irving's driving concentration on prolonged rehearsals. She
writes to Mrs Nettleship:

> June 16 1900 – a little better last eve but oh, I am so tired.
> April 15 1901 – Am far too ill to be up . . . MUST REHEARSE.
> June 24 1901 – Mr Irving is frightfully hoarse tonight – I am
> in consternation! – He is slaving away however.

Letters (mostly undated or only partially so) written from the
1880s to the early 1900s and addressed to another woman friend,
Mrs Bertha Jennings Bramly, give a further running commentary on her life during this period.[10] They can all be dated approx-
imately through internal evidence:

> 23 July 1884 – . . . an apology for loss of voice is given for
> me each night in front of Curtain at the Lyceum. Edie and Ted
> will be home then too – their holidays – *that always* makes me
> well.
>
> [c. Dec 1885] – Dear old Bertha – did you ever feel so

crushed (that's exactly the expression) – I'm not fooling – so crushed out of all individuality that people and all things, seemed unreal, and that it was just impossible to reason or to do reasonable things – oh! how dreadful a time I've passed through – In truth I've been brave in the long-while-ago – through heavy sorrow and trial, and now that theres nothing to bear with, now that the Sun does shine for me, I am in the tight merciless grip of *Melancholy* for the first time in a very long life – Ah! but the terrible time has *past*, only now you will understand me when I tell you I *couldn't* write letters – *couldn't* see people COULD *not* do 'those things which I ought to have done.'

[June 1886] – . . . my *cussed health*!! Last Tuesday and Wednesday I was so weak and worn out that Mr Irving let me off tonight's work and I slipped away down here alone with my maid!

20 June [1890] – This little tour of a month round the Provinces reading Macbeth *ought* to have been most enjoyable – for it was quite marvellous to see the great halls full of people, crowds of working people too, some quite rough and to note how they hung on to the words, and how enthusiastic they all were.[11]

[1897] – Rehearsing every day and every evening 3 plays too. I'm nearly crazy sometimes from just *thinking* = As for my body ——!!!![12]

[*c*. Dec. 1898[So many people who have seen me on the stage, or have passed me in the street *say* they know me quite well, quite marvellous creatures on this earth crawling about, that I can scarcely conceive – One has just written me a letter (no name) signing *herself* 'an American gentleman' telling me I am far too old and fat to be acting, & that no one wants to see me any more on the stage, & warning me not to go to America or I shall be shot! – *I am* fat – & old? (-er than I was yesterday) but surely neither of these are good reasons for

shooting me! On Thursday I had *such* a birthday telegrams –
letters – verses – gifts & flowers everywhere Flowers – Bowers
– & I was so excited, tho' I *am* so old!

Poor H–I has had the 'fluze' *badly* & has gone to Bourne-
mouth to get stronger – Meanwhile Mr Tyars (!) has 'obliged'
– Tell Amy I COULD NOT lie at his feet =

God be with you dearest Bertha

Your old & fat

Nell[13]

[*c*. 1900] You may chance to have a spare hour some evening
to throw away upon me at the Lyceum. If so *do come*. If you
only knew it I have more leasure there than in all my days!!

[Perhaps Oct 1901] This has been a very difficult year for me
– always breaking down in my work.

Writing from Tower Cottage Winchelsea, after one of the last
of her provincial tours with Irving, she writes in relief from the
Kentish countryside: 'All is peaceful once more in Win'sea. I am
nearly always alone.' Letters written to friends during this period
are full of reference to her declining health. On 23 June 1889 she
writes to Mrs Amy Dickens,[14] 'This is the *first season I've not
broken down*. . . . With heavy Lady Macbeth every night – yet it's
because of Lady Mac, I'm alright!! . . . Suffer a great deal with my
eyes lately.' Again she turned to the countryside for rest, writing
to Amy from the Audrey Arms in Uxbridge on 29 November
(no year stated, but presumably in the early 1890s): 'My dear old
thing, I am down here nearly always now, for the town is so
dreary and so noisy and dull – there are lovely bright sunny hours
here in the morning which better fit me for my evening's work.'
Apart from her health, she suffered most when Irving himself was
away from the theatre. To Enid Dickens, daughter of Amy, she
wrote on 23 October 1898:

Sir Henry has been most frightfully ill, and I've been in
despair at the distance between us – I have however heard
news at least three times a day. . . . I was terribly frightened a

20. Ellen Terry as Iolanthe, about 1880

21. Ellen Terry, on tour in Birmingham in about 1881

22. As Juliet in 1882

23. Henry Irving. Portrait by Bastien-Lepage
(*By courtesy of the National Portrait Gallery*).

24. Sargent's sketch of Ellen Terry as Lady Macbeth

25. Ellen Terry and Henry Irving in *Macbeth*. Drawing by Bernard Partridge

26. Ellen Terry as Lady Macbeth, by J. S. Sargent. (*By courtesy of the Tate Gallery.*)

27. Ellen Terry as Catherine Duval in *The Dead Heart*, with Gordon Craig

27a. A scene from *The Dead Heart*

28. Ellen Terry as Queen Katherine in *Henry VIII*, Act II, Scene iv. Drawing by Bernard Partridge

29. *Henry VIII*, Act II, Scene iv. Drawing by Hawes Craven

30. The awakening scene from *King Lear*
Drawing by Hawes Craven

week ago. . . . It will be a long time before he will be strong, I fear. Oh, it is sad, sad, sad.

In another undated letter to Enid, probably concerning the birthday presents she is receiving in February 1889:

> Thanks my dear little Enid for your pretty present – Mr Irving's was the first, yours the second, and then they came pouring in! – Heaps of pretty gifts, from pretty friends – and I got quite excited – though I *am* getting old . . . You can imagine I feel dull at the theatre now King Arthur is away – oh, it has been a trial!! – but he comes back on Saturday.

Another of her friends was Oscar Wilde. He was her junior by seven years, and had left Oxford to live in London in the same year that she had gone to the Lyceum. She had, as we have seen, been touched by Wilde's sonnets – by far the best verse among so much doggerel written in her honour – and Wilde had been invited to one of the grand receptions given on the Lyceum stage. 'The most remarkable men I have known were Whistler and Oscar Wilde. This does not imply that I like them better or admired them more than others, but there was something about both of them more instantaneously individual and audacious than it is possible to describe.' Oscar Wilde and Lillie Langtry had taken the trouble to go to Liverpool to see Ellen and Irving off on their first American voyage; by then Wilde had begun to curl his hair, Ellen noticed, in the style of the Prince Regent, but she thought 'his brown eyes very beautiful'. Like other guests of Wilde, she and Irving had scrawled their signatures on the white panelling of his rooms overlooking the river at 13 Salisbury Street. Wilde was to become the friend of many famous actresses of the day, amongst them Mrs Langtry, Mary Anderson, and, above all, Sarah Bernhardt. After Wilde had married Constance, Ellen and Irving were at times guests at Wilde's house in Tite Street. Unlike Sarah Bernhardt, it was Ellen who was prepared to show sympathy when Wilde was in his deepest trouble in 1895; it would seem that one day between the trials a veiled lady

Q

drove up in a cab and left a horseshoe with a bouquet of violets and a card with the words 'For luck' written on it. It seems, though it cannot be proved, that this veiled lady was Ellen, and that she had meant to rouse him by this small gesture as much as to offer him sympathy and encouragement. She also went out of her way to praise him when even to mention his name in normal society was to risk the severest disapprobation. Irving, too, expressed sympathy for Wilde.[15]

An undated letter from Oscar Wilde to Ellen is preserved at Smallhythe.[16] It was sent from Tite Street:

> Dear Ellen,
>
> Your love is more wonderful even than a crystal caught in bent reeds of gold, and I don't envy Constance any more, for I will wear the love, and no one shall see it. As for the box – it will be the sweetest of pleasures to be the guests of the Goddess – and oh! dear Ellen, look sometimes in our direction, and let us come and pay due homage afterwards to the gracious lady and the great artist we adore.
>
> Always yours,
>
> Oscar.

Apart from the correspondence with Bernard Shaw, only one other volume of her letters has been published. This rare book, *The Heart of Ellen Terry,* appeared soon after her death in 1928 and was compiled anonymously by Stephen Coleridge, who merely called himself 'an intimate friend for half a century', to whom she had written continuously throughout the period of their friendship. 'She was my friend from my early youth until we both became old and had seen our children's children.' Some of these letters to Stephen Coleridge have already been quoted, but here are others which reveal her in the variety of her moods:

Undated, but written sometime in 1881 or 1882:

> Never being able to thank you enough for your very constant care for us all, it seems to me I take refuge in silence and never never express any gratitude at all!!
>
> Oh! dear, Dear, I don't feel as bad as I seem.

Dear Henry is ever the same 'gentle and he's *kind* you'll never never *find* a better dog than poor dog Tray' (Robson's old song).

He'd send his love to you if he knew I was writing but he doesn't, so I send it for him with mine.

The chicks are '*really* having jolly holidays' they say, they and I (and sometimes Booey) go out driving or walking together, and read to them and they to me – in fact we have a rare old time together.

Here's a lot about self. Forgive and love me.

Nell.

Written on 15 February 1892, after he had told her he was to visit Watts, whose friend he was:

You tell me you are going to stay awhile with Mr Watts. The dews of Heaven fall thick in blessings on him.

Where? Not at L.H.H.! At Freshwater perhaps? or – where? *Let me know for I like to picture things.*

(L.H.H. stands for Little Holland House.)

After attending Tennyson's funeral in Westminster Abbey:

The great coffin moving up the centre of the abbey yesterday wrapped in the flag was a harrowing scene. I sat next a sympathetic soul – Mrs Ritchie – and was glad of her. I should have *had* to touch *somebody* and a stranger might have been affronted! I wish you had been with me.

Throughout her career, she was always responding, often unthinkingly, to demands upon her generosity. Having experienced want and debt herself, she could not bear the thought of it for others, with results that were sometimes unfortunate. An early letter to Bertha Bramly dated 3 May and written probably in 1879, shows how she was deluged with appeals: 'This morning's post *alone* brings me *14 appeals for help*! All trouble – and mostly all from *gentle* folk. At times – now – I *can't* study for thinking of the misery.'

On one occasion, her notorious lateness in the theatre was due to an act of generosity. The story is Alice Comyns-Carr's, as she waited one night with Sally Holland, Ellen's dresser, in mounting fear that Irving would discover how late Ellen was:

They always had adjoining dressing-rooms, and most evenings Nell's maid Sally and I waited with quaking hearts for her to arrive at the theatre, knowing that any moment Henry might open the communicating door to see if she were ready. One night at the Lyceum it was only a few minutes before the curtain was due to go up, and still Nell hadn't arrived.

'Miss Terry dressed?' inquired Irving, as he put his head in at the door.

'She ain't come yet, Govenor,' murmured Sally tremblingly.

'Pity,' was Henry's only reply, and it was then I realized how much he cared about Nell, for restraint was never Irving's long suit. At the very last moment she rushed in, cheeks aglow and humming a tune in the way she had when she thought she might be to blame.

'That you, Henry?' she remarked demurely as Irving, watch in hand, came in just as Nell had settled down to 'make up' her face. 'I've been down to the Minories to see a fellow who sent me a begging letter this morning. I just wanted to make sure that it was genuine.'

'The Minories!' grunted Henry. 'A nice place for you at night. I suppose you didn't think of what would happen to the play if you had been attacked by some roughs down there?' But Nell only laughed. 'Why, every man Jack in the crowd knew me or had heard tell. I let down the window of the four-wheeler and shook hands with them all. It's because there were so many that I'm so late.'

'Of course,' Henry muttered laconically, 'it's a good advertisement, but I do wish you wouldn't cut things so fine.'

'Not two minutes to your entrance, Miss Terry,' yelled the call-boy wildly from the passage outside.

'If anybody bothers me I shan't come at all,' Nell replied mildly.

Charlie, the call-boy, was silent, and Sally continued feverishly slipping garments over her mistress's head and fastening them up behind while Nell worked busily with her blacking pencil and hare's foot. From Charlie's movements outside we knew that he was leaning over, listening to the stage.

'Two lines to your speech, Miss Terry, *if* you please.' Nell tore down the narrow staircase, with Sally rushing behind to save her skirts from some irreparable rent. 'The worst "tear-girl" ever I knowed,' said she, on coming back to the dressing-room, as she sank exhausted into a seat.[17]

Most of Ellen's generosity was more concealed than this sudden visit to the Minories. She was always giving money away, usually in secret.[18]

She was always willing to give help, especially to young people. Lewis Carroll was in the habit of approaching her on behalf of stage-struck girls whom he had known as children and who now prevailed on him to get them introductions to the great actress. He was, however, cautious, as a good Victorian should be, and a letter survives written to warn the mother of Dorothea Baird, who was later to marry Irving's son Harry, about the unusual background to Ellen's life. Dorothea, or Dolly as she was called, was a keen amateur actress, who had appeared as Iris in *The Tempest* when it was produced by the Oxford University Dramatic Society in 1893. Lewis Carroll wrote in the following terms to Mrs Baird from Christ Church Oxford on 12 April, 1894:

Dear Mrs Baird,

There are two questions that I want to put before you for consideration.

The first is as to that friend of mine to whom Dolly wishes to be introduced. I have now introduced to her four of the daughters of my friends of ages between 18 and 25; but in every case, *before* doing so, I told the mother the history of my friend and asked her whether, now she knew all the circumstances, she still wished her daughter to be introduced. In each case the answer was 'Yes' – so now, before giving any more promises to introduce Dolly, I would like to know what *you* think about it.

If you already know what is popularly said against my friend (which is usually a good deal more than the truth) and if, knowing it, you still wish Dolly to be introduced, I am quite satisfied and no more need be said.

If you do not know of any such tales, current in society, then I think I had better come and tell you the true history (you yourself, I mean; I had rather not talk about the matter to your daughter) and then you can settle what you wish to be done.

The other question is, may Dolly come and dine with me? I ask this, not knowing your views as to 'Mrs Grundy'. And you may be sure I shall not feel in the least hurt if you think it best to say 'No'. It is only in these last two or three years that I have ventured on such unique and unconventional parties – Winifred Stevens was my first guest.

Believe me sincerely yours,
C. L. Dodgson.

Rather than calling on Mrs Baird, he decided to write down his account of Ellen's background as he saw it:

When she was scarcely more than a child (17, I think), a man nearly three times her age professed to be in love with her. The match was pushed on by well-meaning friends who thought it was a grand thing for her. From the first, I don't think she had a fair chance of learning her new duties. Instead of giving her a home of her own he went on living as a guest with an elderly couple and the old lady was constantly exasperating the poor child by treating her as if she were still in the school-room and she, just like a child, used to go into fits of furious passion.

Quarrels began at once and very soon a separation was agreed on. He cynically told his friends that he found he had never *loved* her; it had only been a passing fancy. He agreed to make her an annual allowance so long as she lived respectably.

This she did for a while, then she rebelled and accepted the offered love (of course without ceremonial of marriage) of another man.

I honestly believe her position was, from her point of view, this: 'I was tied by *human* law to a man who disowns his share of what ought to be a *mutual* contract. He never loved me and I do not believe, in God's sight, we are man and wife. Society expects me to live, till this man's death, as if I were single and to give up all hope of that form of love for which I pine and shall never get from *him*. This other man loves me as truly and faithfully as any lawful husband. If the marriage ceremony were *possible* I would insist on it before living with him. It is *not* possible and I will do without it.'

I allow freely that she was headstrong and wild in doing so; and her only real *duty* was to accept the wreck of her happiness and live (or if necessary die) *without* the love of a man. But I do not allow that her case resembled *at all* that of those poor women who, without any pretence of *love*, sell themselves to the first comer. It much more resembles the case of those many women who are living as faithfully and devotedly as lawful wives without having gone through any ceremony and who *are*, I believe, married in God's sight though not in Man's.

A lady (wife of a clergyman) to whom (before I would introduce her daughter to my friend) I told this story said, 'She has broken the law of man; she has *not* broken the law of God.'

She lived with this man for some years and he *is* the father of her son and daughter. Then came the result she must have known was *possible* if not probable and which perhaps her mad conduct deserved; the man deserted her and went abroad. When her lawful husband found out what she had done, of course he sued for and got a divorce. Then of course she was, in the eye of the law, free to be legally married and if only the other man had been as true as she, I have no doubt, meant to

be to him, they would have married and it would have gradually been forgotten that the children were born before the
ceremony.

All this time I held no communication with her. I felt that
she had so entirely sacrificed her social position that I had no
desire but to drop the acquaintance. Then an actor offered her
marriage and they were married. It was a most generous act,
I think, to marry a woman with such a history and a *great*
addition to this generosity was his allowing the children to
assume *his* surname.

The actor's father, a clergyman, so entirely approved of his
son's conduct that he came from the North of England to
perform the ceremony. This second marriage put her, in the
eyes of Society, once more in the position of a respectable
woman. And then I asked her mother to ask her if she would
like our friendship to begin again and she said 'yes'. And I
went and called on her and her husband.

It really looked as if the misery of her life was *over*. But
another misery came on of quite another kind. The man *drank*.
She knew he was addicted to it before she married him but
she fancied (very foolishly I fear) she could cure him. This got
worse till they had to live apart and I believe he drank himself
to death.

So she is now a widow.[19]

Another letter survives at Smallhythe written to Ellen by
W. S. Gilbert. The letter is of special interest since it concerns the
young and beautiful Julia Neilson, who was in 1891 to marry
Ellen's brother, Fred. She was a protégée of Gilbert's, and had
made her début at a charity matinée of his *Pygmalion and Galatea*
at the Lyceum in 1888. She had been harshly criticized, but Ellen's
constructively critical encouragement had helped her. Gilbert
wrote to Ellen on 9 October 1888:

My dear Miss Terry,
    I can't thank you sufficiently for your kind letter. It will be
invaluable to Miss Neilson who, as you say, stands in every

need of judicious encouragement. I think the press people are hard on her when they tell her that her acting is hopelessly & irredeemably bad. Your opinion of the piece is in the highest degree gratifying & consolatory to her. I am glad you pitched upon the little scene between the two old people, as it always appealed with peculiar force to me. You are quite right of course, in saying that Miss Neilson seems to hold herself too much in check at critical moments. This comes of nervousness, self-doubt. She *can* do better, when she is not affected by these considerations. I cannot tell you how highly I prize your letter, or how greatly it has encouraged the poor girl.

Always sincerely yours

W. S. Gilbert.

In her Memoirs, Ellen herself refers to the help she was able to give to several actresses at the beginning of their careers. She did not try to make it easy for them, and she had to be convinced of their talent and conviction before she let them draw on her encouragement. Among the many actresses she helped were Ellaline Terriss (daughter of William), Violet Vanbrugh, Lena Ashwell, Pauline Chase and Lynn Fontanne. When the talent was there, she recognized it at once; this happened when she first heard Lena Ashwell, who studied elocution at the Royal Academy of Music, and had been commended to Ellen's attention by Joe Comyns-Carr. Ellen wrote of her attempt at a speech from *Richard II*:

She began slowly, and with a most fetching voice, to think out the words. You saw her think them, heard her speak them. It was so different from the intelligent elocution, the good recitation, but bad impersonation of the others. A pathetic face, a passionate voice, a BRAIN, I thought to myself. It must have been at this point that the girl flung away the book and began to act, in an undisciplined way of course but with such true emotion, such intensity that the tears came into my eyes. The tears came to her eyes too. We both wept, and then we embraced, and then we wept again.[20]

Later Lena Ashwell joined the Lyceum company.

Ellen actually gave a home to Lynn Fontanne until she had
found a foothold in the theatre and made her way to the United
States. An entry in Ellen's diaries records: 'Must get Lynn more
money. It's wicked. She is so intelligent.'

Among those for whom she did much were Irving's two sons,
H.B. (Henry Brodribb) and Laurence Irving, who had been
brought up by their mother and as a result had little contact with
their father. Irving's ambition for his sons was at first a negative
one – to keep them away from the theatre. They had both done
well at Marlborough College; on leaving school, young Henry
(known as Harry) had expressed to his father his wish to go on
the stage, which Irving had firmly rejected, persuading him to
go to Oxford. Although Laurence too felt the need to act, his
growing skill in modern languages pointed to a career in the
diplomatic service. Harry, down from Oxford, failed at his first
attempt to go on the stage, and took up the study of law before
returning to the theatre. Laurence served his term in Paris and in
Moscow, where he perfected his knowledge of Russian; he then
returned to London and joined Frank Benson's touring company.
Irving was by then forced to accept the fact that both his sons
would follow him in his profession. Eventually both of them were
to appear with their father; Laurence joined the Lyceum company
in 1895, while Harry made a solitary appearance with him when
Irving and Ellen shared the stage for the last time in *The Merchant
of Venice*.

It was to Ellen that Laurence turned to ease his relations with
his father. It was she who undertook, in the face of Irving's lack
of interest, a single production in Chicago of Laurence's one-act
play, *Godefroi and Yolande*; in this she herself played Yolande.
Irving had rejected the play for the Lyceum; he considered it to
be morbid because its subject involved leprosy; it was based by
Laurence on Swinburne's poem *The Leper*. The revealing correspondence that took place between Laurence (then aged twenty-
three) and Ellen show the hope she both fostered and fulfilled.
Both letters are undated.[21]

My dear Miss Terry,

I cannot tell you how deeply I felt all your generous enthusiasm over my play.

Encouragement such as you gave me will spur me on to renewed efforts so as I may hope to merit it again. I will have another copy of the play got ready and then I will send it to you for the comments you so kindly offered to make. That copy will then be more valuable for your comments than in itself it could ever hope to be. I do not know in what words to tell you how honoured I feel at such an offer from the first of English actresses.

Believe me, My dear Miss Terry, I am very sincerely

Laurence Irving

My dear Miss Terry,

Harry has just told me you have said that *if* I were to ask you to play Yolande in my play you would not refuse: this of course I hasten to do: it would be the making of my play. It is a compliment to myself and my play for which I know not how to thank you. If you will play please Yolande all anxiety is taken off my shoulders: and no time would be too long for me to wait to arrive at such a consummation. It now only remains to persuade my father to play Godefroi. Deeply thanking you for what you have said you will do, as though it were already done.

Believe me, Very sincerely yours,

Laurence Irving.

As if to compensate for his coldness to his own sons, Irving acted like a father to young Teddy. As a child, Teddy could not be unaware of the close relations that had developed between Irving and his mother, for from the earliest times Irving was always calling on them at the house in Longridge Road, as well as spending weekends with them in the country. Gordon Craig wrote later that he believed Irving knew when Godwin lay dying at St Peter's Hospital, London; he had the boy to stay with him and gave him presents of books; one, Southey's *Life of Nelson*, he inscribed, 'To my dear Ted from Henry Irving, 22 September 1886'. When Teddy had grown up and joined the company, he and Edy were allowed to call Irving Henry, as their mother had always done, and in April 1888 Irving gave him the first four volumes of the special Irving Shakespeare inscribed 'To the gay Lord Hamlet'. The following year, as we have seen, he became his godfather, and then at the age of seventeen, Teddy became an apprentice-actor under Irving's professional rule.

Teddy remained with the Lyceum company on and off until 1897. Ellen coached him as best she could, but the instinctive naturalness of her own performance made it difficult for her to act as a good instructor: 'a thing was not good to her . . . if it could not be done easily.' But she knew that Teddy needed male training, and she hired instruction for him in deportment, fencing and French.[22]

During the period 1892 to 1896, Ellen had to face the sorrow of the death of her parents, Sarah in 1892 and Ben in 1896. When Sarah died, Ellen felt unable to appear for a while at the Lyceum. When she returned she found her dressing-room filled with daffodils. They were from Irving: 'to make it look like sunshine,' he said. Ellen was returning from America in 1895 when her father died as the result of pneumonia following a spring cold: the news had to be broken to her in Liverpool when the ship docked. This period, too, saw the beginning of her difficulties with Teddy, who, asserting his independence in his early twenties, was soon to leave her, giving recitals with Violet Vanbrugh (who had once been given a temporary home at Longridge Road before she began work at the Lyceum), and undertaking engagements in repertory when he was not appearing in Irving's company. In 1893 he broke away entirely from the home in Barkston Gardens which he could no longer bear because it was so dominated by women: he lived for a while alone at the Audrey Arms. Above all things, his mother wanted him to become an established actor; she believed in his talent, and so did Irving. But it was in 1893 that he came under the influence of William and Mable Nicholson, and Mable's brother, James Pryde, and through them his interest in wood engraving first developed. Then, on 27 March, he married a young artist, May Gibson. Ellen was distracted by this sudden marriage (May even termed it an 'elopement'), though both she and Irving knew May and Mrs Gibson, the girl's mother. Irving had written very seriously to Teddy urging him not to marry early in life and offering him a splendid future at the Lyceum. But he and Ellen left for America without Teddy, whose marriage soon broke up through youthful incompatibility, though only after four children had been born. Teddy, of course, proved quite incapable of maintaining his wife and children by his casual work as an actor and an artist. 'I marry at twenty-one ... my first female! Rather blundering,' covers his view on the matter. He turned to other loves, and by 1898 the marriage ended in divorce. Ellen paid the alimony for the remainder of her life, and constantly came to the aid of Teddy and his many children. He was at a loose end, and was scarcely to find his feet, or his creative destiny, for many years to come. But in 1900 he met Elena Meo, daughter of the artist Gaetano Meo, who though Italian-born was by this time a naturalized British subject. Elena was to prove the most lasting love of his life, and she became the mother of the two children most closely identified with him, Nelly and Edward Craig.

Edy, tall and handsome, but often distant and painfully analytical with those she loved, created no such difficulties for Ellen. Ellen had spoiled her son and encouraged his self-indulgence precisely because he was the son of Godwin: with Edy the relationship was different because Ellen seemed to see her to some extent as an extension of herself. She exaggerated wildly the scope of Edy's youthful talents – Edy was to be now a great actress, now an outstanding theatrical designer, now a splendid musician. She could, thought Ellen, grow up to become everything that was desirable in a daughter of a Terry and a Godwin.

Edy as a child had developed a sharp eye and a sharper tongue, and her mother was always liable, according to her mood, at one moment to encourage her independence of manner and at the next to scold her for impertinence. She encouraged Edy even

from childhood to make critical judgments about her performances at the Lyceum. Brought up by a small retinue of women in
an atmosphere which combined restriction with indulgence, Edy
became introspective, resentful, mother-proud; at times she was
jealous of her brother, with his almost effeminate good looks and
the attention he excited in a household dominated by the opposite
sex.

Now, in the developing loneliness of the 1890s, Ellen was to
find herself, for the first time, brought face to face with the
problems of living both a domestic and a professional life with a
daughter by no means easy to understand. According to Marguerite
Steen, who knew her well, she was 'emotionally and artistically
... more interested in, and interesting to, her own sex than to the
male'. She also developed certain rather aggressive traits which
held her back in her profession and often made her difficult to
deal with at home. Her undoubted talents never flowered as they
did in her mother and her brother. Twice she was to fall in love
and wish to marry, and twice Ellen stepped in to prevent it, on
the grounds that the men were unsuitable. The first love affair
was with an American painter whom Edy met during the fifth
American tour in 1890; the second, which occurred much later,
was with the composer Martin Shaw, who was badly disfigured
by a birthmark and whom Ellen considered too slovenly to marry
her daughter. According to Marguerite Steen, Edy's close friend
Christopher St John was so upset by the possibility of the marriage
that she threatened to commit suicide. In any event, Edy, at her
best a generous and warm-hearted woman, was to remain a
spinster and to enter upon a period of tense and difficult relationship with her mother, whom she undoubtedly loved but whose
influence she resented at times to the point of bitterness and even
estrangement.

But, after her children, what mattered most to Ellen was her
relationship with Irving. They destroyed almost all the intimate
letters that passed between them; a very few survive and have at
various times come to light.[23] The following letters give some
idea of Irving's feeling for Ellen:

16 Dec 1885 (three nights before *Faust*):

No rehearsal this morning for you, my darling.

Tonight at seven dress,

Last night was a desperate affair from seven till five this morning.

Then only to end of 3rd act.

I left at one.

Today we rehearse several things – Broken scenes etc etc etc.

It was quite amusing last night – the absolute fog of some of 'em.

It will be all right – of course – but it is a stern business.

Yes a good drive today – perhaps you will drive down. But do not wear yourself out – & you shall not tonight either if I can persuade (you) to take it quietly.

What a worry you are you see.

With all my love my dearest dearest.

Between ourselves I think tonight we may struggle through 3 acts – perhaps —

7 June 1887 (after the first night of *The Amber Heart* by Alfred Calmour):

You were very lovely my darling – You yourself – alone – and there is nothing in the world beside you, *but* without you what a sad morning it would have been.

Poor Alfred he thinks its all his own I know and it never will be without you.

I wish we could talk it over now – together – I think I could tell you of the dream of beauty that you realized and were.

A lovely night of rest & peace is the wish of your own fond love.

November 1888 (a month prior to a production of *Macbeth*):

Think Fussie has got wind about going to London for last night, to my intense surprise and indignation, he collared a whole kidney – dispatching it at one bolt and then jumped upon the sofa in the most defiant manner – with head erect and licking lips.

He was proud – very proud of his accomplishment – regardless of consequences . . .

I'm sure it was the thought of seeing you. I'd have done it too had I been Fussie – so, of course, he was forgiven.

The enclosed from that cad Coquelin is too rich. Coquelin as 'Macbeth'. What next?

Goodbye my dearest life for one, two, three days.

Each morning is a bright one now.

Undated Fragment (apparently sent from Dublin):

Soon – soon!
I shall be near you on Sunday.
God bless you my only thought
Your own till Death.

3 June 1891:

My Nell, I thought I should have seen Ted this morning – but I'm glad you took him with you.

The worst will be over now I hope – but you have had a terrible time.

No one thought – nor did I dream how bad you were. Do pray be careful.

I am anxious to see Ted & to hear of you. You gave me a lovely letter to take away with me on Monday – My own dear wife, as long as I live.

12 June 1891:

You are coming back to morrow I hope – I want to see you – & to know & feel that you are getting stronger. Let me know if you are coming & I'll be with you the moment I can . . . we must bring the summer to ourselves by being together as often as we can.

I have not heard today. Telegraph in the morning if you are coming home. You've been a long time away.

Only one letter from Ellen to Irving, written from Brighton and dated 23 October but with no year, shows the manner in which she wrote to him:

Dear – I'm better now and hope to come back to work to-morrow – I was dreadfully ill – but I struggled hard before I broke down – Thank you for *missing* me! and for your loving letter. Your Nell.[24]

That Irving was in love with Ellen – 'the Queen of every woman', 'my own dear wife, as long as I live' – there can be no doubt at all. That she loved him, or accepted him with deep affection as her most intimate male friend, can be proved only by her actions in allowing him, over a period of many years, to visit her incessantly, to go about with her socially, to enjoy holidays with her in England, on the Continent and in North America. But no evidence exists, in spite of her remarks to Marguerite Steen, to justify the assumption that they took the grave risks involved in the final consummation of their love.[25]

Before making the assumption that they did indeed take such a risk, as Marguerite Steen does, one must set aside the restraints imposed by their particular temperaments, by the society in which they moved, and by the particular positions that they occupied together on the English stage. While Ellen was never prudish, her past life had made her prudent and, whatever her inclinations might have been, the last thing she could have risked was yet another proven scandal or, worse still, another illegitimate child. With contraception so unpleasant and so uncertain, the risks of an unwanted pregnancy to a woman in the public eye were far too difficult to face. Nor would Irving, prudish as he was, want to risk the future of so treasured a leading lady in this way. That they indulged in unconsummated love-making is possible, but even this cannot be proved without more evidence. Such written evidence as there might ever have been they were careful to destroy.

When they went on holiday together – for example to Germany in 1885 and later to Canada – they went with other companions.

R

They knew that they were the subject of incessant gossip, but this much they were prepared to weather. Irving knew his wife was on the alert for concrete evidence of his unfaithfulness, and that in any case divorce, no doubt with Ellen publicly cited, could ruin their careers. Everything points to a close and loving friendship of a kind which would justify what Ellen said to young Marguerite Steen, and which was to be the forerunner to Irving's final close relationship with the devoted Mrs Aria.

According to Laurence Irving, it may well be that his grandfather in the first years of his devotion to Ellen, bought in 1882 the house in the village of Brook Green (now absorbed into the ugly sprawl of Hammersmith) in order to provide a house in which he might one day enjoy her company.[26] The Grange, as it was called, was a derelict mansion in a well-shaded garden, and Irving spent money on its furnishing and redecoration. Although he never made the place his home, he spent what leisure time he could there, and entertained many of his guests, including Ellen and the children. Teddy was staying there with him at the time Godwin lay dying in the hospital. But in time the house lost all meaning for its owner, and was abandoned with nothing new to take its place.

It was in the middle-nineties that their love began to cool. The fervent devotion faded, and in its place developed the regard of friends. In December 1894, Ellen began to keep a private diary of her reflections on Irving as an actor and as a man. This splendid analysis is warm, yet accurate, and most courageous in the face of what Ellen realized she must be losing as his affections moved elsewhere.[27] Here are extracts from this diary:

> 1895: He is so careful and cautious. I wish he were more ingenuous and more direct. A thousand little things prove he has no idea of his own beauty – personal beauty. . . . I grant his intellectuality dominates his other powers and gifts, but I have never seen in living man, or picture, such distinction of bearing.

> 12 September 1895: I think it is not quite right in him that he does not care for anybody much. (I think he has always

cared for me a little, very little, and has had passing fancies, but he really *cares* for scarcely any one.) Quiet, patient, tolerant, impersonal, gentle, *close*, crafty! Crafty sounds unkind, but it is H.I. 'Crafty' fits him.

1896: His work, his work! He has always held his life, and his death, second to his work. When he dies, it will be because he is tired out. . . . I have a quick ear for different people's *step*, and a familiar step I generally hear before I see the stepper, but though I have listened for many years for Henry Irving's step, *I have never heard it.*

I consider I have been of a good deal of use to him as a buffer between him and his company.

H.I. is much handsomer now than when I first knew him in 1867. Handsomer, but somehow more furtive-looking. Is his dominant note intellectuality? Yes. I think so. He has so much character. . . .

He is a very *gentle* man, though not in the least a *tender* man.

1897: Very odd. He is not improving with age.

February 1898: His hold upon *me* is that he is INTERESTING no matter how he behaves. I think he must be put down among the 'Greats', and that *that* is his only fault. He is Great. Constantine, Nero, Caesar, Charlemagne, Peter, Napoleon, all 'Great', all selfish, all, but all INTERESTING. Interesting, but terrors in the family.

January 1899: I wonder how his other friends and lovers feel to him. I have contempt and affection and admiration. What a mixture!

He evidently doesn't like taking favours from any of his friends (which he is obliged to do at present). I don't think it *gracious* to be unable to take favours sweetly. He will take them, but will *not* acknowledge them.

He wrote and asked me to go down and see him at Bourne-mouth. I went, and found him looking much better. He wanted to tell me that not only was he broken in health but he was what is called 'ruined'. At which word I refused to shed tears, for, said I: 'As long as you and I have health, we have means of wealth. We can pack a bag, each of us, and trot round the Provinces. Yes, and go to America, Australia, India, Japan, and pick up money by the bushel, even were we to take just the magic book of Shakespeare along with us.' I then asked his plans, and he astonished me by saying: 'That's why I asked you to come down to Bournemouth. (He might have written, but no; he'd not *write* that.) I propose – have in fact written to the managers – going round the English provinces with a very small company, and playing *The Bells, Louis XI, Waterloo,* and perhaps another play.' Long pause. I didn't think it *possible* I heard aright. '*What* plays?' said I. '*Bells, Louis, Waterloo,*' he said irritably. 'Well, and where do I come in?' said I. 'Oh well, for the present, at all events, there's no chance of acting at the Lyceum.' (He looked exceedingly silly.) 'For the present, you can, of course, er, *do as you like!*'

I felt – a good many feelings! At top of all came amusement to save the situation. 'Then,' said I, 'I have in plain terms what Ted would call "the dirty kick out"?'

'Well – er – for the present I don't see what can be done, and I daresay you —' I cut him short. 'Oh, I daresay I shall get along somehow. Have I your permission to shift for myself, and make up a tour for myself?' 'Yes.' 'For how long?' 'Well, I can scarcely say.' 'Until Christmas next?' 'Yes.'

April 1900: H. has sciatica badly. Really he has a very dull time of it, it seems to me, and I believe for the first time begins to appreciate my very long service, to know I am valuable.

October 1900: He has terrified me once or twice by his exhaustion and feebleness. Then he appears grateful to us all, for we *all* give him *all*. But when he gets a little better, anything so icy, indifferent, and almost contemptuous, I never saw.[28]

The draft of a letter from Irving to Ellen survives in a small notebook in which he pencilled his thoughts during 1904 in America when he went on his first and only tour there without her. It shows no diminution in their friendship, though it bears no sign of love:

> As you say how long will this work go on? I would be glad to end now – in Oct 1906 I shall [have] been on the stage 50 years and think that will have been enough.
>
> There is much to be done with properly organized farewell tours – in 2 years or in 4 – and I'm sure if possible we ought to be together, the public want it here and at home.... How beautiful the first *Becket* was in many ways and how impossible to match in any way.
>
> I see that Master Edward is starting a dramatic school not to [be] left out of it. I think you and I should. . . . We should have lots of pupils.[29]

That Ellen, even when approaching fifty, was not free from the embarrassments of gossip is proved by the fact that her name was linked with that of her leading man, Frank Cooper, who returned to the company in 1896 to play Mordred in *King Arthur*. Ellen was thought to be showing him a certain partiality. In 1899, during Irving's illness, she toured the provinces with him independently as her leading man; a descendant of the Kemble family, he was a reflection of Charles Kelly whom she had known for twenty years. The gossip merely amused her, as she wrote to her friend Bertha Bramly from Hull on 30 October during the arduous provincial tour of 1897:

> No – I fear I can't snap up Frank Cooper (!) and marry him, for he happens to have a wife – and she's nice too – so he can't 'cut her throat with a bar of soap' – She is a jealous little lady too, but *not* of me – and I'm fond of her. They marry me to every man I act with – 'She acts so naturally' they say – 'it must be real' – Silly-fool-Asses!!! Mrs Finch Hatton told me a few days since that my Edy was engaged to be married – I knew nothing about it but as Edy is away I sent her congratulations!!!

She thought it very polite of me but knew nothing about the matter.

One of the actresses whom Irving eventually engaged to replace Ellen was Lena Ashwell, whose talent Ellen had recognized at the Royal College of Music. 'She has to work. Her life must be given to it, and then she will – well, she will achieve just as high as she works,' Ellen had written of her in her diary. To the girl who called to see her in Barkston Gardens in a daze of heroine-worship she had said: 'Get experience; do anything, go anywhere, but get experience.' Lena Ashwell's career on the stage began in 1891, and Ellen constantly helped her with recommendations to the actor-managers of the day. In 1895 she joined the Lyceum company and played Elaine in *King Arthur*. When in 1896 she returned to play the Prince of Wales in *Richard III*, she sensed the change that was gradually overtaking the Lyceum: 'The atmosphere was different; the resilience had gone,' she wrote. Irving's ill-health was impeding his mastery of production. She was so upset by the petty rivalries and gossip in the company she had so revered that Irving found her one night quietly weeping beside the stage. 'You know, we were born crying,' he told her in an effort to console. Later still, in 1903, when he was on tour in Glasgow, he summoned her by telegram to come up north to see him. When she came, he offered her during his farewell tours the place in his company which Ellen had vacated.[30]

In effect, Ellen never really left Irving until she finally refused an offer from him of £12,000 to tour the United States in *Dante*.[31] But she was always ready to reappear with him in their old, surviving repertoire, in particular *The Merchant of Venice*. But she realized it was useless to maintain an association which was becoming a burden to them both, and that her future, and those of her many dependents, which now included Teddy's children, required her to try to make a new career for herself.[32] It was a cruel twilight in the evening of her professional life, for she had had no real experience either in management or production, and had little idea of what to do for the best. Meanwhile, there were some minor offers to accept. For example, she appeared as Queen Katherine in Benson's production of *Henry VIII* on Shakespeare's birthday at Stratford.

It was during this period of partial retirement from the Lyceum that she was invited by Beerbohm Tree, perhaps Irving's closest rival, to play Mistress Page in the spectacular production of *The Merry Wives of Windsor* at His Majesty's Theatre in 1902. Mistress Ford had already been given to Mrs Kendal, whom theatrical gossip classed as the actress most jealous of Ellen's position in the theatre. Irving gave her his permission to appear with a rival company and on the opening night sent her a telegram of good wishes: 'Heaven give you many many merry days and nights.' This joint appearance with Madge Kendal and Tree invited a measure of malicious gossip.[33]

In 1902, Ellen moved from Barkston Gardens to No 215 King's Road, Chelsea. She wrote to Stephen Coleridge, who negotiated the purchase for her: 'Please get this 215 house insured for me quickly or the ill-luck of a fire might chance! and my few good pictures? Sorry to be such a trouble.'[34] The year before she had bought Smallhythe.

After her final provincial tour with Irving was over at the end of the year, Ellen decided to enter into management, most of all to help Teddy. In 1903 she took a short lease of the Imperial Theatre, Westminster, and, in April, while Irving was presenting *Dante* at the Theatre Royal, Drury Lane, she presented Ibsen's play, *The Viking's* with sets and production by Gordon Craig. She herself was quite unsuitably cast as Hiordis. The production was an utter failure with the public, lasting only twenty-four performances, and the costs, though not recorded, led her into heavy losses. The theatre had to be changed structurally to accommodate the settings, and new lighting was installed to create the effects that Teddy wanted. *The Vikings* was hurriedly replaced by *Much Ado about Nothing,* in which she naturally appeared as Beatrice with Oscar Asche as Benedick. In his memoirs of the period, Gordon Craig blames the ineptness of the business manager Ellen had insisted on employing. The fault lay probably with all of them, with Teddy's over-ambitious handling of the stage and Ellen's incapacity for either business or publicity.

To recover something of her losses, Ellen undertook a provincial tour without her son, presenting *Much Ado about Nothing* and *The Good Hope*, a play by the contemporary Dutch dramatist Herman Heijermans, which had been translated by Edy's friend, Christabel Marshall (Christopher St John). Apart from these personal connexions, there can have been no other good reason for presenting *The Good Hope*. Once more, Ellen played a part which was scarcely suited to her, that of Kniertje, an elderly woman in a small Dutch fishing village. She claims that this play succeeded in the provinces. After appearing for the last time with Irving in July before he sailed to America without her, all she had in prospect was *Alice-sit-by-the-fire*, a sentimental play which James Barrie wrote in the hope that she would appear in it. She did not enjoy the experience. 'I was never happy in my part, perhaps because although it had been made to measure, it didn't fit me. I sometimes felt that I was bursting the seams! I was accustomed to broader work in a larger theatre.'

Meanwhile, Ted had disappeared to Germany. There, about a year later, he was to meet and fall in love with Isadora Duncan, whom he called Topsy. The relationship lasted, it would seem, until 1906.

In one sense at least, Ellen's heart was still with Irving. She suffered with those that she saw suffering. When Irving fell ill in Glasgow in 1899, she had written of him to Edy:

I am still fearfully anxious about H. It will be a long time at best before he regains strength.... All he wants is for me to keep my health – not my *head*! He knows I'm doing that! Last night I did three acts of *Sans-Gêne* with *Nance Oldfield* thrown in! That is a bit too much – awful work – and I can't risk it again.... A telegram just come: 'Steadily improving'.... You should have seen Norman as Shylock! It was not a bare 'get-through'. An admirable performance as well as a plucky one. H. is more seriously ill than anyone dreams. His look! Like the last act of *Louis XI*.[35]

In the spring of 1905, when she heard he was lying ill in Wolverhampton, she hurried north to see him. She took the precaution of seeing his doctor first, and learned his heart was severely strained, and that he must spare himself. Then she went to see him. It was their last meeting:

He looked like some beautiful grey tree that I have seen in Savannah. His old dressing-gown hung about his frail yet majestic figure like some mysterious grey drapery.

We were both very moved, and said little.

'I'm glad you've come. Two Queens have been in to me this morning. Queen Alexandra telegraphed to say how sorry she was I was ill, and now you – ' . . .

We fell to talking about work. He said he hoped that I had a good manager . . . agreed very heartily with me about Frohman, saying he was always so fair – more than fair.

'What a wonderful life you've had, haven't you?' I exclaimed, thinking of it all in a flash.

'Oh, yes,' he said quietly . . . 'a wonderful life – of work.'

'And there's nothing better, after all is there?'

'Nothing.'

'What have you got out of it all? . . . You and I are "getting on" as they say. Do you ever think, as I do sometimes, what you have got out of life?'

'What have I got out of it?' said Henry, stroking his chin and smiling slightly. 'Let me see . . . Well, a good cigar, a good glass of wine – good friends.' Here he kissed my hand with courtesy. Always he was so courteous; always his actions, like this little one of kissing my hand, were so beautifully timed. They came just before the spoken words, and gave them peculiar value.

'That's not a bad summing-up of it all,' I said. 'And the end. . . . How would you like that to come?'

'How would I like that to come?' He repeated my question

lightly, yet meditatively too. Then he was silent for some thirty seconds before he snapped his fingers – the action again before the words.

'Like that!'[36]

The local doctor in Wolverhampton told her Irving should never undertake the strain of playing Mathias again. This particular performance put the heaviest burden on his weakened body. His heart would throb from the sheer stress of his imagination, and the death of Mathias was performed with fearful physical intensity. In spite of this, later that year at Bradford he insisted on attempting yet another performance in the part. The doctor was right; he lasted only long enough to play *Becket* on the following night, Friday 13 October, barely surviving the performance. Within a few minutes of the curtain-fall he lay dead in the lobby of his hotel. Bram Stoker's description of this moment reads with the shock of real loss:

In the hall were some twenty men grouped round Irving who lay at full length on the floor. . . .

It was almost impossible to believe, as he lay there with his eyes open, that he was really dead. I knelt down by him and felt his heart to know for myself if it was indeed death. But all was sadly still. His body was quite warm. Walter Collinson, his faithful valet, was sitting on the floor beside him, crying. He said to me through his sobs: 'He died in my arms!'

His face looked very thin and the features sharp as he lay there with his chest high and his head fallen back; but there was none of the usual ungracefulness of death. The long iron-grey hair had fallen back, showing the great height of his rounded forehead. The bridge of his nose stood out sharp and high. I closed his eyes myself but as I had no experience in such a matter I asked one of the doctors, who kindly with deft fingers straightened the eyelids. Then we carried him upstairs to his room and laid him on his bed.[37]

Irving had once told Ellen he hoped they would bury him in

Westminster Abbey. This was not said in arrogance, but as a claim for the status of the profession. Ellen attended the funeral service, salving her sorrow at his death with the buoyant thought: 'How Henry would have liked it!' She had memories too, of attending Tennyson's funeral in 1892 with Irving by her side. 'No face there looked anything by the side of Henry's,' she had written then in her diary. Now she was there again, and it was he who lay in the coffin:

> How terribly I missed that face at Henry's own funeral! I kept on expecting to see it, for indeed it seemed to me that he was directing the whole most moving and impressive ceremony. I could almost hear him saying, 'Get on! get on!' in the parts of the service that dragged. When the sun – such a splendid, tawny sun – burst across the solemn misty grey of the Abbey, at the very moment when the coffin, under its superb pall of laurel leaves was carried up the choir, I felt that it was an effect which he would have loved.[38]

IX

SHAW

When George Bernard Shaw wrote his first letter to Ellen Terry in June 1892 he was almost thirty-six and she was forty-five. The heart of the correspondence that followed between 1895 and 1900 is among the most celebrated in the history of British letter-writing. These letters were for Shaw an ideal climax to a long, involved and frequently stormy relationship with women which was only fully revealed well after his death in 1950. However, he had had something to say about this himself, and during his lifetime gave certain details to his principal biographers, as well as publishing some revealing autobiographical essays a year before his death in his book, *Sixteen Self Sketches*.

The Irish romantic in Shaw's complex nature demanded ad-miration from women, while the ascetic in his make-up eventually led him to abandon early in life any further subservience to the physical demands of sex. These demands he quickly exhausted, more especially in his love affairs with the widow Jenny Patterson and the actress Florence Farr.[1] Mrs Patterson, who had money and lived in Brompton Square, was his mother's pupil; she was fifteen years older than Shaw, whom (according to her victim) she seduced on his twenty-ninth birthday. He soon found her to be 'sexually insatiable', and for some years she both attracted and plagued him. He suffered continually from her tormented jealousy, which was aroused by the growing number of women he was encouraging to fall in love with him. In spite of this their relation-ship lasted until 1893, by which time Shaw's passion for philander-ing had brought him intimacy elsewhere.

Florence Farr, an actress of great beauty with progressive views on women's independence, was another woman with whom he consummated love. She was a lady of some means who had been deserted by her actor husband, and Shaw first met her when she was learning embroidery from May Morris, the daughter of William Morris. He was a constant visitor to the aesthete-socialist's luxurious home and, while enjoying a secret understanding with May Morris and contracting what he chose to call a 'celestial marriage' with her, he felt a more earth-like passion for her pupil and turned to Florence Farr for purely physical pleasures after their first meeting in 1890. He wrote parts for her into his plays, *Widowers' Houses* and *The Philanderer;* later she was to appear in *Arms and the Man.* It would seem that Shaw's particular kind of sexuality, which Florence Farr was to describe later as 'passion served up with cold sauce', was insufficient to satisfy her and she turned to others, leaving Shaw to feel jealous; she kept a 'Leporello list' which, Shaw told his biographer Hesketh Pearson, included by 1894 the names of fourteen available men. In the end, she turned from Shaw to W. B. Yeats, who wrote for her his *Land of Heart's Desire.*

From the gentle, tranquil Florence Shaw turned to May Morris and then to a variety of loves including Annie Besant, Karl Marx's daughter Eleanor, and Edith Nesbit, the author of books for children, and Bertha Newcombe. 'Whenever I think of my behaviour in those days I grow afraid of myself,' wrote Shaw. 'I don't know why it was but all the women I really *cared* for were already married.' May Morris eventually married Henry Halliday Sparling, and then left her husband on Shaw's account, though Shaw was never to marry her. Annie Besant, who had deserted her clergyman husband to become, for a while, a militant atheist and propagandist for birth-control, was a close friend of Shaw's in the later 1880s, but lost contact with him when she finally became a convert to theosophy. Eleanor Marx, who was of the same age as Shaw, gave him up to enter a 'free marriage' with the already married journalist, Edward Aveling. Shaw met Edith Nesbit through the Fabian Society; she was unhappy with her husband, who was constantly unfaithful to her. She fell so openly in love with Shaw, also during the 1880s, that he had very firmly to cover his retreat. According to one of his biographers, entries in his unpublished diaries reveal simultaneous 'attachments' in the late 1880s and around 1890 to seven women at one time, some Fabians and some actresses; among the actresses was Janet Achurch, whose marriage became threatened because of her affection for Shaw. But of all these women, Shaw only admitted to having sexual relations with Jenny Patterson and Florence Farr. It would appear that though he was inordinately fond of women he was, like many philanderers, both undersexed and masochistically afraid of the very ardour he set out to encourage. He even inspired the attentions of the well-known Lesbian Kate Joynes, who lived in unconsummated matrimony with his friend Henry Salt, the humanitarian. As for the painter Bertha Newcombe, she was Beatrice Webb's nominee for the position of Shaw's future wife. But he was not to marry her either.

By the time he first entered into correspondence with Ellen, Shaw could claim to be an experienced philanderer and observer of women, though his understanding of love was to some extent limited owing to his insatiable and self-conscious curiosity about it. Though active in the pursuit of all the women who attracted him, he remained, in one sense at least, a voyeur. His initial response to the first lady of the British stage was careful. Their first letters concerned a young singer whom Ellen wanted to help but who, as music critic on *The World,* Shaw felt lacked genuine talent. Ellen expressed her gratitude warmly: 'Thank you. Thank you, *Thank* you for all your beautifulness.' By the time he had reached the third of the letters to her from him which have been preserved, Shaw had decided to send her his book *The Quintessence of Ibsenism,* which had been published in 1891, and was calling her 'irresistible Ellen' and accusing her of wasting herself by playing in such old-fashioned rubbish as *Nance Oldfield* while the new drama stood waiting for her genius to bring it to light. Then the correspondence lapsed for over two years. During this interval, he had himself begun to contribute to the new drama with *Widowers' Houses* and had entered upon his fierce campaign against the conventional drama by becoming in January 1895 dramatic critic for Frank Harris's *Saturday Review*. His main target for attack was Sir Henry Irving, head of the reactionary established theatre, which Shaw regarded as 'childish'. The principal object of his adulation was Irving's leading lady, with whom he renewed his correspondence in July 1895 in an attempt to seduce her from Irving.

This second stage in the correspondence, the heart of it, began when Ellen was at a susceptible period in her life. Her youth, in spite of her beauty and her ageless vivacity, had gone, and her climacteric was approaching. Her health was not very good, and her eyes in particular gave her much trouble. She was already a grandmother, and though delighting in her grandchildren she was very distressed by the irresponsible behaviour of her genius of a son. Her relations with her daughter were difficult; Edy, while loving her mother in her own way, was a self-centred and at times unresponsive girl whose undoubted talents were finding no outlet satisfactory either to herself or to her mother. And her private relationship with Irving was gradually fading no less irredeemably than her partnership with him on the stage. She was more than ready for another man to appear and sweep her off on some magic carpet, more especially if it was a magic carpet which made no physical demands upon her.

Shaw has called his correspondence with Ellen 'a paper courtship', and he regarded it as 'perhaps the pleasantest, as it is the most enduring, of all courtship'. And then he added what for many people has seemed the most inhuman aspect of his celebrated relationship with Ellen: 'We both felt instinctively that a meeting might spoil it, and would certainly alter it and bring it into conflict with other personal relationships. And so I hardly ever saw her, except across the footlights, until the inevitable moment at last arrived when we had to meet daily at the rehearsals of the play I wrote for her: *Captain Brassbound's Conversion*.' This meeting did not take place until 1900, by which time Shaw was already married. There was to be a moment of seeming disenchantment: 'I'm very cold,' wrote Ellen subsequently, 'and they say you could not bear me, when we met, that one time, under the stage.'

But Shaw has made it clear there was no disenchantment, only the natural waning of a friendship which had for a while been the most important one in his life, but which had ceased to have significance once he had married Charlotte Payne Townsend in 1898.

The correspondence resumed after a gap which lasted from July 1892 until March 1895. Shaw, as dramatic critic for the *Saturday Review*, became an ardent member of the audience at the Lyceum – not, as everyone came to realize, because of Irving's art but because of Ellen. When she began to respond to him in letters which were so alive and personal, Shaw realized that Ellen Terry could be the greatest conquest of his career. Ellen was not a member of the circle of intellectual women in which Shaw normally moved; she belonged to an altogether larger sphere, and her beauty and charm were precisely of the unsensual kind most likely to delight him at this stage of his maturity. Shaw was fighting for recognition as a dramatist, and he entertained high hopes of conquering Irving himself with Ellen's help. His approach to her, therefore, had a double purpose – to win both the lady and the actress. Now that she had reached fifty, Shaw doggedly maintained that she stood in need of him and of the new intellectual drama which he represented. And he fully realized that he stood in need of her. She was, after all, the first lady of the London stage. She was obviously intrigued from the start by the impertinently challenging letters she began to receive in 1895, castigating Irving and the Lyceum productions and urging her to take interest in the plays he sent her to read. 'Your lovely letters,' she is writing by May 1896, and the vigorous response she got in correspondence which expanded into fascinating essays on the playing of Shakespeare or on the virtues of Ibsen and the modern drama soon excited her ready interest and finally her affection. They were on first-name terms by the end of the year, and sending each other highly literate kisses through the letter-box.

Shaw's philandering, as much *jeu d'esprit* as it was *jeu d'amour*, exactly suited Ellen's needs at this time. She needed to feel admired and wanted in her private life, and Shaw could fulfil this to an extravagant degree. She also needed a man to challenge her as a woman, to stretch and temper her latent capacities grown slack through the easy adulations of the Lyceum, which no longer made any real demands upon her. Here was the cleverest man of the age about to buzz round her head like a wasp and send her marvellous letters which were full of light and air, and the dry heat of his intellect. Even more delightful still, she was herself to be a match for him; her own letters evidently proved equally marvellous to him as his seemed to her. Indeed they reveal her at the height of her capacity as a woman to respond on an intellectual level to this man who could see through so many pretences in human nature, and who wanted to share with a woman of out-standing intelligence and understanding the revaluations coursing through his mind. 'Part of her remarkable mental endowment was a sure touch with men,' wrote Shaw. The correspondents had an exactly balanced respect for each other as human beings, male and female, and each brought out the very best in the other. When they discovered each other's faults, they commented on them with an exactitude and generosity which could never give offence.

Shaw, it must be remembered, was hated by most people work-ing in the conventional theatre of the period. Irving could never understand Ellen's predilection for this man he called 'Pshaw', who rent the veil of the temple he had dedicated to his own genius. Laurence Irving, whom Shaw, like Ellen, had befriended, told Shaw: 'All my people think you the most appalling Yahoo.' Yet never for an instant did Ellen doubt the sincerity or the capacity of Shaw; as he put it himself, when he was 'posturing as a sort of half-starved Mephistopheles with a success that imposed on the whole theatrical West End, Ellen Terry, without hesitation or effort, went straight through the imposture to the real man and nursed him like a baby, though always taking his judgment seriously even when it did not jump with her own. . . . Shaw made all the world his stage and was not supposed to be acting, in spite of his frequent clownings and the mask of mountebankery which Ellen Terry saw through so easily.'[2]

Shaw was Irish, and this in itself attracted Ellen in the first place. Unlike Irving, Shaw also understood the problems of an ageing actress who remained fixed in established parts most of which were by now far too youthful for her, or was being forced to play new parts of such insignificance that they could only be regarded as an insult to her qualities. Shaw was acutely aware of the difference between Ellen and Irving: 'She, all brains and sympathy, scattering them everywhere and on everybody; he, all self, concentrating that self on his stage as on a pedestal.' Yet, as Shaw observed, the combination worked, until time and Shaw himself came along to undo it. She was lucky, Shaw thinks, in her men, by which he meant Irving and himself: 'If we take it that a clever woman's most amusing toys are interesting men we must admit that Ellen Terry was fortunate in her two dolls.'[3]

Shaw's attacks on Irving were not merely negative, the expression of his reaction against what he held to be Irving's outworn conventions of performance. He recognized in Irving a unique theatrical personality: 'I instinctively felt that a new drama inhered in this man.' Although he found Irving's performance peculiar, if not grotesque, he acknowledged the actor's magnetism, 'which forced the spectator to single him out as a leading figure'. Only Charlie Chaplin had possessed this quality since Irving, Shaw was to write in 1931. To Shaw, Irving's devotion to a kind of melancholy fustian on the stage was a pervasion of his genius, and it was because of this that he castigated him in the *Saturday Review,* while at the same time recognizing all the qualities of his *genre* acting in *The Bells* or *Louis XI.* His performances in Shakespeare he regarded as 'impostures' worked out with awful care to fulfil some fancy of his own; his Hamlet, thought Shaw, was not Shakespeare's, but Irving's. So by the time Shaw became critic of the *Saturday Review* he had come to regard Irving's years at the Lyceum as 'an exasperating waste of the talent of the two artists who had seemed to me peculiarly fitted to lift the theatre out of its old ruts and head it towards unexplored regions of drama'. To present Shakespeare, therefore, especially as Irving presented him, was a waste of time compared with presenting Ibsen, or even his own small curtain-raiser, *The Man of Destiny*, which he wrote for Irving and Ellen and which was to become the cause of so much unseemly haggling between the greatest actor and the greatest playwright in the British theatre at the turn of the century.[4]

According to Shaw he was successful in his seduction of Ellen from Irving:

> This correspondence shows how, because Irving would not put his peculiar talent at the service of the new and intensely interesting development of the drama which had begun with Ibsen, and because he wasted not only his own talent but Ellen's, I destroyed her belief in him and gave shape and consciousness to her sense of having her possibilities sterilized by him. Then her position became unbearable; and she broke loose from the ogre's castle, as I called it, only to find that she had waited too long for his sake, and that her withdrawal was rather a last service to him than a first to herself.[5]

Yet Shaw never ceased to pay tribute to Irving's extraordinary capacities: 'Even to call him eminent belittles his achievement: he was pre-eminent.'

In the letters, however, Shaw constantly attacks Irving. He appears jealous, or mock-jealous, of him: 'I once or twice have met you on Richmond Terrace or thereabouts with him like two children in a gigantic perambulator, and have longed to seize him, throw him out, get up, take his place, and calmly tell the coachman to proceed.'[6] After he and Irving had met to discuss *The Man of Destiny*, Shaw wrote: 'I like Henry, though he is without exception absolutely the stupidest man I ever met. Simply no brains – nothing but character and temperament.'[7] The clue to his acting, according to Shaw, was one of self-hypnosis: 'The condition in which he works is a somnambulistic one: he hypnotizes himself into a sort of dreamy energy, and is intoxicated by the humming of his words in his nose. Besides, he escapes the terrible fatigue of thought and intellectual self-consciousness, through having no brains.'[8] He was well aware that Irving detested him for his eloquent depreciation of everything Irving held most sacred. Having said in the *Saturday Review* that it was a relief to see a production of *Olivia* without Irving for once, Shaw wrote to Ellen:

> There was a terrible thing in that Olivia notice ... that it was a relief to get rid of him for a moment at the Lyceum. It was not so brutal as that; but as he does not understand critical points, and treats all intellectual positions as mere matters of feeling, he probably took it in that way and was hurt by it; and he will perhaps think it unfeeling of you not to be angry with me for saying it. So be kind to him, and if he is clever enough to tell you on that afternoon drive – as I should in his place – that he is giving up the play because he is jealous of me about you, take his part and console him: it is when a man is too much hurt to do the perfectly magnanimous thing that he most needs standing by.[9]

In his championship of Ellen, Shaw saw her as sacrificed on the altar of Irving's dedicated egotism; 'he is an ogre who has carried you off to his cave,' Shaw wrote, 'and now Childe Roland is coming to the dark tower to rescue you.'[10] He sent her the most detailed analysis for the treatment of the various scenes and speeches in *Cymbeline* – an affrontery, it might seem, had not both he and Ellen enjoyed writing their lengthy letters enormously, and had she not found what he said to be both apt and helpful. By now she felt safe enough with him to send him her private analysis of the Lyceum company; 'There's something good in each one,' she added, before making her comments:

Cymbeline (Macklin) Will look superb.
Cloten (Forbes) Has brains.
Posthumus (Cooper) A lovely voice, and never shouts.
Guiderius (Webster) Shouts, but has a sweet face.
Arviraqus (Teddy) Has 'some of the charm which for centuries belonged' to his ma-ma.
Belarius (F. Robinson) 'What a proud stomach!' And one critic

I know will discover that *at last* an actor has arrived in our
midst who can deliver Blank Verse. Looks as if he were going to deliver something else. Oh! and as H.I. says: 'You
can *hear* him' (I wish I couldn't).

Pisanio (Tyars) Well, he always looks well.

Cornelius (Lacy) Was a parson! So he must be 'good'.

Iachimo (H.I.) Well, do you know I think we agree, you and I,
that he's quite a decent actor.

Queen (Gene. Ward) She was the pupil of Ristori. Hang it!

Imogen A painstaking person, but I fear will look a sight.

They *All* work with earnestness, are 'sober, clean' and
perfect (in their words). Except E.T. who will never know
those Confounded Words.[11]

'Tear this up, quick, quick!' she writes on the top of this, though
Shaw fortunately never did so. Of her own shortcomings (as she
saw them) she wrote a remarkably revealing letter on 22 September 1896:

> ... spite of all your goodness to me I shall do nothing to-
> night. It's not because I've left my effects to chance. I've
> settled what I want to try for, but I'm *all earth* instantly I get on
> the stage for this part. No inspiration, no softness, no sadness
> even. Tight, mechanical, *hide-bound*. I feel nothing. I know
> some of myself. In a few days it will all be different. I think it
> is the result of physical weariness. My head is tired. I cant care,
> cant think, cant feel. *Can Not*. After the carefullest thinking
> and practising every detail of my blessed work, something
> comes upon me. (This is when things go well and right. It has
> nothing to do with my will.) I feel exquisitely, and then, I
> realize the situation (in the play) and all is golden.
>
> But no 'gold' tonight. Only dull mud. I cant help it, dear
> fellow. You see it has nothing to do with me. If I ever act well,
> it's accident. It's *divine*, isnt it? There's a double movement
> somewhere, for all the while one is receiving this gracious dew
> from heaven, this fire and warmth, one is turning oneself, as it
> were, to be basted properly.[12]

By May 1897, Shaw's attack on Irving became harsh, almost desperate: 'Your career has been sacrificed to the egotism of a fool: he has warmed his wretched hands callously at the embers of nearly twenty of your priceless years; and now they will flame up, scorch his eyes, burn off his rum-bathed hair, and finally consume him.'[13] In February 1898 he is more analytical of her situation:

> If you once realize that the sacrifice of the other parts is not a conscious, malicious, jealous, direct act of his, but an inevitable condition of his methods and effects, you will see that you, too, must be sacrificed. That he is not crudely jealous is shewn by the fact that he has no objection to your success in *Sans-Gêne* and *Nance Oldfield*, where, since he is not on the stage, your playing does not interfere with his. But the moment he is there, he cannot work out his slow, laboured, self-absorbed stage conceptions unless you wait for him and play to him. This is a frightful handicap for you. Increase it by a bad part and the task becomes impossible.[14]

By February 1900, with Ellen still tied, as he saw it, to Irving's bishop like apron-strings, he seems to accept the inevitable with resignation:

> I have always foreseen, and foretold to you, that when it came to the point, you would find it practically impossible to detach yourself from the Lyceum. And apart from the business reasons, the breaking up of an old partnership like yours and H.I.'s is not a thing to be done except on extreme occasions. It was my feeling concerning this that made me so very determined not to let you interfere in the *Man of Destiny* squabble. I wrote *Brassbound* for you merely for the sake of writing it for you, without any faith in your ever being able to produce it, knowing that the existence of the play would strengthen your hold of H.I. (by making you independent of him if you chose to abandon his ship) and thereby make it doubly certain that he would not let you go for want of asking you to stay – and

obviously if he really wants you to stay, stay you must. Consequently I am in no way disappointed or surprised: destiny has fulfilled itself exactly as I foresaw it would if affairs took their normal course.[15]

During the period when their correspondence was at its height Shaw had sent her his plays to read, and had written two parts specially for her: the Strange Lady in *The Man of Destiny* and Lady Cicely in *Captain Brassbound's Conversion*. He found writing parts for her daunting and difficult: 'Heaven knows how many plays I shall have to write before I earn one that belongs of divine right to you,' he said to her as early as April 1896.[16] Ellen, in 1899, had other ideas: 'Of course you never *really* meant Lady Cicely for me – but to be published along with other Plays. For delight I'd soonest act your Mrs Warren and Cleopatra. For money I'd choose your *You Never Can Tell, The Devil's D,* and *Candida* – (properly acted).'[17] When she read *Candida* in October 1896, she wrote:

> I've cried my poor eyes out over your horrid play, your *heavenly* play. My dear, and now! How can I go out to dinner tonight? I must keep my blue glasses on all the while for my eyes are puffed up and burning. But I can scarce keep from reading it all over again. Henry would not care for that play, I think. I know he would laugh. And that sort of thing makes me hate him sometimes. He would not understand it, the dear, clever silly. *I* cant understand what *he* understands.[18]

Ellen, uncertain of her future at the Lyceum, was anxious only to be loyal – loyal to Irving, loyal to Shaw and all he was trying to tell her about herself and, far behind all this, loyal to her future career, since on this, she now knew, her daughter and her son, and all his children, might well be dependent. Irving naturally resented the attention she paid to Shaw, who wrote to her on March 1897:

> Does H. I. really say that you are in love with me? For that be all his sins forgiven him! I will go to the Lyceum again and write an article proving him to be the greatest Richard ever

dreamed of. I am also touched by his refusing to believe that we have never met. No man of feeling *could* believe such heartlessness.[19]

Ellen fought a rearguard action in defence of Irving, but conceded points to Shaw all down the line. In September 1896 she wrote: '*He* is frightened for everyone but himself, for he has not the ghost of an idea how anyone acts in his theatre, unless he's not in the play.'[20] In May 1897, during Shaw's acrimonious discussions with Irving over *The Man of Destiny,* she wrote: 'H and I are out! A little bit. For he dont tell me things about you, because he's vexed always with people who wont agree always and entirely with everything he says, and although I try not to aggravate him by actually *saying* so, I dont agree with him about you, and he knows it. Have you written to him I wonder? Has he written to you? I never *ask* him things.'[21] And two days later she wrote:

'Be gentle,' you say, 'with H,' I am *always* gentle with him. Better for him if all these years I had acted being something else. It would take too long, and too clever, to tell you the why, but I've spoiled him! I was born meek. (Ugh.) His 'policy of silence' was merely trying to get out of extra trouble, in writing. I do assure you it is *I* all along who wished so hard for the play. He never wishes for anything much outside his own individual effort. I admire him for it, and I hate him for it, that he appreciates NOTHING and NOBODY. You have to poke a play under his nose and read it, and speak of it, and act bits of it, and trouble about it (or rather about his part in it) until you are fagged out, before he'll look at it; and then it takes him a long time to see any good there. But he's worth every trouble, for when once he takes a thing up there's no one like him in mastering the whole affair.

'Gentle!' He wants a good slapping, but *you* must not do that, and *I* wont. I think I'm tired and too indifferent now. It makes me cry to know it, but I'm a patient person.[22]

The previous month on 22 April, she had written:

H. is not jealous of me, I remember he once said: 'The best proof of my love for you is that I am not jealous of you.' (Of course you understand he meant 'jealous of the public liking me!'). He astounded me by saying that. As if one *could* be jealous of such a paltry having! As if one *could* do anything but give and give if one had even a little bit of true love! Ah, he makes me tired and sad and hopeless sometimes, and I do expect always the best from him.[23]

Yet in December 1897, when Irving was ill, she wrote (and meant):

If you worry (or try to worry) Henry, I must end our long and close friendship. He is ill, and what would I not do to better him?[24]

But disillusionment with the Lyceum, if not with Irving personally, is apparent in the letters she wrote in 1898. In March she tells Shaw: 'I cant write to you, cant feel, cant think. I work and work but am ill and hate it all.'[25] In April, during the preparations for *The Medicine Man,* she says: 'It "lunatics" me to watch Henry at these rehearsals. Hours and hours of loving care over this twaddle! He just *adores* his absurd part.'[26] In May 1899, she seems near revolt:

If H.I. gives me only half a fairly good part, I shall play it, but if a part is offered me like the kind of thing I did (or didn't!) in *Peter the Great, Medicine Man,* or *Robespierre* I shall 'refuse to act' (for the first time in my life) and give it all up and come and settle quietly in a place like this [Laleham] and perhaps act sometimes on occasions when I could fit in better than another. I should never say good-bye. Just leave off.[27]

In January 1900, while on tour in America, she admitted again:

My intention (nearly fixed) had been to finish this present tour with H., go back to the Lyceum with him, play there until the Theatre closed in July, and never again to act with H. After a good rest, I should then have announced 'a farewell tour' on my own account and hope to reap, with about two years' work, enough Corn to provide against a Famine in my old age. (And for my children. I feed them all the while, I assure you. . . . .)

In these two years my intention was to provide myself with two or three new plays and re-prepare three old ones and with these 6 to go around the English provinces and through some American and Canadian cities, just saving all the money possible, and then if I lived through it – which I probably should (I'm so tough) – do my best to become a dear old Frump in an arm chair in one of my pretty cottages, and teach Ted's youngest babes to be rather useful and not to trouble about little things.[28]

She had dragged round North America playing a part in 'this beastly *Robespierre*' which any '£10 per week actress' could have 'played well enough'. But Irving still wanted her for the autumn – '*And*, looking at the situation all round, I think I shall come!' She was afraid, she said, of her health failing when she was on her own:

If I did break down the younger people would soon make ducks and drakes of the very moderate sum I have got together by close steady work. I rather dread poverty. My needs are very few; but oh, if I could never help anyone with that *useful stuff*, 'golden ointment', when they were gashed and slashed, in need, it would come very hard to me. . . . Do you call me 'a money-grubber'? A weak, unenterprising, silly fool? An ass? I have not the time, nor the ability, to show you the ins and outs of the whole affair. I appear to be of strange *use* to H., and I have always thought to be *useful, really* useful to any one person *is* rather fine and satisfactory.[29]

The useful actress still, now and for ever.

The same loyalty, the same inability to break away or make a new life for herself, prevailed in her private relations with Irving. In 1898 she learned he was seeing a great deal of Mrs Aria, the

Jewish journalist, and she asked Shaw to find out something about her. Shaw did so, and reported she was 'a good sort'. Her woman's instinct had already sensed she had a rival; in January she wrote from Barkston Gardens: 'Henry is so nice to me lately that I'm convinced he has a new "flame" (he is always nicer then, which I think is to his credit).'[30] She did not indulge in frivolous jealousy, only in curiosity: 'But who is Mrs A.? I only know she is "a journalist" and "a friend" of H.I.'s. I never set eyes on her and she had no idea I know of her. (This is fun, and would be better fun, if I knew something about her.) If you know her personally don't "give away" that I know of her existence.'[31] It is not till November 1900, writing from Liverpool, that she put her position to Shaw once again incontrovertibly:

I feel so certain Henry just hates me! I can only *guess* at it, for he is exactly the same sweet-mannered person he was when 'I felt so certain' Henry loved me! We have not met for years now, except before other people, where my conduct exactly matches his of course. All my own fault. It is *I* am changed, not he. It's all right, but it has squeezed me up dreadfully, and after the long pause of illness, I went back last night, weak and nervous, but looking well and acting well, thank the Lord. Only for the first time not glad to go back to my dear work. I cant speak, you see, so it has been a very tough business. I'm better now, and if I were not a *worm* I'd take my illness as an excuse to outsiders and leave all theatres, Henry, 'and such like trash', behind me and go and live on my farm, but all folk are better working hard, and I know he wants me more than ever in the theatre, so on I go.[32]

Her loyalty to Shaw led her to encourage Irving to produce *The Man of Destiny*, though she kept herself clear of the bitter controversy which developed between the two men about this play. Later, she even discussed with Irving the possibility of producing Ibsen's *The Pretenders* at the Lyceum. 'I am sticking at Henry day and night to do Ibsen,' she wrote from Manchester in 1897. The effect on Irving was extraordinary:

The Pretenders! You should hear him (H.I.) on the subject. Lord, Lord! how funny he is, as he tells of one person after another bounding into his rooms and excitedly roaring '*Pretenders*', until at last *he* got excited too, and all aflame, and (declining to join a gathering where extra superfine incense was to be burned before him) buried himself in the play full of hope and belief that here was the Play at last! And how he was left staring before him all through the night wondering was *he* or all his friends stark staring raving mad! I had only said one word on the subject, that he would play the Bishop to utter perfection. *That* fired him! *Brand* and *Borkman* are really the plays for us now, one thing and another considered. You see as long as we 'go one better' than anybody else, what's the good of suggesting anyone knows better than he?³³

She herself, tutored by Shaw, had come to appreciate Ibsen, but she felt neither the Lyceum nor its audiences to be suitable for 'the tremendously powerful *bare* hardness of Ibsen's *Borkman*. As far as the Lyceum goes, it's much too big a theatre to play delicately any of Ibsen's modern plays'.³⁴

In their private relationship Shaw made it quite clear at the outset that he did not want to be considered a conventional admirer, a solid, ever-present lover. He wanted, he said in October 1896, to be used:

I am not to be your lover, nor your friend; for a day of reckoning comes for both love and friendship. You would soon feel like the Wandering Jew: you would know that you *must* get up and move on. You must enter into an inexorably interested relation with me. My love, my friendship, are worth nothing. Nothing for nothing. I must be *used*, built into the solid fabric of your life as far as there is any usable brick in me, and thrown aside when I am used up. It is only when I am being used that I can feel my own existence, enjoy my own life. All my love affairs end tragically because the women *cant* use me. They lie low and let me imagine things about them; but in the end a frightful unhappiness, an unspeakable weariness comes;

and the Wandering Jew must go on in search of someone who
can use him to the utmost of his capacity. Everything real in
life is based on *need:* just so far as you need me I have you
tightly in my arms; beyond that I am only a luxury, and, for
luxuries, love and hate are the same passion.[35]

He did not want what he now felt to be the one great love of his
life to decline into the empty philandering to which he had become so used. In the same letter he adds:

And now as to all my love affairs. One is just perishing under
a bad attack of the Wandering Jew. Then there is my Irish lady
with the light green eyes and the million of money, whom I
have got to like so much that it would be superfluous to fall in
love with her. Then there is Janet, who, on hearing of the
Irish rival, first demanded, with her husband to witness my
testimony, whether I still loved her, and then on receiving the
necessary assurance, relented and informed me that she had been
faithless to me (with the said husband) to the extent of making
Candida impossible until after next February, when she expects
to become once more a mother. And then there are others
whom I cannot recollect just at present, or whom you don't
know anything about. And finally there is Ellen, to whom I
vow that I will try hard not to spoil my high regard, my worthy
respect, my deep tenderness, by any of those philandering
follies which make me so ridiculous, so troublesome, so vulgar
with women. I swear it. Only, do as you have hitherto done
with so wise an instinct: keep out of my reach. You see, nobody
can write exactly as I write: my letters will always be a little
bit original; but personally I shouldnt be a bit original. All
men are alike with a woman whom they admire. You must
have been admired so much and so often – must know the
symptoms so frightfully well. But now that I come to think of
it, so have I. Up to the time I was 29, actually twenty-nine, I
was too shabby for any woman to tolerate me. I stalked about
in a decaying green coat, cuffs trimmed with the scissors,
terrible boots, and so on. Then I got a job to do and bought a

suit of clothes with the proceeds. A lady immediately invited me to tea, threw her arms round me, and said she adored me. I permitted her to adore, being intensely curious on the subject. Never having regarded myself as an attractive man, I was surprised; but I kept up appearances successfully. Since that time, whenever I have been left alone in a room with a female, she has invariably thrown her arms round me and declared she adored me. It is fate. Therefore beware. If you allow yourself to be left alone with me for a single moment, you will certainly throw your arms round me and declare you adore me; and I am not prepared to guarantee that my usual melancholy forbearance will be available in your case.[36]

Later, in September 1897, he was to warn her again:

It is not the small things that women miss in me, but the big things. My pockets are always full of the small change of love-making; but it is magic money, not real money. Mrs Webb, who is a remarkably shrewd woman, explains her freedom from the fascination to which she sees all the others succumb by saying 'You cannot fall in love with a sprite; and Shaw is a sprite in such matters, not a real person.' Perhaps you can divine the truth in this: I am too lazy to explain it now, even if I understood it. It is certainly true: I am fond of women (or one in a thousand, say); but I am in earnest about quite other things. To most women one man and one lifetime make a world. I require whole populations and historical epochs to engage my interests seriously and make the writing machine (for that is what G.B.S. is) work at full speed and pressure: love is only diversion and recreation to me. Doubtless, dear Ellen, you've observed that you cant act things perfectly until you have got beyond them and so have nothing to fear from them. That's why the women who fall in love with me worry me and torment me and makes scenes (which they cant act) with me and suffer misery and destroy their health and beauty, whilst you, who could do without me as easily as I do without Julia (for instance) are my blessing and refuge, and really care more for *everybody* (including myself) than Julia cared for me. It is also, alas! why I act the lover so diabolically well that even the women who are clever enough to understand that such a person as myself might exist, cant bring themselves to believe that I am that person. My *impulses* are so prettily played – oh, you know: you wretch, you've done it often enough yourself.[37]

It was mainly for these reasons that he determined from the first that Ellen and he should not meet. He wrote as early as 25 September 1896:

Very well, you shant meet me in the flesh if you'd rather not. There is something deeply touching in that. Did you *never* meet a man who could bear meeting and knowing? Perhaps you're right: Oscar Wilde said of me: 'An excellent man: he has no enemies; and none of his friends like him.' And that's quite true: they dont like me; but they are my friends, and some of them love me. If you value a man's regard, *strive* with him. As to *liking*, you like your newspaper, and despise it.[38]

He was often to regret this decision: 'Still I have to dream of my Ellen and never touch her,' he wrote in June the following year.[39] But by November 1900, when Ellen had written that she was concerned Irving 'just hates me', Shaw could reply:

Of course he hates you when you talk to him about me. Talk to him about himself: then he will love you, to your great alarm. I know what it is to be loved. Good heavens! You are a thousand times right to keep me out of reach of your petticoats. What people call love is impossible except as a joke (and even then one of the two is sure to turn serious) between two strangers meeting accidentally at an inn or in a forest path. Why, I dare not for my life's happiness make love to my own wife. A delusion, Ellen, all this love romance: that way madness lies.[40]

Shaw's understanding of a love relationship was of precisely the kind to which Ellen was best able to respond. Of this 'true love' he wrote to her in September 1896 (his place of writing, the London Underground):

> Before the world I must deal sincerely with you, however light a turn I may give my sincerity. I owe that to your dignity as an artist and to my profession. But in private I only want to please you, which makes me a liar and an actor. But you understand all this; only you are not quite as proud as you should be of the fact that you are a fully self-possessed woman and therefore not really the slave of love. You would not delight in it so if it were not entirely subject to your will, if the abandonment were real abandonment, instead of voluntary, artistic *willed* (and therefore revocable) rapture.[41]

He was once more in a train, travelling at midnight to Dorking, when he wrote her one of the most revealing of his letters:

> Yes, as you guess, Ellen, I am having a bad attack of you just at present. I am restless; and a man's restlessness always means a woman; and my restlessness means Ellen. And your conduct is often shocking. Today I was wandering somewhere, thinking busily about what I supposed to be high human concerns when I glanced at a shop window, and there you were – oh disgraceful and abandoned – in your 3rd Act Sans-Gêne dress – a mere waistband, laughing wickedly and saying maliciously; 'Look here, restless one, at what you are really thinking about.' How can you look Window and Grove's camera in the face with such thoughts in your head and almost nothing on. You are worse than Lilith, Adam's first wife.
>
> Oh fie, fie, let me get away from this stuff, which you have been listening to all your life, and despise – though indeed, dearest Ellen, these silly longings stir up great waves of tenderness in which there is no guile. . . . That is the worst of letters: I must say something: I cant in pen and ink rest these bruised brains in your lap and unburden my heart with inarticulate cries. When I can think, when I can write, then my ideas fly like

stones: you can never be sure that one of them will not hurt you. My very love gets knit into an infernal intellectual fabric that wounds when I mean it to caress; and when I am tired and foolish I am flat and apparently bored. Sometimes that happens to my articles; and then I am terrified indeed, and must work fiercely to remedy it. When *you* complain, I am terrified another way, thinking that the end has come, for I have only one thing to say to you, and it must get tedious sooner or later. I am particularly tedious at present in this midnight solitary journey, wanting to sleep, and yet to sleep with you. Only do you know what the consequences would be? Well, about to-morrow at noon when the sun would be warm and the birds in full song you would feel an irresistible impulse to fly into the woods. And there, to your great astonishment and scandal, you would be *confined* of a baby that would immediately spread a pair of wings and fly, and before you could rise to catch it it would be followed by another and another and another – hundreds of them, and they would finally catch you up and fly away with you to some heavenly country where they would grow into strong sweetheart sons with whom, in defiance of the prayer-book, you would found a divine race. Would you not like to be the mother of your own grandchildren? If you were my mother – but I have a lot of things to say and we are at Redhill already.[42]

Later in the year, in September, he is writing: 'I love you soulfully and bodyfully, properly and improperly, every way that a woman can be loved.'[43] But within nine months he had married Charlotte, his Irish millionairess, the 'lady with the light green eyes', and Ellen wrote him a brief, magnificent letter of good wishes:

How splendid! What intrepidity to make such a courageous bid for happiness. Into it you both go! Eyes wide open! An example to the world, and may all the gods have you in their keeping.[44]

Yet her expression of love had been no less than his. 'And so

T

you and I are at the 2 best occupations in this strange old world,'
she wrote to him in September 1896. 'Nothing else worth doing.
Love and Work.'[45] Later in the same month she added: 'I've only
ever met fine fellows and found they were *all* worth knowing,
and have loved them all (dont misunderstand me) and I'm all
tired out with caring and caring.'[46] A month later she is writing:

> With your 3 (or 30?) love affairs on, and the Fabian, and the
> *Saturday* and the etc. etc. etcs., you must be full up and it's
> not my moment. I'll wait until you 'need' me, and then I'll
> mother you. That's the only unselfish love. I've never been
> admired or loved (properly) but one-and-a-half times in my
> life, and I am perfectly sick of loving. All on one side isnt
> fair.[47]

She had a woman's natural fear that age was destroying her power
to attract him. Later in October she confessed this:

> Darling, I've not read your letter, but I must tell you I dislike
> folk who are not reserved, and will tell me of your *Janets* and
> things and make me mad, when I *only* want to know whether
> they think you would if we met, have a horrible dislike of me
> when you found me such an old thing, and so different to the
> Ellen you've seen on the stage. I'm so pale when I'm off the
> stage, and rouge becomes me, and I know I shall have to take
> to it if I consent to let you see me. And it would be so pathetic,
> for not even the rouge would make you admire me away
> from the stage. Oh what a curse it is to be an actress![48]

And she added: 'I cant compete 'cos I'm not pretty.'

She even gave him the advice he sought on his indecisive courtship of Charlotte. 'What does your loving wisdom say to it?',
he asked her in November, and she replied in a letter faithful to
her nature:

> But somehow I think she'll love you quick enough. I *think*
> so, but it's what's in herself. I can tell her, not what is in you.
> How very silly you clever people are. Fancy not knowing!

Fancy not being sure! Do *you* know you love her? 'Cos if so, that would be safe enough to marry on. For if it came to the last second and she didnt love *you*, she couldnt kiss you, and then you'd know quick enough! I'm supposing she's a woman, not a – a – (I dont know what to call the thing I mean) – a 'female that never knows'! Those are often married things, and they have children, and there are many such, but I pity their husbands.

It is borne in upon me that if she is your lover and you hers, I ought not to write to you quite as I do. She might not understand. I should understand it if I were the SHE, but its because I'm not clever. I never was, and sometimes, looking at you all, I hope I never shall be! One thing I am clever enough to know (TO KNOW, mind. I know few things, but I know what I know). It is this. You'd be all bad, and no good in you, if you marry anyone unless you know you love her. A woman may *not* love before marriage and really love afterwards (if she has never loved before). We all love more after union (women I mean, and surely, oh surely men too). *But a man should know.*[49]

She was touched by the agonies of indecision from which she imagined Shaw to be suffering:

You *are* in the blues! You are only a boy. 40 is *nothing* when it's Irish. . . . Be strong. Don't waste your time on any women. Work. Shake the world, you stupid (darling). Give up picture-sitting, writing to elderly actresses (selfish beasts). Give up fooling. It's only because you are a boy, but it's not fair. It's horrid, and like a flirting girl who is more thoughtless, maybe, than wicked. But at 40 you ought to have felt the ache of dead-at-the-heart, the ache of it. I guess you have given it to this poor lady, and you couldnt do that if you knew the pain. But you're only a boy.

Dont be a fool (sweet) . . . Henry married her he knew he didnt love, thought he ought to, and he had better have killed her straight off. For a while at least think only of your dear work. I can scarce bear the reproach in your words: 'I've not missed answering a single letter of yours.' I take your most precious time, although I dont claim your love . . .[50]

This was the vein of her feeling for Shaw during the two years before he finally made up his mind to marry. As for herself, she told him in May 1897: 'No: you have no rivals. You see I have no lovers, only loves, and I have as many of those as I want, and you are the only one I dont benefit! You do things for me. I do things for them.'[51] When he begged her to send him 'one throb' of her heart, she replied:

'A throb of my heart!' Why you dear little stupid you know I havent such a thing about me, at least if I told you I had, you'd laugh and deny it. I wonder will my half century (due in February) finish me up entirely! And end the 'throb' I *do* still feel at a sound, or, most of all, at a touch. . . . I only feel sort of misty-kind about *you*, and a gently warming-all-over-sensa-tion-of-pleasure when I see your writing, and know that 'by and by', upstairs, I'm going to enjoy you, all to myself, linger-ingly and word by word. The woman's voice made my heart 'throb,' or rather stand still, and so would the touch of . . . but I fly from 'throbs' in these days. It is not becoming. It's absurd.

Darling, you are very kind to me. Now dont write again for awhile. I appreciate you and what you do for me very well, but take the time in which you'd be writing to me and rest in it instead. Do nothing for nobody, or rather do that for me! *Rest,* for I know you are tired.

Oh, I am very much yours

E.T.[52]

In September, she allows herself to dream of love with something of the imagery of a picture by Watts:

A Banquet (Oh lor') yesterday, and today I possess a beautiful scarlet and gold-bound tribute to my virtues, beauty, and talent. What a fool one feels, and how silly it all is, and how kind they all were! I sat there for 3 mortal hours, and thought a good deal about you, all the while they were talking and talking. I was thinking you were tired, and breaking your back over those commas and stops, and breaking your head. When will your labour pains be over and that babe be born into the world? Off on a bit of magic carpet would I go if I could, and wave my hands over your blessed head, touch your cerise (?) hair gently with my lips, whisper to you I was there, although invisible, that I love you tho' I could not show you how much (one never does!) and then skip back again on my carpet to – this place.[53]

But such dreams had to fade when Shaw married, though the friendship went on undiminished at least until 1900. The letters became increasingly filled with mutual advice and gossip. Shaw was gaining ground in the theatre while Ellen was losing it. One letter from Shaw, written on 9 November 1913, and excluded from the published correspondence, shows how concerned he was at this time about Ellen's financial position, her need for work and her seemingly endless, self-devouring generosity to Teddy:

Dearest Ellen
    You fill me with concern – with dismay. What am I to do or say? It's as if Queen Alexandra came to me and asked me to get her a place as cook-housekeeper, except that I'm not in love with Queen Alexandra. Nobody dare have you in a cast: *you'd* knock it all to pieces. A tiny yacht may throw its mast overboard and end its day quietly and serviceably as a ferry boat; but a battleship cant do that; and you are a battleship. What parts are there that even the most callous youngster who never saw you could offer you in the ordinary routine of theatrical commerce? Matrons at £15 a week or less. And then the agony of learning a part, and being hustled by a producer, and finally overwhelming everyone on the stage by dwarfing them and mopping up every scrap of interest and attention in the house! Can you wonder that we all recoil, and say 'She would be splendid in it'; and then get some estimable mouse who would give no trouble and spread no terror?

Ellen, Ellen, what has become of all the jubilee money? – for you must be in difficulties or you would never be content with minor work. You are not wildly extravagant: you *dont* keep two motor cars and wallow in sables and diamonds. Do you give it all away; or has Teddy a family in every European capital for you to support? Not my business *isnt it*? Then dont harrow my feelings by telling me that you must get engagements instantly. Must we all sink with 50 starving parasites clutching our hair? I have three letters just received from unfortunate people, pitiable people, nice people, whose only refuge is being adopted by me. I must turn savage and thrust them from my plank into the waves or I shall presently be as desperate as they are. So must you. Well, this isn't very consoling, damn me.

If I were you, I should take the Margate Theatre, and set up a school. Teddy's ambition is to be the successor of Sarah Thorne; but as you gave him your forehead without your chin he will never do it: he will only talk and write beautifully about it, and produce nothing but pretty children with stomachs to fill and backs to clothe. You will have to set up the school yourself as you have had to do everything else; and then you can give him parts to play at thirty shillings a week and use up the children for the pantomime. . . .

Ellen, what a world!

Oh, why cant I write a letter that will make you forget your troubles, instead of rubbing them in?

Oh Lord!

Let us tie ourselves together – close – and give some respectable boatman our last shilling to row us out and drop us into the sea.

G.B.S.[54]

When Irving died, Shaw was invited by the *Neue Freie Presse* of Vienna to write a tribute to him. The article, plainly of an unusual frankness for what was in effect an obituary, recoiled on Shaw's head once the British Press was made aware of the terms

in which it seemed to have been written – judging from trans-
lations of the German text which it quoted Shaw protested in
vain, and subsequently published the original English text to show
exactly what it was he had originally written. He claimed that
Irving's greatest single achievement was to have won social
recognition for his profession, symbolized by his knighthood,
but he criticized him once more for his utter lack of interest in
the modern theatre or in any form of artistry but his own. He
recognized the 'force and singularity' of Irving's personality and
the skilful elaborations of his stage technique, which turned the
defects of his physique and voice into something 'interesting and
characteristic', though it also made him the object of vulgar
ridicule and mimicry. He was, said Shaw, the victim of his own
self-training; Britain, as Shaw reminds his Victorian readers, had
no national theatre to give intellectual and artistic stature to its
drama and stage presentations. A man of Irving's talents had no
standard against which to measure himself, and no school of acting in which he could have learnt to rid himself of the mannerisms
which, Shaw claimed, ultimately destroyed his capacity as an
actor.

Shaw's article excited so much comment that he was invited to
write a sequel on the art of Ellen Terry. This appeared in the
Neue Freie Presse on 24 December 1905. In this he pointed out
the contrast there had been between Ellen and Irving since the
time she had come to find 'life more interesting than art' and,
though 'the most modern of modern women, the most vital of
modern personalities', served out her partnership with Irving 'in
the spirit of a thrifty intelligent housekeeper'. For Shaw, she was
always more interesting as a personality than as an actress appearing
at the Lyceum:

The part she has played in the life of her time will never be
known until some day – perhaps fifty years hence – when her
correspondence will be collected and published in twenty or
thirty volumes. It will then, I believe, be discovered that every
famous man of the last quarter of the nineteenth century –

provided he were a playgoer – has been in love with Ellen
Terry, and that many of them have found in her friendship the
utmost consolation one can hope for from a wise, witty, and
beautiful woman whose love is already engaged elsewhere, and
whose heart has withstood a thousand attempts to capture it.[55]

'She actually invented her own beauty,' he claims, a beauty of a
kind that 'had never been seen in the world before'. She was 'a
new and irresistibly attractive specimen of womankind'. In
addition, she became 'one of the greatest letter-writers that ever
lived. She can flash her thought down on paper in a handwriting
that is as characteristic and as unforgettable as her face.'

With a penetration that came from sharing in part a spirit
similar to Ellen's, Shaw realized the inner nature of her relationship to other people, and contrasted it with Irving's:

> Irving was sentimental and affectionate, and like most senti-
> mental and affectionate people was limited and concentrated in
> his interests. He never understood others, and indeed never
> understood himself. Ellen Terry is not sentimental and not
> affectionate; but she is easily interested in anybody or anything
> remarkable or attractive: she is intelligent: she understands:
> she sympathizes because she understands and is naturally benev-
> olent; but she has been interested oftener than deeply touched,
> and has pitied and helped oftener than loved. With all her
> ready sacrifice of her stage talent and skill, first to domestic
> ties, and then, on her return to the stage, to the Lyceum en-
> terprise, she has never really sacrificed her inner self. In sac-
> rificing her art she only sacrificed a part of herself. Irving's art
> was the whole of himself; and that was why he sacrificed him-
> self – and everybody and everything else – to his art. It is a
> curious piece of artistic psychology, this, and will be misunder-
> stood by stupid people and Philistines; but one does not write
> about artists of genius for people who know nothing about
> genius.[56]

A few months after the publication of this tribute by Shaw,

Ellen was to marry her third husband. The correspondence between her and Shaw more or less ceased, and she lived to see him reach the pinnacle of his great reputation. She never lost her affection for him, and on the scrap of paper found after her death and headed 'My Friends' the name of Bernard Shaw appeared at the head second only to that of Charles Reade.

X

THE SECRET SELF

Only two other actresses of her time, in my opinion – Sarah Bernhardt and Eleonora Duse – have ranked with Ellen either as personalities in the theatre or as performers on the stage. During the 1880s all three reached the top in their profession, although Duse was ten years younger than Ellen and twelve years younger than Bernhardt. Eleonora Duse did not appear on the stage in England until 1893. On her second visit in 1895 Shaw, then a dramatic critic, was able to see Ellen, Duse and Bernhardt perform simultaneously in London. The contrast between these three women could not have been more marked if they had been deliberately brought together for the purpose, yet Ellen became the personal friend of both her great rivals. In 1906, Duse travelled all the way from Florence in order just to stand beside Ellen on the occasion of her Jubilee at Drury Lane.

Duse, like Ellen, was born to a couple of strolling players, Vincenso and Angelica Duse in October 1858. Her grandfather, Luigi Duse, had been a celebrated comedian in the Veneto region in the north of Italy. She was brought up in the theatre, and at the age of six her name appeared on the playbills. While still a child, the parts she played increased in importance; her emotional development was precipitated by the parts she was given, especially Juliet, whom she played at the age of fourteen. She herself seemed to experience directly all the suffering associated with these roles; she made their sorrows her own. At twenty she was fully established, with a naturalistic style of her own which she was prepared to assert against the will of any actor-manager who tried to make her act according to the conventions of the time. She became the mistress of Martino Cafiero, a prominent newspaper proprietor in

Naples who at the age of thirty-five was as famous for his success with women as he was for his artistry and culture. Soon Duse was pregnant.

She gave herself up as completely to her lovers as she did to the characters she impersonated on the stage. When the men she loved, like Cafiero, tired of her or were worn out by her insatiable demands and left her, she could never understand why she had been deserted, and the loss of love sometimes drove her close to suicide. In compensation, she would thrust herself back upon the stage, letting the parts she played express the emotions she felt so intensely. Cafiero's child died shortly after birth; Duse herself carried the small coffin to the grave and watched it sink into the earth in silence. The theatre received her back and helped her to bear her grief. There was another man to whom she could turn, an actor called Tebaldo Chicchi, who loved her with a humble adoration. She married him, and bore him a daughter. But this marriage was a failure; Duse's emotional demands proved too devouring for the kindly, retiring man. It was now that, like Bernhardt, she discovered that she had tuberculosis.

Duse had seen and admired Bernhardt, and in 1884 she added to her repertoire the part of Camille in *The Lady of the Camellias,* the famous melodrama by Dumas fils. She scored a triumph in this part which rivalled that of Bernhardt herself. While on tour she fell in love with the poet and composer Arrigo Boito, who was to become as dear to her as Godwin had been to Ellen. Through him she achieved her ultimate stature as an actress, in 1888, when she triumphed as Shakespeare's Cleopatra in Boito's adaptation of the play. It was not until 1895 that she turned from him to her most famous lover, Gabrielle d'Annunzio. Meanwhile she toured the Americas and Europe, playing such parts as Juliet, Calemil and even Nora in Ibsen's *A Doll's House.* In 1893 she visited America in the wake of Bernhardt and Ellen. She did not enjoy the experience; her work was not fully understood, and she was in low spirits when she finally arrived in London during May. English audiences, too, were slow to respond to her particular style; her subtle quietude and intense concentration made little impression on playgoers who were used to being captured by assault. When she returned in 1895, however, they proved far more receptive. Within a square mile of London, the three greatest actresses of Europe were at work: Ellen at the Lyceum, Duse at Drury Lane, and Bernhardt at Daly's Theatre. The visitors were vying with each other: both were appearing as Camille in *The Lady of the Camellias* and as Magda in Sudermann's *Heimat*.[1]

For Shaw there was no doubt at all which of the visiting actresses he preferred. He found Bernhardt on the stage a purveyor of fake enchantment, each detail of her complexion applied with calculated art:

> Every dimple has its dab of pink; and her finger-tips are so delicately incarnadined that you fancy they are transparent like her ears, and that the light is shining through their delicate blood-vessels. Her lips are like a newly painted pillar box; her cheeks, right up to the languid lashes, have the bloom and surface of a peach; she is beautiful with the beauty of her school, and entirely inhuman and increditable. But the incredibility is pardonable, because, though it is all the greatest nonsense, nobody believing in it, the actress herself least of all, it is so artful, so clever, so well recognized a part of the business, and carried off with such a genial air, that it is impossible not to accept it with a good-humour. . . . She does not enter into the leading character; she substitutes herself for it.[2]

Duse seemed to him to be as intensely real as Bernhardt was unnatural:

> When she comes on the stage, you are quite welcome to take your opera-glass and count whatever lines time and care have so far traced on her. They are the credentials of her humanity; and she knows better than to obliterate that significant handwriting beneath a layer of peach-bloom from the chemist's. . . . I grant that Sarah's elaborate Monna Lisa smile, with the conscious droop of the eyelashes and the long carmined lips coyly

disclosing the brilliant row of teeth, is effective of its kind – that it not only appeals to your susceptibilities, but positively jogs them. And it lasts quite a minute, sometimes longer. But Duse, with a tremor of the lip which you feel rather than see, and which lasts half an instant, touches you straight on the very heart; and there is not a line in the face, or a cold tone in the gray shadow that does not give poignancy to that tremor.... The truth is that in the art of being beautiful, Madame Bernhardt is a child beside her.... Duse produces the illusion of being infinite in variety of beautiful pose and motion. Every idea, every shade of thought and mood, expresses itself delicately but vividly to the eye; and yet, in an apparent million of changes and inflections, it is impossible to catch any line of an awkward angle, or any strain interfering with the perfect abandonment of all the limbs to what appears to be their natural gravitation towards the finest grace.

Duse acknowledged that she suffered with her characters. 'I do not paint my face,' she said, 'I make myself up morally. When I come before the public, my first success is one of ugliness. What difference does it make? I can be beautiful when I want to be.' 'To play,' she once wrote to a critic who had helped her, 'if it were only playing! – I feel I have *never known* and *never will know how to play*. Those poor women of my dramas have so entered my heart and head ... I'm not concerned if they've lied, betrayed or sinned.... Provided I feel they have wept – have suffered for lying, betraying or for loving – I am *with them* and *for* them....' With Bernhardt it was artificial effects which counted – her coloured nails, her jewelled fingers, her spellbound eyes, her drawling 'golden' voice, either gliding smooth and slow or working up to a crescendo. Duse's art was fed by her experience of life, and she portrayed states of emotion of which she seemed to have more than mortal knowledge. She used her body, and especially her hands, to convey the anguish of the spirit in a single gesture, her deepest feeling nakedly revealed in a movement or a glance. Ellen's art lay in its expression of simpler human feeling –

to achieve this with naturalism and ease she gave the greatest care and study to every part, however far it fell beneath the true level of her talents. Her art was neither haunted, like Duse's, nor decorative, like Bernhardt's. It was delicate and lyrical, as generous and human as herself.

For Ellen, these two actresses, though rivals to each other, were in her sight her admired friends.[3] This is her impression first of Bernhardt and then of Duse on the stage:

> How wonderful she looked in those days! She was as transparent as an azalea, only more so; like a cloud, only not so thick. Smoke from a burning paper describes her more nearly! She was hollow-eyed, thin, almost consumptive-looking. Her body was not the prison of her soul, but its shadow.
>
> It is this extraordinary decorative and symbolic quality of Sarah's which makes her transcend all personal and individual feeling on the stage. No one plays a love scene better, but it is a *picture* of love that she gives, a strange exotic picture rather than a suggestion of the ordinary human passion as felt by ordinary human people. She is exotic – well, what else should she be? One does not, at any rate one should not, quarrel with an orchid and call it unnatural because it is not a buttercup or a cowslip.
>
> I have spoken of the face as the chief equipment of the actor. Sarah Bernhardt contradicts this at once. Her face does little for her. Her walk is not much. Nothing about her is more remarkable than the way she gets about the stage without one ever seeing her move. By what magic does she triumph without two of the richest possessions that an actress can have? Eleonora Duse has them. Her walk is the walk of the peasant, fine and free. She has the superb carriage of the head which goes with that fearless movement from the hips. And her face! There is nothing like it, nothing! But it is as the real woman, a particular woman, that Duse triumphs most. Her Cleopatra was insignificant compared with Sarah's. She is not so pictorial.

On the fly-leaves of her lecture notes, written after a lifetime of reflection and practice, Ellen summarized her thoughts about acting:

Get the words into your remembrance first of all. Then (as you have to convey the meaning of the words to *some* who have ears, but don't hear, and eyes, but don't see) put the words into the simplest vernacular. Then exercise your judgment about their sound.

So many different ways of speaking words! Beware of sound and fury signifying nothing. Voice, unaccompanied by imagination, dreadful. Pomposity, rotundity. Imagination and intelligence absolutely necessary to realize and portray high and low imaginings. Voice, yes, but not mere production. You must have a sensitive ear, and a sensitive judgment of the effect on your audience. But all the time you must be trying to please *yourself*.

Get yourself into *tune*. Then you can let fly your imagination, and the words will seem to be supplied by yourself. Shakespeare supplied by oneself! Oh! Realism? Yes, if we mean by that real feeling, real sympathy. But people seem to mean by it only the realism of low-down things.

To act, you must make the thing written your own. You must steal the words, steal the thought, and *convey* the stolen treasure to others with great art.[4]

Ellen had reached her position of eminence during a period which saw the virtual transformation of British society. During her lifetime the population of Britain doubled; it was barely 20 million when she was born, and over $1\frac{1}{2}$ million were paupers living on relief. London, with around 2 million inhabitants, was expanding rapidly, and there was a severe cholera epidemic in 1849, the year after her birth, with over 13,000 dying during the summer. There was another outbreak in 1865, leading to the introduction of new regulations covering public health.

Ellen's earlier life, therefore, was spent during the mid-Victorian period of expansion and reform. While the Terry family were living the simple, almost primitive life of strolling players, the nation to which they belonged was creating an economy which was to make Britain a centre for world trade and at the same time introducing the reforms which are the foundation of our modern society. Exports trebled between 1850 and 1870. But the Victorians engaged in the expansion of industry were materialists who saw their drive and ruthless initiative as an outcome of their firmly-entrenched Christian beliefs, as expressed through the teaching of the various sects. They allied their conscience with their material progress, promoting missionary work among the heathen and believing themselves and their society the most powerful and God-fearing on earth. The new rich were essentially philistine (as Matthew Arnold was among the first to point out) and faced men and women of taste with a hard crust of indifference to any aspect of art and culture which did not seem to reflect their wealth, power and piety. Many of them were among the regular patrons of Irving's lavish productions at the Lyceum. Conspicuous comfort, not beauty, characterized the architecture and furnishing of the period. It was this that Ellen, under Godwin's influence, re-sisted with such fervour. Poverty, though relieved by the exercise of charity, was despised as the visitation of God for the most part on the idle and unemployable. Yet the latter part of the nine-teenth century saw the introduction of many much-needed re-forms in conditions of employment and housing, as well as in public health and education. Ellen, as compassionate as she was generous, gave lavishly to people in distress, and visited the poverty-stricken areas of London. But she did not sweep in like some grand lady bent on dispensing charity. She would stop and talk to the ragged children in the streets as if they were members of her family.

At the head of this ebullient and thrusting nation presided a woman, Queen Victoria, who, after an initial period when the monarchy was frequently under bitter attack, became from the 1860s an emotional symbol for her people. This new feeling for the Queen made the Golden Jubilee of 1887 and the Diamond Jubilee of 1897 occasions for a glittering celebration of imperial splendour, and established the modern, more sentimental, response

31. Ellen Terry as Rosamund in *Becket*, 1893

31a. Henry Irving in *Becket*
(*By courtesy of Pamela Hansford Johnson*)

31b. A scene from *Becket*

32. Ellen Terry as Imogen in *Cymbeline*, 1895

32a. George Bernard Shaw in the 'nineties

33. Ellen Terry as Catherine in *Madame Sans-Gêne*, 1897

34. Ellen Terry as Volumnia in *Coriolanus*, 1901

35. Ellen Terry as Lady Cecily Waynflete in *Captain Brassbound's Conversion*, 1906

36. James Carew with Ellen Terry at Smallhythe, shortly after their marriage in 1907

37. Film stills from *The
Invasion of Britain*, 1918. Ellen
Terry as the Mother receiving
news of her son's heroism and
immediately afterwards the
telegram announcing his death
(*By courtesy of the National Film
Archive.*)

38. Film stills from *The Bohemian Girl*, 1922. Ellen Terry as the Nurse appealing to her master after the loss of his child (*By courtesy of the National Film Archive*.)

39. Smallhythe, photographed by Ellen Terry's great-granddaughter, Helen Craig

40. The garden at Smallhythe. Photograph by Helen Craig

41. Ellen Terry in 1917, wearing her Nance Oldfield dress

of the British people to the Royal Family. There was no doubt
about the loyalty and affection felt by both Irving and Ellen
for the Queen and the Prince of Wales.

Yet the nineteenth century was still a period of grave restrictions
on the rights of women, who remained throughout second-class
citizens. They had only one main object in life: marriage, the
management of a husband's home under his more or less stern
eye, and the bearing and upbringing of his children. As Florence
Nightingale wrote in 1851: 'Women don't consider themselves as
human beings at all. There is absolutely no God, no country, no
duty to them at all, except family ... I know nothing like the
petty grinding tyranny of a good English family. And the only
alleviation is that the tyrannized submits with a heart full of
affection.' It was through marriage, and marriage alone, that a
woman achieved social status; her only legal status was as an
adjunct to her husband. If she were a middle-class or upper-class
girl, her education was designed to make her attractive to men so
that she might, as soon as suitable, be asked in marriage. Clever
and exceptionally well-informed women were not generally
popular with either sex; they were labelled 'blue stockings', which
meant they should be avoided socially. The spinster who did not
achieve a man or by some misadventure lost one became an object
of pity and even ridicule, with little or no opportunity to find
herself interesting employment; she became a governess, perhaps,
helping to raise the children of women who had been more fortunate than herself. The exploitation of timid and ill-paid 'gentle-
women' who obtained positions as governesses became notorious,
all the more so because they were often quite unqualified for the
work. Ellen was in most respects a model employer of her many
grades of domestic help; she was, in fact, indulgent to a fault
until in old age and failing health she became more difficult.

Most married women, though their social status was assured
and often powerful, had to endure the prolonged period of child-
bearing which seemed right and natural in Victorian society. It
was only to be expected that some of a woman's children would
be stillborn or die prematurely, and large families were the only

insurance against the poor health of the period. The risks and pains of childbirth were great (they were, indeed, regarded as part of the will of God), and it was only when Queen Victoria asked for chloroform during two of her confinements that the use of anaesthetics, available to pregnant women by the 1840s, became accepted by married couples with more advanced views.[5]

Once she accepted marriage a woman ceased to exist in law separately from her husband. All her property was immediately merged with his and could be disposed of as he willed; if she earned money, as a writer, for example, or as an actress, he could claim it, even if he had deserted her, and he could take the children of the marriage from her if they were separated. But Ellen's children, being illegitimate, were never legally tied to Godwin, and even when Ellen married Kelly and became Mrs Wardell, the children, though taking the name of Wardell, did not, of course, come under Kelly's full legal control. However, Ellen's possessions and earnings technically became his property, and after their separation she was not only being generous but also formally correct in sending him money for his support.

Yet Ellen's household, with or without a man in residence, was utterly untypical of the period. The great Victorian middle-class family with a flock of children, unattached relatives, and staffs of ill-paid servants, was normally ruled by the pater familias in the spirit of sectarian religion. If the pater familias were a man of goodwill and affection, he became the centre of an admiring flock of playful daughters and rather more distantly respectful sons. If he were harsh or tyrannical, the family would live in dread of his arrival home in the evening, his disciplinary administration alleviated only by the submissive affection of his wife, unless she too became a tyrant. Discipline was only too often punitive, with constant caning and flogging of children both at home and in the schools. What was important was that the family unit should be maintained by law, and every item of possession lay ultimately in the hands of the head of the household.

For the young Victorian girl sewing and letter-writing to

friends and relatives became a consuming pastime; the arrival of the penny post in 1840 encouraged the endless exchange of confidences through correspondence. She might also learn sketching and elocution, music and singing to enhance her social attractions, and she probably kept a more or less secret diary. Enterprising mothers introduced their daughters to household management and economy, and many books were published to show how to make the best of lower middle-class incomes of £200 and £300 a year. Mrs Beeton, whose celebrated cookery book appeared in 1861, was the wife of Samuel Beeton, the editor of a household journal for women, *The Englishwoman's Domestic Magazine,* which was first published in 1852. If a young lady had a taste for outdoor exercise she would learn how to ride side-saddle, skate, play croquet, or, later in the period, run long-skirted round the tennis-courts. As for other amusements, there were always fashionable balls in the season, for which she had to learn how to dance, as well as theatres, concerts, exhibitions and the many popular shows of the period. There was no shortage of 'pastimes' for her, provided she could persuade her father to pay whatever it might cost to indulge in them.

But the fact always remained that she was a dependant – first on her father and then, if she married, on her husband. Until the passing of the Married Women's Property Act in 1881, when Ellen was thirty-six, no married women could own property, though they could benefit under a trust. The law came just in time to help Ellen when she was receiving what was probably the highest salary earned by a woman in Britain during the late nineteenth century – £200 a working week, together with lump sums acquired from benefit performances.

It was, therefore, during Ellen's lifetime that women in Britain achieved the right to a basic formal education (Ellen herself, as we have seen, had had none), the right to own property, the right to divorce undesirable husbands, and in 1918, when she was over seventy, the right to vote. Ellen herself took no militant part in supporting women's rights, but she exemplified in her own way of life how utterly independent a woman of character could become.

She was used from childhood to earning (though not owning) money, and free almost entirely from the sense of economic dependence on men which other women either accepted or endured. It is true that her brief retirement from the stage during her marriage to Watts and her alliance with Godwin made her temporarily dependent, but she always knew that she could return to the stage and support herself and later on her children as well. And this in fact she did, earning a handsome income throughout the 1880s and 1890s which made her at that time a very rich woman. Her position, however, changed radically in the early years of the new century.

At the time of Irving's death, Ellen had been playing in *Alice-sit-by-the-Fire,* the play specially written for her by James Barrie, who was already well-established as a novelist and dramatist with such plays as *The Little Minister* (1847), *Quality Street* and *The Admirable Crichton* (both 1902) and *Peter Pan* (1904). His instinct for dramatic effect combined with his impish sentimentality was everything that the more comfortable theatre-goers wanted at the turn of the century; it reassured them at a time when the society they most valued was being eroded or re-examined by the newer writers and dramatists such as Ibsen, Shaw, Harley Granville-Barker (*The Voysey Inheritance* 1905) and John Galsworthy (*The Silver Box* 1906).

Barrie, the son of a handloom-weaver in Forfarshire, was forty years of age in 1900. Irving had considered producing *The Professor's Love Story,* one of Barrie's earlier plays, at the Lyceum, but had finally rejected it, as he so often rejected the work of contemporary dramatists, because he found it lacked the scale and *panache* which he needed to satisfy his theatrical instinct. Ellen herself had first made Barrie's acquaintance when she had written to him to say how much she had enjoyed his story, *Sentimental Tommy.* Their friendship was to be lifelong.

In 1906 Ellen, at the age of fifty-nine, was honoured by the profession with a great Jubilee performance on 12 June at the Theatre Royal, Drury Lane. She had been on the stage for fifty years, almost half of which she had spent with Irving. The general committee sponsoring the performance was made up of over a hundred names representing the nobility and men of distinction in every branch of public life. The executive committee, whose chairman was Arthur Pinero, all came from the theatrical profession. Both these committees were composed entirely of men.[6]

Had Irving lived to appear beside her, his own fiftieth anniversary would have occurred in the same year. It would have been an occasion unequalled in English theatrical history. As it was, with Ellen standing alone to receive the homage of those who loved her as fellow-players and as members of her public, the occasion was extraordinary. It began before noon and lasted until past six o'clock. It was, she said herself, a 'mammoth matinée'. Duse, as we have seen, came from Florence to be present at the reception with which the programme of nearly twenty items concluded. Caruso, accompanied by Tosti, sang for her; so did her friend from the music halls, Gertie Millar. Réjane came from France, and Coquelin and his son appeared in a scene from Molière's *Le Marriage Forcé*. W. S. Gilbert presented *Trial by Jury*, his production crowded with celebrities from the theatre and the arts; the Jury alone included Conan Doyle, Comyns-Carr and Anthony Hope. A series of twelve *Tableaux Vivants* was presented by over fifty actresses, among them Mrs Tree, Mrs Langtry, Kate Rorke, Violet and Irene Vanbrugh, Ellaline Terriss, Gertrude Elliot, Constance Collier, Lillian Braithwaite, Lena Ashwell and Julia Neilson. Seymour Hicks and 'all the Bath Buns' appeared in a scene from *The Beauty of Bath*. Mrs Patrick Campbell and Lewis Waller recited. Sir Charles Wyndham offered a scene from *The School for Scandal,* and the 'Leading Comedians of London' gave a Minstrel Entertainment. Ellen herself appeared as Beatrice in the first act of *Much Ado About Nothing,* with Beerbohm Tree as Benedick and Forbes-Robertson as Claudio. The scenery was designed by Gordon Craig, and every available member of the Terry family joined in this performance – Fred as Don Pedro, Marion as Hero, Kate as Ursula, and many of the younger generations (including Edy and Kate Terry Gielgud, and Gordon

Craig's children, Rosemary, Robin and Peter) appeared as dancers, torch-bearers and pages. Gordon Craig's masked dance concluded the scene, and a host of famous names joined the Terrys to fill the stage with movement and colour, among them Henry Ainley, Gerald du Maurier, Harcourt Williams, Matheson Lang and H. V. Esmond. In the cast itself both Irving's sons were featured, together with Henry Neville, Oscar Asche and Edmund Gwenn. This great assembly of artists, whose combined careers were to span over a century of active work on the English stage, had never been matched in one single performance. The sum raised for Ellen was nearly £6,000. She was by now in some need of money.[7]

The draft of Ellen's speech survives written in her bold handwriting. She began by saying: 'I will not say goodbye – It is one of my chief joys today that I *need* not say goodbye – just yet – but can still speak to you as one who is still among you on the active list – Still in your service – if you please.'[8]

The only significant absence from the Jubilee was that of Gordon Craig, who was in Berlin. He wrote in his old age that he had resented the whole affair at the time:

> Somehow this Jubilee thoroughly upset me – because my father, E.W.G., was forgot – like the Hobby-horse! My father, my master and I, all loved the same woman – and we all left her for the same reason – a commonplace one: our work called to us, and we went. But we did love her. Strange, it was she who could not follow us. My father died in 1886, my master in 1905, and I still live on – older now than they were when they died. Both died tired out. Of us three, my master was the greatest man. Both he and my father did more for her than ever I did: yet I believe she loved me most: how strange. I alone live on now to write of this. I older than all three. It seems queer to me: it seems all wrong: but as it is an old story, ever being retold and rehearsed, it can hardly be quite all wrong. I was the least of the three, the weakest and the smallest: is that why she loved me most? Yes and no: for in loving me so much she loved my father at the same time.[9]

After it was all over, Ellen had to face a regular evening performance at the Court Theatre. She says she did not feel sad; she was not, as she noted in her speech, retiring from the stage. Referring to her own performance at Drury Lane, she wrote: 'I believe I played Beatrice as joyfully as at any time in my life. . . . there being no sadness of farewell in this commemoration of my Jubilee.' But with the audience dispersed and the players hastening away to their various dressing-rooms in other theatres in London, Ellen was finally left alone with Edy. The stage-door keeper called up a four-wheeler to take them to the Court in Sloane Square. When they left there was still a crowd outside to raise a cheer for Ellen.

The play in which she was appearing at the Court was Shaw's *Captain Brassbound's Conversion*. Ellen's talent had at last yielded to Shaw's ten-year siege. After the single copyright performance she had undertaken for him while on tour in Liverpool in October of that year, just before leaving for America, she undertook to play Lady Cicely Waynflete, the part he had originally written for her in 1899, and which she had found, after all, she 'adored'. Now, in 1906, it was she who was in search of suitable characters to play. On 20 March she had appeared in the first of a series of six matinées devoted to Shaw's play which, to her surprise, developed the following month into a full twelve-week season. She was sufficiently pleased with the result to present the play subsequently on tour both in Britain and in the United States. This colourful piece, though certainly not Shaw at his best, nevertheless had wit, style, and an exotic setting in North Africa; it also offered a fashionably pro-feminine theme, and an admirable male part for a comedian in the Cockney seaman, Drinkwater. Ellen could scarcely fail as the all-charming disposer of men's lives and morals, but the London season was only barely successful. She and Shaw had better fortune with the play in the provinces and the United States.

In the cast for *Captain Brassbound's Conversion* at the Court was an American actor, James Carew. He was of German-Jewish origin, and had changed his real name, which was Usselman.

According to Shaw, an enthralled spectator now safely married, Ellen took one glance at this actor who had been engaged to play the minor part of the American Captain Kearney, and claimed him for her own, though he was so many years her junior: 'So swift a decision by a huntress who, far from being promiscuous in her attachments, was highly fastidious, made me marvel and say to myself "There, but for the grace of God, goes Bernard Shaw".'[10]

Carew, like Kelly, was another plain, honest and handsome man. Born in Indiana during the 1870s, he had seen Ellen and Irving perform in Chicago, and determined as a result to go on the stage. He made his way to England, and after some hard work shaping his modest talent, he had first appeared at the Court in 1905 as Hector Malone in Shaw's *Man and Superman*. Overwhelmed by the attentions of this famous and beautiful actress, he became a constant visitor both at King's Road and Smallhythe. A sentence in a letter from Shaw written on 16 March 1906, four days before the opening of the play, gives his view of the situation: 'I am furiously jealous of Carew, with whom you fell in love at first sight.'

The following year Ellen took him with her to America as her leading man, her Captain Brassbound, and on 22 March, a year after she had first met him, she married him secretly in Pittsburg. She kept her marriage concealed from everyone, and especially from Edy, but she wrote to Shaw a fortnight or so later – 'James Carew goes on trying and striving and acts better and better every week. He is a splendid fellow and adores you, *and me!*' Ellen returned to London during the summer as Mrs James Carew, and the family struggles began afresh.

The relationship between Edy and her mother had become involved and difficult, though Ellen adored her daughter: Teddy had gone his own way, leaving his mother to shoulder many of his responsibilities. Now that Irving was dead, the great masculine prop of her life was gone and she felt an ageing but still attractive woman's need for the presence of a strong man who would be prepared to cherish her. Carew, a supporting actor suddenly elevated to the position of a leading man, found that he was also to be cast as a supporting husband. He loved her as well as any man in his thirties can love a beautiful woman in her late fifties. But it would seem he had not reckoned with marrying her, and it was only on her insistence that he consented to do so. She wanted, she said, to avoid any more gossip attaching itself to her name.

But, consciously or unconsciously, there seems little doubt that Ellen felt she needed this kindly man's protection from the complications with which her daughter sought to surround her. Edy expressed violent resentment whenever her mother showed any inclination for male company. Her aggressive and domineering nature was the very opposite of Ellen's, whose interest in people and events increased rather than lessened with age. Ellen, who was used to the admiration of men and women who occupied the highest and most responsible positions in society and culture, appreciated increasingly the value of her male friends, more especially as her self-fulfilment in the theatre decreased. These closer friends, in addition to Stephen Coleridge, Sir Albert Seymour and Graham Robertson, included Norman Forbes and Tom Heslewood.[11] Edy resented these friendships as an intrusion upon the in-growing devotion of mother and daughter.

Ellen in her fifties and Edy in her thirties loved and quarrelled with equal fervour. Their life, though sometimes idyllic, was also one of recurrent rows and reconciliations. Then Edy began to acquire intimate women friends whose society she wanted to impose upon her mother. The foremost of these friends was Christabel Marshall. Chris, according to Marguerite Steen, who knew her, liked to be thought the illegitimate daughter of the Victorian novelist, Emma Marshall, though she was in fact quite securely legitimate. She was a cultured girl with a gift for writing, but she suffered from an embarrassing impediment of speech which had an effect on her pronunciation similar to that which is caused by a cleft palate. She fell deeply in love with Edy, and gave both her and her mother a lifelong, but demanding, devotion. When she eventually joined the Catholic Church, she changed her name to Christopher St John.

It was as a young girl in 1890 that she had first seen Ellen on the stage at the Prince's Theatre, Bristol and, in her own words, 'forthwith fallen in love with her'. She was among the many promising young people to whose ardour Ellen responded with friendly letters, though she did not meet her until 1896. With her heart thumping she was swept by Sally Holland from the stage-door of the Lyceum up the stairs into Ellen's dressing-room, 'inhaling for the first time in my life the air of a theatre, back-stage, air laden with the aroma of rope, canvas, glue, size, grease-paint and, at this period, gas'. There she found Ellen, swathed in an old grey flannel dressing-gown, vigorously washing her face before making up. It was her first sight of Ellen's passion for cleanliness. Ellen, drying her face with a rough towel, told her not to wear her heart upon her sleeve; this referred to the ardour of her letters, but she followed this almost immediately by complimenting her on her cleverness. 'I never read a letter from you without wishing I had had a better education,' she said.

A woman, whom she had at first thought to be Ellen, had swept past her as she entered the dressing-room. The play to be performed was *King Arthur,* and the girl was dressed for Guinevere. But her eyes, unlike Ellen's, were dark. This was Edy dressed to double for Ellen in the Prologue. Chris was allowed to watch the play from the wings.

She did not meet Ellen again for three years, when, after a period of study at Oxford, she was working in London as a secretary and journalist. She then paid a second visit to Ellen in a theatre in Fulham, and found herself in the care of Edy, who was mending a mitten. As she shook hands, Edy's needle pricked her. 'Cupid's dart,' wrote Chris, 'for I loved Edy from that moment.' She was invited to a midnight meal at Barkston Gardens, where she enjoyed kidneys specially grilled at table by Ellen herself in a chafing-dish, followed by creamed rice and 'superb Mocha coffee'.

Chris was working intermittently as secretary to Lady Randolph Churchill and her son Winston. The following day, Edy stood waiting outside the Churchill residence in Great Cumberland Place to take her out to lunch. She describes her at this period:

She had not yet reached her thirtieth birthday, but in her dark hair, nearer black than brown, there was already one white lock. Her brown eyes, set wide apart, were perhaps the most beautiful feature of her face. The nose was rather too long, though its upward tilt deceived one about that. The straight lips were a fault in her mouth, which otherwise was very like her mother's. She had a lovely slender figure in these days, and looked taller than she was (about 5ft. 8in.) owing to her elevation. Her carriage was perfect in its grace.... In repose she was as graceful as in movement.... Edy's control of her limbs might not have been so remarkable if she had not been trained as a fencer and a dancer. Edy had a beautiful voice 'quite her own, unlike anyone else's', Bernard Shaw, who once engaged her for a part on the strength of it, limited himself to saying. How wise, for a voice eludes description. Warm, mellow, deep, resonant give only faint clues to what Edy's voice was like. It had a penetrating timbre, rather like that of an oboe.[12]

In the autumn of 1899, while Ellen was touring in the United States with Irving, Edy and Chris started their life together in Smith Square, Westminster. They were to remain there for six years, though on Chris's own admission, there was at one time a grave crisis in their relationship:

This first phase in my long friendship with Edy cannot be epitomized as an idyll. It came near to being a tragedy. Of that Edy never spoke in after years. I think our life together subsequently was all the happier, because we did not break open the grave of a thing past which had threatened to separate us.

This was a reference to one of Edy's unhappy attempts to achieve a normal love affair. This, we have seen, occurred during the fifth American tour, when Edy accompanied her mother and fell in love with an American painter, Joe Evans, of whom Ellen for some reason disapproved. Ellen, as she sometimes did when she had worked herself up to do so, asserted her full authority, which seemed all the more harsh because of the serious distress it caused her. This opposition, whether well- or ill-considered, only served to increase Edy's sense of frustration, and force her to find consolation in the devotion of the friend whose torturing jealousy was raised by this threat of marriage.

Edy, like her brother, was seldom to achieve economic independence from her mother. Although Gordon Craig was making some money on the Continent, he left his wife and family in England unsupported, and Ellen assumed the responsibility of paying his alimony. She was also responsible for supporting Edy's small business as a theatrical costumier. In return, Edy gave her mother a form of affection which became increasingly 'protective'. The situation is described frankly by Chris:

Edy's devotion to her mother was not manifest to everyone. To me it became clearer and clearer as time went on that she loved her mother more deeply, more entirely, than anyone else. It was a maternal love. Often when I was with them, Edy seemed to me the wise mother, and Ellen Terry the wayward child. A child Edy would not spoil. 'She doesn't spoil me,' Ellen Terry wrote to Shaw, 'but let anyone try to hurt me! Murder then, if it would save me.' I am convinced now that Edy always acted in her mother's interests, and that her separate ménage with me, far from separating them, brought them into a closer relationship. . . . She did not grudge me my place in Edy's life and love, and soon gave me one in her own. This was perhaps the happiest period in my long friendship with Edy. The period when I was a member of Ellen Terry's company first at the Imperial Theatre, later on tours in the provinces and America. The period when I became Ellen's literary henchman, and helped her to write her memoirs.

Ellen gave them a small cottage, Priest's House, in Smallhythe, which formed part of her property and was situated a hundred yards or so from her own farmhouse.

This initial period of close and friendly relationship – which included Chris's editorial work on Ellen's book *The Story of My Life*, which was published by Hutchinson in 1908 – was ruptured by Ellen's sudden and secret marriage. As Chris says:

This lovely, pleasant carefree period came to an end, shortly after the celebration of Ellen Terry's jubilee, with her third marriage. Edy was blamed for the estrangement from her mother which ensued, but could the whole sad story of it be told, she would be vindicated by an impartial judge. She lost many friends at this time. We grew accustomed to being ostracized.

That Ellen was concerned about Edy and her career is evident in her correspondence with Shaw. ('I wish you'd marry her,' she writes in October 1896. 'Nobody else will. The ninnies are frightened at her!') In a letter of troubled and penetrating analysis written on 4 November, she tries to understand her daughter:

Edy *looks* a tragedy, and is about the most amusing, funniest creature living, a casual wretch. Oh she is odd. . . . She says she could not live with any set of people in the world, that no one would put up with her but me. ('Put up' with her!) She'll try and go away for a whole month sometimes, and hates it, and always gets into a difficult corner. . . . She's high, she's low. She's a perfect Dear. She loathes emotional people, yet adores me. I scarcely ever dare kiss her, and I'm always dying to, but she hates it from anyone. It 'cuts both ways' I assure you, the having an impersonal person for a daughter. . . . But oh, she's really sweetness and softness indeed. Only she's odd. . . . I've prayed she might love, but I don't pray for that now. I'll tell you some day when we've time to meet.

She realized by 1896 that Edy 'will never get a chance of distinguishing herself' at the Lyceum, though 'she can, and must, and will'. She begged Shaw to give her a chance to develop as an actress. 'If only she had nobody to help her she would get on fast enough,' replied Shaw, who thought she was inhibited by being

Ellen Terry's daughter; nevertheless, through his influence, she was engaged in 1897 by Janet Achurch and her husband to play Prossy in *Candida*. 'She is like a boy in her youth and virginity,' he wrote in July, when Edy was twenty-seven. Ellen, missing her when she was away on tour, thought it 'good for her to feel the struggle of life alone for a while. She has always thought it so easy'. Later in the year she found 'the *loneliness* mixed up with *jealousy*' oppressive. 'I think she is the only one I was ever jealous about. Folk think she cares for me. I don't. I never plague her with my love, but oh how she cuts my heart to ribbons sometimes, and very likely she doesnt intend to be unkind.' Yet, the following year in April she writes: 'I'm Edy's Mother, and I so fear I don't know the people I adore . . . I *do* wish someone would hasten and offer her (Edy) a *London* engagement. It is *so* bad for her to be far from me for a long time.

Edy, unemployed, became in effect Ellen's personal manager, looking after her both inside and outside the theatre. This is evident in Allan Wade's description of them behind the scenes during the run of *Captain Brassbound's Conversion* at the Court. Allan Wade had a small walking-on part in the production.

One might almost have thought that the roles of mother and daughter had been reversed – and the 'daughter' was sometimes headstrong and by no means easy to control. Miss Terry, coming down from her dressing-room on the first floor, would in the kindness of her heart, stop to chat with anybody she met – stage-hand, dresser, understudy – there was always something to say. She had discovered, how I don't know for I certainly never told her, that I had been a subscriber, for some years earlier, to Gordon Craig's magazine *The Page* which he had illustrated with his own woodcuts, and so I became for her 'a friend of Teddy's' – though actually it was many years later that I first met him. 'Oh yes – you are a friend of Teddy's; I heard from him last week.' 'Come *on*, mother,' Edy's voice would be heard from the stage-door. 'Oh, that's Edy,' Miss Terry would say with an even sweeter smile. 'I mustn't keep her waiting!'

And then, perhaps, she would meet somebody else coming up from the stage below and have another little talk. To my interested observation Miss Craig, as I then thought of her, seemed genial, a little brusque in speech, somewhat impatient, and certainly a very dominant personality.[13]

Edy always excited different reactions; she was whatever you saw her to be. For Chris, she was 'a saint', full of faults, she admits but free from 'self-love', wonderful in her 'magnanimity', her 'humility', her 'unworldliness', her enthusiasm for her work, her radiant enjoyment. For others, she was a feminist, militant about women's rights though not an active suffragette, a member of the Women's Freedom League and of the Actresses' Franchise League. But, for all her prickly humanity, she had no tact and was regarded by many as a trouble-maker and a dangerous woman at all costs to be avoided. This aspect of her nature ruined a career which otherwise might have been brilliant. She had a lively sense of humour; she was kind and patient with children, and above everything she wanted to be helpful, but her helpfulness always took the unfortunate form of organizing other people's lives for them to the point of causing resentment and pain. Ellen, extravagantly prejudiced, regarded her as 'something better than the best actress in the world'. Harcourt Williams, who came to know her well when he joined Ellen's company, praised her as a stage director:

> Her flair for costume and colour was inimitable. Her stage craft, always sound, frequently touched brilliance. Her criticisms were trenchant and often brusque, but so vital and finally good-humoured that none but a fool or a coxcomb could resent them. Her outbursts at rehearsal came and went like summer storms and left no trace of malice or aftermath of ill-temper. Her mother, who sometimes encountered these squalls with the rest of us, knew so well how to weather them. . . .[14]

Gordon Craig gives a remarkable and revealing picture of Ellen and Edy rivalling each other at the piano:

My mother, who could and couldn't play, knew what it was to attack a difficult piece of music, and they often played together. When Mother attacked, she was resplendent, and Edy gave up. Duets they played – and Edy, despairing to improve my mother, took to arguing; and the fierce torrent of music ceased, and logic took its place. Edy utterly annihilated Mother with her logic: she explained that if a piece was written to be played slowly and with such and such emphasis, it was not being polite to the composer, especially if his name was Brahms, to . . . Here Mother peered at the music to see the name of this celebrated being: 'Yes – it *is* Brahms.' All this gently murmured while Edy's scathing logic marched on. At the end of the speech, Mother would say: 'Let's try it again.' . . . And again Mother dashed in and on, and Edy came following after. Again a traffic jam. 'What's the matter?' 'Twice too fast,' said Edy. . . . And the funny thing was that she was right and Mother couldn't believe her own daughter's ears. 'Once more!' cries Mother. And this time Edy only pretended to play and let E.T. go ahead as fast as she liked – to the end of the piece.

The marriage with James Carew could not last. Ellen was, as her son put it, 'unmarriable'. It seems the marriage was never consummated; all Ellen wanted was a man about the house. She would not have dreamed of going to bed with him. But no man, least of all the uncomplicated Carew, could understand the jealous tensions that were roused by the particular relationship between Ellen and Edy. Edy could not bear the sight of Ellen in a state of matrimony, consummated or not, and the gap in the hedge which allowed a path to join the two properties of Smallhythe and Priest's House became overgrown through disuse. She refused to have anything to do with her mother, and the estrangement became a matter of gossip and intrigue in their wide circle of female friends and acquaintances. Ellen, doubly unhappy at the loss of both her beloved children in circumstances of such difficulty, did not prove an easy wife for any man to understand and tolerate. That there was affection between her and her husband is proved by the fact that they remained warm friends for the rest of their lives. But the relationship as a marriage could not last. A judicial separation was arranged two years later, and James moved out of the household. The gap in the hedge was reopened, and Edy returned triumphantly to power. She became her mother's 'manager' for the rest of her life – capable up to a point, long-suffering, exasperating, driving Ellen ultimately either mad or mischievous with her uncompromising, domineering demands. Ellen's self-protection began to take on oblique forms; she became more wayward, more evasive, blind and deaf to what she did not want to see or hear, and, unfortunately, less responsible in the handling of her affairs. Edy was forced to accept that certain of Ellen's male friends had to be admitted to King's Road or to Smallhythe – Sir Albert Seymour, with his charm, his humour, his high-pitched voice, his stutter, or Graham Robertson, the wealthy painter, dark and distinctive in his aestheticism. Occasionally there were signs that Teddy might sweep back to England. Edy, full of love–hate for her brother, would willingly have barred the door to him if only she could. If it had not been for the constant presence of Edy, Gordon Craig would probably have let his small daughter Nellie come to live with her grandmother far earlier than he did. And Ellen would have liked nothing better.

Professionally, Ellen was living on her 'image'. So strong was her position as a 'personality' that there was no time throughout the rest of her long life when she could not excite attention through her public appearances. The tragedy lay in the lack of any real need for her in the theatre. Her work was done. But for the sake of money it was necessary to keep herself employed. She had insufficient income for her needs and those of her many dependants. Ellen, incurably generous, kept a secret list of needy people to whom she sent small but regular sums of money. This she would consult, sending the maid out to the post with the envelope in which she had tucked the money. Edy mustn't know about this.

Edy made it her business to see that Ellen was kept as constantly engaged as possible. As a result, Ellen was afflicted with a long

x

trail of engagements in spite of her failing health, her poor eye-
sight, and in later years her wandering attention. To Graham
Robertson's delight she agreed to appear in his play for children,
Pinkie and the Fairies, the outcome of his affection for his ward
Marion Melville, the little daughter of his friend and artistic
partner, Arthur Melville, a painter and illustrator who had died
of typhoid contracted in Spain during 1903. In 1908 'Binkie', as
Marion was called, was six, and she had Ellen for her godmother.
Ellen, ceaselessly patient with children but ever-insistent about
the correctness of their speech and deportment, had begun by
teaching four-year-old Binkie how to play her old part of
Mamillius at the time she was herself preparing to play Hermione
for Tree at His Majesty's in 1906. Robertson wrote his fairy
play for Binkie, and it was set to music by Frederic Norton. In
October 1908, Tree offered to produce it at His Majesty's. Ellen,
who knew the script, wrote to Robertson from Smallhythe on 9
November:

> Blow the trumpets, beat the drums! I am delighted, my
> dear. Did you read it to Tree? I do like Tree, he *does* things.
> But take care. You must have your say in all of it or — I'd so
> much like to see your alterations (cuts, I suppose) in the last
> Act. Keep well and let me help you in bits of your work if
> I can.[15]

The play opened at Christmas with Ellen in the cast. Her reception was tumultuous, as Robertson describes:

> My chief memory is of the terrific outburst of applause that
> greeted Ellen Terry. She had not been seen for some time, and
> when she stepped upon the stage a storm seemed to break. It
> crashed out suddenly, like a thunderclap directly overhead,
> pealed on for a few moments, then settled into a steady roar
> which rolled on and on with a rhythmic throb like the beating
> of great drums and seemed as though it would never cease.

This was to be the pattern of Ellen's final years as an actress,
a respected public figure appearing in parts of ever-decreasing

importance until she was reduced, in more advanced years still, to one-night stands in the provinces through which she staggered, sustained by Edy's indomitable will. But throughout these final indignities she never lost her hold on the public imagination owing to the undying largeness of her personality. And, between 1916 and 1921, she was to appear in five films.[16]

The only work of distinction that she undertook after the end of her appearances for Tree were the series of Shakespearean lecture-recitals she gave between 1910 and 1921, when she was between the ages of sixty-two and seventy-three. In these she was able to relive momentarily many of her greatest moments on the stage. The written text of these recitals was carefully prepared with the help of Chris, and the scripts were marked up like any of her play scripts at the Lyceum: 'take time', 'quiet', 'keep still', 'low voice', 'with humour, rather reckless', 'dark, fierce, ardent', 'whisper', and so on. Chris says she was recalled to Ellen's side (having been 'banished', as she puts it, like one infectious since her marriage) in order to help her once again with her writing. The popularity of these lecture-tours gave Ellen a profound satisfaction, while the high fees made a substantial addition to her income. Again according to Chris: 'The proposal that she should lecture on Shakespeare came at a moment when she was puzzled, disheartened and disappointed at her failure to maintain her position. Time was pushing her into retirement.'[17]

The lecture-tours, suggested initially by the literary agent Curtis Brown, began in America in 1910, opening on 3 November in the form of a matinée at the Hudson Theatre, New York. Ellen had preceded the tour with a single appearance in London, the success of which encouraged her. She was not in very good health, as she wrote to Stephen Coleridge from on board the *Oceanic:* 'I can get through so little nowadays. . . . My heart has played me horrid tricks lately and frustrated all I undertook. . . . The first time I am making this long journey *alone* – and I feel strange.'[18]

Everywhere she went in the United States she was fêted. She did not return to England until the spring of 1911. Once

home again, a second tour was arranged for her in England. The
lectures were so successful that the following year Albert Chevalier
arranged a three-week season for her at the Savoy, her recital
placed between two short plays, one of which was Barrie's
Pantaloon.

Edy assisted her mother with the formal presentation of these
lectures in England, which Chris describes as follows:

> Aided by her daughter, she created 'scene' on the platform
> with dark green curtains, bunches of flowers and ingenious
> lighting. She wore flowing robes of crimson, or white or grey,
> the colour being determined by the mood of the discourses in
> her repertory and of the scenes she read, or acted, to illustrate
> them. For a lectern, she used one of the decorative desks, made
> for Irving and her in the year 1889 when they gave readings of
> 'Macbeth'. She had several copies of each lecture printed in a
> type large and bold enough for her to read the text without
> spectacles, and these folios were finely and solidly bound.[19]

'This discoursing is exhausting work,' wrote Ellen when it was
proposed she undertake a world tour, starting in Australia in 1914,
'far more exhausting that playing a part, for I have to sustain the
burden of the whole entertainment for nearly two hours. And
then there is the travelling'. Although warned against the tour on
the grounds that her heart was showing signs of strain – 'a kicking
Donkey', she called it, she did so partly because, according to
Chris, she was determined to maintain the financial help she
gave so constantly, especially to Edy and her grandchildren. If
she were to die, it was all the more necessary, in her view, for her
to leave the family a reasonable competence. The tour opened in
Melbourne in May 1914, when she was sixty-six. Edy did not go
with her. Her diaries and her letters home from Australia and
New Zealand show her reactions:

> First lecture in Australia. Very ill, very nervous, but I let
> myself go! I don't think they liked it much, however. After the
> Juliet scene, a lot of floral tributes and applause, but also God

Save the King, and every one went out before I had nearly finished!

My blessed old Edy, how hard I've been trying to keep going at my work, you'll never know, but it was no use trying, and on the conclusion of my last performance in Sydney, the doctor flatly told me I must not appear for a fortnight at least. I had to give in, and then we went over the water to Auckland, twelve hundred miles or so. I was worse than ever when I got there, but I landed in a dear little hotel, and was just nursed through my great weakness by the kind landlady, and now I think I'll get through the rest of the lectures easily.[20]

After war had been declared she wrote while staying with Melba in Coldstream, Victoria, that 'all engagements are being cancelled'. She accompanied Melba, giving free recitals to help war charities. Of Melba and her home she wrote: 'This (Melba's cottage at Coldstream) is an ideal spot, and Melba makes it an ideal home. She is so strong in body and character – a *splendid* woman, a magnetic one. She is thinking out kindnesses every hour of the day. I just love her now.' But Ellen's heart was in Kent, which she now imagined to be threatened by invasion by the German army: 'Maybe they are in Kent by now, perhaps inhabiting *our cottages*! And perhaps you may be giving them some tea! The horrors of this war for a few minutes now and again make me crazy, when I dare think, but I *darent*, and only pray that no harm comes near you, and that somehow or another we meet at home before Christmas.'

She did not return to England until May 1915, travelling by way of America where she gave more recitals to cover her expenses. On 27 February her left eye was operated on for cataract in New York, but she was recovered sufficiently by April 23 (Shakespeare's birthday) to make what was to be her final appearance in the United States at the Neighbourhood Theatre, New York. 'Nervous and weak at first,' she wrote. 'Soon inspired by the warmth of the audience.' It was, of course not recognized as a farewell appearance in the United States, and everyone radiated happiness. A First Folio of Shakespeare, lent by J. P. Morgan for a foyer exhibition, was brought to her in her dressing-room into which many people crowded to talk with her as she examined it. She was to leave America at the end of the month. She was offered a suite on the *Lusitania* by a friend of Charles Frohman, who was himself sailing on it, but she preferred for safety's sake to sail on a neutral American liner, the *New York*. By the time she landed in Liverpool the *Lusitania* had been sunk.

What delighted her most during these years was the company of her friends and, above all, of her grandchildren. Of the children born as a result of Ted's initial marriage and succession of love affairs, none appealed to her more than Little Nelly and Little Teddy, her grandchildren by Elena Meo. She shared with Isadora Duncan the tragic loss of Deirdre, another grandchild (whom she had never seen), when, with her half-brother Patrick, the child was drowned in a car which plunged out of control into the Seine.

Elena was to be the constant love of Ted's life. She alone understood him and, like Ellen, accepted him as he was, selflessly and generously. Unlike his former wife, she came from a true artist's background; she was used to the conversation of such constant visitors to her father's house as Samuel Butler, Burne-Jones and Swinburne. Also, she had an Irish mother, and when Ellen came to know her intimately in later years, she loved Elena and made her her companion and confidante. Elena's children were born in a flat in Southminster, Nellie on 11 January 1904 and Teddy on 3 January 1905, when his father was on the Continent with Isadora Duncan. However, when Ted learned of the birth of his son he hurried back to be with Elena. She became used to these sudden, unannounced visits; however much he was distracted by sudden passions for other women, Elena was the one woman to whom he always returned and the mother of the children who remained close to him throughout his life.

Ellen did not see her new grandchildren immediately. Ted first brought them to meet her around 1908, before spiriting them away for a period on the Continent, where they lived intermittently in Paris and Florence, returning to London according to Ted's preoccupations of the moment. But soon Elena and they were to become a most welcome part of Ellen's household, delighting her heart. In a notebook entry which appears to belong to 1914, Ellen writes: 'For the last four years Elena and her two wonderful children, my most beloved grandchildren, have lived with me, and I am most happy, and not alone. Ted comes and goes from his work in Italy, and this must soon fix them all up there. Meanwhile, they are my joys.'[21] This idyllic relationship, in which Edy joined, lasted until 1917, when Ted once more withdrew Elena and the children and took them back to Italy.

Ellen always loved her son's peripatetic entrances into her life. He arrived suddenly like some laughing demon king wrapped in his cloak, his long hair only half-concealed under his broad-brimmed hat. He was the genius she had created out of her love for Godwin. She knew he was irresponsible; perhaps she considered his irresponsibility to be part of the birthright she had given him herself, reserving the responsible part for Edy, who increasingly resented her brother's unforeseen incursions. They were so often associated with wild projects in which Ted, brimming over with excitement, would try to involve his mother. Edy knew only too well that they always meant fresh demands on Ellen's resources. Ellen would laugh uproariously at Ted's outrageous jokes, while Edy, angry and mortified, grew ever more bitter and spinsterly in her reproaches. But Elena was there now, Elena who had the kind of woman's understanding that Ellen most appreciated. She was, says Chris, 'daft about Elena'. Together they shared their unceasing devotion to Ted, whatever he might choose to do once he had left them, disappearing with a flash of lightning back to the Continent. Edy was thrust more and more into the bosom of her women friends, who were later to include Radclyffe Hall, the author of *The Well of Loneliness,* the writer Cecily Hamilton, Una Troubridge and, during and after the First World War, Clare (Tony) Atwood, the artist, with whom Edy and Chris formed the celebrated household of three on which Shaw was to make his pointed comment: 'You ought to write a history of that *ménage à trois,*' wrote Shaw ironically to Chris after Edy's death in 1947. 'It was unique in my experience.'[22] They retained the flat in Bedford Street as well as the Priest's house in Smallhythe.

Edy shared with Ellen a love for the children. For Ellen it was as if little Edy and little Ted had returned from the past to light up the long days of her later years. Indeed she would often make the mistake of calling little Nellie by Edy's name. Harcourt Williams, a constant visitor to Smallhythe, remembers a birthday party for Little Teddy:

> A little stage deftly arranged between the sitting-room and the kitchen at Yew Tree Cottage, opposite the Farm. The proscenium no wider than a doorway, but, for an audience of three or four, Edy made it seem big enough. There were comic interludes and other matters which have faded from my mind, but what glows there still is the picture of the boy, Teddy Craig, dressed in a snow-white farmer's smock, holding a shepherd's crook in his hand and in the bend of his arm a china lamb, whilst Ellen Terry read Blake's poem 'Little Lamb, who made thee?' Teddy had thick, longish hair, and the bend of his small head towards the lamb was simple and very beautiful.[23]

James, the household husband, had long since gone, though he remained a friendly visitor in the childhood memories of the grandchildren who did not lose touch with him when they reached maturity. But it was Ellen who shared with the devoted Elena the upbringing of the children during the war. She wanted, as always, to give both Teddy and Nellie a basic training for the stage, and they made walk-on appearances in plays during the war period.[24] She took them constantly to the theatre and to the music halls, which were now rapidly declining in number as the popularity of the cinema grew. While she was living in the King's Road she loved to cross the street in the evening to visit the Chelsea Palace music hall. The manager, resplendent in top-hat, white tie and tailcoat, always delighted to receive her. 'This way, Miss Terry,' he would say, guiding her along to a private box, usually with Little Teddy bringing up the rear, his eyes fascinated by the great watch-chain suspended in a loop across the manager's white waistcoat. Sometimes Ellen would meet Marie Lloyd, who usually kept a bottle of gin in her large handbag. 'D'you fancy a drop, dearie?' she would say to Ellen, who always said 'no' with a laugh, as she never drank spirits. Champagne was more to her taste.

When the air-raids came to London, Ellen calmed the timid servants when they all hurried down to the ground floor room, which was considered safest in these unknown dangerous circumstances. Ellen did not mind sleeping on the floor; she liked lying on a hard surface, and so did Teddy, lying back-to-back with Granny during the long, exciting nights. Teddy remembers their poor old cook coming up from the kitchen, crying in sheer despair at the awful stories of atrocity she had picked out from the papers. She stood there, old and weeping, with Ellen trying to comfort her. 'If they come here, ma'am, will they cut me breasties off?'

After the children had gone, Ellen suffered acutely from their loss. Perhaps she had loved them too possessively while they were there; she had not liked sparing them for an instant, even when they went off to visit their other grandparents, Gaetano Meo and his wife in Hampstead. Ellen occupied herself with a series of performances of scenes from Shakespeare starting at the Coliseum in November 1917 and continuing subsequently in the provincial music halls under Oswald Stoll's management. The scenes were from *The Merchant of Venice* and *The Merry Wives of Windsor*. A very young actress, Edith Evans, appeared as Mrs Ford. Later, in 1919, her memory sadly astray, she appeared as the Nurse in *Romeo and Juliet*.

Ellen's appearances in films began in 1916. She was invited by the British Ideal Film Company to star in a production called *Her Greatest Performance,* in which Edy was also offered a supporting part. The film, which was released in January 1917, was produced by Fred Paul, an actor who had become an established producer-director. Apart from the fact of Ellen's appearance on the screen in the part of a retired actress, Julia Lovelace, the film had no distinction. Julia Lovelace relives her former successes, which are somewhat similar to those of Ellen herself, in the triumphs of her widowed son, Gerald, a well-known actor. Gerald is wrongfully accused of the murder of his friend, Stephen Brinton, and imprisoned for manslaughter. The identity of the real murderer is known to Julia's former dresser, Mrs Carter, now an alcoholic; this was the part played by Edy. After Mrs Carter on her death bed has confessed her knowledge to Julia, the old actress impersonates the dead women in order to enforce a confession from the real murderer. 'It will be my greatest performance,' says Julia, looking upwards. 'Grant that it may be my most successful.' That she is successful goes without saying. The fact that this sentimental melodrama was created specially to suit Ellen's talent and background does not prevent it from being a sad début to the screen. However, like Duse, who made her only film, *Cenere* (Ashes), in Italy that same year, she lent the qualities of her personality to this impoverished material, though she scarcely did more than gain some casual enjoyment as well as some useful money from the experience. She liked the opportunities to meet and talk to people which film-making offered, and Bernard Shaw visited her on the set. She made much of Joan Morgan, who played the part of her grandchild in the story, Gerald's daughter. But the technique of film production, which involved creating a part scene by scene between what seemed to be lengthy waits spent sitting in a chair, soon began to bore her.

Though she did not enjoy the process of film-making, she did enjoy going to see films. She admired *The Cabinet of Dr Caligari*, and wished that Irving could have played the part of the sonambulist in which Conrad Veidt appeared. She enjoyed *Blood and Sand*, and thought Valentino had the ideal poise for Romeo. She celebrated her birthday in 1924 by going to see Chaplin's new film, *A Woman of Paris*; she had loved Chaplin's films ever since seeing *The Kid*. During the war she had taken Little Teddy to see Griffith's great films *The Birth of a Nation* and *Intolerance*, and they had impressed her as much as everyone else with the capacity of the screen to present action on a scale impossible in the theatre.

The next film in which she appeared was *The Invasion of Britain,* which was an official production sponsored by the Ministry of Information in 1918. The scenario was written by the popular novelist Hall Caine, and the film was directed by Herbert Brenon. This ambitious production was never shown because Brenon took so long to complete it that the war was over before it was finished. Fortunately, a sequence has been reserved in which Ellen, playing the part of a mother whose hero-son is killed at the front, is seen receiving the news of his death from her daughter-in-law, played by José Collins. Here we are able to see something at least of Ellen's art: limited to mime, she uses her hands and the movement of her head to express the devastation of a mother's grief. Though the scene lasts barely two minutes, it matches for these brief moments the screen achievement of Duse. And it reveals her great command of pathos.

Ellen's later appearances on the screen, apart, that is, from several in the newsreels, occurred in three further films, *The Pillars of Society* (1921), *Potter's Clay* (begun in November 1921, and first shown in March 1922), and *The Bohemian Girl* (1922). A complete print of the last film, directed by Harley Knowles, fortunately survives, and shows Ellen in a gracious but otherwise undistinguished performance as the nurse, Buda, who is responsible for the loss of Count Arnheim's child, Arlene, who is abducted and brought up by the gypsies. The cast of this well-made film was an interesting one: it included Gladys Cooper, Constance Collier, Ivor Novello and C. Aubrey Smith.

According to Chris, Ellen found it difficult to take direction in films, with the result that she was only able to give what was needed emotionally in flashes. Too often she found that these moments of concentration to order were beyond her control, and the methods of work in the studios and on location were quite alien to her. For example, says Chris, 'she saw in the trial scene in *Her Greatest Performance,* when a mother has the terrible experience of seeing her son, of whose innocence she is certain, made to appear guilty through a weight of incriminating evidence, her best opportunity for acting. But throughout the scene, the camera was picking out the prisoner, the witnesses, the judge, and members of the jury as well as the distraught mother. The scene was not moving in the same way or at the same pace as it was in Ellen Terry's imagination, with the result that when she was "shot" she was often expressing an emotion inappropriate at the particular moment.' She became more accustomed to film-making with time, and Chris believes her best scene was in the prologue to *The Pillars of Society*. Unfortunately, no print of this film is known to have survived.

It must be remembered that Ellen was in her seventies when she worked in these last three films. 'She's just past taking direction,' said one of the executives to Douglas Payne, the assistant producer on *Potter's Clay*.[25] According to Payne, Edy pleaded with him to let Ellen work only half days, as she was tired, and he rearranged the shooting schedule with some difficulty to meet her demands, only to discover subsequently that Edy had arranged for her to work in some other studio during the period she was released from *Potter's Clay*. Edy is remembered by Joan Morgan as a dominant figure in the studios during the filming of *Her Greatest Performance;* she watched over her mother with a fierce protective loyalty which did not endear her to the film-makers. Ellen, of course, was charming to everyone, though often nervous when it came to the crucial moment of performance before the cameras.

But, like her lecturing engagements, these films produced useful money to supplement her depleted income. Her appearances in the theatre remained transient. In 1915 she appeared for a charity matinée at the Haymarket in a ballet-pantomime based on a story by Hans Andersen, *The Princess and the Pea*, in which both Little Teddy and Nellie 'walked on' with her. Barrie created the new part of the old housekeeper, Darling, in *The Admirable Crichton*, especially so that she might play it in another charity matinée the same year. In 1919 she played the Nurse in *Romeo and Juliet* to Doris Keane's Juliet, and this was to be her last appearance in a full-length Shakespearean production. 'I'm keeping all the rude bits in,' wrote Ellen to her young friend Marguerite Steen.

By this time her finances were in so precarious a condition that she was forced by Edy in 1921 to give up the house in Chelsea, though she retained Smallhythe. She was still carelessly generous over money, in spite of Edy's attempts at strict surveillance. Her health by now had deteriorated, and her sight was very poor. It came as a profound shock to her when many of her most precious possessions at King's Road were sold and, after a period in Small-hythe, she was moved by Edy to a small three-roomed flat in St Martin's Lane; this was at Burleigh Mansions, a block with a grim and gloomy entrance. In her diary for 26 April 1921, Ellen wrote: 'I am unhinged (*not* unhappy) and comfortable. I wonder where everything is. Cannot remember new things. All is changed. Change at 73 puzzles the will. I live in puzzledom.'[26] Edy was not far off in Bedford Street, and James Carew, his friendship still surviving the broken marriage, lived in effect next door to her. The theatres, the restaurants she loved, and many of her friends were near her, but servants and companions began now to find her difficult and would not stay long in her service. According to Marguerite Steen, she even showed signs of panic and, in spite of her frailty, was only too ready to accept any kind of work which would bring in money for herself and her dependants. In July 1921, Marguerite Steen accompanied her to the Gaiety Theatre, Manchester, where she had been offered £100 and expenses to appear twice daily for a week in scenes from her 'repertoire'; in spite of the heat, she managed to fulfil the engagement, appearing between films (ironically enough, the theatre was celebrating its conversion into a cinema) and reciting 'The Quality of Mercy' and other speeches and poems with the help of Marguerite Steen's anxious prompting. Ellen gave the fee to Edy, who had been unable at the last minute to accompany her mother as she normally would have done, nursing her through her performances.

Following her succession of films Ellen made other spasmodic stage appearances which culminated in her final performance in the theatre; this was in Walter de la Mare's play *Crossings,* in which she played Susan Wildersham at the Lyric, Hammersmith, during 1925. Chris, who was present at a rehearsal, records the effect she created: 'I was standing in the stalls at the Lyric Theatre, Hammersmith, when Ellen Terry made her first entrance. The vision of this fragile creature, far advanced in years, yet somehow not old, tremulously gliding across the stage with loving arms outstretched, all earthiness purged away by time, the spirit of beauty, rather than beauty itself, filled the spectators with a strange awe. A long sighing 'Oh!' arose from them all, and the sound was a more wonderful tribute than any applause I have ever heard.'[27]

So, to the last possible moment, she carried her youth with her. Her hair, luxuriant still, flowed about her head as if it were yellow, not white; her face seemed smooth under its careful, unobtrusive dusting with French chalk, and her lips were touched with a special coloured salve supplied to her from Paris in small jars, the lids of which were always decorated with an ornamental flower. She had become thin again to the point of frailty; her slender figure enhanced the impression of youthfulness, and her voice remained fully toned, deep and clear with fine enunciation. On the stage she retained command of her movements; only in strange surroundings did she become hesitant, feeling her way among the unfamiliar tables and chairs, revealing the extent to which her sight had dimmed. Her mental perception came and went during the last few years of her life.

She outlived Bernhardt, Duse, even Isadora Duncan. She saw Bernhardt for the last time in London in a play called *Daniel,* in which she impersonated a young man in a wheelchair; they had met afterwards in Sarah's dressing-room, where Ellen praised her performance. When Sarah died in 1923 Ellen attended a Requiem mass at Westminster Cathedral, taking care to hold herself upright, though by now her back was weakened by age.

Duse appeared for the last time in London in 1923; Chris was sent on to meet her at Victoria station with a bunch of red roses, presenting them to her with Ellen's love. Duse, exhausted after a long illness, looked as if she would be unable to act, but at the sound of Ellen's name Chris saw her face become 'young and radiant'. Ellen went to see her in a matinée performance of Ibsen's *The Lady from the Sea*. 'Oh! she was Perfection!' wrote Ellen in her diary. 'I took her some flowers and she used them in the play. Afterwards I went round to see her. She seems even nobler now than when she was young. Was warmly affectionate to me and to my Edy.'[28] Duse died while on tour in America in April the following year.

Isadora Duncan's death followed in 1927. Ellen had seen her perform her dance of the Revolution at the Queen's Hall in June 1921 before she had left for Russia. 'I never saw *true* tragedy before,' wrote Ellen. At the end Isadora had spoken from the stage and invited her audience to acknowledge the presence of Ellen among them. After her passionate love affair with Teddy, Isadora Duncan had written affectionate letters to Ellen. Among some unpublished correspondence from her preserved at Smallhythe, there is an undated letter (which from internal evidence must have been written round 1908) which reveals how much she had felt herself at that time to be a member of Ellen's family:

Dearest and Sweet Nell. My heart leapt for joy when I saw your letter – How gracious and kind of you to write —

I don't know where to write to Ted – he did not answer my last letter so I think did not receive it —

Whether I write or no my heart goes out to him always wherever he is – I long for him just as I long always to see his Baby but I don't dare to think of it – or I shouldn't be able to live at all – That there is a Glorious Future waiting for him of that I never have had a doubt – It has seemed a long time for him to wait but it will only be the greater when it comes.

I will sail about Dec. 20th and dance in Paris – January – then to Budapest – February till March I go to Russia – I hope to steal a little time and come over to see you – Perhaps Ted might be there too – what a rejoicing we could have —

Where shall I write to Ted – I feel so much about him that I can't write – when I take up a pen – it all comes over me – choking – I can't write – Well perhaps we can all sit about the same table some day soon and drink to his Health and Glory.

He always looks wonderful – All the light and beauty of the World – That's what he is – *You* are the only one who understands how I love him – it will all come right some day.

With all my love. Isadora.

When Ellen's grandchild by Isadora had been drowned in Paris, the family link was severed. But their friendship remained. Isadora herself died in Nice a year before Ellen; she was strangled to death and her neck broken when the end of her long trailing scarf caught in the wheel of a car in which she was being driven.

After an interval, which to many of her admirers seemed a national disgrace, Ellen was made a Dame Grand Cross in 1925. Though she was pleased with the distinction it brought both to her sex and to her profession, she did not like the idea of the title itself; she did not want to be called a 'Dame'. At the investiture, which was held in private at Buckingham Palace, she was accompanied by Edy. When she was received by the King, Edy described her 'wonderful curtsy on entering – slow, stately, very expressive'. She was seventy-eight. When she left she had to be assisted; she was groping to find her way. Then suddenly she laughed outright, 'I quite forgot to walk out backwards,' she said to Edy. The King, who was just behind her, laughed with her. Then she met Queen Mary, who remembered her so well from the days of the Lyceum.

During these last years Ellen became the object of yet another factional struggle. When Edy and Teddy as small children had attended a mixed school together, Edy had made friends with a girl who shared the same first name, Edie Lane. This friendship survived into adult years but was later to develop into a bitter enmity. Edie had married H. A. (Taffy) Gwynne, who was eventually to become editor of the *Morning Post,* and the break in the friendship with Edy occurred at the time of the marriage. The fierce difference between the two women broke out afresh when, during the 1920s, Edie Gywnne did all she could to expose what she claimed to be Edy's vicious exploitation of her mother's helpless position and the mismanagement of her affairs. What Edie Gwynne tried so passionately to do was to dispossess Edy and take over the management of Ellen herself. She failed in this, but only after creating an unpleasant amount of gossip, and winning over as many supporters as she could.

There were always others who, without belonging to Edie Gwynne's faction, disagreed with Edy's conduct of her mother's affairs. There had even been some suggestion in about 1924 among Edy's circle at Priest's House that Ellen should be placed in a 'mental institution'; she was considered a danger to herself, for she would wander about the house at Smallhythe during the night, talking to herself and tracing the fading memories of the past which were enshrined in the objects in every room or looked out at her from portraits and pictures hanging upon her walls. She could not sleep, and she would wander out in the garden in search of the moon as Godwin had told her to do. It would have been merciless to part her from the treasures of house and garden, and Fred Terry among others intervened vehemently to prevent it. It was Hilda Barnes, Ellen's last companion and nurse, who watched over her during these final, difficult years, and withstood even Edy's attempts to have things her own way. So long as 'Barney' remained at Smallhythe there was no need to sever Ellen from the place she loved. She was even well enough in February 1928 to travel a short distance and stay with her friend Lady Mabel Egerton at Wateringbury.[29] Graham Robertson wrote to Kerrison Preston saying he had seen her and that she looked 'very frail', but a few weeks earlier she had been 'wickedly funny' when she had told him all about her sister Marion's recent visit to Smallhythe and her ladylike behaviour. 'It was a mercy *you* weren't there,' Ellen had said, 'or I should certainly have got the giggles and disgraced myself.' However, at the end of February, Graham Robertson wrote that 'the Lady' was 'drifting away into a strange vague world where nothing is real and people bear no names'. She was still at Wateringbury being protected, as Graham

Robertson puts it, from Edy and Ted, about whom, he says, his language had become 'forcible'. Early in March he spoke to James Carew, who had recently been to visit Ellen and told him about her reaction to seeing the man who was still her husband:

She had a flash of recognition and was pleased to find him there, 'Tell me, Jim,' she said clearly, 'I can't quite remember – did I kick you out or did you kick me out?' 'Well, dear,' said poor Jim cautiously, 'I think we arranged it between us, didn't we?' 'Yes, so we did,' said Nell. Then, after a pause: 'Dam' fools, weren't we?'

Slowly the time to die approached. She spent her last months in 1928 at Smallhythe, her mind veiled, her strength fading. Then the news came in July that she had had a stroke. Ted, fortunately, was on one of his rare visits to London; his son Teddy was already in England, having left Italy the year before to make his own career in London. They were both summoned by Edy to Small-hythe, and they were there with her and Barney when Ellen died early in the morning of 21 July. The sun was shining and the garden thick with flowers. It was the height of summer, and a good day to die.

Ellen herself had made it clear that she wanted 'no funeral gloom'. Her pall was made of cloth of gold from India.[30] Edy put a sprig of jasmine in her folded hands, and the family and friends stood by her in turns as she lay surrounded with flowers, her face lit by candlelight through the night watches.

Graham Robertson came to Smallhythe for the funeral. '*She* would not care whether one went or not,' he wrote to Kerrison Preston, 'one cannot associate her with funerals.' It took place at the little village church, and then the cortège covered with the golden pall and decorated with flowers travelled to Golders Green for the cremation. The church bells were asked to ring out, not to toll, their last greetings to her. People lined the way of the sixty-mile journey to London. They brought their flowers and threw them in tribute to her. Her last bouquets.

What she would have enjoyed during all this public parade of death, the services, the processions, the crowding photographers and reporters, the sightseers gathered to watch the solemn movement of coaches and cars during the long ride through countryside and town to the fires of Golders Green, would have been what Barney said as they left the church at Smallhythe – how glad she was they had played Ellen's favourite tune, the 'Dromedary' Air. How she would have laughed at Ted's remark when he grew excited at seeing so many of his relatives gathered round him. Clutching his sister's arm as they led the procession of mourners behind their mother's coffin, he said in a voice that everyone could hear: 'We must have more occasions like this.' They had become close now and for the moment reconciled.

Bernard Shaw had written while Ellen was at the height of her powers: 'Ellen Terry is the most beautiful name in the world; it rings like a chime through the last quarter of the nineteenth century.' Now, in our century, to which she also belonged, her ashes are kept in the actors' church, St Paul's in Covent Garden.

NOTES

The principal published sources for this book are the writings of Ellen Terry herself, notably her *Memoirs* in the edition edited by her daughter, Edith Craig, and by Christopher St John and published in 1933, and her correspondence with Bernard Shaw, edited by Christopher St John and published in 1931. Other important sources include two early biographies, *Ellen Terry* by Charles Hiatt (1898) and *Ellen Terry and her Sisters* by T. Edgar Pemberton (1902), the study of her written by her son, Edward Gordon Craig, *Ellen Terry and her Secret Self* (1931) together with his own autobiographical notes, *Index to the Story of my Days* (1957) and, for the period Ellen Terry was working at the Lyceum with Irving, Laurence Irving's meticulous study of his grandfather, *Henry Irving: the Actor and his World* (1951). I am also indebted for many points of detail to Marguerite Steen's picturesque account of the whole Terry family, *A Pride of Terrys* (1962). For details of theatrical history I have naturally turned to many books which are listed in the bibliography and referred to in the Notes below.

Evidence given to me personally by Ellen Terry's grandson, Edward Craig, has been of inestimable value throughout the preparation of this book. So too has the information I have obtained from Irving's grandson, Laurence Irving. The help I have received from other special sources, notably the Ellen Terry Memorial Museum at Smallhythe, the British Theatre Museum and the Library of the British Drama League, are acknowledged elsewhere.

In the notes below, the following initials are used: Ellen Terry appears as E.T., Gordon Craig as E.G.C., Edward Craig as E.C. and the author as R.M.

CHAPTER I: BEGINNINGS

Apart from E.T.'s *Memoirs*, the principal published sources for this chapter include the books already listed by E. G. C., Hiatt, Pemberton and Marguerite Steen. Among the sources used for background, I have drawn especially on Prof. Allardyce Nicoll's *A History of Late Nineteenth-Century Drama 1850–1900*, two volumes (1949).

1. When the children were very small, cradles were improvised for them in

the drawers of the chests of drawers common in Victorian bedrooms. The drawers were pulled out for the babies to sleep in.

2. See E.T. *Memoirs*, pp. 44 and 54. In a later passage, p. 65, the younger daughters, Marion (Polly) and Floss (Florence), are referred to as attending school.

3. E.T. told her grandson, E.C., that her mother changed her name when she went on the stage in order to avoid offending her Scottish relations.

4. See Steen, *A Pride of Terrys*, p. 46.

5. See Nicoll, *op. cit.* I., pp. 45 *et seq*.

6. Kean's spectacular productions with their emphasis on archaeological exactness had been anticipated in certain of Macready's productions. Charles H. Shattuck has published a facsimile of Macready's prompt-book for his production of *King John* at Drury Lane in October 1842, together with the drawings and watercolours of the original designs for sets and costumes. The sets were designed by William Telbin under the influence of Clarkson Stanfield (1793–1867), the painter who also worked for the theatre; the drawings are preserved in the Folger Shakespeare Library in Washington. The book, sponsored in 1962 by the University of Illinois Press, also contains for comparison reproductions of designs for Charles Kean's final London production of 1858. Telbin's designs to a large extent anticipate those created for Irving over thirty years later. I am grateful to Laurence Irving for help in the preparation of this note.

7. E.C. told me that E.T. taught him to dance the hornpipe in just the same spirit more than fifty years later.

8. E.T. would teach E.C. as a child to walk with a pack of cards stacked on his head.

9. See ET., *Memoirs*, p. 18.

10. Hiatt says this accident took place not at the Princess's Theatre but when the company was on tour playing at the Theatre Royal, Manchester. But E.T. in her *Memoirs* implies it was at the Princess, since she adds: 'Mr Skey, of Bartholomew's Hospital, who chanced to be in a stall that very evening, came round behind the scenes and put my toe right. He remained my friend for life.' (p. 17).

11. E.T. *Memoirs*, p. 28.

12. E.T. *Memoirs*, p. 23.

13. For this and other reviews quoted see Pemberton, *op. cit.*, pp. 34–6, and Hiatt, *op. cit.*, pp. 33–4.

14. See *Charles Reade, a Memoir*, by Charles L. Reade and the Reverend Compton Reade, Vol. II, p. 259.

15. See Steen, *op. cit.*, p. 71. The sum amounted probably to a few hundred pounds, though Fred Terry was to claim later that it was a few thousand pounds.
16. See E.T. *Memoirs*, pp. 33–34. E.T. was, of course, 14 years old.

CHAPTER II: CHILD ACTRESS AND CHILD WIFE

Ellen Terry's *Memoirs* remain the principal source for this chapter, supplemented by the books of Pemberton and Hiatt. Godwin's life story has been told by Dudley Harbron in *The Conscious Stone* (1949), and the facts concerning Watts appear in Ronald Chapman's *The Laurel and the Thorn* (1945), supplemented by David Loshak's detailed study of E.T.'s relationship with Watts in an article published in *The Burlington Magazine* (November 1963). A useful background source for the whole Terry family at this time is the *Diaries of Lewis Carroll* (1953).

I am grateful to Wilfrid Blunt, the Curator of the Watts Gallery, and to Kerrison Preston, friend and literary executor of Graham Robertson, for the help and advice they have given me. There are important references to E.T.'s relations with both Watts and Godwin in Kerrison Preston's edition of the *Letters* Graham Robertson sent him (published 1953), as well as in the E.T.– Shaw *A Correspondence*.

1. E.T. in her *Memoirs* says she 'wore a short tunic which in those days was considered too scanty to be "quite nice"' when she appeared as Cupid (see p. 37).
2. Pemberton, *op. cit.*, p. 62.
3. See E.T. *Memoirs*, p. 35. The quotation that follows can be found on pp. 36–37.
4. E.T. *Memoirs*, p. 38. E.T. was 15, not 16.
5. See Pemberton, *op. cit.*, p. 76. The quotation following is on p. 78.
6. There is a record, noted by Pemberton (*op. cit.*, p. 90) that she also appeared as Desdemona at the Princess's Theatre in June 1863. Othello, it appears, was played by Walter Montgomery.
7. See E.T. *Memoirs*, pp. 50–52.
8. Watts painted a fine portrait of her around 1860, which can be seen at the Watts Gallery, Compton, Surrey. She appears proudly beautiful, a little contemptuous and rather aloof; Roger Fry regarded the portrait as one of the 'finest achievements of English art for all times'. During the same period

Mrs Thoby Prinsep posed for a picture which was called *In the Time of Georgione*; it is reproduced in Chapman's biography. It is characteristic that both these pictures remained unfinished for some thirty years, Watts only getting round to completing them in the 1890s. Nevertheless, the brief period of his marriage to E.T. was the start of what Wilfrid Blunt regards as his best period for portraiture.

9. Little Holland House had associations with Cromwell and, among others, with Caroline Fox, Macaulay, Coleridge and Jeremy Bentham.

10. Chapman, *op. cit.*, p. 49.

11. Chapman, *op. cit.*, pp. 62–63.

12. See E.T. *A Correspondence* with Shaw, p. 122. For the additional unpublished text I am grateful to E.C. E.T., of course, was nearly 17.

13. See *Letters of Graham Robertson*, p. 409, and Loshak, *The Burlington Magazine*, November 1963, p. 479, note 6. (See also Steen, *op. cit.*, p. 96.)

14. See E.T. *Memoirs*, p. 42. Among the many rumour-spreaders was Frank Harris, who wrote in *My Life and Loves*: 'What caused the rupture between them he never told me, and she was almost as reticent – though once she admitted that she "never loved Watts", which was perhaps confession enough. "He was charming," she said, "and I loved the pictures he made of me, but I never cared for him."' (Vol. V, Chap. XII.)

15. See Chapman, *op. cit.*, p. 67. For the marriage-night gossip, see Steen, *op. cit.*, p. 96.

16. All these pictures, as well as others, are reproduced in the *Burlington Magazine*, November 1963. See also Wilfrid Blunt's volume in the *Masters* series. The original of *Choosing* is in the possession of Kerrison Preston; *The Sisters* is owned by the Hon. Mrs E. Hervey-Bathurst. Graham Robertson, who first came to know E.T. when she was thirty-nine, received her confidence on certain matters connected with her private life. In his letters written many years later to Kerrison Preston he makes his own comments on her relation with Watts, whom he also knew well. He wrote to Kerrison Preston in 1939: 'If Watts thought he could mould that vital and radiant creature into what he wished her to be, he did not show much intelligence' (pp. 409–10). When in 1934 Kerrison Preston acquired Watts's portrait of E.T., *Choosing*, Graham Robertson wrote: 'It is a great joy to me that the picture has come to you. It was Ellen Terry's favourite of all the portraits painted of her. And I'm glad the Watts self-portrait hangs by it. They were much misrepresented to each other by kind friends, and they both knew it afterwards. But of course they could never have settled comfortably down together. To marry Ellen Terry was an absurd thing for any

man to do. He might as well marry the dawn or the twilight or any other
evanescent and elusive loveliness of nature' (p. 316). In other letters he made
other references to this picture. In 1938 he writes: '. . . that throat is Ellen
Terry's throat, the eager, impulsive movement entirely hers, the whole
thing inspired by her. When E.T. first told me about the picture, she called
it "Choosing" and described the scentless camellias and the violets. She
wanted to take me to see it, but we never made the visit' (p. 401). Also: 'It
is curious that Watts, who apparently understood her so little, should have
painted by far the truest portraits of E.T.' (p. 323). In another letter (p. 403)
he states that many of the portraits of E.T. were not painted as such, but
were subject pictures for which she acted as model.

17. This portrait, which is a distortion rather than a likeness of E.T.'s features, is
preserved in the Print Room of the British Museum.
18. Quoted by Loshak in the *The Burlington Magazine* (Nov. 1963).
19. Quoted by Loshak from A. M. W. Stirling, *Life's Little Day* (1944), p. 219.
20. E.C. tells me this photograph was taken in the bathroom of Tennyson's
house on the Isle of Wight.
21. E.T. *Memoirs*, pp. 44–5.
22. *Diaries of Lewis Carroll*, Vol. I, p. 225.
23. E.T. *Memoirs*, pp. 46–47.
24. See *The Heart of Ellen Terry*, p. 35. The friend was Stephen Coleridge (see
page X).
25. See E.T. *Memoirs*, p. 47.

CHAPTER III: GODWIN

In addition to E.T.'s *Memoirs* and the biographies already cited, primary sources
for this chapter include E.T.'s unpublished letters to Mary-Anne Hall preserved
at the British Theatre Museum, the diaries of Lewis Carroll, E.G.C's *Index*, and
Bancroft's *Recollections of Sixty Years* (1909). I have also drawn on the books by
Marguerite Steen and Dudley Harbron already cited, Graham Robertson's
Time Was, Alice Comyns-Carr's *Reminiscences*.

1. E.T. *Memoirs*, p. 48.
2. This, and subsequent letters to Mary-Anne Hall, are all in the British
Theatre Museum archive.
3. E.T. *Memoirs*, p. 54. It is perhaps of some significance that in her own
edition of *The Story of My Life* (the Memoirs in the form published during

her lifetime) preserved at Smallhythe, E.T. scribbled in the margin of p. 113 concerning Tom Taylor: 'Sweet fellow: Kate should tell of him for he cared for *her* more than he cared for me.'

4. In a letter to Mary-Anne Hall dated 6 June, E.T. refers briefly to this forth-coming single appearance.

5. I can find no satisfactory record of these appearances. Kate played her final London season at the Adelphi, so no doubt E.T. made her usual brief appearance in support of some benefit performance for her sister in both Bristol and London. But Marguerite Steen quotes an undated letter in which Polly and Nellie join to report to their mother on some engagement in the provinces with Ben. The town was probably Bristol, and the date pre-sumably 20 February 1866. (See Steen, *op. cit.*, p. 107.)

6. Carroll, *op. cit.*, I, p. 233.

7. *Cox and Box* (originally called *Box and Cox*) by F. C. Burnand and Arthur Sullivan originated as an amateur production at Moray Lodge, the house which was to become Kate's home after her marriage to Arthur Lewis in October the same year.

8. Pemberton, *op. cit.*, p. 131.

9. In a letter dated 11 Jan. 1867 to Mary-Anne Hall, E.T. writes: 'Really dreadful cough . . . my "shrewishness" will be *tame* tonight.'

10. E.C. says that she undoubtedly did meet Godwin again at Little Holland House, and that E.T. could proudly claim him as her friend among the overwhelming number of cultured and famous people introduced by the Prinseps. But the old story accepted uncritically by Godwin's biog-rapher, Dudley Harbron, and repeated by Marguerite Steen in *A Pride of Terrys*, which asserts that E.T. while still at Little Holland House deserted her husband to spend a night away nursing Godwin during an illness, appears to be so much moonshine. According to this account, E.T. was met on the mat in the morning by a reception party composed of Mrs Prinsep, Watts, and her father and mother, all of whom accused her of immoral behaviour. E.T.'s unusual life was to excite constant speculation in London society, and there were only too many people prepared to gossip about her and pass on their inventions about her private life. This particular story appears to have originated with Lady Duff Gordon, who in her book *Discretions and Indiscretions* (1932) claims that E.T. told her that Godwin 'had been on friendly terms with the family for years and both my husband and I were on terms of the most informal intimacy with him; we used to run in and out of his house whenever we wanted'. According to Lady Duff Gordon, E.T. told her that, after having been taken to task at Little Holland

House, Godwin became 'her only refuge, and I went back to his house'. Godwin had no residence in London during the period E.T. and Watts were married, and indeed his own wife was still alive and living with him in Bristol.

11. It could well be that this friend was not Godwin, but Charles Reade. This is the view of E.C. He considers that E.T.'s account implies, that her 'friend' was familiar with Paris and spoke French, whereas there is no evidence that Godwin had visited France before or knew the language. On the other hand, E.C. knows for a fact that E.T. went to Ireland with Godwin on one of his many professional visits to this country. Ellen would particularly value the opportunity to visit the home-country of the Irish.

12. E.T. *Memoirs*, p. 65.

13. There is no reference in Lewis Carroll's diary to seeing E.T. again until her return to the stage in February 1874, but he kept in fairly close touch with both Stanhope Street and Moray Lodge, visiting both on occasion, going to the pantomime with Polly and Flo in January 1868, and to the Christie Minstrels with Sarah and the children in September the following year. Later he went several times to the theatre to see Flo and Polly (Marion) on the stage.

14. E.T. *Memoirs*, p. 66.

15. According to Marguerite Steen, *op. cit.*, p. 124, Godwin was away from home at the time of the birth of his first child. The local doctor, Dr Rumball, delivered the child. His wife was later to become one of E.T.'s closest companions (see text, p. 79). According to Marguerite Steen, E.T. told her that she nearly left Godwin when he reproved her roughly for harnessing the pony when she was pregnant. (See Steen, *op. cit.*, p. 125.)

16. This work, carried out in the inadequate artificial light of the period, is believed to have been the initial cause of E.T.'s severe eye trouble in later life. See page 75.

17. Robertson, *Time Was*, pp. 140–1. The quotations that follow are at pp. 142 and 143. Robertson also quotes a letter from E.T. in which she rejoices in being able to share her experience of moonlight with her grandson, Little Teddy: 'Good Lord, that November moon! I had to pull little Teddy out of his bed one night so that he should not miss the teeming loveliness. His face in the pale light I shall never forget. The delicacy of it – so grave and so adoring! His morning reading has been a great bond between us, but the Moon — He made me promise to wake him up once a month to see the sight' (p. 143). E.C. remembers these moonlight experiences vividly; they often had to be kept secret from Edy.

18. E.T. seems to imply that she attended the village church at Fallows Green. This she could do under her 'guise' of being Mrs Godwin. But in later life she was never to be a churchgoer, though she believed in God, kept a Bible by her and read such books of religious meditation as that by Thomas à Kempis, whom she called by the pet name Kempy. Godwin used to practise on the organ in the church at Harpenden, and had an organ installed in his house. E.C. tells me there was a monkey kept at Harpenden which would sit on Godwin's foot when his legs were crossed.

19. The conversation is recorded by E.T. herself. (See *Memoirs*, p. 69.)

20. See E.T. *Memoirs*, p. 70. Marguerite Steen, without giving her source, says the whole family openly moved to London. But E.C. has told me of certain letters, now destroyed, which E.T. sent from London to Harpenden addressed to a Miss Bindloss, who was at this time governess to the children. The letters were full of distressing references to Godwin and to E.T.'s difficult situation. The Bindloss letters were destroyed by her nephew, a clergyman, as he thought them of too private a nature to preserve.

21. See E.T., *op. cit.*, pp. 78–81; the passages following, giving Reade's view of E.T. and hers of him, appear on pages 75 and 71 respectively of the *Memoirs*. The Reade letters are still preserved in the archives at Smallhythe; some are signed 'Papa'. E.T.'s personal copy of Reade's biography referred to is in the library at Smallhythe.

22. See Forbes-Robertson, *Under Three Reigns*, pp. 66–7.

23. E.G.C. in his various books always expresses great antipathy to Reade, largely because of Reade's known antipathy to Godwin. For the relations between E.T. and Mrs Seymour, see E.T. *Memoirs*, p. 85. She 'liked' Mrs Seymour.

24. See Hiatt, *op. cit.*, p. 20. Cp. *Mr and Mrs Bancroft on and off the Stage* (1889), p. 208.

25. Bancroft divided the play into seven scenes to avoid a set-change in view of the audience. The scenes were: Under the arches of the Doge's Palace; Belmont; Lanes in Venice (morning); Lanes in Venice (evening); Belmont; the Sala della Bussola; a Garden. During the intervals between these scenes, views of Venice, painted by Gordon, were displayed. (See *Mr and Mrs Bancroft*, p. 211.)

Godwin's article on the architecture and décor for *The Merchant of Venice* was reprinted by his son, Gordon Craig, in a double issue of his journal, *The Mask*, May–June 1908. This article (there was a second on costume) was originally published in 1875 in *The Architect*. It began with an analysis of the double plot of the play which, Godwin maintained, should be treated as taking place contemporaneously with the composition of the play, namely during the 1590s. Architectural ground-plans are given for a public place in Venice incorporating the exterior of Shylock's house, a hall of Justice in the Doge's Palace, and a stateroom in Portia's house at Belmont.

Godwin goes on to determine the exact appearance of houses and palaces in Venice in the 1590s, and how any scene-painter should seek to represent the city. He then explains how each element making up his sets should correspond to Venetian originals. He thinks, for example, bearing in mind the delimitation of a stage, the Court of Justice would be more appropriately based on the relatively small Sala dello Scrutinio in the Doge's Palace than on the great Sala del Maggior Consiglio. In the trial scene, he considers the disposal of the groups surrounding the plaintiff and defendant as well as the Doge and his fellow dignitaries, and how their seats and other furnishings should be devised, down to the smallest detail: the bond, the scales, the knife, etc. The trial, in other words, is not treated as a theatrical fantasy but considered as actually taking place in the Venice of the 1590s. For Portia's room, he refers the scene painter for details to the paintings of such artists as Ghirlandaio and Bazzi, and considers in great detail an ornate contemporary design for the caskets.

In the subsequent article on costume, he describes Portia's dresses with great care. Among the points he makes are: 'Portia would do her shopping in Padua, and would therefore follow the fashions of the mainland. The chief difference we have to note is the absence of the square-cut body. High-necked bodies, with fine cambric ruffs, was the everyday attire usually worn by Paduan ladies of noble birth. . . . There is also a marked difference to be observed between the dresses of a maiden and that of a married woman, and there is no question that the Paduan ladies (wives or not) indulged in a considerably extensive wardrobe. So, too, there was more than one mode of dressing the hair . . . Rings were worn on the first, third and fourth fingers.' And so on.

26. Pemberton, *op. cit.*, p. 147.
27. Alice Comyns-Carr, *Reminiscences*, p. 31. Beerbohm Tree's reaction, recorded in his diary, is interesting. 'I cannot understand how she can smile so naturally. Her by-play was marvellous. She looked like one of Leighton's women, queen-like. In the trial scene she astonished me by putting on the manners of a youth . . . like a young barrister of the present day.' See Hesketh Pearson, *Beerbohm Tree* (1956), p. 11.
28. E.T. *Memoirs*, pp. 86–7.

29. E.T. *Memoirs*, p. 89.
30. See Terry-Shaw, *A Correspondence*, p. xxxii.
31. E.G.C. *Index*, p. 21.
32. This letter, preserved in the archive at Smallhythe, is addressed to 'Dear old Bobbie' and written from Barkston Gardens on 8 September 1890. The recipient is marked in the handwriting of Christopher St John – 'an old friend'. The singleness of E.T.'s love for Godwin is also referred to in a letter from Graham Robertson to Kerrison Preston written in 1931: 'Though I know most people would not think so, Ellen Terry was a "one man" woman. She loved (in the true sense of the word) one man only – and for ever' (*Letters*, p. 260).
33. Divorce in England before 1857 was only possible by a private Act of Parliament. By the Marriage Act of that date a petition for divorce could be submitted to the civil courts and, if granted, took six months to be declared absolute. Legal costs were high at this time.
34. E.T., like all players, was always ready to help her fellows by appearing in their benefit performances. On 1 March 1877 she took part in a performance of part of Lytton's play *Money* for the benefit of Henry Compton, and on 20 June she appeared at the Gaiety as Lady Teazle in *The School for Scandal* for the benefit of Charles Lamb Kenney. (See Hiatt, *op. cit.*, pp. 93–4, and Pemberton, *op. cit.*, p. 161.)
35. Terry-Shaw *Correspondence*, p. xxxii.
36. E.T. *Memoirs*, p. 116.
37. E.G.C. *Index*, p. 49.
38. See E.T. *Memoirs*, p. 118.

CHAPTER IV: THE LYCEUM

In addition to the books by E.T., E.G.C., Hiatt, Pemberton and Graham Robertson already cited, in this and succeeding chapters I have drawn continuously on Laurence Irving's biography, *Henry Irving*. I have also used Bram Stoker's *Personal Reminiscences of Henry Irving*, A. E. Wilson's *The Lyceum*, Henry James's *The Scenic Art*, Allardyce Nicoll's *A History of Late Nineteenth Century Drama* and Clement Scott's *Drama of Yesterday and Today*, among many other books.

1. He adopted the name partly in tribute to one of his favourite authors,

Washington Irving, and partly in recognition of the Northumbrian preacher, Edward Irving. (See Irving, *op. cit.*, p. 62.)

2. After Irving's death, a photograph of Nellie Moore was found in his pocketbook pasted back-to-back with a portrait of himself taken in 1868.

3. Laurence Irving, *op. cit.*, p. 308. The letter is dated 25 August 1878. The 'half-clear' benefit in the terms settled with Irving means E.T. was to receive half the takings of a benefit performance during the season, clear of any deductions.

4. E.T. *Memoirs, op. cit.,* p. 102.

5. For example, Lewis Carroll in his *Diaries*, Vol. II, p. 377, says: 'Irving rather spoiled Hamlet by his extraordinary English.' For discussion of Irving's manner of speech see James, *The Scenic Art*, p. 139, E.T. *Memoirs*, p. 123, E.G.C.'s *Henry Irving*, pp. 62–9, and Laurence Irving's *Henry Irving*, p. 284.

6. James, *op. cit.*, p. 139.

7. E.T., *op. cit.,* p. 106. For the quotation that follows below, see pp. 119–20. For E.T.'s ambitions for herself, see also p. 100 and p. 120.

8. For E.T.'s interest in lighting, see Chapter V, p. 146.

9. E.T. *Memoirs*, p. 131.

10. E.G.C., *Irving*, pp. 58–61.

11. For the amusing story of Irving purloining for himself the cloak that E.T. had hoped to wear, see E.T., *op. cit.*, p. 123.

12. Pemberton, *op. cit.*, p. 225.

13. Kelly only appeared at the Lyceum with E.T. once, in a benefit performance for a sick actor, Henry Marston. For this and other facts concerning the provincial tours see Hiatt, *op. cit.*, pp. 123, 130–2, 147.

14. They also appeared together in a single performance of the first act of *Richard III* on 25 July 1879 on the occasion of Irving's 'benefit'. E.T. played the Lady Anne, and Irving, of course, Gloucester. This first season benefit brought him £250, and that for E.T. £233. See Chapter V, Note 4. After the theatre was enlarged, E.T.'s benefits materially increased. In later years she records getting £430 from a single benefit. See Terry-Shaw *A Correspondence*, p. 296.

15. James, *op. cit.*, p. 122.

16. Stoker, *op. cit.*, Vol. I, p. 170.

17. This privately printed copy of *Charles I* is preserved at Smallhythe.

18. Hiatt, *op. cit.*, p. 128.

19. For a very full description of Irving's performance as Shylock, see Laurence Irving, *op. cit.,* pp. 339–444.

20. Robertson, *op. cit.*, pp. 54–55.
21. Kate Terry Gielgud, *Autobiography*, p. 90.
22. James, *op. cit.*, pp. 143–4.
23. Hiatt, *op. cit.*, pp. 137–8.
24. Laurence Irving, *op. cit.*, p. 346.

CHAPTER V: THE NEW LIFE

In addition to the books by E.T. and E.G.C. already cited, I have drawn for this chapter on Laurence Irving's *Henry Irving*, Henry James's *The Scenic Art*, Coquelin's *The Art of the Actor* (1894; translated into English 1932), Frank Benson's *Memoirs* and Martin Harvey's *Autobiography*.

1. E.G.C. *Index*, p. 182.
2. E.T. *Memoirs*, p. 149.
3. E.G.C. *Ellen Terry and Her Secret Self*, p. 14.
4. Laurence Irving has presented a set of the regular Lyceum account sheets prepared by Bram Stoker for his grandfather to the British Theatre Museum. An undated example that went astray is discussed by Maurice Willson Disher in *The Last Romantic*, p. 96; this shows E.T. to be earning £200 a week. It is difficult to determine exactly when E.T. was promoted to this high salary, plus the seasonal benefits, since the company's salaries were normally totalled together. But it would seem just to assume that she reached this level early in the 1880s when the success of the Lyceum was fully established and she was free of her separate provincial tours with Kelly. Her annual income must have been in the neighbourhood of £9,000 a year throughout the 1880s and 1890s.
5. E.G.C. *Ellen Terry*, p. 22.
6. See the note to this effect by Christopher St John and Edith Craig, E.T. *Memoirs*, p. 185. Also see p. 139, quoting E.T.'s letter to Shaw. E.T. calls Kelly 'a male Julia' (*Correspondence*, p. 137); for the significance of this, see below Chapter IX, note 1.
7. E.T. *Memoirs*, p. 113.
8. See E.T. *Memoirs* pp. 116–17 and the Terry–Shaw *A Correspondence* (p. 137) for the comments on Kelly made in this paragraph.
9. E.G.C. *Ellen Terry*, p. 9. E.G.C. says Rose Cottage was given up round 1880. It may not have been given up quite so soon as this. See E.T. *Memoirs*, p. 163.
10. E.T.'s letters, apart from those to Shaw have yet to be collected and pub-

lished. This will be a considerable task. There are many still in private hands, many in public collections (for example, at the British Theatre Museum and at Smallhythe). Some have been sold to America, and a collection of letters primarily to Laurence and Mabel. Irving were formerly in the possession of Bernard Miles. The great collection written to Stephen Coleridge, which he claims amounted to fourteen bound volumes, were the source for the only others so far published; these appear in *The Heart of Ellen Terry*, published in 1928 shortly after her death. Some of these are quoted later in this paragraph. The volume contained only twenty-six letters. The Hon. Stephen Coleridge was the son of the Lord Chief Justice and became E.G.C's godfather, much to Ted's distaste. (See E.G.C. *Index*, pp. 59–60, 66.) The artists, Ella and Nelia Casella and Ellaline Terriss, daughter of William Terriss, were also amongst E.T.'s regular correspondents.

11. Cited by E.G.C. *Ellen Terry*, p. 49.
12. E.G.C. *Ellen Terry*, p. 10.
13. Inspired by Laurence Irving (*op. cit.*, p. 673; cp. Pemberton *op. cit.*, pp. 22–3), I have made an attempt to trace the 'lineage' in British acting from the time of Shakespeare to that of Irving and E.T. See page 102.
14. E.T. *Memoirs*, p. 134.
15. James, *op. cit.*, pp. 142–3.
16. Coquelin, *The Art of the Actor*, p. 31. For next quotation see p. 78. For Coquelin's observations on E.T., see Laurence Irving, *op. cit.*, p. 327.
17. James, *op. cit.*, pp. 128–9.
18. See Chapter VIII pp. 224–5 for amusing accounts of Bernhardt being entertained by Irving in the Beefsteak Room at the Lyceum, see Alice Comyns-Carr, *op. cit.*, p. 217, and E.T. *Memoirs*, p. 168. According to Alice Comyns-Carr: 'Brilliant and interesting companion that the Divine Sarah was, her views and her illustrations of them were not always in what more prudish English people considered good taste. Indeed, in her choice of examples she was sometimes like a fishwife.' Graham Robertson, who became a close friend of Bernhardt in spite of the difference in their ages, describes her in great detail in *Time Was*. E.G.C. claimed that 'her methods were quite Irvingesque' and that this 'suited her'.
19. This description was Oscar Wilde's.
20. Hiatt, *op. cit.*, p. 164. The Meiningen company, their *ensemble* productions forecasting one work of the Moscow Arts Theatre, had appeared in London in 1881.
21. E.T. *Memoirs*, p. 167.
22. E.T. (*Memoirs*, p. 171) recalls it as the *Electra*. But see Benson *Memoirs*, pp.

z

117, 151. For Benson's recollections of meeting E.T. at the Lyceum, see p. 129.

23. See Martin Harvey, *Autobiography*, pp. 92–3.

CHAPTER VI: NORTH AMERICA

In this chapter, in addition to the E.T. *Memoirs* and Laurence Irving's *Henry Irving*, I have drawn primarily on Joseph Hatton's book, *Henry Irving's Impressions of America* (1884), which was so successful it had to be reissued in a cheap edition. Lengthy extracts from reviews of the Lyceum productions by the American press appeared regularly in the *Illustrated London News* in what would be called now 'advertisers announcements'. In other words, they were paid insertions to keep the British public informed of the Company's progress during their first visit to the United States.

1. See below, Chapter X, p. 302. The later American tours which E.T. undertook with Irving are listed in Note 29 of Chapter VII. In addition to these official tours, E.T. made private visits to the United States, and toured on her own account. See below, Chapter X, pp. 313, 315.

2. For this and the quotation from the *Tribune*, see Hatton, *op. cit.*, pp. 37–8.

3. Hatton, *op. cit.*, pp. 46–7.

4. E.T. *Memoirs*, pp. 202–3.

5. Hatton, *op. cit.*, p. 105.

6. Hatton, *op. cit.*, p. 118.

7. E.T. *Memoirs*, p. 223.

8. Hatton, *op. cit.*, p. 237.

9. Hatton, *op. cit.*, pp. 236–7.

10. E.T. *Memoirs*, p. 220.

11. Hatton, *op. cit.*, p. 221.

12. Hatton, *op. cit.*, p. 324.

13. Laurence Irving, *op. cit.*, p. 449.

14. Laurence Irving, *op. cit.*, p. 450.

CHAPTER VII: SHAKESPEARE, MY SWEETHEART

The principal sources for this chapter are the E.T. *Memoirs*, the books already cited by Hiatt, Pemberton, E.G.C., Laurence Irving, Graham Robertson and Alice Comyns-Carr. I have also drawn on E.T.'s unpublished notes on *Macbeth* preserved at Smallhythe, and on her published *Four Lectures on Shakespeare* (1932).

1. See Alice Comyns-Carr, *op. cit.*, p. 155 for this quotation and the one immediately below.

2. Quoted by Hiatt, *op. cit.*, p. 188–9.

3. A week earlier, on 1 June, another special matinée was staged. This was Byron's *Werner*, in which Ellen appeared as Josephine. Irving played Werner.

4. According to Alice Comyns-Carr, Irving went to Paris with her husband on a number of occasions. One of Irving's favourite pastimes was to visit the Morgue to watch the reactions of the men and women who were brought in to inspect the dead bodies. Joe, however, insisted on taking Irving to the Moulin Rouge.

5. E.T. *Memoirs*, p. 231.

6. Sarah Siddons's observations on Lady Macbeth were originally published by her biographer Thomas Campbell. See *Life of Mrs Siddons* (1834), Vol. II, pp. 10–34.

7. E.T.'s notes on the essay in the *Westminster Review* are preserved at the British Theatre Museum in a specially bound copy of the article. See also Laurence Irving, *op. cit.*, p. 500.

8. For Irving's two letters quoted here, see E.T. *Memoirs*, pp. 232–3.

9. Quoted in Hiatt, *op. cit.*, p. 202.

10. Alice Comyns-Carr, *op. cit.*, pp. 211–12.

11. Alice Comyns-Carr, *op. cit.*, pp. 299–300.

12. See Laurence Irving, *op. cit.*, p. 504.

13. See Hiatt, *op. cit.*, pp. 206 *et seq.* for the reviews quoted.

14. I am grateful to Mrs Molly Thomas, Curator at Smallhythe, for discovering this letter.

15. See Hesketh Pearson, *The Life of Oscar Wilde* (Penguin edition), p. 120. The Sargent portrait, which was owned initially by Irving, hung in the Beefsteak Room at the Lyceum when it was not on loan for public exhibition. After Irving's death it was auctioned at Christie's and bought by Sir Joseph Duveen and presented to the Tate Gallery. For the sketches made by Sargent, see E.T. *Memoirs*, p. 248.

16. E.T. *Memoirs*, p. 245. The letters to Amy Dickens are preserved at the British Theatre Museum.

17. Twelve, if the single appearance as the Lady Anne in *Richard III* be included.

18. E.T. *Lectures*, pp. 130–1.

19. For the elaborate preparations for the décor of this production of *Henry VIII* under the supervision of Seymour Lucas, see Bram Stoker, *op. cit.*, Vol. I, pp. 113 *et seq.* Cp. E.T. *Memoirs*, pp. 240–1.

20. *The Heart of Ellen Terry*, p. 49.

21. Graham Robertson, *op. cit.*, p. 287.

22. Hiatt, *op. cit.*, p. 242.

23. Graham Robertson, *op. cit.*, p. 153.

24. E.G.C. *Index*, p. 128.

25. Terry-Shaw, *A Correspondence*, p. xxxvii.

26. Miss Maud Gibson of Tenterden recollects the gusto with which E.T. spat on the iron. Then she would look up at Maud in the box near the proscenium and wink, because Maud's mother had told her to be sure and spit on the iron like a professional washerwoman.

27. See Bram Stoker, *op. cit.*, Vol. I, p. 261 *et. seq.* for Irving's devices for concealing his height and for 'fleshing' and dressing the part of the Emperor.

28. These Command performances are described by Laurence Irving, *op. cit.*, pp. 512, 582 and 585. Irving played *Waterloo* before King Edward VII in 1902. See also E.G.C. *Index* p. 143. Perhaps the most entertaining account from the point of view of E.T.'s participation in these Command entertainments is that for 1889 written by Bram Stoker, *op. cit.*, Vol. II, pp. 213 *et seq.*

29. Provincial tours took place in 1891, 1894, 1897, 1898, 1899, 1900 and 1902, all with E.T. participating.

30. A summary of the facts concerning the later American tours, derived from Laurence Irving's biography, is as follows:
    Tour of 1893–4:
    Starts on 4 September at the Grand Opera House, San Francisco. Other places included were Portland, Seattle, Tacoma, Minneapolis, Chicago (when the World Fair was taking place), New York, Boston, Philadelphia, Washington, and cities in Canada. The plays included *Becket, Henry VIII, Nance Oldfield* and *The Bells*. The Company returned to London in time to start the new season at the Lyceum in April with revivals of *Becket* and *Faust*. The profits from this tour were £24,330.
    Tour of 1895–6:
    Starts on 16 September at the Academy of Music, Montreal. Other places (often involving two separate visits) included Toronto, Boston, New York, St Louis, Baltimore, Philadelphia (where Duse was also playing), New Orleans, Memphis (including an adventurous journey across the Mississippi floods), Cincinnati (where Henry Howe died at the age of eighty-four).

The tour involved some dozen productions, including *Faust*. The Company returned in May. The profits this time were barely £6,000.

Tour of 1899–1900:

Starts on 30 October at the Knickerbocker Theatre, New York. The tour included some thirty cities in the United States and Canada, including Baltimore, Brooklyn and Cleveland. Irving toured five productions, *Robespierre*, *The Bells*, *The Merchant of Venice*, *Louis XI* and *Madame Sans-Gêne*. The profits to Irving personally amounted to £24,000. Irving had undertaken five weeks' provincial tour of Britain before the American tour, and followed it on his return in May by further provincial tours later in the year.

Tour of 1901–02:

Starts on 21 October at the Knickerbocker Theatre, New York. Irving was back in Britain in time for a season in London starting in April. The productions given in America included *Charles I*. The profits to Irving personally amounted to £12,000.

Irving's final tour in the United States was undertaken without E.T. in 1903.

31. Laurence Irving, *op. cit.*, pp. 640–1.
32. Even during the period she played Mrs Page for Beerbohm Tree E.T. continued to appear for matinees at the Lyceum of *The Merchant of Venice* and *Charles I*. Of all the plays, only *The Merchant of Venice* enjoyed an unflagging success. This Irving and E.T. played with great popularity for over twenty years.

CHAPTER VIII: QUEEN OF EVERY WOMAN

In addition to the E.T. *Memoirs* and the works of E.G.C., I have also drawn for this chapter on the books already cited by Bram Stoker, Graham Robertson, Alice Comyns-Carr and Marguerite Steen, and on Lena Ashwell's *Myself a Player*. I have also used the collections of E.T.'s letters preserved at Smallhythe, the British Theatre Museum (B.T.M.), and in the Enthoven Collection at the Victoria and Albert Museum, as well as those published in *The Heart of Ellen Terry*.

1. E.T. *Memoirs*, p. 194.
2. This letter is part of the Morris Collection at the British Theatre Museum.
3. E.T. *Memoirs*, p. 196.
4. For the relations of Mrs Godwin and Whistler, see James Laver's biography

of Whistler (Penguin edition, 1942), p. 129. Godwin's funeral, according to Laver, 'was turned into a kind of picnic. Whistler, Mrs Godwin, and Lady Archibald Campbell attended it, riding in a country wagon, and the second lady was quick to notice that her companions already seemed very fond of one another.'

5. Letter in the Morris Collection, B.T.M. It is addressed to 'Georgina'.

6. E.T. *Memoirs*, p. 243.

7. Alice Comyns-Carr, *op. cit.*, p. 216.

8. Graham Robertson, *op. cit.*, p. 293.

9. All these letters to Mrs Nettleship are preserved in the Enthoven Collection. E.G.C. writes of his mother's attitude to dress: 'She never looked on herself as clever or as a beauty, so she was never vain, and ever lovely. She liked to dress well, but liked her dresses not to irk her – they had to be easy – so that she was on the side of untidy, preferring that to being too spick and span. She never fussed about her appearance' (*Index*, p. 131.)

10. The letters to Bertha Bramly are preserved at Smallhythe.

11. Written during a provincial tour with Irving giving recitals from *Macbeth*.

12. Another hand (probably Mrs Bramly's) has noted the three plays to be *Cymbeline, Olivia*, and *Madame Sans-Gêne*.

13. Irving was convalescing in Bournemouth after contracting pleurisy and pneumonia while on tour in Glasgow. Frank Tyars took over to complete the tour. See Laurence Irving, *op. cit.*, p. 623.

14. The letters to Amy and Enid Dickens are preserved in the Morris Collection at the B.T.M.

15. See Hesketh Pearson, *The Life of Oscar Wilde* (Penguin edition) pp. 303 and 327, and Steen, *op. cit.*, p. 206.

16. A copy of Wilde's play *Vera*, which he had privately printed in 1880, is preserved at Smallhythe. It is inscribed: 'For Miss Ellen Terry from her sincere admirer, the Author.' A letter accompanies it (undated) from Tite St: 'Dear Miss Ellen Terry, Will you accept the First copy of my First play – a drama on modern Russia – perhaps one day I shall be fortunate enough to write something worthy of you playing. We all miss you so much, and are so jealous that the provinces should see you in all the great parts you are playing before we do – so please come back quite soon. Believe me, Yours sincerely, Oscar Wilde.'

17. Alice Comyns-Carr, *op. cit.*, pp. 209–10.

18. In a British Theatre Museum exhibition, 1966, a letter was on loan from the Belmore family revealing that E.T. had made a gift in 1893 to George Belmore, a member of Irving's company, when he had been robbed.

19. I am grateful to Laurence Irving for giving me the text of this letter prior to its publication in his book, *The Successors*.

20. See Lena Ashwell, *Myself a Player*, pp. 54–5.

21. Both letters are preserved at Smallhythe. Dame May Whitty and her husband Ben Webster were friends both of Ellen and Edy. They helped with the production of *Godefroi and Yolande* in Chicago during the 1895–6 American tour. Later, Dame May wrote the following just before her death: 'Ellen Terry had promised Sir Henry's son, Laurence, that during the tour she would produce his play *Godfroi and Yolande*, based on Swinburne's poem of *The Leper*, which in turn was adapted from an old French legend. Sir Henry was definitely against it – "an unpleasant subject – we have a repertory of fourteen plays – surely enough work!" But Ellen was determined; she had promised. She enlisted the help of many of the company, and, rather reluctantly, the stage hands. Luckily for this enterprise there were few if any unions in those days. Edy devised the scenery, the clothes, the effects; it had to be done with very little expenditure, and she gathered up the scenery from odd bits from the other plays, also costumes which she seemed to transform into something quite different. Ellen Terry made her first entrance along a balcony at the back of the scene leading to a flight of steps where she stood clad in a scarlet gown, part of her Portia dress – completely changed – scarlet flowers in her red hair, an absolutely white face, those strange eyes and her beautiful mouth that so easily took on the lines of the tragic mask. I, as a lady-in-waiting, had to follow, but I remember standing there transfixed by her strange loveliness, and the scene itself so rich, so beautifully composed. We played the play in Chicago, and as far as I can remember it met with much enthusiasm, and we repeated it several times' (*Edy*, p. 52).

In 1897, Laurence Irving wrote his melancholy play *Peter the Great* and through this joined the Lyceum company. The play, though heavy, was sufficiently worthy to attract some praise, even from Bernard Shaw, though E.T. disliked her part in it. Laurence Irving proved sufficiently capable an actor to take his father's place upon the stage when he had lost his voice, playing the Czar before the Prince and Princess of Wales, though Shaw was not at all impressed. The play lasted only for thirty-eight performances. Laurence translated *Robespierre* for his father and once more, when his health failed, took his place upon the stage.

22. See E.G.C., *Ellen Terry*, pp. 85–7 for a description of how E.G.C. and his mother used to travel together to the theatre.

23. Some of these letters appear in E.G.C.'s *Index*, as follows: letter of 16

December 1885, p. 67; of November 1888, p. 87; of 3 June 1891, p. 125; and of 12 June 1891, pp. 126–7. The originals of all these letters, initially in the possession of E.G.C., are now in private ownership in the United States. The original of the letter dated 7 June is in the possession of E.C., and I am grateful to him for permission to reproduce it. The undated fragment seemingly written from Dublin is at Smallhythe. Also preserved at Small- hythe is a bound copy of the Lyceum *Hamlet*, inscribed: 'My fairest – sweet- est loveliest Ophelia. Only this, *Your* Hamlet.'

24. This letter is preserved in the Morris Collection, B.T.M.

25. Marguerite Steen in *A Pride of Terrys* feels that she has proved that E.T. was Irving's mistress, yet the only hard evidence she produces is the the remarks E.T. made to her when she was the ageing actress's youthful companion. Of these, the principal is as follows: 'The conversation had turned on some troublesome affair of my own, and led to my asking Ellen point-blank whether she had ever been Irving's mistress. She answered without hesitation. "Of course I was. We were terribly in love for a while. Then, later on, when it didn't matter so much to me, he wanted us to go on, and so I did, because I was very, very fond of him and he said he needed me."' As against this, both E.C. and Laurence Irving, grand- sons of the persons involved and steeped in the history of their respective families, are convinced to the contrary. So are others of the Terry family, including Olive Chaplin, E.T.'s niece, who was for a while Curator at Smallhythe.

E.T. was always reticent about her private life and probably spoke most intimately about it to Elena Meo, the mother of Nelly and Edward Craig, during the years they lived together. It is scarcely characteristic that she would speak more openly to her young friend, and I am inclined to think that she meant no more than that Irving and she were 'lovers', and much together, but *not* that she had at any period actually *consummated* the rela- tionship. But that they indulged in minor physical intimacies does not seem to be in doubt. E.C. remembers her telling him that on one occasion when Irving's feet were cold she let him warm them back to life by holding them to her stomach under her dress.

All that arises from this is that we must wait for incontrovertible evidence before stating that E.T. was actually Irving's mistress in the fullest sense as distinct from being his close and affectionate companion.

26. Laurence Irving tells me that for a while during the 1880s his grandfather conducted continuous, discreet negotiations to achieve legal separation from his intransigent wife. It is of interest to note that the garden at the

Grange was, according to Christopher St John, 'Laid out on the lines of Ellen Terry's garden at Harpenden.' See E.T. *Memoirs*, p. 195.

27. See E.T. *Memoirs*, pp. 269–74.

28. See also passage from Terry–Shaw *A Correspondence*, pp. 387–8, quoted below, p. 273.

29. This pencil draft is preserved in a notebook at the B.T.M.

30. See Laurence Irving *op. cit.*, p. 595 and Lena Ashwell, *op. cit.*, pp. 85–7.

31. Marguerite Steen quotes this figure without giving a source. See *A Pride o Terrys*, p. 257.

32. E.C. tells me that E.T. paid her son's alimony to May Gibson for the rest of her life. It was reduced only in 1921, when E.T.'s financial affairs underwent a drastic overhaul. She also made E.G.C. an allowance of some £2 or £3 a week most of the time, at least in the later years before and during the war.

33. See E.T. *Memoirs* p. 86, and Laurence Irving, *op. cit.*, pp. 643–4. According to Oscar Asche in his *Life*, he was responsible for the initial suggestion that E.T. and Madge Kendal should appear together, and he meant it as a joke. Tree, however, was taken with the idea, but was careful to give Madge Kendal the first choice of part (see p. 101).

34. *The Heart of Ellen Terry*, p. 61.

35. E.T. *Memoirs*, p. 259.

36. E.T. *Memoirs*, pp. 261–2. In her edition of *The Story of my Life* preserved at Smallhythe, E.T. wrote in the margin on p. 338 beside this account of her visit to Irving: 'We were both gravely smiling all the while – and both spoke very slowly – very quietly.' Of Irving she also wrote in this book: 'I doted on his *looks*.'

37. Stoker, *op. cit.*, Vol. II, pp. 357–8.

38. E.T. *op. cit.*, p. 263. E.T. was on tour in Manchester in Barrie's *Alice-sit-by-the-Fire* at the time of Irving's death. Laurence Irving tells me the news was broken to her by Hilda Trevelyan the following morning in her hotel. James Agate (*Ego*, p. 146) claims to have seen E.T. break down during her performance in Manchester that night when she had to speak the line, 'I had a beautiful husband once.' After attending the funeral service at Westminster Abbey, E.T. had to return to Manchester for the evening performance. She travelled with Martin-Harvey and his wife, Eleanor da Silva. Apparently E.T. was 'like a cat on hot bricks', reacting against any direct expression of emotion. She seemed 'wildly elated'. (See Maurice Disher, *The Last Romantic*, p. 176.) In E.T.'s copy of *Becket* at Smallhythe she wrote against Becket's final line, 'Into Thy hands, O

Lord, into Thy hands!', her own comment: 'The *last words* spoken by Henry Irving – on the stage – at Bradford Theatre.' When asked by an interviewer what she felt after Irving's funeral, E.T. said: 'He was a great actor, a great friend and a good man. What more is there to say?' (See *We Saw Him Act*, p. 250.)

Additional Note to Chapter VIII. According to Charles Tennyson in his biography of Lord Tennyson, his grandfather saw much of E.T. during the autumn and winter of 1890–91. She sent him a New Year greeting in which she called him the King of Poets and thanked God he was alive whilst she and her children lived. When he died in October 1892, she attended the funeral service in Westminster Abbey with Irving. That night, she wrote of Tennyson in her diary: 'His majestic life and death spoke of him better than the service . . . The music was poor and dull and weak, while he was *strong*. The triumphant should have been the sentiment expressed. . . . No face there looked anything by the side of Henry's. . . . He looked very pale and slim and wonderful.'

CHAPTER IX: SHAW

The principal source for this chapter is naturally the Terry–Shaw *A Correspondence* (1931), edited with notes and comments by Christopher St John and Bernard Shaw. Details of Shaw's life come from his *Sixteen Self Sketches*, from his principal biographers, Frank Harris (writing in 1931), Archibald Henderson (writing finally in 1932), Hesketh Pearson (1942) and St John Ervine (1956), and from C.G.L. Du Cann's *The Loves of Bernard Shaw* (1963). I am indebted to Laurence Irving for certain other biographical facts.

1. Jenny Patterson, who died in 1924, has been identified with Blanche Sartorius in *Widowers' Houses* and Julia Craven in *The Philanderer*. (Hence E.T.'s reference to Kelly as 'a *male* Julia', *A Correspondence*, p. 137). Grace Tranfield is equated with Florence Farr. According to *The Serpent's Eye*, Shotover in *Heartbreak House* was Shaw's conception of Godwin (see foreword by Cecil Lewis to this book by Donald P. Costello of Notre Dame, Indiana). Annie Besant was said to be the model for Raina in *Arms and the Man* and for Mrs Clandon in *You Never Can Tell*.

2. *et seq.* Terry–Shaw *A Correspondence*. The quotations that follow with reference numbers occur on the following pages: 2, pp. 14–16; 3, p. 16; 5,

p. xxxix; 6, p. 44; 7, p. 88; 8, p. 228; 9, p. 192; 10, p. 57; 11, p. 65; 12,
p. 73; 13, p. 204; 14, p. 299; 15, p. 373; 16, p. 29; 17, p. 338; 18, p. 107;
19, p. 165; 20, p. 60; 21, p. 196; 22, p. 199; 23, p. 194; 24, p. 276; 25, p. 303;
26, p. 309; 27, p. 324; 28, pp. 369–70; 29, pp. 370–1; 30, p. 291; 31, p. 301;
32, p. 345; 33, pp. 265–6; 34, p. 151; 35, pp. 96–7; 36, pp. 98–9 (in this
letter, 'my Irish lady' is Charlotte Frances Payne-Townshend, who later
became Mrs Bernard Shaw, and Janet is the actress Janet Achurch); 37,
pp. 253–4; 38, pp. 82–3; 39, p. 215; 40, p. 389; 41, p. 71; 42, p. 216–17; 43,
p. 256; 44, p. 313; 45, p. 45; 46, p. 84; 47, p. 100; 48, p. 110; 49, pp. 120–
1; 50, pp. 123–4; 51, p. 209; 52, p. 224; 53, p. 257.

4. During the period of his relationship with E.T. Shaw wrote, in addition to
The Quintessence of Ibsenism (1891), his articles for the *Saturday Review*
(1895–8), *Widowers' Houses* (produced in 1892), *The Philanderer* and *Mrs
Warren's Profession* (1893; both banned by the censor), *Arms and the Man*
and *Candida* (1894), *The Sanity of Art* (1895) and *The Man of Destiny* (1895),
Plays Pleasant and Unpleasant (published in 1898, and including in two
volumes, in addition to the above plays, *You Never Can Tell*), *The Devil's
Disciple* (1896), *Captain Brassbound's Conversion* and *Caesar and Cleopatra*
were completed before the end of the decade.

54. I am grateful to Laurence Irving for letting me have the text of this letter
which was omitted from the published correspondence, but privately
printed.

55. Shaw, *Pen Portraits and Reviews*, p. 165.

56. Shaw, *Pen Portraits and Reviews*, p. 167.

CHAPTER X: THE SECRET SELF

The principal sources for this chapter, in addition to the books by E.T. and
E.G.C., are the Terry–Shaw *A Correspondence*, Shaw's *Dramatic Opinions and
Essays*, *Edy* (edited by Eleanor Adlard), *Wings of Fire* by Frances Winwar, *Time
Was* and *Letters* by Graham Robertson, and Marguerite Steen's *A Pride of
Terrys*. The E.T. *Memoirs* finish at 1906, but are continued in biographical
form by Edith Craig and Christopher St John in the 1933 edition. E.T.'s Jubilee
was commemorated in a special hard-backed illustrated book which acted also
as a programme and gave many details concerning her career as well as listing
the many contributors to the performance at Drury Lane. For personal information concerning this period I am specially indebted to Edward Craig from
whom many of the details in this chapter derive. I am also grateful to Kerrison

Preston, Joan Morgan, Colin Ford of the National Film Archive, John M. East, and to Laurence Irving for help over points of detail.

1. Sudermann's *Heimat* (*Home*), called in English *Magda*, the name of the principal character, concerns a girl whose father has turned her out of his house for defying his authority. Her final success as a singer is preceded by a period of misfortune as an unmarried mother whose lover has deserted her. Later, when she is famous, she revisits her home only to find her former lover has become a friend of the family. In the final act she is confronted by him.

2. See Shaw, *Dramatic Opinions and Essays* (Constable, 1913, Vol. I, pp. 136–8) for this and the quotation that follows.

3. See Duse's correspondence with E.T. in the *Memoirs*, p. 183. E.T.'s description of the actresses which follows is on pp. 168–9.

4. E.T. *Lectures*, pp. 14–15.

5. Fanny Kemble wrote at about the time of her first confinement: 'I cannot believe that women were intended to suffer as much as they do, and be as helpless as they are, in child-bearing. In spite of the third chapter of Genesis, I cannot believe that all the agony and debility upon the entrance of a new creature into life was ordained.' E.T., writing to Shaw on 10 October 1896, said that whilst reading William Morris's *The Watching of the Falcon* she forgot her pangs 'on a certain bitter-sweet night in December' when Edy was born. (*A Correspondence*, p. 94.)

6. According to Marguerite Steen, this was because of Edy's 'difficult' reputation in the profession. If women had been invited to serve, Edy's presence would have been inevitable.

7. In all, E.T. received some £9,000–£6,000 from the commemoration performance, and £3,000 from the Ellen Terry Jubilee Celebration Fund inaugurated by the Liberal journal of the period, *The Tribune*. The Jubilee was also celebrated by a public dinner at which Winston Churchill presided. (See E.T. *Memoirs*, pp. 279–80; *A Correspondence*, p. 430).

8. At the time of writing, E.T.'s draft, like too many of her letters and other documents, was in the salesroom.

9. E.G.C. *Index*, pp. 287–8.

10. Terry–Shaw *A Correspondence*, p. xliv.

11. Heslewood was a stage designer, Forbes an actor.

12. For this and immediately succeeding quotations see *Edy*, pp. 20–30.

13. *Edy*, pp. 67–8.

14. For this and the quotation immediately following, see *Edy*, pp. 47 and 35–6.

15. *Time Was*, p. 316.

16. For these films, see pp. 319–22. For the occasional appearances of E.T. in the theatre during these later years, see *Memoirs*, pp. 283, 300.

17. E.T. *Memoirs*, p. 286.

18. *The Heart of Ellen Terry*, p. 67.

19. E.T. *Memoirs*, p. 287.

20. E.T. *Memoirs*, pp. 290–1.

21. E.T. *Memoirs*, p. 297. There is a discrepancy here concerning dates. E.C. tells me he did not actually go to live with his grandmother until the war years. Prior to this, he and his sister lived with their parents in various places on the Continent.

22. See Steen, *Pride of Terrys*, p. 326.

23. *Edy*, pp. 49–50.

24. See E.T. *Memoirs*, pp. 297–8. Both Little Nellie and Little Teddy were screen-tested with E.T. for the film, *Her Greatest Performance*. See p. 319.

25. I am grateful to John M. East for information concerning *Potter's Clay*.

26. E.T. *Memoirs*, p. 302.

27. E.T. *Memoirs*, p. 300.

28. E.T. *Memoirs*, p. 319.

29. For E.T.'s visits, see *Letters from Graham Robertson*, pp. 196–9. E.T. was a frequent visitor to Graham Robertson's house, Sandhills near Witley in Surrey. She was staying there on her birthday in February 1926, when the house was besieged by the Press. When leaving after what proved to be her last visit, she burst into tears, saying: 'I shall never be here again – I know it.'

30. This gold tissue material was already in the house, the gift of an actor who had brought it back from India so that E.T. might have a dress made from it. See E.T. *Memoirs*, p. 337.

Additional Note. E.T.'s ashes were enclosed in a silver casket designed by E.G.C.'s boyhood friend, Paul Cooper. A second memorial, quite distinct from that in St Paul's, Covent Garden, was commissioned by Edie Gwynne and her friends and executed by Gilbert, the monumental sculptor. This was erected in Little Easton Church, near Dunmow in Essex. A death mask was cast by Miss Margaret Winser, as well as a cast of E.T.'s hands, and these are kept at Smallhythe.

ELLEN TERRY'S NOTES FOR THE
INTERPRETATION OF LADY MACBETH

Ellen Terry's notes on the playing of the part of Lady Macbeth are
scribbled over the blank interleaves of Irving's private edition of the
play and on the pages carrying the printed text. She filled two copies of
the play with her notes, and the more general observations she made on
the characters of Macbeth and Lady Macbeth have already been quoted
in Chapter VII. What follows is a selection of the notes written alongside the text of the two copies. The notes were also adapted for a
broadcast by the author in the B.B.C. Third Programme, and appeared
in this form in the *Listener* on 2 February 1967.

   Ellen Terry's notes on individual scenes naturally concentrate on the
major appearances of Lady Macbeth in the play. All her speeches are
carefully marked for inflexion, level and, above all, attitude of mind,
and one can trace almost line by line how she approached the part. As
she enters reading Macbeth's letter she writes, 'Steady. Breathe hard.
Excited. Not too quick,' and 'It is wretched to be *discovered* on the
stage. She shd be reading *at the back* by the fading light, and then
come forward to the firelight to see better.' Of the lines. 'This have I
thought good to deliver thee, my dearest partner of greatness' she
marks the level for the word 'good' as 'subdued also quite low in tone
excited' and has the words 'my dearest partner of greatness' marked
with a query, 'linger on this? smiling'. After reading the letter she sits
down saying, 'Glamis thou art, and Cawdor' and then whispers, 'and
shalt be/What thou art promised.' The following lines, beginning 'Yet
do I fear thy nature,' she marks as, 'He puzzles her', the speech becoming
Lady Macbeth's unresolved attempt to analyse her husband's weakness
of character as she sees it. When the messenger arrives to interrupt her
thoughts with the news of Duncan's intended stay at her castle, Ellen
Terry marks in, 'Pause. Tremble. Breathe. Take time.' in reaction to
this fortuitous news, and adds, 'Don't believe him except for the first
moment.' When Lady Macbeth finally takes it in and says 'He brings/
great news', she notes 'High. Breathless. Slow'.

Ellen Terry realizes that the great 'unsexing' prayer that follows is the first exacting test of her as a tragic actress. She notes, 'I *must* try to do this: 2 years ago I could not *even* have tried.' Of Lady Macbeth at this moment she says: 'She goads herself on to crime. She feels she has only a *woman*'s strength and calls on "Spirits".' Then she adds: 'The tale of the witches fired her imagination, and kindled her hopes. Under her lonely battlements she dreamed of future splendour – she did *not* realize the measure of the crime.' In the speech itself 'remorse' is marked. 'Keep *that* from me!' the 'compunctious visiting of nature' are marked 'Action of pushing it away –' while the word 'nature' is noted. 'She dreads *that*'. The climax of the speech – 'Nor heaven peep through the blanket of the dark/ To cry "Hold, hold!"' is marked, 'Keep voice down'.

When Macbeth arrives, there are many directions how Lady Macbeth should behave. Before she says of Duncan, 'And when *goes* hence?' Ellen Terry writes 'Right hand eagerly on M.'s breast. Action first', and adds that the line should be 'slow' and that she should 'smile', her hand drawn back sharply from Macbeth on the lines, 'O, never/ Shall sun *that* morrow see'. Alongside the 'beguiling' speech, during which she begins her temptation of Macbeth to commit the murder of Duncan, Ellen Terry suggests: 'Smile at him. Bright. Quick! Aflame! Alert.' Against the final lines beginning. '*Only* look up clear . . .', she writes, 'Closer in, she too plotting. Charm. Serpent.' Then she adds: '*He* can't face things and *talk* of 'em, but he can *do* them. *She* can talk and plan but shd not be able *to do* so easily.' In the brief scene of greeting to Duncan that follows, she notes that Lady Macbeth should be, 'Most modest, knowing her place,' that she should 'Speak it musically' and act like 'the innocent flower'.

The next major scene involves the final spurring on of Macbeth to kill Duncan. 'I love this scene,' she notes, and calls Lady Macbeth 'the spur'. The margin is covered with single words revealing the attitude she should adopt to Macbeth. 'Severely; sarcasm; cold; distant; quiet; dangerous; accusing'; 'Stand still and look at him,' she says at one point. But everything should be kept quiet until the lines, 'What *beast* was't then/ That made you break this enterprise to me?' Here, she notes, a change should begin, but there should be 'no rant'; only 'amaze'. The voice should be kept 'deep' and 'low', taunting him for his cowardice; after all, as she puts it, 'He suggested the murder and she caught on.'

Ellen Terry interprets, 'You are a coward, that's what all this means.' The lines, 'I have given suck, and know/How tender 'tis to love . . .' are marked, 'Only an exaggeration, as she is in a fury', and she adds, 'She loved her babies and she could not kill the man who looked like her Father. (*Woman*)' – doubly underscored, that! Even the climax – '. . . and dash'd the brains out, had I so sworn as *you*/ Have done to this,' are marked 'Low down voice always'. She notes as a plea to Irving that he should cut in quickly with the point, 'If we should fail?' Her immediate response to this is annotated, 'Strong downward inflection' – '*We fail*'; here she follows Mrs Siddons's final interpretation of resignation, but she marks the follow-up lines: 'But screw your courage to the sticking-place,/ And we'll not fail . . .' as requiring a 'Slow change developing into a "great change".' 'All women are clever at *contriving* merely,' she adds in the margin. Lady Macbeth then starts on the detailed planning of the murder in order to give him the courage to carry it out: 'Be damned *charming*,' she adds with a touch of the Terry humour. 'Now see – here is a beautiful plan which your wife has thought all out (the hell-cat).'

When Lady Macbeth comes to support her husband in the very act of murder, Ellen Terry makes the point that she is 'excited by wine' and she notes the 'horrid smile' adopted by Mrs Siddons. She must use this smile herself when saying the lines, 'I have drugg'd their possets —' 'Smile. Devil,' she notes. When Macbeth cries out off-stage, the 'agony of suspense' begins for her; she has to fight back her own weakness for so long as Macbeth proves weak. This is the whole tenor of the notes. He comes back: 'Together now,' writes Ellen Terry, 'she is relieved.' She also has to cope with Irving, who she guesses will take no notice of Lady Macbeth's interruptions as Macbeth dwells obsessively on what he has just done. 'He is sure to go on here,' she notes. She also has to cope with the demonstrative Victorian audiences. When Irving will finally have reached the climax, 'Macbeth shall sleep no more', she notes. '*If* applause *wait* petrified and *then* shake off and say "who was it that . . ." If *not* applause say *at once* "who was it" the *right way*'. As for the right way, she notes that Lady Macbeth's attitude during her speech must express initially 'torture' and 'alarm'. She writes further: 'Watching him she thinks on – "Why he is quite ill! Come. Come. The danger's *past now* — Consider it not so *deeply*." This last not stern and angry, but with some feminine consideration mixed with alarm.' Then she adds another point: 'Remember the murder is done – not *heavy*. A little flutter and whisper, but he's been a good fellow – he has not *failed* – don't press him too far – bear with him – humour him.'

The solution for Lady Macbeth at this moment of crisis, according to Ellen Terry's notes, is for her to overcome her innate 'fear of possible defeat' and 'summon a *tone* to work on him. Upon my soul, you should be ashamed. You want shaking.' She puts this against the line, 'Go get some water . . .' She puts 'angry' against the line, '*Why* did you bring these daggers from the place?' and 'Grandly, I'll do it' against the exclamation, 'Infirm of purpose!' 'Nothing else for it. I must do it myself,' she adds. The lines, 'If he do bleed . . .', she marks, 'This should be to herself, I think.' Her return from the murder-chamber is marked 'Creep on', and her lines, 'My hands are of your colour,' are noted 'Sarcastic; keep cool'. Her voice must be kept 'low' and 'quiet' and, since Macbeth will be transfixed with guilt, she must '*push* him *pull* him off the stage'. Against the line: 'Methought I heard a voice cry "Sleep no more . . ."' she writes, 'The most awful line in the play if one realizes what it means to his guilt-burdened mind. Poor wretch, he does not sleep after this.'

This reading of the part makes Lady Macbeth's faint in the following scene a natural one, claims Ellen Terry. 'She faints 'cos she *may*,' is how she puts it. When Lady Macbeth comes on following the alarm caused by the discovery of the murder, she notes: 'Play here not the loud-voiced commanding Queen but the frightened "innocent flower".' She prepares carefully for Lady Macbeth's reaction to her husband's able and self-possessed command of the situation: 'She stands dead still listening. She is *not* (in truth) horrified by this news – "*Anything, anything to be safe.*" Strung up, past pitch, she gives in at the *end* of his speech when she finds he is safely through his story, and *then she faints, really*. Strung up at first she relaxes when all seems safe and they swallow her husband's masterly explanation. Listen until her ears crack, or she faints (which she *does*) – faints after pent-up agony and anxiety, *from relief*.'

On her first appearance as the Queen, Lady Macbeth is preoccupied and depressed. 'Naught's had, all's spent,' she says, and against this line, E.T. notes, 'Hands to head. Albert Dürer's Melancholy. Express here (when *alone*) a "rooted sorrow" – a half-dulled knowledge of the fact of her husband having been all the while deceived in her. She sees clearer now, knows she has missed what she had hoped to gain. I sometimes think she is rather stupid!!' Then she adds: 'Beware of showing the pathetic result of trouble upon a *good* woman. Lady Macbeth is not too good. Grief and trouble softens I think a *good* nature but hardens a bad one.' Lady Macbeth should be 'Rossetti-mournful', she says, when speaking the lines leading up to, 'What's done is done.' Then she adds, 'Cautious but not repentant, but let everything be damned before we give up now.' During Macbeth's speech beginning, 'We have scotch'd the snake, not kill'd it . . .', she suggests: 'She looks frightened at him'; then, 'During this she pities him and turns more tender. His trouble affected her – for she loved him.' Alongside Lady Macbeth's line, 'Gentle my lord, sleek o'er your rugged looks . . .' she paraphrases: 'Come. Come. You must pluck up courage. Remember the tea-party tonight', and adds: 'Mournful. Gentle. Forced cheerfulness. Kisses his head. Soothe him. Deep voice.'

Mrs Siddons made Lady Macbeth responsible for suggesting to Macbeth that Banquo and Fleance should be murdered through the way she said the single line, 'But in them nature's copy's not eterne'. Ellen Terry will have none of this; her reaction is merely feminine, and she paraphrases the line with yet another touch of Terry mischief: 'Don't trouble so, for they cannot live for ever – that fellow Banquo may die any day – *why not!* and the boy may have whooping cough in such a climate as this – and we keep all the whisky to ourselves – I lock up the cupboard every night.' Nevertheless, she ends the scene with the note: 'Nervous clutch at his sleeve. Henry goes out first. *Sit still*, I think and try to find the meaning of his words. Anxious. Uncertain and rather ill.'

The banquet scene – what she calls the royal 'tea-party', follows. This social event at a time of deep misgiving should begin with 'double acting', at once 'royal' and yet revealing to the audience very clearly Lady Macbeth's 'secret uneasiness'. When Macbeth toasts her 'brilliantly' (her word), Lady Macbeth 'drinks *deep*' (doubly underlined in the margin). Banquo comes in – a solid ghost gliding unobserved to his place, as she notes, adding: 'First – the ghost might look like an ordinary man and then *develop* into ghost-like appearance by lighting (Lime)'. Mrs Siddons, by the way, let Lady Macbeth see the ghost at the same time as her husband; not so Ellen Terry, who made Lady Macbeth rise to the occasion in just the same way as she did after the murder of Duncan. 'How he *will talk!*' she mutters in the margin when Macbeth goes out of his way to challenge the dead Banquo to come to the feast; says Ellen Terry, 'She *knows* he is hysterical, and "giving way" to "*acting*" before people. He "shows off". When the guests are departed he drops it all.' Meanwhile, when Macbeth says, 'The table's full', Lady Macbeth is drinking again, but stops at once when he starts to address Banquo. She takes the situation, E.T. notes, 'with *great* – quick – decision. *Then* except for pausing entirely hide all emotion – Smile.' She comes down-stage, taking command at once, 'turning some of the women bodily round' – 'Feed, and *regard him not*'. Then she whispers hoarsely into Macbeth's ear, 'peevish and scornful' – '*O proper stuff!* (doubly underlined). 'When all's done,/ You look but on a *stool*' is paraphrased: 'A chair. A fine thing to be frightened of.' On 'Fie, *for shame!*' (whispered), she writes: 'She shd fill his place.' Then she adds: 'Catch the eye of First Lady Guest and go to her. Then speak to all the others and call for wine.' She notes that the lines, 'My worthy lord,/ Your noble friends do lack you' should be 'Not severe but with playful amazement are you deaf or blind. Don't you see your noble friends do lack you?' The lines, 'Think of this, good peers,/ But as a thing of custom:'tis no other/ Only it spoils the pleasure of the time', she annotates, '"pleasure" Oh Lor' how grim. I wonder she don't go mad.' But the lines, she says, should be spoken, 'Sweetly but with a ghastly mouth. The *mouth* tells all the pain and the effort and the madness.' In the end, When Lady Macbeth says, 'You have displaced the mirth, broke the good meeting,/ With most admired disorder', Ellen Terry writes 'She allows the guests here to *see* that she reproves him – but not *before*. She settles that something must be done so does not return to her seat, but says goodnight to some of the guests and gets rid of them.' By now she is really frightened: 'Stand not upon the order of your going/ But go at once', is said with 'voice choked. Alarm. Hurry. Convulsive fear.' Nevertheless, she manages to 'smile and smile' as they go.

When she is at last alone with Macbeth, her fear may be allowed to show itself fully; she has almost nothing left to say. Ellen Terry writes: 'She goes to the window for air and falls all of a heap, and sees "it is almost at odds with morning which is which" . . . She is now beginning to know him well and is thoroughly frightened at him. I think she feels pretty frail – and that her *reason* here begins to be shaken.' She adds: 'Notice he never speaks harshly to his "chuck". By suffering at this point she pays penance and repents – all is forgiven. First thing she does is take off her crown. How about trying to ease his head by taking off his crown – which he the more firmly plants *on his* head.' This is her last moment on the stage before the sleepwalking scene, and her distressed state of mind must be shown. 'Now – she knows him,' writes Ellen Terry. '*Now Lady* Macbeth shall sleep no more – for she is at last – *frightened*!' 'We are yet but young in deed', says Macbeth, but E.T. comments, '"Young in deed." *He* to go off full of vigour, *blood – more blood*!! *She*, left behind – dazed – turn weary – faint – and stagger to the throne – Alone – *Isolation* – *On* the throne – Crown on her lap. laugh? Dark. *Curtain*.'

The sleepwalking scene is now fully anticipated, but Ellen Terry prepares herself for it in her notes. 'She took to sleepwalking when Macbeth went into the field. Remember she is weak and asleep. Macbeth preyed on her mind more than the deed. *This* might be some time afterwards and grey hair would be pathetic. For both of them have gone through enough to *make* 'em grey.' Her entrance is marked as 'hurried and excited', her actions undertaken with 'trembling hands – she is very weak. Rub the *Palms* of hands.' (Mrs Siddons scooped up imaginary water with one hand and poured it over the other.) The words 'Out, damned spot', are marked: 'Out, *damned* (high voice; pause) spot (pause) out, I say! One: two: (low and long) why, then 'tis time to do't (whisper).' The line, 'The thane of Fife had a wife' is marked: 'Horror! One of the murders Macbeth never told her about'; 'Where is she now?' is a whisper. When she re-enacts the murder scene, her deepest anxieties are revealed as the root of her madness.

When she leaves the stage after this, the notes on the playing of the individual scenes finish. Lady Macbeth does not appear again.

PAGES FROM ELLEN TERRY'S
ANNOTATED COPY OF *MACBETH*

*Do. he "pretend" to live?
I think not – only "a silly
cuss" to expect the others".*

When we have mark'd with blood those sleepy two
Of his own chamber and us'd their very daggers,
That they have done't?
   Lady M.   Who dares receive it other,
As we shall make our griefs and clamour roar
Upon his death?
   Macb.   I'm settled, and bend up
Each corporal agent to this terrible feat.
Away, and mock the time with fairest show:
False face must hide what the false heart doth know.
                            [Exeunt.

[Handwritten annotations:]

X to L ♀

She gives him courage =

Lady M comes back
& goes out R.E —

She loved her babies
& she could not kill
The man who looked
like her Father =

(Woman .)

(in truth)

⊖ She is not horrified by
this news - "Any thing -
Any thing to be safe" -
Strung up, part pitch, she
gives in at the end of his speech
- when she finds he is safely
through his story + then
+ She faints Really -
Strung up at first she
relaxes when all seems
safe & then swallow her up
masterly. EXPL - it!

[right margin, vertical:]
the danger to another now that it was past - as it does most One - money with women "Once - (under five stages).

There's nothing serious in mortality:
All is but toys: renown and grace is dead;
The wine of life is drawn, and the mere lees
Is left this vault to brag of.

Enter MALCOLM and DONALBAIN.

Don. What is amiss?

Macb.   You are, and do not know't:
The spring, the head, the fountain of your blood
Is stopp'd—the very source of it is stopp'd.

Macd. Your royal father's murder'd.

Mal.   O! by whom?

Len. Those of his chamber, as it seem'd, had
        done't:
Their hands and faces were all badg'd with blood;
So were their daggers, which, unwip'd, we found
Upon their pillows:
They star'd, and were distracted; no man's life
Was to be trusted with them.

Macb. O, yet I do repent me of my fury,
That I did kill them.

Macd.   Wherefore did you so?

Macb. Who can be wise, amaz'd, temperate and
        furious,
Loyal and neutral, in a moment?   No man:
The expedition of my violent love
Outran the pauser, reason.—Here lay Duncan;—
His silver skin lac'd with his golden blood,
And his gash'd stabs, look'd like a breach in nature,
For ruin's wasteful entrance: there the murderers,
Steep'd in the colours of their trade, their daggers
Unmannerly breech'd with gore: who could refrain,
That had a heart to love, and in that heart,
Courage, to make's love known?

Lady M.   Help me hence, ho!

Ban. Look to the lady.

[Lady MACBETH is carried out.

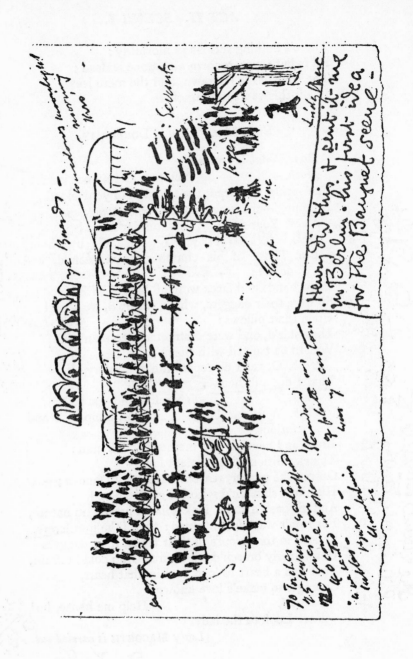

THE PARTS PLAYED BY ELLEN TERRY AT THE LYCEUM IN ASSOCIATION WITH HENRY IRVING

Date	Play	H.I.	E.T.
30.12.78	*Hamlet*	Hamlet	Ophelia
17. 4.79	*Lady of Lyons*	Melnotte	Pauline
6. 6.79	*Eugene Aram*	Eugene Aram	Ruth
27. 6.79	*Charles I*	Charles I	Henrietta Maria
4. 7.79	*The Lyons Mail*	Dubosc and Lesurques	Jeanette
25. 7.79	*Richard III* (Act I)	Gloster	Lady Anne
	Raising the Wind	Jeremy Diddler	Peggy
1.11.79	*The Merchant of Venice*	Shylock	Portia
20. 5.80	*Iolanthe*	Count Tristan	Iolanthe
3. 1.81	*The Cup*	Synorix	Camma
16. 4.81	*The Belle's Stratagem*	Doricourt	Letitia Hardy
2. 5.81	*Othello*	Othello/Iago	Desdemona
23. 7.81	*The Hunchback* (scene)	Modus	Helen
8. 3.82	*Romeo and Juliet*	Romeo	Juliet
11.10.82	*Much Ado about Nothing*	Benedick	Beatrice
14. 6.83	*Robert Macaire*	Robert Macaire	Clementine
8. 7.84	*Twelfth Night*	Malvolio	Viola
27. 5.85	*Olivia*	Dr Primrose	Olivia
19.12.85	*Faust*	Mephistopheles	Marguerite
1. 6.87	*Werner*	Werner	Josephine
29.12.88	*Macbeth*	Macbeth	Lady Macbeth
28. 9.89	*The Dead Heart*	Robert Landry	Catherine Duval

Date	Play	H.I.	E.T.
20. 9.90	*Ravenswood*	Edgar	Lucy Ashton
5. 1.92	*King Henry VIII*	Cardinal Wolsey	Queen Katherine
10.11.92	*King Lear*	King Lear	Cordelia
6. 2.93	*Becket*	Becket	Rosamund
12. 1.95	*King Arthur*	King Arthur	Guinevere
22. 9.96	*Cymbeline*	Iachimo	Imogen
10. 4.97	*Madame Sans-Gêne*	Napoleon	Catherine (Mme Sans-Gêne)
1. 1.98	*Peter the Great*	Peter the Great	Catherine
4. 5.98	*The Medicine Man*	Dr Tregenna	Sylvia Wynford
5. 4.99	*Robespierre*	Robespierre	Clarisse
15. 4.01	*Coriolanus*	Coriolanus	Volumnia

Without Irving, Ellen Terry appeared with the Lyceum company in:

7. 6.87	*The Amber Heart*	Ellaline
20. 7.93	*Nance Oldfield*	Anne Oldfield
Early 1895	*Godefroi and Yolande*	Yolande

NOTES ON THE PRINCIPAL
NON-SHAKESPEAREAN PLAYS
IN WHICH ELLEN TERRY
APPEARED AT THE LYCEUM

THE AMBER HEART (Alfred C. Calmour). Produced for a single performance at the Lyceum on 7 June 1887 and revived for a short season in May 1888. The dramatic copyright of this play, described as 'a graceful trifle', was presented to Ellen Terry by Irving.

BECKET (Alfred, Lord Tennyson; 1884). First produced at the Lyceum in 1893. The action of the play turns on the dispute between Henry II, originally played by William Terriss, and Becket which leads finally to the Archbishop's assassination. Ellen Terry played the very subsidiary part of Rosamund, the King's mistress, whom Becket protects from the jealous plots of Eleanor, Henry's Queen.

THE BELLE'S STRATAGEM (Hannah Cowley; 1780). First produced at the Lyceum in 1881. Doricourt returns from his travels to fulfil an arranged marriage with Letitia Hardy. He receives her coldly, and she sets out to win his love, first of all by assuming a hoydenish manner in order to affront him, and then taking him by storm with a sudden switch-over to charm and vivacity. She succeeds.

CHARLES I (W. G. Wills; 1872). First produced at the Lyceum in 1879. A romantic historical play originally written for Bateman. It presented the King in a sympathetic light in his losing struggle, more especially with the harsh character of Cromwell and the treachery of the Earl of Moray. The play aimed at pathos at the expense of history, and finished with the parting of Charles and his Queen prior to his execution.

THE CUP (Alfred, Lord Tennyson; 1881). First produced at the Lyceum in 1881. A two-act tragedy concerning the plot of the Galatian Synorix to murder Camma's husband Sinnatus in order to obtain her for himself. Camma takes refuge as a priestess in the temple of Diana, where she poisons her suitor by inducing him to drink poisoned wine in

libation to the goddess. After this, she poisons herself. The play was put
on initially along with *The Corsican Brothers*, and later with *The Belle's
Stratagem*.

THE DEAD HEART (Watts Philips). First produced at the Adelphi
in 1859, and at the Lyceum in 1889. The story is set against the background of the French Revolution. Robert Landry, the hero, is a sculptor in Paris. Before the Revolution, he and the Count de St Valéry had
both been in love with Catherine Duval. Catherine is tricked by the
villain, the Abbé Latour, into marrying the Count, believing Landry,
whom Latour has contrived to imprison in the Bastille, to be dead.
The Count dies, but leaves her with a son, played at the Lyceum by
Gordon Craig. The play turns on Landry's revenge when he is released eighteen years later after the storming of the Bastille. At the end,
he discovers Catherine, learns the truth, and saves the young Count
from the guillotine by taking his place.

EUGENE ARAM (W. G. Wills; 1873). First produced at the Lyceum
in 1879. Based on Thomas Hood's poem, and written during the
period of Bateman's management of the Lyceum in order to provide
Irving with the part of another man, like Mathias of *The Bells*, who
is haunted by his evil past. Irving was fond of reciting Hood's poem.
Ellen Terry played the small but sympathetic part of Ruth Meadows,
the clergyman's daughter whom Eugene secretly loves.

FAUST (W. G. Wills). Commissioned by Irving, and produced in
1885. The story followed the pattern of Gounod rather than of Goethe.

IOLANTHE (W. G. Wills; 1849). First produced at the Lyceum in
1880. A one-act play, taken from a Danish original, *King René's
Daughter*. There were several versions on the Victorian stage of this
play by Henrik Hertz, and the title-role was played by Mrs Charles
Kean, Helen Faucit, and others. The central character is Iolanthe, the
blind daughter of the King, whose sight is miraculously restored. Its
main appeal was pathos. Irving played Count Tristan, Iolanthe's lover.

KING ARTHUR (J. Comyns-Carr). A play in blank verse written in
1894 for Irving, the story loosely taken from Malory rather than from
Tennyson. It concentrates on the love of Guinevere for Lancelot (originally played by Forbes-Robertson) and the injury she does her blame-
less husband. The play was produced in 1895.

THE LADY OF LYONS (Lord Bulwer-Lytton; 1838). Produced at
the Lyceum in 1879. A romantic period play, originally produced by
Macready in 1838 with Helen Faucit. The central character is Pauline

Deschappelles, who was supposed to be a proud, if hysterical woman. Ellen Terry played her for pathos and fragility in her unhappy relations with her erring and rhetorical lover, Claude Melnotte, whom Irving played as 'deeply tragic, absorbed and highly nervous'.

THE LYONS MAIL (Charles Reade; 1854). Produced at the Lyceum in 1879. Adapted from a French original, *Le Courier de Lyons* (and called at first *The Courier of Lyons*), this romantic melodrama originally written for Charles Kean, centres on an actual robbery near Paris in 1796 of the mail carrying the pay for Napoleon's troops in Italy. Mystery surrounds the identity of the robber. There was evidence against Lesurques, a businessman who was accused and sentenced to the guillotine; later a gang-leader, Dubosc, became suspected as the real culprit. Confusion was further caused by the men's resemblance to each other, and this gave Irving his opportunity to exploit his virtuosity in a double role. He played Lesurques for innocence and Dubosc for sardonic, drunken villainy. Ellen Terry played the subordinate part of Jeanette, Dubosc's mistress, and the play ended with a last-minute reprieve for Lesurques. MADAME SANS-GÊNE (Victorien Sardou and Emile Moreau; 1893). Translated for Irving by J. Comyns-Carr in 1897. The title-role was created in London by Réjane. Catherine, a spirited French washer-woman, becomes a duchess in Napoleon's court. She retains her old, blunt ways, and is ordered by Napoleon to divorce her husband and retire from court. But she reminds Napoleon of the days of struggle in which she shared, and of the laundry bill he still owes her. The Emperor relents, and reinstates her. The play was produced at the Lyceum in 1897.

THE MEDICINE MAN (H. D. Traill and Robert Hitchens). Written for Irving, and produced in 1898. The central figure of this play was a wealthy, West-End doctor who disguises himself and uses hypnotism in the course of trying to conduct social reform in the East-End, where he works with London's poor.

NANCE OLDFIELD (Charles Reade). Nance Oldfield was a popular actress of the early eighteenth century. In the play she tries to cure the romantic love which a young man conceives for her through seeing her on the stage by pretending to be a tom-boyish hoyden when she is off it. It gave Ellen Terry an opportunity to display her high spirits and sense of comedy, as well as her charm. Produced at the Lyceum in 1893.

OLIVIA (W. G. Wills). Based on Goldsmith's story, *The Vicar of Wakefield*, the plot of the play turns on the seduction of Olivia

daughter of the kindly parson, Dr Primrose, by the villainous Squire
Thornhill. Produced at the Lyceum in 1885.

PETER THE GREAT (Laurence Irving). Produced at the Lyceum in
1898. This play turned on the unhappy relations between the overbear-
ing Czar and his weak, retiring son, on whose irresolute nature the
intrigues of the court depend. Ellen Terry played Catherine, the Czar's
second wife.

RAVENSWOOD (Herman Merivale). Produced at the Lyceum in
1890. Adapted from Scott's *Bride of Lammermoor* Irving, working with
Merivale, was forced to truncate the plot. Edgar of Ravenswood (Irving)
falls in love with Lucy Ashton (Ellen Terry), daughter of Sir William
Ashton, who has ruined Ravenswood's father so that the son is deprived of his title. Ravenswood vows revenge. Lucy's mother, who
is opposed to Ravenswood, tricks Lucy into marriage with the laird
of Bucklaw. Lucy, on learning the truth, goes mad, Ophelia-like, and
dies. Ravenswood dies too, caught in quicksands. The story is well
known now to opera-goers.

ROBESPIERRE (Victorien Sardou). A play commissioned by Irving
and translated by Laurence Irving. A political melodrama written to
give Irving, who naturally played Robespierre, a grandiloquent part in
the setting of the French Revolution. Ellen Terry's part was the very
subsidiary one of Clarisse.

SELECT BIBLIOGRAPHY

ADLARD, ELEANOR (Editor). *Edy, Recollections of Edith Craig.* (London: Muller, 1949.)

ARCHER, WILLIAM. *The Theatrical World.* Vols. for 1893 to 1897. (London: Walter Scott.)

ASCHE, OSCAR. *Life.* (London, 1929.)

ASHWELL, LENA. *Myself a Player.* (London: Michael Joseph, 1936.)

BABLET, DENIS. *Edward Gordon Craig.* (London: Heinemann, 1966.)

The BANCROFTS: *Recollections of 60 Years.* (London: Murray, 1909.)

BENSON, FRANK. *My Memoirs.* (London: Benn, 1930.)

BEERBOHM, MAX. *Around Theatres.*

BLUNT, WILFRID. *Watts.* (London: The Masters series, Purnell and Sons, 1966.)

CARROLL, LEWIS. *The Diaries of Lewis Carroll*; edited by Roger Lancelyn Green. Two vols. (London: Cassell, 1953.)

CHAPMAN, RONALD. *The Laurel and the Thorn:* a study of F. G. Watts. (London: Faber and Faber, 1945.)

COMYNS-CARR, ALICE. *Reminiscences.* (London: Hutchinson, N.D.)

COQUELIN, C. *The Art of the Actor.* Translated by Elsie Fogerty. (London: Allen and Unwin, 1932.)

CRAIG, EDWARD GORDON. *Henry Irving.* (London: J. M. Dent and Sons, 1930.)

CRAIG, EDWARD GORDON. *Ellen Terry and her Secret Self.* (London: Sampson Low, Marston and Co., 1931.)

CRAIG, EDWARD GORDON. *Index to the Story of my Days.* (London: Hulton Press, 1957.)

DISHER, MAURICE WILSON. *The Last Romantic.* (London: Hutchinson, N.D.)

DU CANN, C. G. L. *The Loves of Bernard Shaw.* (London: Barker, 1963.)

DUNBAR, JANET. *The Early Victorian Woman.* (London: Harrap, 1953.)

374   *Ellen Terry*

FORBES-ROBERTSON, JOHNSTON. *A Player under Three Reigns*. (T. Fisher Unwin, 1925.)

GIELGUD, KATE TERRY. *An Autobiography*. (London: Max Reinhardt, 1953.)

HARBRON, DUDLEY. *The Conscious Stone*. (London: Latimer House, 1949.)

HATTON, JOSEPH. *Henry Irving's Impressions of America*. (London: Sampson Low, Marston, Searle and Rivington, 1884.)

HIATT, CHARLES. *Ellen Terry and her Impersonations*. (London: Bell, 1900.)

IRVING, LAURENCE. *Henry Irving: the Actor and his World*. (Faber and Faber, 1951.)

JAMES, HENRY. *The Scenic Art*. (London: Hart-Davis, 1949.)

LAVER, JAMES. *Whistler*. (Penguin Books, 1942.)

LUCAS, E. V. *Prologue to Ellen Terry's Bouquet*. Illustrations by Laura Knight. (Privately printed; 1917.)

MARTIN-HARVEY, JOHN. *Autobiography*. (London: Sampson Low, Marston and Co., N.D.)

NICOLL, ALLARDYCE. *A History of Late Nineteenth-Century Drama*. Two vols. (Cambridge University Press, 1949.)

PEARSON, HESKETH. *Bernard Shaw*. (London: Collins, 1942.)

PEARSON, HESKETH. *The Life of Oscar Wilde*. (London: Methuen, 1946.)

PEARSON, HESKETH. *Beerbohm Tree*. (London: Methuen, 1956.)

PEMBERTON, T. EDGAR. *Ellen Terry and her Sisters*. (London: C. Arthur Pearson, 1902.)

PERRY, EDWARD. *Remember Ellen Terry and Edith Craig*. (London: English Theatre Guild, 1948.)

READE, CHARLES L. and the Rev. COMPTON READE. *Charles Reade; a Memoir*. Two vols. (London: Chapman and Hall, 1887.)

RICHARDSON, JOANNA. *Sarah Bernhardt*. (London: Max Reinhardt, 1959.)

ROBERTSON, GRAHAM. *Time Was*. (London: Hamish Hamilton, 1931.)

ROBERTSON, GRAHAM. *Letters from Graham Robertson*. Edited by Kerrison Preston. (London: Hamish Hamilton, 1953.)

ROWELL, GEORGE. *The Victorian Theatre*. (Oxford University Press, 1956.)

SAINTSBURY, H. A. and PALMER, CECIL. *We Saw Him Act: a*

Symposium on the Art of Sir Henry Irving. (London: Hurst and Blackett, 1939.)

SCOTT, CLEMENT. *The Drama of Yesterday and Today.* (London: Macmillan, 1899.)

SHAW, BERNARD. *Dramatic Opinions and Essays.* (London: Constable and Co., 1913.)

SHAW, BERNARD. *Pen Portraits and Reviews.* (London: Constable and Co., 1932.)

SHAW, BERNARD. *Sixteen Self-Sketches.* (London: Constable and Co., 1949.)

STEEN, MARGUERITE. *A Pride of Terrys.* (London: Longmans, 1962.)

STEEN, MARGUERITE. *Looking Glass: an Autobiography.* (London: Longmans, 1966.)

STOKER, BRAM. *Personal Reminiscences of Henry Irving.* (London: Heinemann, 1906.)

TENNYSON, CHARLES. *Alfred Tennyson.*

TERRY, ELLEN. *The Story of my Life.* (London: Hutchinson and Co., N.D., but published in 1908; reprinted Gollancz, 1933.)

TERRY, ELLEN. *The Russian Ballet,* with drawings by Pamela Colman. (London: Sidgwick and Jackson, 1913.)

TERRY, ELLEN. *The Heart of Ellen Terry.* (London: Mills and Boon, Ltd., 1928.)

TERRY, ELLEN, and SHAW, BERNARD. *A Correspondence.* (London Constable and Co., 1931.)

TERRY, ELLEN. *Four Lectures on Shakespeare.* (London: Martin Hopkinson Ltd., 1932.)

TERRY, ELLEN. *Memoirs:* with Preface, Notes and Additional Biographical Chapters by Edith Craig and Christopher St John. (London: Gollancz, 1933.)

TREWIN, J. C. *Mr. Macready.* (London: Harrap, 1955.)

WILLIAMS, HARCOURT. *Four Years at the Old Vic.* (London: Putnam, 1955.)

WINWAR, FRANCES. *Wings of Fire.* (London: Alvin Redman, 1957.)

INDEX

This Index incorporates names and principal references except for the plays and parts in which E.T. appeared, which are included in a separate Index. Principal references appearing in the Notes are included in both indices.

INDEX

Principal Plays and Parts in which Ellen Terry appeared